How Monetary Policy Got Behind the Curve—and How to Get Back

The Hoover Institution gratefully acknowledges the following individuals and foundations for their significant support of the ECONOMIC POLICY WORKING GROUP *and this publication:*

Lynde and Harry Bradley Foundation

John A. Gunn and Cynthia Fry Gunn

Preston and Carolyn Butcher

Sarah Page Herrick

Gail A. Jaquish

Koret Foundation

How Monetary Policy Got Behind the Curve—and How to Get Back

EDITED BY

MICHAEL D. BORDO
JOHN H. COCHRANE
JOHN B. TAYLOR

CONTRIBUTING AUTHORS

James Bullard
Jennifer Burns
Richard H. Clarida
Tyler Goodspeed
George J. Hall
Beth Hammack
Arvind Krishnamurthy
Mickey D. Levy
John Lipsky
Ellen R. McGrattan
Monika Piazzesi

Charles I. Plosser
Randal Quarles
Joshua Rauh
Ricardo Reis
Condoleezza Rice
Thomas J. Sargent
Tom Stephenson
Lawrence H. Summers
Christopher J. Waller
Kevin Warsh
Volker Wieland

HOOVER INSTITUTION PRESS
STANFORD UNIVERSITY   STANFORD, CALIFORNIA

hoover.org

Hoover Institution Press Publication No. 730
Hoover Institution at Leland Stanford Junior University,
Stanford, California 94305-6003

First printing 2023
29 28 27 26 25 24 23   7 6 5 4 3 2 1

Manufactured in the United States of America
Printed on acid-free, archival-quality paper

Library of Congress Cataloging-in-Publication Data
Names: How Monetary Policy Got behind the Curve, and How to Get Back (Conference) (2022 : Hoover Institution on War, Revolution, and Peace), author. | Bordo, Michael D., editor. | Cochrane, John H. (John Howland), 1957- editor. | Taylor, John B., editor.
Title: How monetary policy got behind the curve—and how to get back / edited by Michael D. Bordo, John H. Cochrane, John B. Taylor.
Other titles: Hoover Institution Press publication ; 730.
Description: Stanford, California : Hoover Institution Press, Stanford University, 2023. | Series: Hoover Institution Press Publication ; no. 730 | Proceedings of the conference How Monetary Policy Got behind the Curve, and How to Get Back held May 6, 2022 at the Hoover Institution. | Includes bibliographical references and index. | Summary: "Proceedings from the 2022 Hoover Institution monetary policy conference examine recent inflation in the wake of fiscal and other shocks and measures by the Federal Reserve intended to counter inflation"—Provided by publisher.
Identifiers: LCCN 2022045696 (print) | LCCN 2022045697 (ebook) | ISBN 9780817925642 (cloth) | ISBN 9780817925666 (epub) | ISBN 9780817925680 (pdf)
Subjects: LCSH: Monetary policy—United States—Congresses. | Inflation (Finance)—United States—Congresses. | LCGFT: Conference papers and proceedings.
Classification: LCC HG540 .H68 2023 (print) | LCC HG540 (ebook) | DDC 332.4/973—dc23/eng/20221129
LC record available at https://lccn.loc.gov/2022045696
LC ebook record available at https://lccn.loc.gov/2022045697

Contents

• •

FISCAL POLICY AND OTHER EXPLANATIONS

• •

THE FED'S DELAYED EXITS FROM MONETARY EASE

• • • • • • • • • • • • • • • • •

INFLATION RISKS

· ·

WORLD WARS: FISCAL-MONETARY
CONSEQUENCES

· ·

TOWARD A MONETARY POLICY
STRATEGY

Preface

Michael D. Bordo, John H. Cochrane, and John B. Taylor

The thoughtful policy papers and the thorough policy discussions in this book come at a very important moment for economic policy. The inflation rate in the United States and many other countries had been rising for over a year and was nearing double digits as the conference began. It was clearly time to discuss the situation with policy makers, market participants, the financial press, and academic researchers in person and in the same room, and with others online and around the world. Moreover, with a dozen Hoover monetary policy conferences completed, there was a special need to come together again, as the last two years had seen a hiatus in the conference series due to the pandemic that broke out in the spring of 2020.

The message from the conference participants was nearly uniform. As the conference and book title indicates, "Monetary Policy Got Behind the Curve," with interest rates very low, a greatly expanded balance sheet, and with money growth high. These indicators of monetary ease did not correspond with the high inflation rate nor with the evidence that the recovery from the deep recession in 2020 was well under way. To be sure, there was debate about the reasons for this lack of correspondence at the conference. Some argued that expectations of higher future short-term interest rates increase the interest rate on longer-term securities, through the term structure or the futures market, and this implies that the Fed was not behind.

There was also a focus on the other theme of the conference, "How to Get Back." Indeed, soon after the conference, the Fed began to change policy substantially with a historically large 75-basis-point increase in the Fed's interest rate instrument, the federal funds rate. The Fed also indicated that more federal funds rate increases were on the way. Moreover, the Fed, in its *Monetary Policy Report* released on June 16, put back in a whole section on policy rules, including the Taylor rule as number one on the list. It included statements that: "Simple monetary policy rules, which relate a policy interest rate to a small number of other economic variables, can provide useful guidance to policymakers." And that "simple monetary policy rules considered here call for raising the target range for the federal funds rate significantly."

The analyses presented at the conference—all recorded and summarized in this volume—are timely and original. We are confident that the message and the style is creeping through to policy actions. Indeed, with three current members of the Federal Open Market Committee (FOMC), along with two very recent members of the FOMC present and speaking, and many members of the press broadcasting or writing from the conference, we know the message of the meeting was conveyed to the Federal Reserve and to other central bankers in Europe, Asia, and the Southern Hemisphere.

The conference opened with a presentation by Condoleezza Rice, director of the Hoover Institution and former US secretary of state and national security advisor. Director Rice began by connecting the recent developments to those of terrible shocks of September 11, 2001, then to the financial crisis of 2008—which destabilized the international economy—and finally to COVID-19, which "turned out to be not just a health crisis but a crisis in every aspect of our lives: social, educational, and especially economic."

She also delved into the connection between the economic problem, and the worsening of that problem, by the war in Ukraine. "Just as the world was beginning to recover from the COVID-19 crisis, another enormous shock has occurred in the Russian war on Ukraine. The idea that a large powerful state like Russia would decide to simply absorb its neighbor and do so by brutal military measures makes one think we are living in 1939 instead of 2022." She argued that NATO would emerge as a much stronger alliance after this episode, and that it is likely that we will see a major reshuffling when it comes to energy supply.

Following the opening by Director Rice, the conference proceeded with its first monetary policy panel, entitled "What Monetary Policy Rules and Strategies Say." The presider was the chair of the Hoover Institution Board of Overseers, Tom Stephenson, and the panel consisted of presentations by Richard Clarida, Lawrence Summers, and John Taylor.

Clarida gave the opening remarks, as he did at the 2019 Hoover conference. Having served on the FOMC during the start of the pandemic, he described what life was like on the FOMC during the "public health calamity and economic catastrophe that would, months later, befall the economy as a consequence of the COVID-19 pandemic." He then described the quick recovery and the pressing need for policy to get back to normal. The year 2021 saw "vaccines, economic recovery, and repercussions flowing from the policy response."

By the fall of 2021, monetary policy rules of his own and others were suggesting that it was time to lift off. "The Taylor-rule arithmetic is both simple and compelling: if PCE inflation a year from now is running at, say, 3%, a policy rate reaching 4% would be implied by the Taylor principle" as well as by the policy rule Clarida outlined in his opening remarks at the 2019 Hoover conference three years ago.

Lawrence Summers then made several points. He argued that the current high inflation was predictable a year ago and that the United States is now experiencing a very tight labor market, indicating that "low levels of unemployment are significant predictors of future recessions, implying a significant risk of a hard landing for the economy." He noted that there are confusions at the Fed about nominal and real interest rates and, in a practical sense, "the epistemic approach taken by the Fed using specific numerical targets for forward guidance undermines its credibility."

Summers argued for a monetary policy with "broad objectives clearly stated," efforts to rely on "forward-looking anticipations in policy," avoidance of "specific doctrines that must be displaced when unexpected shocks occur," and utilization of "policy rules to signal when [the Fed] needs to change course."

John Taylor emphasized the advantages of thinking of and conducting monetary policy as a rule in which the interest rate reacted in predictable ways to inflation and real GDP. His paper examined the recent deviation from rules-based monetary policy in the United States, especially during the year 2021 and continuing into this year. He proposed a way for the Federal Reserve to return quickly to a more effective rules-based policy.

His paper reviewed the impact of the COVID pandemic on the economy, and the key monetary policy developments that led to an increase in inflation and today's precarious economic situation. His review set the stage and suggested ways for the Federal Reserve to improve economic performance and achieve low inflation by getting back to more rules-based policy decisions.

The next panel was on "Fiscal Policy and Other Explanations" of the increase in inflation, with presentations by John Cochrane, Tyler Goodspeed, and Beth Hammack.

Cochrane emphasized that the initial cause of our current inflation was a fiscal shock, approximately $5 trillion in newly created reserves and Treasury borrowing, mostly sent as transfer payments. The "behind the curve" question is whether the Fed's slowness to react is causing additional inflation.

Rather than simply presume the Fed is making a gargantuan and evident mistake, Cochrane presented a simple model that encompasses that traditional view, as well as the view embodied in the Fed's projections, which makes sense of the Fed's decisions. The model contains expected inflation. If one assumes that expected inflation is whatever inflation was last year, we obtain the view of many conference participants: that the Fed's slow reaction indeed produces spiraling inflation in response to this fiscal shock. But if expected inflation in the model is equal to the model's prediction for next year, then inflation dies away even if the Fed does nothing. This version of the model fits the Fed's projections. Cochrane noted that the forward-looking model is consistent with the quiet inflation of the zero-bound era. Equivocating on which is the right model, Cochrane pointed us to this central underlying assumption.

Cochrane also addressed how higher interest rates might end inflation. He cautioned that monetary policy without fiscal backing cannot durably lower inflation, and that only a joint monetary, fiscal, and growth-oriented microeconomic reform will do so. He argued that the tax reforms and deregulation of the 1980s were crucial parts of that stabilization.

Goodspeed also emphasized that pandemic fiscal policy was the underlying shock, in particular transfers to individuals. He noted that inflation is much larger in the US than the rest of the world, while supply-chain and other explanations are global. In particular, he noted the $1.9 trillion American Rescue Plan, which arrived in March 2021 as the economy was already swiftly recovering and added to already abnormally high savings and bank account holdings that were ready to be spent.

Goodspeed noted "supply" problems, in particular the large numbers of Americans who had retired or otherwise left the labor force. He pointed to continuing subsidies that disincentivize work, and the remarkable outward shift in the Beveridge curve: the number of job openings is very high for any level of unemployment. He closed by reminding us how similar today's mindset is to that of the 1970s.

Hammack offered her view of how financial market participants who watch the Fed see the unfolding of events. She noted that Fed "dot plot" projections of future interest rates have risen substantially, along with a view that there will be one year of substantial 4.3% inflation.

Hammack noted how the unexpected emergence of inflation, and the change in expectations of Fed policy, have coincided with patterns in securities markets that were not typical of the stable expectations era. The sharp rise in long-term Treasury yields has coincided with a rise in credit spreads and a fall in the stock market. Normally higher yields come during an expansion and with lower credit spreads. The signs of a potential recession are already showing. "Yields are up, volatility is up, spreads are wider, and equities are down. The exit from the pandemic economy is quite unique, but this confluence of moves is tightening financial conditions and signaling a very challenging growth outlook at the same time." Hammack noticed a rise in risk aversion, "increased investor demand for cash," a shift from growth to value, and sharp decline in new issues, all leading to a reduction in investment. Hammack stressed the adverse effects of volatility and uncertainty in the Fed's plans on capital markets. However, she noted that the same reserves of cash that lead some to worry about inflation yet to come when it is spent, also provide a cushion against a recession induced by tighter financial conditions.

This was followed by the paper by Michael Bordo and Mickey Levy and the discussion by Jennifer Burns. Bordo and Levy studied the Fed's current delayed exit from extended monetary ease through the lens of history. They examined the Fed's exit record from 1920 to the present. They compared the timing of changes in the Fed's policy instrument relative to the business cycle trough with the timing of changes in inflation and unemployment relative to the troughs. Their empirical analysis, accompanied by historical narratives, showed that in the vast majority of cases, the Fed waited too long to tighten to stem inflationary pressure, and when it did tighten, it usually led to a hard landing, i.e., a recession.

Bordo and Levy then examined, in considerable detail, the Great Inflation period from 1965 to 1983, when the Fed's "behind the curve" policies led to a pattern of rising inflation and then recession, which has considerable resonance to the present.

They attributed the Fed's behind the curve actions to three forces. The first was the evolving and often flawed doctrine (the gold standard and real bills before World War II, Keynesian economics and the Phillips curve in the 1960s and '70s, focus on Japan's early 2000s experience with deflation and the ZLB, and the Fed's recent flexible average inflation targeting since 2020). The second force was the misreading of economic and inflation conditions, especially very inaccurate forecasts. The third was the political pressure from the executive and legislative branches of government.

They concluded that the record of too many "unforced errors" calls for a monetary policy reset—more systematic rules-based guidelines to avoid the flaws of the discretionary policies that generally followed.

Jennifer Burns in her comment focused on the Great Inflation episode. She reexamined the famous 1960 Samuelson and Solow article that posited the Phillips curve trade-off between unemployment and inflation that was used by the Kennedy and Johnson administrations and the Fed to justify inflationary policies. She then turned to Arthur Burns's role in worsening the Great Inflation in the 1970s. Despite his personal connection to Milton Friedman, Burns downplayed the role of monetary policy in causing inflation and attributed the run-up in inflation to cost-push forces. He forcefully made the case for the adoption of wage-price controls, which in the end just made things worse.

This was followed by "The Burst of High Inflation in 2021–22: How and Why Did We Get Here?" by Ricardo Reis, and the discussion by Volker Wieland. Reis told the story of how central banks let inflation emerge through the perspective of the modern Phillips curve, which is how central bankers view the economy. Inflation today is driven by expected future inflation, by the deviation of output from its potential, and by shocks away from these forces, in theory a "markup shock that introduces a gap between the potential and efficient levels of output."

First, central banks mistook the pandemic for a "demand" shock like the 2008 financial crisis and expected it to lead to years of stagnation. Governments met it with immense fiscal and monetary stimulus. It was a transitory "supply" shock, leading to a V-shaped recession. Output and employment almost completely recovered while the Delta wave of COVID was still surging.

Supply-chain problems soon emerged. Central banks interpreted this as a "transitory" shock that did not require higher interest rates, a "markup shock" in Reis's framework. They did not see the event as output persistently greater than potential, which would demand higher interest rates.

Then energy prices rose. Central banks again treated it as a temporary markup shock, to be ignored. They also had in mind the experience of the 1970s, during which higher energy prices raised inflation, central banks tightened, and the action led to recessions.

Three times in a row, then, central banks misdiagnosed the situation—perhaps understandably, as things are hard to see in real time. But this set the stage for expectations to rise.

The strategy of ignoring temporary shocks requires that the first term of the Phillips curve, expected inflation, remains "anchored." Central bankers noticed the remarkable stability of inflation expectations during the decades of little inflation and gained too much faith that those expectations could not move. The median value of survey forecasts and financial indicators also showed unchanged expected inflation through the first few shocks. Reis shows, however, how one can see expectations becoming unhinged by looking at the dispersion in survey forecasts and signals from the option markets. Also, people tend not to pay much attention to inflation when it is low, leading central banks to overestimate how sticky expectations really are. A boat may be still because it's anchored or because it is simply in calm waters.

Finally, central banks had settled too long into battling the perceived danger of a deflation spiral, and downward drift of expectations. Much of this fear came from the steady downward drift of r-star (r*), the neutral real rate of interest on government bonds, pushing actual interest rates to the zero bound. But Reis points out that the rate of return on physical capital did not decline. This fact means that monetary policy raising the rate on government bonds may have less effect on the real economy than central bankers believe.

In his discussion, Volker Wieland told how both the European Central Bank (ECB) and the Fed regarded inflation as "transitory" and that inflation would pass on its own through 2021. Wieland went on to question the conventional wisdom that the central bank should "look through" or ignore cost-push shocks. He considers a simple model and adds the possibility that current inflation also depends on past inflation in the Phillips curve. He contrasted a Taylor rule that pays conventional attention to output with an output-focused rule that pays eight times more attention to the output gap, dramatically lowering interest rates to fight a recession and keeping interest rates low until output fully recovers. With the traditional forward-looking Phillips curve, this output focus and consequent delayed reaction do little harm. But as the Phillips curve adds a backward-looking term, the delay in raising rates causes more and more inflation. This finding mirrors Cochrane's analysis in which a fully backward-looking Phillips curve demands immediate and large interest rate responses to inflationary shocks to keep inflation from spiraling out of control.

Wieland extended Reis's point that central bankers had become too focused on fighting perceived deflation risks. He pointed out that the Fed's strategy explicitly called for an asymmetric, inflation-biased response, and shifted to fighting output "shortfalls" rather than symmetric deviations of output from potential. He also applied Reis's insight on the distribution of inflation forecasts and the influence of r* and zero-bound thinking to the ECB.

This was followed by the paper "Financing Big US Federal Expenditures Surges: COVID-19 and Earlier US Wars" by George Hall and Thomas Sargent, and the discussion by Ellen McGrattan.

Hall and Sargent noted that the rate of spending during the pandemic is as large as in World Wars I and II. They compared how the government financed pandemic spending to how it financed the world wars, as well as the Revolutionary War, the War of 1812, and the Civil War. That comparison can give us historical precedent for how things might turn out, and particularly how the inflation we are now experiencing contrasts with inflation following the previous wars.

The US financed the wars and the pandemic largely by issuing money and debt, not by raising taxes. Hall and Sargent summarized: "Increases in tax revenues covered 20.8% of the cost of World War I, 30.2% of the cost of World War II, and only 3.5% of the war on COVID-19. Money growth covered 6.9% of the cost of World War I, 10.1% of the cost of World War II, and 18.5% of the cost of the war on COVID-19."

Inflation also rose during the world wars. Indeed, the current inflation neatly tracks with the early years of both wars, each of which resulted in a halving of the real value of bondholders' debt. The comparison is chilling.

Hall and Sargent pointed out the "ratchet effect," that the overall size of government rose in each war and seems to be doing so again. They also noted that, unlike in the earlier wars, the gap between forecast tax revenue and expenditures has also grown, with no sign of a return to small, steady primary surpluses.

Financing a war or pandemic transfers by taxation, borrowing, or money creation, and whether to repay, default, or inflate away debt ex post are all choices. Each choice sets up reputations that frame later possibilities. Hall and Sargent took conference participants on a brilliant tour of these choices, as interpreted by economic theory. Hall and Sargent also showed how each era's accumulation of experience led to different choices. Perhaps their longer history will help our leaders to make wiser choices.

The UK famously financed much of the Napoleonic Wars by issuing notes no longer convertible to gold. By presiding over a postwar deflation, they rewarded noteholders and earned a reputation useful for later borrowing.

The aftermath of the US Revolutionary War was different, and more subtle than the common impression. Yes, Hamilton prevailed, and the US assumed state debts. It thereby rewarded "speculators" who had bought debt at a discount, but those "speculators" are the next-time's bond buyers. But the US also inflated away its paper money, the "continentals," exactly the opposite action of the UK's. This move "was designed to intentionally poison the US government's reputation for servicing some types of debt (the despised paper money known then as 'bills of credit') while simultaneously enhancing its reputation for servicing other types of debt (interest-bearing medium- and long-term obligations, especially to foreign creditors)." The founders of Hamilton's era wanted to preclude future paper money issuance, especially interest-paying money.

Already in the War of 1812, the Madison administration thought differently. It did reward holders of short-term debt and refrained from the money issuance that the US had used in the Revolutionary War. That changed the US reputation. The Civil War was financed with both debt and paper money, greenbacks. The latter depreciated during the war, but the US eventually redeemed greenbacks at par, though only after a long and contentious political debate. The post–Civil War US had a different view of the desirability of paper money, and of establishing a reputation for maintaining a steady value of money rather than poisoning that well: "In 1790, people deplored federal paper money as 'not worth a continental'; after 1879, people trusted greenbacks to be small-denomination warehouse certificates for gold. Reputational considerations were very much on the minds of public officials in both periods."

Wartime inflation does not always lead to a permanent price level rise as it did after the world wars. Governments can acquire a different reputation for different classes of debt, sold to different investors. Our government's desire for a reputation in upholding the value of paper currency, interest-bearing reserves, indexed and nonindexed treasury debt, and domestically vs. to foreigners as the "reserve currency" (really "reserve debt") will be important to determining how the current episode works out.

Conventional theory predicts tax smoothing, that wars should be financed by debt that is slowly repaid by higher taxes. It also predicts Lucas-Stokey defaults, that inflation (or default) occurs on the outbreak of war, not afterwards, as a form of insurance. Hall and Sargent note that we do not see this pattern. In part, debt was small on the outbreak of previous wars. (Perhaps some of our current inflation can be read as a Lucas-Stokey default on the large debt outstanding before 2020.) But "Early American policy makers did not see it [this] way. Influenced by the repudiation of the Continentals, they saw inflation as a deplorable way of abrogating contracts."

The lessons of previous episodes guided leaders:

> Memories of how the Continental currency that had financed the War of Independence from Great Britain had eventually depreciated to one penny on the dollar convinced War of 1812 decision makers to take steps to avoid that outcome. Non-callable federal bonds issued to pay for the Mexican-American War appreciated in value after the war when interest rates fell, creating ex post regrets that the bonds had not been bundled with call options, something that the Union would do early in the Civil War. . . . Rising prices and thus rising nominal interest rates after World War I delivered nominal capital losses to owners of the Liberty Bonds that had been used to finance the war, teaching Captain Harry Truman a lesson that he would remember when, as president, he insisted that the Treasury and Federal Reserve manage interest rates after World War II to prevent that from happening again.

With this learning from experience in mind, it is interesting that the Fed, ECB, and other central banks today seem to have abandoned the standard interpretation of the 1970s and 1980s, that central banks should react quickly and systematically to inflation. The experience of the zero-bound era may be more salient. Hall and Sargent's point, though, is that a much longer experience, involving the joint fiscal and monetary policies behind inflation, will also be necessary going forward.

A broader puzzle remains. If money holders and bondholders since World War I on have routinely lost via inflation after wars, why do they continue to buy debt and hold money at the beginning and middle of wars? Why does inflation not come sooner?

Hall and Sargent close with an essential bit of wisdom: "Confused monetary-fiscal coordination creates costly uncertainties."

In her discussion, Ellen McGrattan first questioned the analogy between the pandemic and the world wars. First, the pandemic was much shorter lived. So much so, in fact, that the huge spike in spending largely disappears when one looks at annual rather than quarterly data. The pandemic looks like a larger version of the 2008 financial crisis recession. Some of the spending measured as a percentage of GDP in quarterly data looks large by the collapse in GDP, but the latter only lasted a few quarters. Second, "The main spending of World War II was purchases of goods and services by the military," along with soldiers' salaries. Much of this wartime spending was also clearly temporary, lasting only the duration of the war. By contrast, "The main spending of the pandemic is in the form of transfers and subsidies," some of which "will be hard to discontinue." Considering "who will pay," McGrattan opines that the most likely outcome is individual taxpayers, but in the far future.

The conference then turned to a monetary policy panel with current and former members of the FOMC, entitled "Toward a Monetary Policy Strategy."

The president of the Federal Reserve Bank of St. Louis, James Bullard, presented his paper, "Is the Fed 'Behind the Curve'? Two Interpretations." He started by observing that US inflation is indeed exceptionally high, and similar to that of the years 1974 and 1983. He noted that standard Taylor-type monetary policy rules still recommend substantial increases in the policy rate, even if they are based on a very low interpretation of the persistent component of inflation. This provides one definition of "behind the curve," and the Fed is far behind.

However, Bullard also pointed out that modern central bankers are more credible than their corresponding central bankers in the 1970s: they use forward guidance. If forward guidance is credible, then market interest rates will increase substantially in advance of actual actions by the Fed. This alternative view provides another definition of "behind the curve." The Fed is not so far behind the curve if the distance in the concept is measured with this alternative definition.

Former Fed governor Randal Quarles then presented his paper, "Strategy and Execution in US Monetary Policy 2021–22." He began by recalling the titles of the conference—"How Monetary Policy Got Behind the Curve—and How to Get Back"—and of his panel—"Toward a Monetary Policy Strategy." This contrast of titles, Quarles argued, clearly presupposes that "the Fed is currently on the wrong track, but that it may not be too late to redeem the day by shifting course."

Quarles made the case that such a judgment is premature, in part because "the Fed's strategy is misunderstood." Those who said the Fed should have tightened in early 2021 were too early, "and while with the benefit of hindsight I think it is clear the Fed did move too slowly in late 2021 and early 2022 to raise interest rates (a misstep that I supported at the time), this was an error of execution, not of strategy—a tactical misjudgment in the fog of war—and what is more, it is an error that the Fed can correct, and is correcting, effectively and with dispatch."

The interest rate increases that the Fed has begun, if continued as outlined, will be quite effective, Quarles argued. "In an environment where economic actors and market participants have been conditioned for almost 15 years to expect extremely low interest rates," he argued "even modest nominal rate increases will result in quite high percentage increases in debt service, and the effect on the economy should be both swifter and more powerful than in many prior cases of the Fed's response to inflation."

He continued, "I think it will be clear by the fall that inflation is heading into the pen, and by the first part of next year it should be effectively corralled. There are lessons to be learned from this episode, certainly. But I think it is premature to conclude that one of those lessons is that either of the two operative principles of the monetary policy framework adopted by the Fed in August 2020 was a mistake or has become outmoded."

Fed governor Christopher Waller then presented "Reflections on Monetary Policy in 2021," in which he focused on the question: How did the Fed get so far behind the curve? His response relates to how his view of the economy changed over the course of 2021, and he explained how that evolving view shaped his policy position.

When thinking about the policy question, Waller argued that there are several points that need to be considered: "First, the Fed was not alone in underestimating the strength of inflation that revealed itself in late 2021. Second, to determine whether the Fed was behind the curve, one must take a position on the evolving health of the labor market during 2021. Finally, setting policy in real time can create what appear to be policy errors after the fact due to data revisions."

In the final session, "Inflation Blues: The Fortieth-Anniversary Revival?," Monika Piazzesi made a clever analogy with the legendary blues musician B. B. King, whose song "Inflation Blues" from 1983 "mirrored Americans' struggle to pay the bills and their frustration with the government's inability to address the rising costs of living. This was just after inflation soared to more than 14% at the dawn of the decade, while unemployment peaked at about 11% during 1982. Now, 40 years after its vinyl debut, King's 'Inflation Blues' is threatening an encore."

Piazzesi asked: "Are we in a time machine on our way back to the 1970s?" A quick glance at rising ratios of house prices to rents seems to suggest that the answer to this question may be yes. However, she noted that uncertainty in the United States is relatively low now. The public still trusts the Fed to rein in inflation. Consequently, the ratio of equity values to dividends manages to stay high despite the currently high inflation. That is different from the 1970s.

"The big question in coming weeks," she argues, "will be whether the Fed will lose its reputation as an inflation fighter, especially if there are signs that inflation pressures may be more persistent." Right now, short-run inflation expectations are elevated, but "the public believes the Fed will take us back to 2% inflation over the longer run."

Let us hope she is correct, and that this belief makes the disinflationary process easier.

CHAPTER ONE

Introductory Remarks

Condoleezza Rice

The work of the Economic Policy Working Group at the Hoover Institution is long running, and it has profoundly impacted economic policy debate in our country and abroad. Today, given these unprecedented times, I cannot think of a better moment to discuss the Federal Reserve, its current and potential policies, and the general state of the economy.

The United States and the world have experienced a number of shocks over the last twenty years. I was national security advisor and John Taylor was under secretary of the Treasury for the Bush administration when we experienced the terrible shock of September 11. The United States had not been attacked on its territory since the War of 1812, and it was a day that we thought we would never see. Facing attacks on New York, the Pentagon, and potentially the White House, the country soon found itself suddenly at war, which was an enormous shock with repercussions that would continue to follow long after.

Before we would leave office, the global financial crisis of 2007–8 occurred. This was another crisis that seemed to destabilize the international economy as we knew it, a crisis that some would say was a black swan event but nevertheless was a huge shock to the American and global economies. Then, in 2020, we would learn the name of a virus that would launch a pandemic. COVID-19 turned out to be not just a health crisis but a crisis in every aspect of our lives: social, educational, and especially economic.

Just as the world was beginning to recover from the COVID-19 crisis, another enormous shock has occurred with the Russian war on Ukraine. The idea that a large, powerful state like Russia would decide to simply absorb its neighbor and do so by brutal military means makes one think we are living in 1939 instead of 2022. It is hard to understand that Vladimir Putin has launched this war because it is his aspiration and his intention to reestablish the Russian Empire—not the Soviet Union, but the Russian Empire. This reality has implications for Europe that are beyond anything that anyone can predict.

During all these crises, of course, the role of the Fed and monetary policy will be under a microscope for the short-term effects. But it is also critical to remember the potential long-term effects of the shock that we are seeing in Europe.

We must remember that this war in Europe is essentially a geopolitical earthquake. It is reshuffling the deck in terms of security in Europe. NATO will emerge a much stronger alliance after this. Finland and Sweden, countries that not too long ago maintained strict neutrality policies, are now seeking full membership in the NATO alliance. In just a few weeks, Vladimir Putin ended German pacifism and Swedish neutrality.

Given these shifts in attitudes on neutrality and pacificism around Europe, it is likely that there will be extraordinary pressures on national budgets for huge increases in defense spending going forward. The Germans sometimes talk about as much as doubling their defense budget. While it is hard to imagine that this will be achieved, the very fact that a long-term reshuffling of European security is occurring and being intensively discussed means that nations are going to be forced to spend more on defense. These effects will certainly have impacts on debt ceilings and national economies.

Secondly, it is likely that we will see a major reshuffling when it comes to energy supply. As much as the world might like to make a quick, uninterrupted transition to a low-carbon or carbon-free economy to fight climate change, hydrocarbons are still a big part of our energy mix in the short term, especially in transportation. Indeed, the question of how countries provide those hydrocarbons is now not just a question of energy but also a question of energy and its relation to national security.

A number of countries have found themselves overly dependent on Russian oil and gas, and after Russia's invasion, they are now trying to end or at least minimize that dependence. Some countries have already successfully done it. Poland, for instance, after the 2014 Russian invasion of Crimea, started changing its energy sources, significantly decreasing its dependence on Russian oil and gas. Due to these proactive measures, the announcement by Vladimir Putin that Russia was going to cut off natural gas to Poland and Bulgaria was barely an issue for them. They had already made the necessary arrangements to not be negatively impacted by these potential scenarios with Russia, which are now reality.

The Germans, however, who have been warned since Ronald Reagan was president about their dependence on Russian pipelines and Russian oil and gas, find themselves in a difficult situation by having also decided not to use nuclear energy. The French, on the other hand, get 80% of their generating power from nuclear sources, allowing them to mitigate the impacts of the loss of Russian energy supplies.

This leads to perhaps the most important point: Russia under Vladimir Putin is going to be isolated from the international economy for the foreseeable future. No matter how long the war with Ukraine continues, sanctions are unlikely to be lifted anytime soon. The self-sanctioning that is taking place by companies and countries around the world who do not want the reputational risk or uncertainties of dealing with Vladimir Putin's Russia will leave Russia with very little international business engagement or investment for a long time to come.

With Russia's likely long-term isolation, at least from the West, there will be new questions on where those hydrocarbon resources will come from moving forward, which will drive new decisions about energy supply and the production of oil and gas in North America. I agree with the view that if you are going to continue to need hydrocarbons, let's make sure that they come from North America, not from Iran, Russia, and even to a certain extent, Saudi Arabia. In addition, when energy prices are up, we see other impacts on the economy, including on food supply, which is often overlooked. I was secretary of state in 2007 when oil prices rose to over $140 a barrel and transportation costs spiked over 50%. Consequentially, food riots occurred in places like Egypt, which is completely dependent on the import of food. The transportation costs from energy shocks will lead to new supply-chain issues, including on food, which could potentially lead to increased instability in various places around the world.

I want to underscore how dramatic what we are seeing in the world today really is. We have never tried to isolate an economy of Russia's size and importance from the international economy. Back in the days of the Soviet Union, it was self-isolating. The Soviet Union never accounted for more than 1% of its GDP in international trade. By contrast, the modern Russian economy, in fact, has been very integrated into the international economy.

We have isolated economies before. We isolated North Korea with sanctions. But there was very little, if any, impact on the American or global economy given that the North Koreans produce and sell counterfeit cigarettes, counterfeit dollars, and nuclear parts. The Trump administration isolated the Iranian economy and the Iranian Central Bank, something that the Bush administration chose not to do because of its potential shock to the economy.

But the Russian economy on any given day, whether you think of it as the eleventh or fifteenth largest economy in the world, is fully integrated. Russia and Ukraine combined account for almost 30% of the world's wheat supply. Russia accounts for 20% of titanium, and Russia and Belarus account for 40% of potash and thus, fertilizer.

Therefore, it seems the international community does not yet fully understand the potential unintended consequences of the medium-to long-term isolation of the Russian economy.

This isolation of Russia, as long as Vladimir Putin is in power, will also have an effect on Russia itself. A brain drain has already occurred, with approximately 500,000 people having left Russia since the war began on February 24, and the number will continue to grow. They are among the country's best and brightest—its entrepreneurs, its software engineers, and its intelligentsia. This exodus of the sort of talent that drives a country's development forward will have a long-term impact on Russia, perhaps for generations to come. Russian oil fields, even if sanctions are lifted, will suffer, because the major oil companies of the world are not going back. And without their technology, Russia cannot develop some of its most vulnerable and older oil fields in places like Sakhalin Island.

And so, as we go back and look at all the shocks that we have experienced over the last twenty years, the shocks that have been thoroughly discussed through these conferences, it is important to understand the magnitude of the geopolitical earthquake that the world is currently experiencing. The global economy is in uncharted waters, experiencing inflation and pressures on growth.

Major economies across the world will be reacting to what has happened in Europe for some time to come. With that in mind, this is an important time to consider the Fed and how far it may already be behind the curve, and where we go from here.

....

WHAT
MONETARY
POLICY RULES
AND
STRATEGIES SAY

.

CHAPTER TWO

PERSPECTIVES ON US MONETARY POLICY

Richard H. Clarida

I would like to thank John Taylor, John Cochrane, and the other organizers for inviting me to participate, once again, in the Hoover Monetary Policy Conference. When this group last convened in May 2019, none of us anticipated—nor really could have foreseen—the public health calamity and economic catastrophe that would, months later, befall the economy as a consequence of the COVID-19 pandemic. The pandemic, and the mitigation efforts subsequently put in place to contain it in 2020, delivered the most severe blow to the US economy since the Great Depression. GDP collapsed at an annual rate of over 30% in the second quarter of 2020. More than 22 million jobs were lost in just the first two months of the crisis, and the unemployment rate rose from a 50-year low of 3.5% in February to a postwar peak of almost 15% by April of 2020. A precipitous decline in aggregate demand pummeled the consumer price level and inflation fell sharply in 2020. The resulting disruptions to economic activity significantly tightened financial conditions and impaired the flow of credit to US households and businesses.

The monetary and fiscal policy response to the COVID crisis in the United States, and in many other advanced economies, was unprecedented in its scale, scope, and speed.[1] Legislation passed by Congress in March 2020, December 2020, and March 2021 provided

---

1. Richard H. Clarida, Burcu Duygan-Bump, and Chiara Scotti, "The COVID-19 Crisis and the Federal Reserve's Policy Response," Finance and Economics Discussion Series 2021-035, Board of Governors of the Federal Reserve System, Washington, DC, June 2021.

a total of nearly $5.8 trillion in fiscal support to the US economy—about 28% of US GDP. The Federal Reserve acted decisively and with dispatch as it deployed all the tools in its conventional kit—cutting the federal funds rate to the zero lower bound (ZLB), launching large-scale purchase programs for Treasury and mortgage-backed securities, and providing outcome-based guidance for the future path of the policy rate. And it did this while designing, developing, and launching a series of temporary backstop facilities to support the flow of credit to households and businesses in a matter of weeks.

But if 2020 was the year of the pandemic, economic collapse, and the policy response, then 2021 was the year of vaccines, economic recovery, and repercussions flowing from the policy response. In 2021, the real side of the economic recovery was about as good as it gets with strong growth and robust hiring. And in the first half of the year, this rapid return to the economy's potential was accompanied by indicators of underlying inflation that remained consistent with the Fed's 2% objective. But in the second half of 2021, and continuing into 2022, there was a surge in inflation that was about as bad as it gets, not only in the United States but also in many other countries. It was certainly not moderate, nor foreseen in the Fed's Summary of Economic Projections, and it is turning out to be distressingly persistent and increasingly broad based as evidenced in both price and wage data.

Speaking for myself, I entered 2021 with the assumptions that inflation expectations were well anchored, that in the aggregate there remained substantial slack in the economy, and that there were also some significant, but likely short-lived, sectoral imbalances between supply and demand that would require large increases in some relative prices—for example, the relative prices of durable goods versus contact intensive services.[2] As a starting point, with well-anchored inflation expectations, the textbook monetary policy response

---

2. Richard H. Clarida, "US Economic Outlook and Monetary Policy," speech at the 2021 Institute of International Finance Washington Policy Summit, Washington, DC (via webcast), Board of Governors of the Federal Reserve System, March 25, 2021.

would be to look through such relative price changes caused by supply shocks as long as inflation expectations stayed well anchored and economic slack remained evident. That was certainly my view in the spring of 2021, since it was not inconsistent with the data on price and wage inflation available at the time. It was also the view of virtually all private sector forecasters as documented in the *Wall Street Journal, Bloomberg*, and *Survey of Professional Forecasters* surveys, which were conducted in the first half of 2021.

But of course, these assumptions proved to be wrong, and beginning in the summer of 2021, the incoming data—for example, the data on trimmed-mean inflation calculations, on wage and compensation dynamics, and on unit labor cost trends—began to reveal, at least to me, that the balance of risks to the inflation outlook were skewed decidedly to the upside. I indicated as much in remarks delivered at the Peterson Institute for International Economics event in August.[3]

It was taking longer to reopen and rebalance the $20 trillion economy than it did to shut it down. The US labor market tightened much faster than the Fed and most others had been expecting in the spring, and the cause of the aforementioned sectoral imbalances was revealed to be due more to excess demand than to transitorily depressed deficient supply.

Certainly by the fall of 2021, the monetary policy rules I consult based on my research with Mark Gertler and Jordi Galí—for example as highlighted in a presentation I delivered (virtually) to a Hoover seminar in January 2021 and as studied in a recent paper by David Papell and Ruxandra Prodan—were indicating that liftoff from the ZLB was or soon would be warranted (figure 2.1).[4]

---

3. Richard H. Clarida, "Outlooks, Outcomes, and Prospects for US Monetary Policy," speech delivered (via webcast) Peterson Institute for International Economics, Washington, DC, August 4, 2021.

4. Richard H. Clarida, Jordi Galí, and Mark Gertler, "The Science of Monetary Policy: A New Keynesian Perspective," *Journal of Economic Literature* 37 (December 1999): 1661–707; Richard H. Clarida, Jordi Galí, and Mark Gertler, "Monetary Policy Rules and Macroeconomic Stability: Evidence and Some Theory," *Quarterly Journal of Economics* 115,

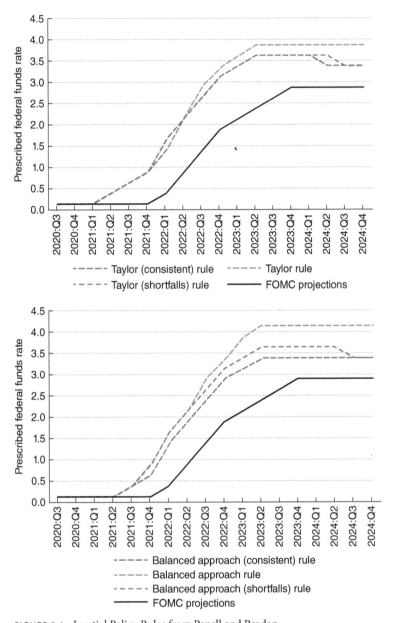

FIGURE 2.1. Inertial Policy Rules from Papell and Prodan

Source: David H. Papell and Ruxandra Prodan, "Policy Rules and Forward Guidance following the Covid Recession," University of Houston Department of Economics, May 1, 2022.

Subsequently, the FOMC began pivoting in the fall of 2021 to end quantitative easing earlier than expected. It also commenced rate hikes sooner than had been expected, signaled a faster pace of policy normalization than had been previously projected, and made it clear it was also likely to commence balance sheet normalization much sooner and at a much faster pace than was the case following the global financial crisis of 2008. Taken together these actions have tightened financial conditions considerably and pushed nominal (but not real) bond yields and mortgage rates to levels last seen at the peak of the previous rate hike cycle when the fed funds rate reached 2.5%, roughly equal to the FOMC's current assessment of long-run neutral. Indeed, there appears to be broad support on the Committee to return the funds rate "expeditiously" to neutral.

But I judge, at least from my vantage point back at Columbia University, that simply and even expeditiously "getting to long-run neutral" will not be enough to return inflation over the forecast horizon back to the 2% longer run goal during this cycle. And let me be clear, even if through good policy or good luck inflation does return to 2% over the forecast horizon, average personal consumption expenditures (PCE) inflation as calculated using either backward- or forward-looking windows of two, three, even five years will work out to be well above 2%.[5] That was another point I made in my August 2021 Peterson Institute remarks. Because of the size and nature of the pandemic shock and the monetary and fiscal policy response to the shock, the ZLB in this cycle did not turn out to have been ex post a binding constraint on the ability of monetary and

---

no. 1 (2000): 147–80; Richard H. Clarida, "The Federal Reserve's New Framework: Context and Consequences," speech delivered (via webcast) at "The Road Ahead for Central Banks," a seminar sponsored by the Hoover Economic Policy Working Group, Hoover Institution, Stanford University, January 13, 2021; David H. Papell and Ruxandra Prodan, "Policy Rules and Forward Guidance Following the Covid Recession," University of Houston Department of Economics, May 1, 2022.

5. Federal Reserve Bank of Atlanta, Underlying Inflation Dashboard, https://www.atlantafed.org/research/inflationproject/underlying-inflation-dashboard.

fiscal policy to return inflation to 2% from below, or for inflation to average 2% over time. And monetary policy should, I argued, reflect this reality.

In practice, this will mean that, even under a plausible best case scenario in which most of the inflation overshoot in 2021 and 2022 turns out to have been transitory, the funds rate will, I believe, ultimately need to be raised well into restrictive territory—by at least a percentage point above the estimated nominal long-run neutral rate of 2.5%—for inflation to be credibly projected to return to 2%. The Taylor-rule arithmetic is both simple and compelling: if PCE inflation a year from now is running at, say, 3%, a policy rate reaching 4% would be implied by the Taylor principle and the policy rule I outlined in my 2021 Hoover remarks.

The policy path for the funds rate I have just described does not incorporate the possible additional tightening of financial conditions that could arise as the Fed allows its balance sheet to shrink over time, although bond yields have likely already priced in some assumptions about the ultimate destination for the size of the balance sheet and duration of the program. Were the term premium to increase substantially from current levels—due to the Fed's balance sheet policy, coupon supply, a decline in the value of Treasuries as a hedge against equity risk, or a global rise in term premia as major central banks shrink their balance sheets in tandem—the required rise in the funds rate to return inflation to 2% could be somewhat smaller than indicated by popular policy rules.[6] On the other hand, if the consensus and SEP forecast that inflation will fall below 3% in 2023 turns out to be overly optimistic, then the tightening of monetary policy required to return inflation to the 2% longer run goal would be greater than in the baseline scenario that is consistent with the SEP projections and many private sector

6. Richard H. Clarida, "Monetary Policy, Price Stability, and Equilibrium Bond Yields: Success and Consequences," speech delivered at the High-Level Conference on Global Risk, Uncertainty, and Volatility, Zurich, Switzerland, November 12, 2019.

inflation forecasts. And of course, r-star itself is unobserved and time varying and could turn out to be higher than the committee expects, in which case the peak funds rate in this cycle that would be consistent with returning inflation to 2% would be higher than indicated in figure 2.1.

In closing, the Fed in March 2020 faced a "whatever it takes" moment and I believe, without any pretense of impartiality, that history will judge that it rose to that challenge. Today, the Fed faces a different challenge, that of insuring that the hard-won battles under Paul Volcker and Alan Greenspan to achieve price stability are not squandered. The Fed has the tools to meet this challenge, officials understand the stakes, and are determined to succeed. But the Fed's instruments are blunt, the mission is complex, and difficult trade-offs lie ahead.

CHAPTER THREE

A Labor Market View on Inflation

Lawrence H. Summers

This paper presents four arguments relating to the Fed's response to recent inflation. First, using a simple output-gap framework, I argue that inflation should have been predictable in early 2021. Second, given the extremely elevated level of job vacancies and quits, I show that labor markets are currently extraordinarily tight, and the non-accelerating inflation rate of unemployment (NAIRU) has likely risen substantially. This suggests the labor market is significantly tighter than would have previously been implied by the current unemployment rate. Third, high levels of inflation and low levels of unemployment are significant predictors of future recessions, implying a significant risk of a hard landing for the economy. And fourth, I argue that the epistemic approach taken by the Fed using specific numerical targets for forward guidance undermines its credibility, and that it should return to a more modest framework with broad, clearly stated objectives.

THE OUTPUT-GAP VIEW OF INFLATION

The output gap, defined as the difference between actual output and potential output, is a useful indicator for the degree of inflationary pressure in the economy. In the first quarter of 2021, measures of the output gap were already sending an alarming signal about the

I would like to thank Alex Domash for assistance in preparing this paper.

possibility of an overheating economy in the near future. The best estimate for the 2021 gap was about $600 billion (or $50 billion per month), based on the Congressional Budget Office's (CBO) July 2020 projections and economic data released in late 2020. At the same time, $2.8 trillion of fiscal stimulus was being delivered to the economy between the $900 billion COVID-19 Relief Bill passed in December 2020 and the $1.9 trillion stimulus package passed in March 2021. Depending on the precise multiplier used, this translated to approximately $150 billion per month in fiscal stimulus—or three times the size of the output gap.

Figure 3.1 puts the magnitude of the fiscal stimulus into perspective by comparing it to the 2009 stimulus package created in response to the Great Recession. In 2009, the output gap between actual and estimated potential output was about $80 billion a month, according to CBO projections. The 2009 stimulus measures provided an incremental $30 billion to $40 billion a month during 2009—an amount equal to about half the output shortfall. Relative to the size of the output gap addressed, the COVID stimulus was essentially six times as large as the 2009 stimulus package.

These estimates of the output gap are meant to be illustrative rather than precise—as well-known estimates of potential GDP may be inaccurate since the potential output cannot be observed directly (see Williams 2017 or Powell et al. 2021). Yet, there was good reason to believe that the fiscal stimulus in 2021 would overshoot the output gap by even more than projected. At the time, households had amassed nearly $2 trillion in excess savings, most of which had been deposited in checking accounts (Greig and Deadman 2022). Monetary policy was also much more expansionary than in 2009, with nominal interest rates at the zero lower bound and the Fed balance sheet expanding at a record pace. Even without COVID-related supply shocks or adverse impact on potential output, the output gap was signaling a substantial risk of overheating.

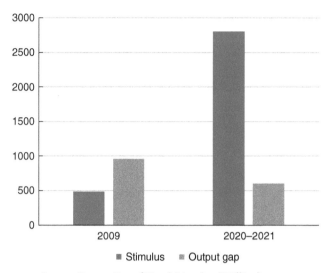

FIGURE 3.1. Output Gap vs. Size of Fiscal Stimulus ($Billion)
Sources: Congressional Budget Office, "Estimated Impact of the American Recovery and Reinvestment Act on Employment and Economic Output in 2014" and "An Update to the Budget Outlook: 2020 to 2030."

Despite the above, the Federal Open Market Committee's March 2021 economic projections had personal consumption expenditures (PCE) inflation at 2.4% in 2021 and 2.0% in 2022. One reason these projections likely underestimated the possibility of inflation is the nature of the Fed's primary macroeconomic model, the FRB/US. Figures 3.2 and 3.3 show the results of a simulation of the FRB/US model under the assumption that the economy had $2 trillion of GDP (about 9%) in extra government spending maintained for the next six years. The figures show that inflation would rise by only 70 basis points at the end of the six years—which suggests a significant limitation in the model's ability to detect inflation stemming from expansionary fiscal policy.

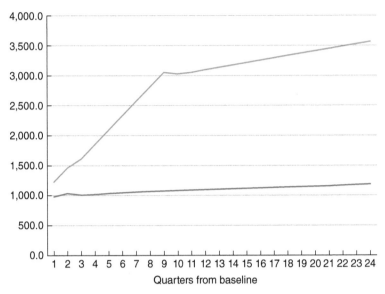

FIGURE 3.2. Federal Spending ($Trillion)
Source: Federal Reserve, FRB/US dataset.

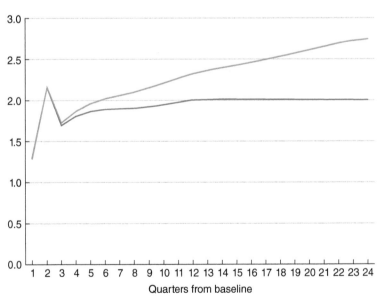

FIGURE 3.3. Inflation Rate (%)
Source: Federal Reserve, FRB/US dataset.

THE LABOR MARKET VIEW OF INFLATION

Another way to understand the inflationary pressure in the economy is to estimate the degree of slack in the labor market. Today, the US labor market is extraordinarily tight. Figure 3.4 shows that the number of job vacancies per unemployed is higher than it's been in seventy years. In April 2022, the vacancy-to-unemployment (v/u) ratio was at 1.92 (after reaching a high of 1.99 in March). For perspective, the v/u ratio has averaged 0.65 since the 1950s and reached a pre-pandemic peak of 1.5 in 1969. The quits rate in the US is also at a historic high of 2.7%, compared to a historical average of 1.8% and a pre-pandemic peak of 2.2%.

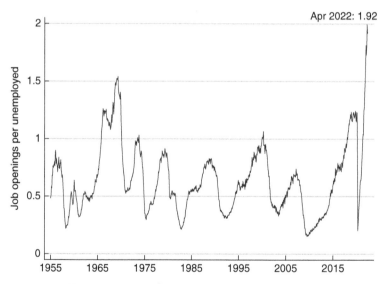

FIGURE 3.4. Vacancy-to-Unemployment Ratio, January 1955–April 2022

Sources: Bureau of Labor Statistics (BLS) Current Population Survey (CPS) and Job Openings and Labor Turnover Survey (JOLTS) via Federal Reserve Economic Data, Federal Reserve Bank of St. Louis (FRED), Barnichon (2010); author's calculations.

Notes: Vacancy data before 2001 uses vacancy estimates constructed from Barnichon (2010) using the Help-Wanted Index published by the Conference Board. All values are seasonally adjusted.

The surge in demand-side labor market measures like the vacancy rate and quits rate since the outset of the pandemic has led to a significant outward shift in the famous Beveridge-type curves, which relate demand-side and supply-side labor market measures. Figure 3.5 shows how the relationships between the job vacancy rate and the unemployment rate, and the quits rate and the unemployment rate have deviated significantly from their historical trends. This suggests that the labor market is significantly tighter today than implied by the unemployment rate.

The relevant question for determining the inflationary pressure in the labor market is how much the non-accelerating inflation rate of unemployment (NAIRU) has increased as a result of the outward shift in these Beveridge-type curves. In what follows, I present a very crude analysis that suggests that it is plausible the NAIRU has increased somewhere between 1.5 and 2.5 percentage points.[1]

One way to crudely estimate the rise in the NAIRU is to calculate the unemployment rate that is consistent with the current measures of the job vacancy rate and the quits rate. In a recent paper (Domash and Summers 2022), we calibrate a model of the unemployment rate on the log of the vacancy rate and the log of the quits rate using monthly Job Openings and Labor Turnover Survey (JOLTS) data from January 2001 to December 2019. We then use this model to predict what rate of unemployment is consistent with current levels of vacancies and quits post-2020. Figure 3.6 shows the difference between the actual and predicted unemployment rates, using a model with twelve-month lags and a time trend. Given the historical relationship between the unemployment rate and the vacancy and quits rates, the unemployment rate consistent with the current levels of vacancies and quits is between 1.5 and 2 percentage points lower than its current value.

---

1. I am currently working on a more sophisticated analysis with Olivier Blanchard and Alex Domash that incorporates changes in the labor matching process to estimate the increase in the NAIRU.

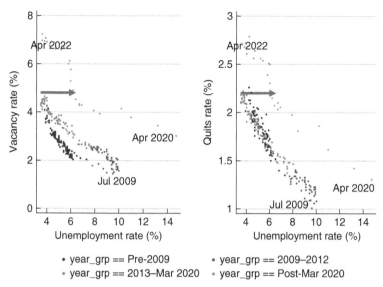

FIGURE 3.5. Beveridge-Type Curves, January 2001–April 2022
Sources: BLS and JOLTS; author's calculations.

Another way to roughly estimate the increase in the NAIRU is to calculate the unemployment rate needed to bring the vacancy and quits rates back to their December 2019 levels. The red arrows in figure 3.5 visually depict this. They conceptually are equivalent to asking where on the new Beveridge-curve line (highlighted in orange in figure 3.5) the December 2019 values of the vacancy rate and the quits rate fall. Estimating a basic model of the unemployment rate on lagged log vacancy rate and log quits rate between April 2020 and April 2022 indicates that the unemployment rate implied by December 2019 levels of quits and vacancies is 6.7%. This suggests a substantial increase in the NAIRU and a labor market that is significantly tighter than the current unemployment rate would have implied in the past.

The historically tight labor market has corresponded with record levels of wage inflation. According to the best available wage data from the Federal Reserve Bank of Atlanta, which matches the hourly

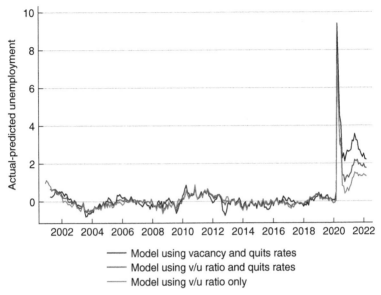

FIGURE 3.6. Residual from Firm-Side Unemployment Regressions

Sources: BLS and JOLTS; author's calculations.

Notes: Predicted unemployment rates are estimated using a model with 12-month lags of each slack variable and a time trend. The model is trained on data from January 2001 through December 2019, and then predicts out-of-sample estimates post-2020. The vacancy and quits rates use JOLTS data, and the v/u ratio is calculated as total vacancies/total unemployed.

earnings of individuals across twelve months, median year-over-year wage inflation in May 2022 reached a series high of 6.6% (using the weighted 3-month moving average of median wages). This series is shown in figure 3.7, going back to 1997. Other wage series show a similar story. According to the Employment Cost Index for private-sector workers, wages and salaries increased by an annualized rate of 5.2% in the first quarter of 2022. The average hourly earnings for all private-sector production and nonsupervisory employees from the Bureau of Labor Statistics shows that month-over-month wage inflation (using a 3-month moving average) reached 5.6% in May 2022.

Historically, wage inflation is highly correlated with price inflation. While the precise relation depends on productivity growth

FIGURE 3.7. Weighted 3-Month Moving Average of 12-Month Percentage Change in Wages
Source: Atlanta Federal Reserve Wage Tracker.

and margins, the empirical evidence suggests that wage inflation usually runs about 1 percentage point higher than price inflation. Tables 3.1 and 3.2 below show the relationship between wage inflation (measured using the Atlanta Wage Tracker and Employment Cost Index) and price inflation over the last two decades, using both core PCE and CPI. Since 2001, annual wage inflation has been 0.6 percentage points higher, on average, than the CPI using the Employment Cost Index and 1.3 percentage points higher, on average, using the Atlanta Wage Tracker. Current levels of both the ECI and the Atlanta Wage Tracker imply price inflation of around 5 percent. This evidence implies that it is highly improbable average price inflation will fall below 3% without a significant slowdown in wage growth from its current levels.

TABLE 3.1. Average Difference between Wage and Price Inflation, 2001–20

Wage Measure	Core PCE				CPI			
	Avg.	SD	Highest	Lowest	Avg.	SD	Highest	Lowest
Employment Cost Index (ECI)	0.9	0.6	2.3	–0.04	0.6	1.1	3.1	–2.2
Atlanta Wage Tracker	1.7	0.8	3.5	0.05	1.3	1.3	3.9	–1.8

Sources: BLS via FRED; Atlanta Federal Reserve; author's calculations.

Notes: Calculations show the difference between nominal wage growth and price inflation, using quarterly data from 2001 to 2020. The Employment Cost Index (ECI) uses the total compensation for all civilian workers, seasonally adjusted. The Atlanta Fed series is the weighted 3-month trailing average of median wage growth. Core PCE uses the personal consumption expenditures excluding food and energy, and CPI uses the Consumer Price Index for all urban consumers.

TABLE 3.2. Predicted Price Inflation Based on Wage Inflation, March 2022

Wage Measure	Wage Inflation (2022 Q1)	Predicted Core PCE	Predicted CPI
Employment Cost Index (ECI)	5.2	4.3 (0.6)	4.6 (1.1)
Atlanta Wage Tracker	6.6	4.9 (0.8)	5.3 (1.3)

Sources: BLS via FRED; Atlanta Federal Reserve; author's calculations.

Notes: Predicted price inflation is calculated using the average difference between wage inflation and price inflation from 2001 Q1 to 2020 Q4. The Employment Cost Index (ECI) uses the total compensation for all civilian workers, seasonally adjusted. ECI inflation in 2022 Q1 is calculated using the percent change from the previous quarter (annualized). The Atlanta Fed series is the weighted 3-month trailing average of median wage growth. Predicted PCE uses the personal consumption expenditures excluding food and energy (Core PCE), and predicted CPI uses the Consumer Price Index for all urban consumers. Standard errors are shown in parentheses.

THE RISK OF A HARD LANDING IS SUBSTANTIAL

Given the extraordinarily tight labor market and high inflation levels, the likelihood of a soft landing for the economy is very low. Table 3.3 looks at quarterly data going back to the 1950s and calculates the probability that the economy will go into recession within the next one to two years, conditioning on alternative measures of

TABLE 3.3. Historical Probability of a Recession Conditional on Different Levels of CPI Inflation and Unemployment, 1955–2019

	Avg. Quarterly Inflation above:	Avg. Quarterly UR below:	Probability of Recession over Next 4 Quarters	Probability of Recession over Next 8 Quarters	Number of Quarters	When Did US Economy Most Recently Cross Threshold?
Inflation only	3%	#N/A	27%	48%	95	Q2 2021
	4%	#N/A	37%	59%	51	Q2 2021
	5%	#N/A	45%	62%	29	Q3 2021
UR only	#N/A	6%	25%	47%	142	Q2 2021
	#N/A	5%	31%	57%	83	Q4 2021
	#N/A	4%	42%	69%	26	Q1 2022
Inflation and UR	3%	6%	43%	75%	53	Q2 2021
	3%	5%	54%	85%	26	Q4 2021
	3%	4%	54%	85%	13	Q1 2022
	4%	6%	59%	89%	27	Q2 2021
	4%	5%	73%	100%	11	Q4 2021
	4%	4%	57%	100%	7	Q1 2022
	5%	6%	83%	100%	12	Q3 2021
	5%	5%	100%	100%	5	Q4 2021
	5%	4%	100%	100%	3	Q1 2022

Sources: BLS via FRED; author's calculations.

Notes: The calculation for the probability of recession over the next 4 quarters and 8 quarters excludes quarters when the US economy is already in a recession. Recession is defined using NBER-based recession indicators for the United States from the period following the peak through the trough. The measure of inflation used is the Consumer Price Index for all urban consumers.

price inflation and unemployment. The results indicate that lower unemployment and higher price inflation significantly increase the probability of a recession. Historically, when average quarterly inflation is above 4%, and the unemployment rate is below 4%, a recession has always started within the next two years.

Measuring labor market tightness with the job vacancy rate rather than the unemployment rate yields nearly identical probabilities for the risk of recession over the next one and two years. Using the Core PCE or nominal wage growth to measure inflation, rather than using CPI inflation, also shows similar results. Given the few business cycles from which to draw data for the US, this analysis is repeated across thirty member countries of the Organisation for Economic Co-operation and Development (OECD). Table 3.4 presents the results, which largely corroborate the findings that high inflation and low unemployment are strong predictors of future recessions. Across the OECD, when countries experience inflation above 5% and unemployment below 5%, the probability of recession within the next two years is 90%. This cross-country historical evidence strongly substantiates the claim that a soft landing will be very difficult.

Some have argued that there are grounds for optimism on the basis that softish landings have occurred several times in the post-war period—including in 1965, 1984, and 1994. But inflation and labor market tightness in each period had little resemblance to the current moment. Table 3.5 summarizes the labor market conditions during these alleged soft landings. In all three episodes, the Fed was operating in an economy with an unemployment rate significantly higher than today, a vacancy-to-unemployment ratio significantly lower than today, and wage inflation still below 4%. In these historical examples, the Fed also raised interest rates well above the inflation rate—unlike today—and explicitly acted early to preempt inflation from spiraling, rather than waiting for inflation to already be excessive. These periods also did not involve major supply shocks such as those currently being experienced in the US.

Another argument that has been made in favor of the soft-landing view is that given the extremely elevated levels of job openings, the Fed may be able to curb demand in such a way that job openings fall considerably without a corresponding increase in unemployment. Unfortunately, this claim also goes against the historical evidence. Table 3.6 shows that the vacancy rate has never come down in a significant way without large increases in unemployment. For each of the previous nine vacancy rate peaks, the table calculates the increase in unemployment that follows a substantial fall in the vacancy rate. To be conservative in the estimate, we look at a 20% decline in vacancies,

TABLE 3.4. Historical Probability of a Recession for OECD Countries, Conditional on Different Levels of CPI Inflation and Unemployment, 1955–2019

	Avg. Quarterly Inflation above:	Avg. Quarterly UR below:	Probability of Recession over Next 4 Quarters	Probability of Recession over Next 8 Quarters	Number of Quarters	When Did US Economy Most Recently Cross Threshold?
Inflation only	3%	#N/A	38%	65%	841	Q2 2021
	4%	#N/A	37%	64%	559	Q2 2021
	5%	#N/A	38%	65%	392	Q3 2021
UR only	#N/A	6%	42%	68%	872	Q2 2021
	#N/A	5%	46%	73%	545	Q4 2021
	#N/A	4%	48%	75%	292	Q1 2022
Inflation and UR	3%	6%	53%	81%	275	Q2 2021
	3%	5%	56%	85%	188	Q4 2021
	3%	4%	52%	80%	124	Q1 2022
	4%	6%	57%	82%	157	Q2 2021
	4%	5%	57%	85%	100	Q4 2021
	4%	4%	51%	80%	71	Q1 2022
	5%	6%	64%	88%	104	Q3 2021
	5%	5%	66%	90%	70	Q4 2021
	5%	4%	63%	86%	51	Q1 2022

Sources: OECD; author's calculations.

Notes: The table includes data from 30 OECD countries from 1960 to 2019, where data is available. Lithuania, Latvia, Iceland, and the Netherlands are excluded due to lack of available data. The analysis also excludes Japan and Mexico. The unemployment rates are OECD seasonally adjusted harmonized unemployment rates. Recession data uses the OECD Composite Leading Indicators dataset, which identifies business cycles and turning points based on a growth cycle approach. Inflation is measured using the CPI for all items and taking the 4-quarter percentage change on the same period from the previous year. All data comes from the OECD.

TABLE 3.5. Labor Market Conditions Today Compared to Past Periods

	1965	1984	1994	Today
Unemployment rate	4.9%	7.9%	6.6%	3.6%
Vacancy-to-unemployment ratio	0.7	0.5	0.5	1.9
Wage inflation	3.6%	3.8%	2.5%	6.6%
Interest rate > inflation rate?	YES	YES	YES	NO

Source: BLS.

Note: This table uses quarterly averages from the first quarter of the tightening cycle.

TABLE 3.6. Change in Unemployment Rate (pp) after Vacancy Rate Falls 20% from Its Peak, 1950–2019

Month of Peak Vacancy Rate	Vacancy Rate (%)	Unemployment Rate (%)	Number of Months to Reduce Vacancy Rate by 20%	Sacrifice Ratio: Increase in Unemployment (pp) to Reduce Vacancy Rate by 20%
March 1953	4.4	2.6	4	3.3
February 1956	3.5	3.9	18	3.6
February 1960	3.1	4.8	8	2.3
May 1969	5.2	3.4	11	2.7
July 1973	4.8	4.8	14	5.2
April 1979	5.2	5.8	12	2.0
October 1988	4.4	5.4	22	1.5
February 2000	4.1	4.1	14	1.8
June 2007	3.1	4.6	12	4.9
March 2022	7.2	3.6	#N/A	#N/A
AVERAGE			13 months	3.0pp

Sources: BLS, JOLTs, Barnichon (2010); author's calculations.

Notes: The sacrifice ratio is calculated as the difference between the highest unemployment rate within one year after the vacancy rate falls by 20% and the unemployment rate when the vacancy rate is at a peak. The vacancy rate is calculated as the total number of nonfarm job openings divided by the size of the labor force. Job vacancy data from 2001 onward uses estimates from JOLTS, while vacancy data before 2001 uses job vacancy estimates constructed from Barnichon (2010) using the Help-Wanted Index published by the Conference Board. All values are seasonally adjusted.

which would bring the vacancy rate down from its March 2022 peak of 7.2% to a still-elevated level of 5.6%.

The results show that each time the vacancy rate falls by 20% from its peak, the unemployment rate increases substantially. On average, a 20% decline in vacancies requires a 3-percentage point increase in the unemployment rate. The smallest increase in unemployment associated with a 20% drop in vacancies in the postwar period was 1.5 percentage points. The largest increase occurred in the mid-1970s when unemployment rose by more than 5 percentage points.

According to the Sahm rule, a recession starts when the three-month moving average of the national unemployment rate rises by 0.5 percentage points or more relative to its low during the previous twelve months. Based on the evidence provided above, it seems highly plausible that the economy will pass this threshold over the next year or two.

While none of the evidence asserts with certainty that a recession will start, the historical experience strongly suggests that recession risks are substantially greater than is commonly thought likely.

OBSERVATIONS ON FED TACTICS

Finally, I conclude with a few comments on the specific tactics used by the Fed. Given the need to change policy in the face of changing data, the idea of providing forward guidance by setting specific numerical targets around price stability and through the provision of dot plots is problematic. Central banks can't know what they will do in the future—they must constantly react to incoming data. However, when the Fed gives specific forward guidance, it feels constrained to follow through on it, and so it diverts policy from what would otherwise be the optimal path. A more prudent path forward would be a return to a more modest framework with broad objectives clearly stated and a reliance on forward-looking anticipations in policy. The Fed should use policy rules to signal when it needs to change course, rather than constructing specific doctrines that must be displaced when unexpected shocks occur.

Moreover, by not setting policy on an anticipatory basis, the Fed acted too slowly in responding to credible inflationary threats in the economy. The first two sections of this chapter showed that inflation should have been predictable in early 2021 using basic forecasts of the output gap and by looking at tightness in the labor market. The amount of stimulus being pushed through the economy amounted to approximately three times the size of the output gap. The outward shift in the Beveridge curve signaled that the NAIRU had likely risen substantially, and that the labor market was significantly tighter than implied by the unemployment rate. These strong inflationary indicators should have justified action far sooner than the actual point when the Fed acted—which would have helped to avoid the need to engineer an extremely difficult disinflation over the coming years.

References

Barnichon, Regis. 2010. "Building a Composite Help-Wanted Index." *Economics Letters* 109, no. 3:175–78.

Bureau of Economic Analysis. 2022. "Table 1.15. Price, Costs, and Profit Per Unit of Real Gross Value Added of Nonfinancial Domestic Corporate Business." National Income and Product Accounts. February 24.

Domash, Alex, and Lawrence H. Summers. 2022. "A Labor Market View on the Risks of a US Hard Landing." National Bureau of Economic Research Working Paper No. 29910.

Federal Open Market Committee. 2021. "Summary of Economic Projections." Board of Governors of the Federal Reserve System. March 17. https://www.federalreserve.gov/monetarypolicy/files/fomcprojtabl20210317.pdf.

Federal Reserve Bank of Atlanta. 2022. "Wage Growth Tracker." https://www.atlantafed.org/chcs/wage-growth-tracker?panel=1.

Greig, Fiona, and Erica Deadman. 2022. "Household Pulse: The State of Cash Balances at Year End." JPMorgan Chase Institute.

Powell, Tyler, Louise Sheiner, and David Wessel. 2021. "What Is Potential GDP, and Why Is It So Controversial Right Now?" Brookings Institution. February 22.

Williams, John C. 2017. "The Perennial Problem of Predicting Potential." Federal Reserve Bank of San Francisco Economic Letter. November 6.

CHAPTER FOUR

IT'S TIME TO GET BACK TO RULES-BASED MONETARY POLICY

John B. Taylor

For several years, starting around 2017, the Federal Reserve began to move back to a more rules-based monetary policy, which had worked well in the United States in the 1980s, 1990s, and in other years. Many papers written at the Fed and elsewhere reflected this revival and showed the benefits of rules-based policies. In July 2017, when Janet Yellen was chair, the Fed began to include a whole section on rules-based monetary policy in its *Monetary Policy Report*, and many policy makers made favorable comments about rules-based policy. The evidence was that the move toward rules-based policy was beneficial and economic performance improved.

The Fed halted that move in early 2020 when the COVID-19 pandemic hit the American economy and many other economies around the world. The Fed stopped reporting on monetary policy rules in the July 2020 *Monetary Policy Report*. It also embarked on new efforts to deal with the effects of the pandemic-fueled crisis on the economy, including a rapid reduction in the federal funds rate, large-scale purchases of Treasury and mortgage-backed securities, which led to a large expansion of the Fed's balance sheet, and a sharp increase in the growth rate of the monetary aggregates. These actions were special and were not generally consistent with rules-based policies.

In February 2021, however, the Fed began to put monetary policy rules back in its *Monetary Policy Report*. Though the section on policy rules was back in the *Report* and remained there through July 2021, there was little evidence that actual monetary policy decisions followed those rules. Thus, a gap developed between the reported rules-based policy and the policy actions of the Fed. Inflation began to rise.

Perhaps seeing this gap, the Fed then reversed again, removing the section on policy rules from the *Monetary Policy Report* in February 2022. In a congressional hearing on March 3, 2022, several members of Congress asked Fed Chair Jerome Powell questions about why the policy rules section was missing. Fed Chair Powell responded that the Fed would aim to put the rules section back in the *Report* later in the year, perhaps in the July *Monetary Policy Report*. And, true to Powell's word, on June 17, 2022, soon after this Hoover conference took place, the Fed put policy rules back in the *Report*. However, only small changes have occurred in actual monetary policy.

A big gap thus still exists between most measures of rules-based policy and actual policy actions. When this gap occurred before, it was accompanied by the rise of inflation. Thus, we are in, and will remain in, a high-inflation era unless the Fed and other central banks take sensible actions to bring policy in line with known policy rules and strategies. Recent events in Ukraine have raised measured inflation of many goods, such as gasoline, but have not changed this basic story.

A REVIVAL OF RESEARCH ON MONETARY POLICY RULES

Monetary policy rules were the subject of much research in the 1970s through the early 2000s. For the next several years, there was a lull in policy rule research and applications, but starting in 2017, there was a big pickup, and there is plenty of evidence for this revival. As mentioned above, a new section on monetary policy rules for the instruments appeared in the Fed's *Monetary Policy Report* with five different policy rules presented and compared with actual policy. In addition, papers were presented at a monetary policy conference at the Hoover Institution at Stanford University in May 2019, at the Federal Reserve Review conference in Chicago in June 2019, and at the Macroeconomic Modelling and Model Comparison Network conference in Frankfurt, also in June 2019. There are many takeaways, but that there was a revival of research on monetary policy rules is quite evident.

At the Stanford conference, for example, Mertens and Williams (2020) evaluated different policy rules for the interest rate with a New Keynesian model. They considered three types of monetary policy rules. The first was a standard inflation-targeting interest rate rule in which the Fed reduces its response to higher inflation and output to bias the economy toward higher interest rates and inflation and thereby reduces the probability of hitting the lower bond. The second was a rule in which the average inflation target is higher than the one used with standard inflation targeting, though the strength of responses to deviations is unchanged. The third was a price level targeting rule, in which the Fed allows substantial inflation after a low-inflation episode, until the price level recovers to its target, and vice versa.

Cochrane, Taylor, and Wieland (2020) evaluated rules with seven different models. These rules include the Taylor rule, a "balanced-approach" rule, a difference rule that responds to growth rather than levels of inflation and unemployment, and two rules that take particular account of periods with near-zero federal funds rates by implementing a forward-guidance promise to make up for zero bound periods with looser subsequent policy. The paper evaluated these monetary policy rules in seven well-known macroeconomic models—a small New Keynesian model, a small Old Keynesian model, a larger policy-oriented model, and four other models from the Macroeconomic Model Data Base. The robustness across models was an essential part of the evaluation process.

At the conference at the Federal Reserve Bank of Chicago, Sims and Wu (2019) evaluated different monetary policy rules with a new structural model, and Eberly, Stock, and Wright (2019) evaluated monetary policy rules using the Federal Reserve Board/ United States (FRB/US) model. At the conference in Frankfurt, Andreas Beyer (2019), Gregor Boehl (2019), and many others evaluated interest rate rules in specific models. These included interest rate rules as well as rules for purchases of assets and the corresponding expansion of the central bank's balance sheet. Of particular note is the paper by Nikolsko-Rzhevskyy, Papell, and Prodan (2021), which compared policy rules and discretion historically, using new econometric techniques. Their paper considered a specific policy rule for the interest rate and measured discretion as a deviation of the actual interest rate from that rule. They did calculations for 400 rules and found the average loss in high-deviation periods was greater than the average loss in low-deviation periods. Some researchers, including Belongia and Ireland (2019), looked at other instruments such as the money supply, but most continued to look at interest rate instruments.

An important example of this revival of research on policy rules is the paper by Bernanke, Kiley, and Roberts (2019a), which examined the stabilizing properties of ten different monetary policy rules for the instruments using the FRB/US model. Figure 4.1 shows seven of these ten interest rate rules, using the notation of Bernanke, Kiley, and Roberts (2019b). The symbol i_t^{Tay} is the nominal interest rate implied by the Taylor rule, r^* is the real natural rate of interest (assumed to be 1%), π^* is the inflation target (assumed to be 2%), π_t is the inflation rate defined as the four-quarter percentage change in core consumer price index, and $\hat{y}_t$ is the output gap. In addition, i_t^{FPLT} is the flexible price level targeting rule, i_t^{KR} is a rule for the interest rate proposed by Kiley and Roberts (2017), and P_t is the deviation of the consumer price index from its target level, assumed to grow by 2% each year. Two of the policy rules (the Taylor rule and the Reifschneider-Williams rule) are shown by the arrows in figure 4.1. The other three rules

$$i_t^{Tay} = r^* + \pi_t + 0.5(\pi_t - \pi^*) + \hat{y}_t \quad \leftarrow \text{Taylor rule}$$

$$i_t^{iTay} = \rho i_{t-1} + (1 - \rho)[r^* + \pi_t + 0.5(\pi_t - \pi^*)] + \hat{y}_t]$$

$$i_t^{FPLT} = r^* + \pi_t + 0.5(\pi_t - \pi^*) + \hat{y}_t + P_t$$

$$i_t^{iFPLT} = \rho i_{t-1} + (1 - \rho)[r^* + \pi_t + 0.5(\pi_t - \pi^*) + \hat{y}_t + P_t]$$

$$i_t^{FTPLT} = \rho i_{t-1} + (1 - \rho)[r^* + \pi_t + 0.5(\pi_t - \pi^*) + \hat{y}_t + \alpha TP_t]$$

$$\boxed{TP_t = \Sigma_{j=t1}^{m}(\pi_j - \pi^*)}$$

$$i_t = \max\left\{0, i_t^{Tay} - \Sigma_{j=t1}^{t-1}(i_j - i_j^{Tay})\right\} \quad \leftarrow \text{Reifschneider-Williams rule}$$

$$i_t^{KR} = i_{t-1}^{KR} + \alpha[(\pi_t - \pi^*) + \hat{y}_t]$$

Plus 3 TPLT rules, which are like i^{Tay} except for an ELB threshold

FIGURE 4.1. Policy Rules Studied by Bernanke, Kiley, and Roberts
Source: Bernanke, Kiley, and Roberts (2019b).

considered by Bernanke, Kiley, and Roberts (2019b) are temporary price level targeting rules (TPLT) that are very similar to these seven rules but take into account the effective lower bound (ELB) of zero in the interest rate.

What explains this revival? One explanation is a revealed preference for such research on the part of monetary policy officials and others interested in monetary policy making. At the Chicago Fed conference, Cecchetti and Schoenholtz (2019) shared that they found, "The most frequently mentioned topic is the desirability of having a clear understanding of policy makers' reaction function." There were also statements by central bank leaders. Raghuram Rajan, former governor of the Reserve Bank of India, said, "What we need are monetary rules." Mario Draghi, then president of the European Central Bank, said, "We would all clearly benefit from . . . improving communication over our reaction functions." Jay Powell, chair of the Federal Reserve Board, said, "I find these rule prescriptions helpful."

Another explanation for the revival was the desire to figure out how to deal with the effective (or zero) lower bound on the interest rate. There was genuine concern about the lower bound in the case of a need for substantial easing. How else can one evaluate alternative proposals for "lower for longer" policy, such as the Reifschneider and Williams (2000) proposal, than with a rule? This is also a huge motivation behind the work by Lilley and Rogoff (2020).

Another possible explanation was the disappointment with monetary policy leading to the Great Recession, especially the deviation from rules in the 2003–5 "too low for too long" period. Yet another explanation was the recognition that rules are necessary to evaluate quantitative easing proposals. At the Chicago conference, for example, Brian Sack said, "Talking more about the policy rules . . . is appropriate to guide future bond purchase programs and improve their impact." Perhaps concern about proposed policy rules legislation that was circulating around Congress in 2017–18 led the Fed to talk more openly about policy rules in the *Monetary Policy Report*.

A RETREAT FROM POLICY RULES

The pandemic that started in the first quarter of 2020 with COVID-19 was a jolt to the American economy and many other economies. It interrupted the revival of rules-based policies as many central banks, including the Fed, took special actions to deal with the effects of the health crisis on the global economy.

In the US, these actions included a rapid reduction in the target for the federal funds rate during the period around March 2020, as shown in figure 4.2. It also included large-scale purchases of Treasury and mortgage-backed securities causing a large expansion of the Fed's balance sheet as shown in figure 4.3. Total assets at the Fed rose from $3.8 trillion to $8.9 trillion. Both M1 and M2 measures of the money supply also grew rapidly. As mentioned above, the Fed

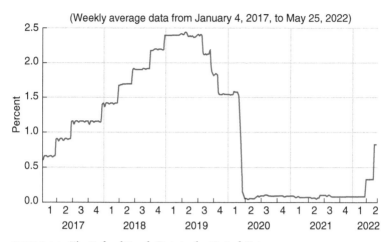

FIGURE 4.2. The Federal Funds Rate in the United States
Source: Federal Reserve Economic Data, Federal Reserve Bank of St. Louis (FRED).

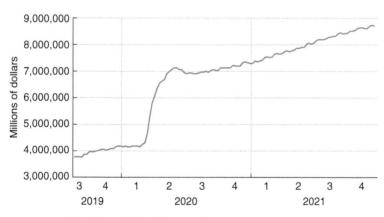

FIGURE 4.3. Total Assets Federal Reserve System
Source: FRED (Wednesday Levels).

also stopped reporting on rules-based policy in its *Monetary Policy Report* with the July 2020 issue.

By many accounts, these actions were discretionary and were not consistent with rules-based policies. Indeed, as would be expected from the large difference between these interest rate actions and a

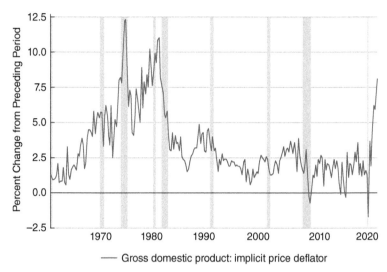

FIGURE 4.4. Inflation Reached 8.1% in Early 2022
Source: US Bureau of Economic Analysis (BEA) via FRED, myf.red/g/O6K4.
Note: Shaded areas indicate US recessions.

more rules-based policy, the inflation rate rose. As measured by the GDP deflator, the inflation rate shown in figure 4.4 rose by very large amounts. The inflation rate as measured by the consumer price index rose to 8.5% in March 2022.

AVERAGE INFLATION TARGETING: A FURTHER RETREAT?

While these changes in inflation were beginning, the Fed and other central banks began to review their monetary policy strategies in light of COVID-19 as summarized in Taylor (2020). One of the first to complete this review was the Fed, which decided to move to a new "flexible form of average inflation targeting," as Fed Chair Jerome Powell described it at the annual Jackson Hole monetary policy conference in August 2020. European Central Bank President Christine Lagarde explained at the annual ECB and Its

Watchers conference in September 2020, that the ECB was in the middle of its own "monetary policy strategy review." At the Bank of Japan, Governor Haruhiko Kuroda was involved in a similar discussion with the government of Japan.

In fact, it looked like there was a move underway to reform the entire international monetary system, with each country or region taking actions similar to the Fed, though attuned to its own circumstances. It did not turn out that way. "At the very least," argued Otmar Issing, a former chief economist and former member of the ECB Board who was largely responsible for charting the original course of ECB policy making, "other central banks should not blindly follow the Fed's new strategy."

Others criticized the Fed's new approach to average inflation targeting. In early September 2020, Robert Heller, former Federal Reserve governor, argued in a letter to the *Wall Street Journal* that the Fed should "not target an average inflation rate of 2%." At a virtual conference convened by Stanford University's Hoover Institution, Charles I. Plosser, a former president of the Federal Reserve Bank of Philadelphia, and Mickey D. Levy, of Berenberg Capital Markets, criticized the Fed for not being specific about the timespan over which average inflation is measured. Is it one year or several years?

Chair Powell acknowledged this lack of specificity at the Jackson Hole conference in August by saying, "We are not tying ourselves to a particular mathematical formula that defines the average." He added that, "Our decisions about appropriate monetary policy . . . will not be dictated by any formula." Then, in a press release the same day, the Fed's Board of Governors explained that policy decisions depended on "assessments of the shortfalls of employment from its maximum level" rather than by "deviations from its maximum level," as it had previously stated.

Partly because of the difficulty distinguishing "deviations" from "shortfalls," this new approach added uncertainty. There was no mention of how monetary policy could create higher inflation.

In adopting this "flexible" approach, the Fed seemed to shift further away from the more rules-based policy that it had been pursuing since 2017. As mentioned, the *Monetary Policy Report* dropped the section on monetary policy rules, in contrast to previous *Reports*, which had featured a whole section on rules. This made it difficult to compare rules with actual policy.

It is understandable that Issing and others would be reluctant to go along with the Fed's apparently more discretionary approach, especially when there were alternatives that other central banks could pursue. Rather than casting about for something new or simply different from the Fed, they looked for a rules-based policy path that the Fed itself was on before the pandemic struck.

When it was first developed, the Taylor rule used an average inflation rate. However, the Taylor rule defined the "average" as "the rate of inflation over the previous four quarters." In other words, the Fed could still switch to a specific average-inflation approach.

Moreover, the formal policy rules previously listed in the *Monetary Policy Report* had variables to account for factors other than the inflation rate, such as the unemployment rate or the gap between real and potential GDP. These variables could be included in any new strategy without neglecting the inflation target, as could policy rules, to deal with asset purchases and their eventual unwinding. Developing such an approach would not be difficult to do.

The large increase in the inflation rate in 2021 and 2022, shown in figure 4.4, raised an even more basic question about the average inflation targeting. With the current inflation rate well above the level needed to raise average inflation by a small amount, the focus of everyone became how to reduce the current inflation rate rather than simply allowing the average inflation rate to rise.

That policy rules reentered the Federal Reserve's *Monetary Policy Report* on February 19, 2021, was a welcome development. It reinitiated a helpful reporting approach that, as mentioned earlier, began in the July 2017 *Monetary Policy Report* when Janet Yellen was Fed chair but was dropped in July 2020.

Five rules were in the February 2021 *Monetary Policy Report* on pages 45 through 48. To quote the *Report*, these include "the well-known Taylor (1993) rule, the 'balanced approach' rule, the 'adjusted Taylor (1993)' rule, and the 'first difference' rule." In addition to these rules, and this is very important, there is a new "'balanced approach (shortfalls) rule,' which represents one simple way to illustrate the Committee's focus on shortfalls from maximum employment."

Figure 4.5 shows the five rules from the July 2021 *Report*. Even though these were not in the February 2022 *Monetary Policy Report*, they state where the Fed was most recently regarding rules. Moreover, the Fed chair suggested the rules would be in future *Reports*. There were also five rules in the earlier *Reports*, but one was out, and a new one—the balanced-approach (shortfalls) rule—was in. This new modified simple rule would not call for increasing the policy rate as employment moves higher and unemployment drops below its estimated longer-run level. This modified rule aims to illustrate, in a simple way, the Committee's focus on shortfalls of employment from assessments of its maximum level.

In figure 4.5, the notation is standard: The symbol r is the interest rate, π is the inflation rate, u is the unemployment rate, and the superscript LR means the long run. How different would the shortfalls rule be compared to the regular balanced-approach rule? The 2021 *Report* endeavored to answer this question. The balanced-approach (shortfalls) rule was below the regular balanced-approach rule in 2017 through the start of the pandemic in 2020. Thus, the shortfalls rule did not increase the interest rate, as does the balanced-approach rule without the shortfall. The shortfalls and the non-shortfalls rules then move together during the start of the pandemic as the unemployment rate rises well above the long run rate. The adjusted Taylor rule stays above zero, but then stays low for longer than the Taylor rule.

A. Monetary policy rules

Taylor (1993) rule	$R_t^{T93} = r_t^{LR} + \pi_t + 0.5(\pi_t - \pi^{LR}) + (u_t^{LR} - u_t)$
Balanced-approach rule	$R_t^{BA} = r_t^{LR} + \pi_t + 0.5(\pi_t - \pi^{LR}) + 2(u_t^{LR} - u_t)$
Balanced-approach (shortfalls) rule	$R_t^{SBA} = r_t^{LR} + \pi_t + 0.5(\pi_t - \pi^{LR}) + 2\,min\{(u_t^{LR} - u_t), 0\}$
Adjusted Taylor (1993) rule	$R_t^{T93\,adj} = max\{R_t^{T93} - Z_t, \text{ELB}\}$
First-difference rule	$R_t^{FD} = R_{t-1} + 0.5(\pi_t - \pi^{LR}) + (u_t^{LR} - u_t) - (u_{t-4}^{LR} - u_{t-4})$

FIGURE 4.5. Five Policy Rules from the July 2021 *Monetary Policy Report*
Source: Federal Reserve, *Monetary Policy Report*, July 9, 2021, 44.

The useful contribution of this new shortfalls rule is that one now had an explicit way to think about the Fed's new "shortfalls from maximum employment" approach. One can see if the new rule performs better than the balanced approach or the modified Taylor rule, for example, by simulating various models. It was disappointing that, as the *Report* says, the aims "of having inflation average 2% over time to ensure that longer-term inflation expectations remain well anchored, is not incorporated in the simple rules analyzed in this discussion."

To summarize, the analysis in this section takes into account the shortfalls of unemployment rather than deviations, and focusses on the average inflation rate by looking at moderate inflation rates slightly higher than the long-run target inflation rate. Nevertheless, the results are similar to what one finds by looking at the regular Taylor rule. The results can be compared by looking at the average gap in percentage points between the Federal Open Market Committee (FOMC) interest rate and the settings of the three rules.

REENTRY INTO A MONETARY STRATEGY

It is good that rules were in the Fed's *Monetary Policy Report* in 2021, and it is good that they might be back in future *Monetary Policy Reports*. It would be more helpful if the Fed incorporated some of these rules or strategy ideas into its actual decisions. Apparently, this has not yet happened, as I show below by comparing the interest rate path and policy rules for the interest rate.

One reason that there was little, or no action, is that the Fed viewed the resurgence of inflation as "transitory." It was very low in previous years and supply chains seemed to be a special factor. While there have been effects on commodities from supply shortages and the war in Ukraine, the major effect on inflation has been due to monetary policy. The Fed's plan to halt or slow the purchases of Treasuries and mortgage-backed securities seemed like it might reduce inflation, but a policy rule was not part of the strategy.

This is illustrated in figure 4.6, which is based on the data as of April 10, 2021; thus, the graph illustrates that the Fed has been behind the curve for a quite a while. The three lines in figure 4.6 show the federal funds rates from three policy rules using the same parameters as those in the Taylor rule, which is discussed in the February 2021 *Monetary Policy Report.*

The so-called equilibrium interest rate is reduced from 2% to 1% in the calculations in figure 4.6. Such a reduction in the equilibrium interest rate was suggested by staff at the Fed but may be larger or smaller than assumed here. The policy rules use the four-quarter inflation rates of the GDP price index, the personal consumption expenditures (PCE) price index, or the core PCE price index, based on the February 2021 Congressional Budget Office (CBO) projections. They use the same percentage deviation of real GDP from potential GDP as in the CBO report. Other economic forecasters have inflation and real GDP forecasts close to those of CBO.

Even with this smaller equilibrium real interest rate (1% rather than 2% in the original Taylor rule), the FOMC's path for the federal funds rate is well below any of these policy rules. There is a difference in the first quarter of 2021, and the difference grows over time. Consider for simplicity's sake the average of the interest rates for the three different inflation rates in the final quarter of each

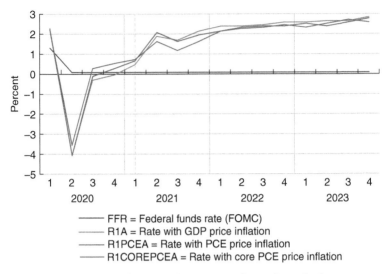

FIGURE 4.6. Federal Funds Rate and Monetary Policy Rules with Three Inflation Rates

Notes: The lines show the federal funds rates from three policy rules using the same parameters as those in the Taylor rule as discussed in the Fed's February 2021 *Monetary Policy Report*. The flat blue line shows the Fed's projection in April 2021.

year. If we average the three values, we get 1.9% in 2021Q4, 2.5% in 2022Q4, and 2.7% in 2023Q4.

There has been little mention of why the discrepancy existed between the Fed's actual decisions reported here and the policy rules. Did this mean that the Fed actually intended to keep the rate this low under these circumstances regarding real GDP and inflation? Would it then raise the rate sharply in 2023 or 2024?

Now consider the current situation. Table 4.1 was created from the Fed's dot plot, which shows individual FOMC member views about future values of the federal funds rate. Table 4.1 shows the value at the end of different calendar years corresponding to different meeting times.

Note that the rates are higher than the blue line in figure 4.6, and that they rise over time at each meeting. The top line shows

TABLE 4.1. FOMC Projections of the Federal Funds Rate at Different Meeting Dates

Year	2021	2022	2023	2024
March 15–16, 2022	—	1.9	2.8	2.8
December 14–15, 2021	0.1	0.9	1.6	2.1
September 21–22, 2021	0.1	0.3	1.0	1.8

Source: Fed *Summary of Economic Projections* for dates shown.

Notes: The projections for the federal funds rate are the value of the midpoint of the projected appropriate target range for the federal funds rate or the projected appropriate target level for the federal funds rate at the end of the specified calendar year. "Appropriate monetary policy" is defined as the future path of policy that each participant deems most likely to foster outcomes for economic activity and inflation that best satisfy his or her individual interpretation of the statutory mandate to promote maximum employment and price stability.

the values at the meeting in March of 2022. According to the dots, the federal funds rate will be 1.9% at the end of 2022, and then will rise to 2.8% at the end of 2023 and at the end of 2024.

The averages in table 4.1 have been calculated from the projections of each FOMC member at various meetings. For example, the average at the December 2021 meeting for the end of 2022 is 0.9% and then rises over time. The averages at the more recent meeting in March 2022 are higher as both the dots and the averages rise over time. Looking out into the later periods in 2023 and 2024, the results are higher in each row of table 4.1.

The solid red line in figure 4.7 is the Taylor rule recommendation from over a year ago in April 2021. The green and orange asterisks are the forward-looking estimates of the FOMC in September 2021 and December 2021, respectively. The blue circles are from the FOMC meeting in March 2022. The FOMC values have been increasing toward the Taylor rule values during this period.

While the blue dots are close to the policy rule, the inputs to the policy rule have changed since a year ago and these have lead to a higher rules-based interest rate. Most important is that inflation has continued to rise. The 4-quarter average inflation rate was 4.575%

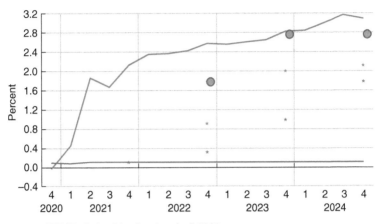

FOMC - federal funds rate - April 2021
* FOMC - federal funds rate - December 2021
* FOMC - federal funds rate - September 2021
Taylor rule - federal funds rate - April 2021 (R* = 1, CBO; Defl & Gap)

FIGURE 4.7. Taylor Rule as of April 2021 and Average of FOMC Dot Plots

Notes: The red line is from the Taylor rule as presented in the Fed's February 2021 *Monetary Policy Report.* The other points are as in table 4.1.

as of the 3rd quarter of 2021, which implies the interest rate should be about 6% even with a GDP gap of −1.6%. That is, the Taylor rule rate is: $r = 6 = 4.575 + 1 + 0.5*(4.575 − 2) + 0.5(−1.60)$.

If the average inflation rate is rounded down to 4%, then the interest rate should be 5%. If you look at the July 9, 2021, *Monetary Policy Report* version of the Taylor rule, and plug in an inflation rate over the past four quarters of 4%, the gap between GDP and its potential of about −2%, a target inflation rate of 2%, an equilibrium interest rate of 1%, you get a federal funds rate of 5%. Recall that this assumes an equilibrium interest rate of 1% rather than 2%. These calculations use an average inflation rate over four quarters, consistent with a form of "average inflation targeting." Even if the inflation rate falls sharply to 2% by the end of 2022, and output equals potential, the federal funds rate should be about 3%. So, the Fed is still behind.

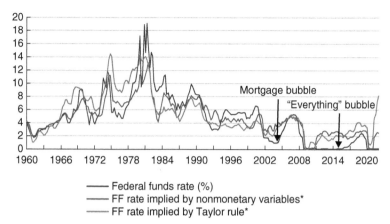

FIGURE 4.8. Federal Funds Rate and Taylor Rule

Source: Hussman (2022) from Federal Reserve data.

Notes: Nonmonetary explanatory variables include the real GDP output gap, inflation as measured by the core PCE deflator, and current and lagged growth rates of real GDP, non-farm payroll employment, and real retail sales. Implied federal funds rate reflects a rolling regression to each date. Taylor rule estimates based on the real GDP output gap and core PCE inflation.

These types of calculations and estimates have now become very well known and have appeared in many places. An excellent recent example is shown figure 4.8. It is a time-series chart reproduced from research conducted by John Hussman (2022), which he recently published in the *Financial Times*. It shows the federal funds rate and an estimate of that rate from the Taylor rule. It is based on up-to-date information, and it shows the ideal rules-based policy interest rate may even be higher than in the above calculations.

CONCLUSION

This paper has examined reasons for returning to a rules-based monetary policy in the United States and has outlined a method for doing so. By reviewing the years leading up to the present monetary situation, it provides the background needed for analyzing current and future monetary policy decisions.

The answer to the key question, "Are We Entering a New Era of High Inflation?" is clearly "yes," unless monetary policy makers change policy. There are now more reasons than ever for central banks to use a more rules-based policy. Central banks should start now with rules that markets understand. The policy interest rate would then increase as inflation rises, as has already happened. It would of course be a contingency plan, as are all rules. But this would greatly reduce the probability of a large damaging change later.

Having a clearly stated policy rule would prepare the Federal Reserve and others for such a strategy, in practice. Moreover, explaining how its policy rule or strategy would be consistent with its flexible average inflation targeting statements would further clarify the Fed's monetary policy and facilitate market adjustments. It would remove uncertainty and remaining inconsistencies.

References

Belongia, Michael T., and Peter N. Ireland. 2019. "A Reconsideration of Money Growth Rules." Boston College Working Papers in Economics, No. 976.

Bernanke, Ben S., Michael T. Kiley, and John M. Roberts. 2019a. "Monetary Policy Strategies for a Low-Rate Environment." American Economic Association Papers and Proceedings, Vol. 109, May, 421–26.

———. 2019b. Online Appendix for "Monetary Policy Strategies for a Low-Rate Environment." Finance and Economics Discussion Series 2019-009. Washington, DC: Board of Governors of the Federal Reserve System. http://doi.org/10.17016/FEDS.2019.009.

Beyer, Andreas. 2019. "Financial Stability and Monetary Policy—An Augmented Taylor Rule for the Euro Area." European Central Bank. Presented at the Third Research Conference of the Macroeconomic Modelling and Model Comparison Network (MMCN), Frankfurt, June 13–14.

Board of Governors of the Federal Reserve System. 2017b, 2018a, 2018b, 2019a, 2019b, 2020a, 2021a. *Monetary Policy Reports*. Washington, DC: Board of Governors.

Boehl, Gregor. 2019. "A Structural Investigation of Quantitative Easing." Presented at the Third Research Conference of the Macroeconomic Modelling and Model Comparison Network (MMCN), Frankfurt, June 13–14.

Cecchetti, Stephen G., and Kermit Schoenholtz. 2019. "Improving US Monetary Policy Communications." CEPR Discussion Paper, No. DP13915, August 2019.

Cochrane, John H., and John B. Taylor, eds. 2020. *Strategies for Monetary Policy*. Stanford, CA: Hoover Institution Press.

Cochrane, John H., John B. Taylor, and Volker Wieland. 2020. "Evaluating Rules in the Fed's Report and Measuring Discretion." In *Strategies for Monetary Policy*, edited by John H. Cochrane and John B. Taylor. Stanford, CA: Hoover Institution Press. https://www.hoover.org/sites/default/files/research/docs/chapter_5.pdf.

Eberly, Janice C., James H. Stock, Jonathan H. Wright. 2019. "The Federal Reserve's Current Framework for Monetary Policy: A Review and Assessment." Prepared for the Conference on Monetary Policy Strategy, Tools, and Communication Practices, Federal Reserve Bank of Chicago, May 24. https://www.chicagofed.org/~/media/others/events/2019/monetary-policy-conference/review-current-framework-eberly-stock-wright-pdf.pdf.

Hussman, John. 2022. "The Fed Policy Error That Should Worry Investors." *Financial Times*, January 25, 2022.

Kiley, Michael T., and John M. Roberts. 2017. "Monetary Policy in a Low Interest Rate World." Brookings Papers on Economic Activity. Spring: 317–96.

Lilley, Andrew, and Kenneth Rogoff. 2020. "The Case for Implementing Effective Negative Interest Rate Policy." In *Strategies for Monetary Policy*, edited by John H. Cochrane and John B. Taylor. Stanford, CA: Hoover Institution Press.

Mertens, Thomas M., and John C. Williams. 2020. "Tying Down the Anchor: Monetary Policy Rules and the Lower Bound on Interest Rates." In *Strategies for Monetary Policy*, edited by John H. Cochrane and John B. Taylor. Stanford, CA: Hoover Institution Press, 103–54.

Nikolsko-Rzhevskyy, Alex, David H. Papell, and Ruxandra Prodan. 2014. "Deviations from Rules-Based Policy and Their Effects." *Journal of Economic Dynamics and Control*, December, 49: 4–17.

———. 2021. "Policy Rules and Economic Performance." *Journal of Macroeconomics*, Vol 68. https://www.sciencedirect.com/science/article/abs/pii/S0164070421000045?dgcid=rss_sd_all.

Papell, David. 2020. "Discussion of Evaluating Rules in the Fed's Report and Measuring Discretion." In *Strategies for Monetary Policy*, edited by John H. Cochrane and John B. Taylor. Stanford, CA: Hoover Institution Press.

Reifschneider, David, and John C. Williams. 2000. "Three Lessons for Monetary Policy in a Low-Inflation Era." *Journal of Money, Credit and Banking* 32, no. 4, part 2: 936–66.

Sims, Eric R., and Jing Cynthia Wu. 2019. "Evaluating Central Banks' Tool Kit: Past, Present, and Future." Presented at the Conference on Monetary Policy Strategy, Tools, and Communication Practices, Federal Reserve Bank of Chicago, June 2019. https://papers.ssrn.com/sol3/papers.cfm?abstract_id=3416343.

Taylor, John B. 1993. "Discretion versus Policy Rules in Practice." Carnegie-Rochester Conference Series on Public Policy 39: 195–214. Amsterdam: North-Holland.

———. 2020. "Who's Afraid of Rules-Based Monetary Policy?" Project Syndicate October 16, 2020. https://web.stanford.edu/~johntayl/2020_pdfs/Who_s_Afraid_of_Rules-Based_Monetary_Policy-Project_Syndicate-10-16-20.pdf.

———. 2021. "The Optimal Reentry to a Monetary Policy Strategy." Presented at the Graduate Center, City University of New York, April 13, 2021.

GENERAL DISCUSSION

TOM STEPHENSON (INTRODUCTION): Welcome to the first session of Hoover's 2022 Monetary Policy Conference. Due to the impact of COVID-19, it's been several years since we've held this conference. Our introductory session this morning is entitled "What Monetary Policy Rules and Strategies Say" and features three extremely well-known experts in the field, Larry Summers, Richard Clarida, and John Taylor.

Larry, whom I've known dating back to his days as president of Harvard University, has subsequently served as secretary of the Treasury in the Clinton administration, director of the National Economic Council from 2009 to 2010, and is now the Charles W. Eliot [University] Professor at Harvard University.

Richard Clarida is a well-known economist who most recently served as the vice chair of the Federal Reserve from 2018 to 2022. He is currently a professor of economics at Columbia University.

John Taylor, of course, needs no introduction to this group, as he is the [Mary and Robert] Raymond Professor of Economics at Stanford University, the George P. Shultz Senior Fellow [in Economics] at Hoover, and the former under secretary of the US Treasury for International Affairs during the George W. Bush administration.

US monetary policy is an extremely timely but very complicated subject, and we are most fortunate to have three insightful experts with us this morning to help us better understand just where we are or should be as a country on this subject. Larry Summers has been particularly outspoken for a number of months on stagflation and its impact on our economy in both the short and longer term if we don't take corrective action. Richard Clarida, having only recently stepped down from his post at the Fed, has been on the front line in analyzing and battling the threat of inflation. And, of course, John Taylor and his superanalytical and closely followed "Taylor rule" for coherent monetary policy is looked to by all who seek to understand and manage interest rate policy and monetary flows at the national level.

Larry will lead off our discussion, to be followed by Richard Clarida and John Taylor, in that order, and then we will open it up to questions from the audience and our panelists to create what I'm sure will be a very interesting conversation. Larry, please.

* * *

ROBERT HALL: I taught Larry Summers a bit of macro in 1975 at MIT. This is the first time in my career that I just absolutely enthusiastically agreed with everything that Larry is saying. And I think it's really, really important for everyone to listen. The fact that there's a consensus between Larry and John Taylor is remarkable. Let me try to restate it in just the simplest possible way. We're about four percentage points above target on the inflation rate. The Taylor principle says raise the funds rate by 1.5 times the gap. So what's 1.5 times 4? It's 6. We should have raised the funds rate by 600 basis points to deal with the inflation situation, and instead, we got 50 basis points. So, cheer if you agree with these economists. [Laughter]

TERRY ANDERSON: Hi, Terry Anderson, senior fellow at Hoover. A question for Larry. Many years ago, I had the pleasure of fly fishing with Paul Volcker on a stream in Montana. Because I was teaching economics at that time, I asked Paul, "What do I tell my students are the constraints on what the Fed can do?" I expected him to say, "A call from the president or somebody with political powers rules." He said, "It's all in whether I can convince the press that what I'm doing is the right thing." And I think he did that. If he's still right today, how do rules apply, when it seems the press has been convinced that we need to have the Fed do what it thinks is best to stabilize our economy? How can a group like this, and the consensus people in this room seem to share, communicate that there needs to be limits—rules—on what the Fed can do?

JOHN TAYLOR: So let me say something very brief. I've never seen so much reference to rules. Isn't the last six weeks or two months just amazing? I have a whole long list of things. I think that's an indication that there's somebody paying attention, and I think it's affecting policy.

KRISHNA GUHA: Krishna Guha with Evercore Partners. Question for everyone on the panel, if I may. So it's very clear we need a more systematic approach to monetary policy at this juncture. But the debate today—with the exception of a small aside from Rich— was about only one of the two instruments that the Fed is using to tighten the stance of policy going forward, namely rates and the balance sheet. So my question to each of you is, how would you integrate the balance sheet tightening in a systematic rule, and what difference would it make to the recommendations for rate policies in the current environment? Thank you.

LAWRENCE SUMMERS: I'll give a kind of extreme answer to that question as a place to start the conversation. If the Federal Reserve engaged in very large-scale operations that purchased $10 bills with $100 bills, I would expect that to be an irrelevance from the point of view of the economy. That's because $100 bills and $10 bills are essentially perfect substitutes. You can use either of them for pay. Ten-year bonds and 3-month bills are not perfect substitutes. But they're pretty good substitutes, because you can buy a sequence of 3-month bills and hold it for ten years. And so I think that something that is underappreciated in all of the conversation is that in a world where money pays interest, which is what happens when deposits at the Fed are remunerated, essentially all the Milton Friedman intuitions about money as a hot potato become wrong. And the right way to think about things is as shifts in the balance sheet between assets that are very close substitutes.

So I think that QE, aside from conditions of heavily distorted markets, heavily disrupted in illiquid markets, is a much smaller deal than most market participants think, because I think they have underinternalized the significance of the fact that we now pay interest on reserves.

The Jay Powell rough statement that all the QT was going to be the equivalent of one 25-basis-point tightening, seemed to me to be of the right order of magnitude.

. . . QE is very much like when the government issues a ton more long-term debt. If the price pressure effects that Bernanke emphasized on this topic were true, you would expect that there'll be a massive increase in term premiums associated with the huge run-ups in debt associated with major moments of deficit. And we mostly don't see that in the aftermath of either 2009 or in the aftermath of 2020. What I think gets too little attention is the fact that one should at least pause and ask the question: at a moment when every homeowner in America is shifting from a variable-rate to a fixed-rate mortgage, at a moment when every corporate treasurer in America is terming out their debt, is it really a great idea for taxpayers to be terming in their debt because of a financial policy made up by unelected officials? I was struck when I was in the White House in 2009 and 2010 that it seemed to me there was utter foolishness going on. That we had simultaneously, on a nearly monthly basis, the chairman of the Fed explaining how they were doing QE in order to reduce term premiums and whatever and stimulate the economy. And we had the Treasury department simultaneously announcing that we were terming *out* the debt in order to take advantage of the low rates. And it seemed to me that the only people who were really benefiting from this policy were the private-sector intermediaries, who were intermediating these transactions as the government went in opposite directions. And we had the president of the United States announcing that they were public enemies number one as large sources of systemic risk.

So in general, I think the only other thing I'd add to that is it is hard to imagine something more foolish than last December the Federal Reserve, in the name of stability, in large scale buying mortgage-backed instruments at a moment when housing prices were rising faster than they had ever risen before, and causing the mortgage-Treasury spread to be unusually small. So I think that QE should be conceptualized in a much more limited way as a tool for responding to disorderly and disrupted markets in some way. We should think of intervention in the bond market in the same kind of way we think about the Strategic Petroleum Reserve—as something we use in response to a particular kind of contingency, not as an ongoing policy instrument.

RICHARD CLARIDA: Let me just say a bit on that. This has been an excellent panel. Not surprisingly, I've learned a lot from both Larry and John. I'll make two comments on the term premium question specifically. And then on the related point that came up about the Greenspan and Volcker approach, especially the Greenspan approach to price stability.

On the term premium, I'm very sympathetic, Larry. I think I have some sense about what the sign of QT is, I have no idea about the magnitude. I do think term premia are important, but they may shift not because of QT but because of other factors I alluded to in my speech. For example, one of the reasons term premia have compressed in the last twenty years is because of the success of monetary policy to reduce inflation and risk premiums. So when Larry and I were in graduate school together, there was a significant part of what we call a term premium, which really was just an inflation risk premium term. And with price stability, that risk premium got compressed. So in a world where John and Larry worry about where the Fed does not succeed in maintaining price stability, that inflation term premium could come back, and obviously that would be a nominal as well as a real factor pushing up bond yields.

The other point, and I'll just stand on my soapbox here for a moment, the term premium in the Treasury market is a global general equilibrium outcome. It depends as much on what is going on in Japan, the Euro zone, China, and the Middle East as it does on what is going on in the US. And so term premia are important but perhaps not solely because of QT. I also wanted to second something Larry said and I think John alluded to. And I've grown to appreciate it more now than I did some years ago. Chair Greenspan, of course, was notoriously averse to ever signing on to a numerical inflation target. Roughly, Greenspan's definition was that price stability is achieved when no one's really thinking about inflation. And I think what we're observing now is what happens when that threshold is crossed. Ricardo Reis and others have written about rational inattention, but certainly the possibility that there are nonlinear responses to discrete moves in inflation outside of whatever the comfort zone is, I believe is a very important issue as it relates to inflation expectations.

ELLEN MEADE: Thank you. This has been a really interesting conversation. If we think for a minute about Fed communications and the kinds of sequencing steps that are necessary before you can actually raise the fed funds rate—that is, communicating about ending asset purchases and then not ending them immediately but tapering them off, and all the forward guidance and communications around ending the forward guidance—there was a tremendous number of hurdles that were in place before the Fed could take action. And I'm wondering to what extent you see those hurdles, which were useful in the post-GFC recovery environment, as not being so useful this time around? I'm wondering to what extent you see those as having posed a problem? I'd like to hear from all of you but am particularly interested to hear what Rich has to say in response, given his role at the Fed during this episode. Thank you.

CLARIDA: Well, truth in advertising, Ellen was my senior adviser at the Fed and did an incredible job. So let me be very concise.

Forward guidance, like everything in economics, has benefits and costs. I think the academic literature, which I contributed to, has at times been a bit off point, in the sense that it has talked about the cost of forward guidance if it's not credible, if it's not time consistent. But there's another dimension to forward guidance: if there's guidance that a committee feels bound to honor, that can complicate sequencing or timing of policy. It's not a deep point, but it's not an irrelevant point.

SUMMERS: I think it's one of those clever ideas that has been taken far too far. What I'm going to say now is an overstatement, but not that much of an overstatement. Forward guidance is goofy. The market doesn't believe you, so it doesn't have much effect. You believe yourself, so it constrains you down the road. So you get constraints down the road without substantial ex ante benefits. And so, except in quite extraordinary circumstances, it is not likely to be a good idea.

I think the two most successful bits of financial communication in the last twenty-five years, last thirty years, were Mario Draghi's statement that he would do whatever it takes, which produced a seismic and immediate and effective interaction in the direction that he wanted; and Bob Rubin's ending of the cacophony surrounding the dollar exchange rate at a time when that was a much more salient issue than it is today, by saying a strong dollar is in our national interest. "What's your definition, Secretary Rubin, of a strong dollar?" "A strong dollar is in our national interest." "How would you know if the dollar became weak?" "A strong dollar is in our national interest." "Are you concerned about a weak yen?" "A strong dollar is in our national interest." And that's in a sense repeated, and the unwillingness to say anything else about the topic—if he had said, "Well, the context in which we favor a strong dollar is that we have been studying this recent study on pass-through impacts, and in the context of our current analysis of pass-through impacts, and we're going to give forward guidance based on a review of a variety of different officials' view as to what the ideal level of the dollar would be for the next nine months"—it would have been far less effective.

So I think the message is, I think if there's any disagreement on this panel, and I think it's a small one because I think we're in broad agreement, it's the primacy of rules versus the primacy of resoluteness. And I believe that what's necessary is the primacy of resoluteness. And I think rules can be a contributor to that. But as we saw with the various rules that were adopted during the flexible average inflation targeting enthusiasm, rules can also be a bit problematic. And I think we need to be aware that rules are only as good as the parameters that enter into them, and the parameters are hard to estimate and all of that. But I think, in a way, this is a case where you kind of need a yardstick, not a micrometer, to perceive that there have been significant errors in the recent past.

Fiscal Policy and Other Explanations

CHAPTER FIVE

INFLATION PAST, PRESENT, AND FUTURE: FISCAL SHOCKS, FED RESPONSE, AND FISCAL LIMITS

John H. Cochrane

As figure 5.1 reminds us, we are in the midst of an inflation surge that started in January 2021. Reaching an 8.5% inflation rate (March 2022) is unquestionably a major institutional failure, given that the Fed's first mandate is "price stability." What went wrong? What caused inflation? Will it continue, get worse, or subside? Why is the Fed reacting slowly? Will the Fed's slow reaction spur greater inflation? How will inflation end? What policies will work, and what will not?

I start by documenting the fundamental fiscal source of our current inflation. We had a $5 trillion fiscal helicopter drop. Inflation need not have been a surprise. I also document that the Fed is, by historical standards, reacting very slowly to this inflation.

Does the Fed's slow reaction amount to additional stimulus, that will unnecessarily boost inflation beyond this initial impulse? Why do the Fed's projections indicate that inflation will fade away without sharp interest rate rises? I write a simple model that unites two views of this question. If expectations are adaptive, reacting to past inflation, then I replicate the traditional view that the Fed is horribly behind the curve and inflation will explode unless it raises interest rates swiftly. However, if expectations are forward looking, if the Phillips curve is centered on expected future inflation, then

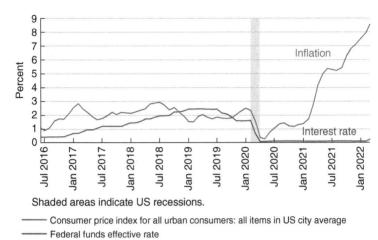

FIGURE 5.1. Inflation and Federal Funds Rate
Source: Bureau of Labor Statistics (BLS), Board of Governors via Federal Reserve Economic Data, Federal Reserve Bank of St. Louis (FRED).

I replicate the Fed's projections. Inflation may indeed fade on its own, without a period of high interest rates. The Fed's projections, and its relatively slow reaction to inflation are not, thus, inconsistent or incoherent. They come from a standard, well-developed view of the world, embodied in New Keynesian models for the last three decades. That view is also consistent with the zero-bound experience. By writing a model that encompasses Fed and traditional views, we can understand underlying assumptions and more productively debate which is right.

Next, I ask, how long will inflation persist? One might think that once the fiscal or monetary stimulus is over, inflation will end. I show that with sticky prices, inflation has considerable persistence. This persistence holds even with totally forward-looking sticky prices—it does not require indexation, slow pass-through, or other sources of momentum, although those features add to inflation persistence. The Fed's projections imply relatively flexible prices, a steep Phillips curve. With somewhat stickier prices, then, inflation can continue a good deal longer than the Fed's projections.

I then consider how Fed reaction might tame inflation. Given that inflation was sparked by fiscal policy, given the large amount of debt outstanding, and given persistent primary deficits, fiscal constraints on monetary policy and monetary-fiscal coordination will be crucial to answer this question.

I document a form of "unpleasant arithmetic" in interest-rate-based economic models. With no change in fiscal policy, by raising interest rates the Fed can lower inflation now, but only by raising inflation later. Rather than a short spike of inflation, the Fed can produce a longer period of moderate inflation. Such smoothing is valuable, and lowers the output impact of a fiscally inevitable inflation.

However, this discussion presumes there are no further shocks. War, a resurgent pandemic, or financial trouble can always boost inflation beyond such forecasts.

I then ask, what will it take to durably disinflate? Suppose, either by present dynamics or future shocks, we get to 1979. Can we and must we repeat 1980? Could it be worse this time? Or are there better options? Fiscal constraints will make a disinflation harder this time. In 1980, the debt-to-GDP ratio was 25% and the entitlement crisis was decades away. Now the debt-to-GDP ratio is 100%, the underlying inflation is more clearly fiscal, and we face large structural deficits and looming entitlements. Raising interest rates will increase debt service costs, and lower inflation will require a bondholder windfall. I show that without coordinated and durable monetary, fiscal, and microeconomic reform, a purely monetary stabilization will fail.

On the other hand, the lessons of the ends of hyperinflations, the lessons of the inflation target episodes, and the insights of economics since the 1980s suggest that such a stabilization can be much less painful than 1980.

However, once fiscal shocks are past, the very-long-run price level always remains in the Fed's control.

WHERE DID INFLATION COME FROM?

In my view, the underlying source of the current inflation is straightforward: Our government printed about $3 trillion in extra money, and sent it out as checks. It borrowed another $2 trillion and sent more checks. (The figures are taken from Cochrane 2022a and Cochrane 2022b, which explore the argument in more depth.) It was a classic helicopter drop. Figure 5.2 illustrates these events.

It was a *fiscal* helicopter drop. Imagine that the Fed had increased the monetary base by $3 trillion, by buying existing debt, and there was no deficit. Surely that would not have had the same effect. Inflation comes from the vast expansion in the overall amount of government debt, not just from a mistaken composition of that debt; not from too much overnight debt (reserves) and not enough longer-term debt (Treasury debt). Contrariwise, imagine that the Treasury had sent people shares in a mutual fund backed by Treasury debt, with thereby no direct increase in reserves or M2. Surely that would have had much the same effect.

This is not an outlandish view, nor one only available with 20/20 hindsight. For example, Summers (2021) wrote presciently the same view in early 2021. So did Cochrane and Hassett (2021), but our view is much less influential. Summers changed his mind from a decade of advocacy for greater fiscal stimulus in order to beat "secular stagnation." His analytical framework was disarmingly simple: Multiply the deficit by something like 1.5, compare it to any reasonable estimate of the GDP gap, and you see inflation coming.

The reigning alternative theory is that inflation came from a "supply shock." Much of this discussion confuses individual supply curves and relative prices with aggregate supply curves and overall inflation. A supply shock can raise the price of affected goods relative to others, and prices relative to wages. It does not raise all prices and wages together. At least not directly. One has to work the supply shock into a Phillips curve. It has to become part of the wage

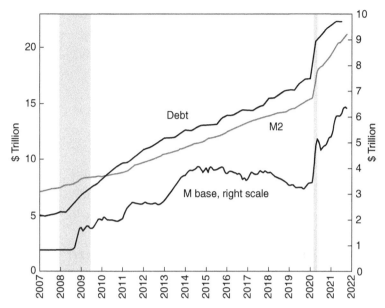

FIGURE 5.2. Money and Debt in the COVID Recession and Aftermath
Source: Reproduced from Cochrane (2022b).

and price stickiness of the economy. The obvious story—it's hard to import chips so the price of chips goes up, causing inflation—is wrong. A shift in demand from services to goods raises the price of the latter, but lowers the price of the former.

There is nothing unusual about the interest-rate part of monetary policy until inflation broke out in January 2021. It's hard to make a case that interest rate policy *sparked* this inflation.

"Monetary policy" is responsible to the extent that the Fed participated in the creation and helicopter drop of $3 trillion of reserves. Here, one may fault the Fed along with the Treasury for misdiagnosing the recession as a "demand" shortfall, rather than the "supply" effects of the pandemic. Restaurants were not closed because people didn't have enough money to go out to dinner, but because a pandemic was raging. Likewise, once the pandemic eased, the economy bounced back faster than any previous recovery. It was the economic equivalent of a snowstorm, not a repetition of 1933 on a grand scale. Here, one may fault the Fed for not "normalizing" interest rates more quickly; or for not following a Taylor rule that reacts more promptly to unemployment. But this is really just a restatement of the joint fiscal-monetary shock view of what got inflation going.

Shocks and Forecasts

The Fed's failure to control inflation was undeniably partly due to a failure of perception: The Fed failed to see inflation coming, and through the year 2021, the Fed failed to see that inflation would endure.

But whether the cause was fiscal policy or pandemic-related supply shocks, inflation was not *unknowable*. The fiscal shock was known. Pandemic-induced supply shocks should not surprise the largest and most sophisticated inflation-forecasting institution in the world. If the Fed was surprised that TVs could not get through the ports, it wasn't looking.

If inflation was indeed foreseeable—whether it came from a supply shock or from fiscal stimulus that ran into the aggregate supply constraint—clearly the Fed's inflation forecasting procedures need to think harder about what external shocks can cause inflation, where supply constraints are, and monitor their state. Summers suggests that the Fed, like any other institution suffering a major failure, begin a formal after-action inquiry into just what is wrong with its forecasting procedures.[1] The Fed seems uninterested in that project, but it is open to us.

---

1. "Soft Landing: Larry Summers on Inflation, Debt and a Looming Recession," an interview with John H. Cochrane, Niall Ferguson, H.R. McMaster, Bill Whalen, and Larry Summers on *GoodFellows: Conversations from the Hoover Institution*, April 13, 2022, https://www.hoover .org/research/soft-landing-larry-summers-inflation-debt-and-looming-recession.

Perhaps inflation *was* unknowable, and those of us who forecast it just got lucky. Perhaps six percentage point forecast errors are inevitable. In that case, the Fed should be rethinking its procedures to rely less on projections and more on timely real data. Why is the Fed speaking confidently today of policy based on its projections for inflation, given the massive failure of those projections only last year?

IS THE FED BEHIND THE CURVE?

The main issue for Fed policy in the last year and today is not root cause or shock, and not its failure to forecast inflation and react ahead of time, but whether its slow response is making inflation worse. The issue is largely whether the Fed should have, and should still react more and more promptly to observed inflation, no matter what is the shock that set inflation off.

A Slow Response

By historical standards, the Fed is moving quite slowly. Inflation broke out in February 2021. The March 2022 CPI was 8.5% and core CPI was 6.5%. Yet the Fed waited until March 2022, budging the interest rate up to 0.33%, moving again in May with an additional half a percentage point.

The Fed is even slow by contrast with the late 1960s and 1970s, as shown in figure 5.3. In each of the four surges of inflation, the Fed raised interest rates one-for-one or more with inflation. The 1970s Fed is generally criticized because it *only* raised rates one-for-one. But even in the 1970s, the Fed never waited a whole year, or let inflation get 8% above the federal funds rate. In the four tightenings since 1980, the Fed raised interest rates promptly and more than one-for-one with inflation.

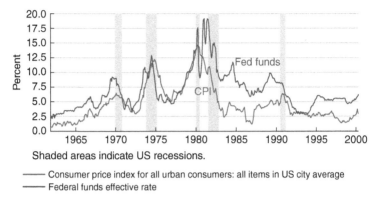

Shaded areas indicate US recessions.

——— Consumer price index for all urban consumers: all items in US city average
——— Federal funds effective rate

FIGURE 5.3.   Inflation and Federal Funds Rate in the 1970s
Source: BLS, Board of Governors via FRED.

The Fed is even slow by comparison with its last tightening start-ing in 2016, shown in figure 5.1. In that event, the Fed started gently tightening as inflation broke its 2% target, with a view that low unemployment might signal inflation ahead. The Fed now sees that event as its institutional failure, because inflation did not break out. The event provoked the Fed's strategy change to average inflation targeting with forward guidance. I remain puzzled by this reaction. Why does the Fed not declare that its prescient tightening fore-stalled inflation, and pat itself on the back for a perfect soft landing?

Why did the Fed react so slowly in 2021–22? In part, the Fed clearly misperceived inflation and thought inflation would go away on its own, despite the experience with "transitory" and "supply" shocks in the 1970s. In part, the Fed may have been worried about its reputation. Having made forward guidance promises not to raise rates, having announced a new strategy focused on employment and waiting for a long time to react to inflation, the Fed would have looked foolish if it abandoned that strategy quickly. Perhaps the new strategy was a grand Maginot Line exquisitely constructed to com-bat deflation, but like the original lacking a contingency plan for an unexpected attack from a different direction. If so, moving to state-based rather than time-based guidance, adding that contingency plan—doing any contingency planning for unforecasted outcomes rather than making projections and acting as if they are known—and rethinking the strategy are in order.

But I want to consider a different, radical possibility. Perhaps reacting slowly makes sense given the Fed's current view of the economy, which is shared by the equations of essentially all modern macroeconomic models. (I write "the equations," as authors' intuitive views are often quite different from the equations of the models.)

A Model Justifying Slow Response

Does the slow response matter? History provides us with the Fed's past habits, but not with counterfactuals. Suppose inflation broke out for whatever reason; fiscal shocks or supply chain shocks. Suppose that "stimulus" or shock is over. Will the Fed's historically slow *response* act as additional monetary stimulus, driving up inflation even further? When we look for reasons for the Fed's slow action, must we jump immediately to its failure to see inflation emerge to a policy mistake? Yes, if the slow response spurs more inflation, but perhaps not if there is a sensible view of the world in which the Fed's slow reaction does *not* spur inflation ever higher. There is.

What does the Fed think will happen? Figure 5.4 presents the Fed's projections from the March 15, 2022, outlook.[2]

This projected scenario is dramatically different from a repetition of the 1970s with surging inflation, or of 1980 in which inflation went away after a sharp rise in interest rates. *The Fed believes inflation will almost entirely disappear on its own, without the need for any period of high real interest rates to bring inflation down.*

The Fed's inflation projection continues through 2022 and a bit into 2023. Thus, we cannot understand the Fed's projections as simply a onetime price level shock, a view that expected future

---

2. Board of Governors of the Federal Reserve System, "March 16, 2022: FOMC Projections," accessible at: https://www.federalreserve.gov/monetarypolicy/fomcprojtable20220316.htm.

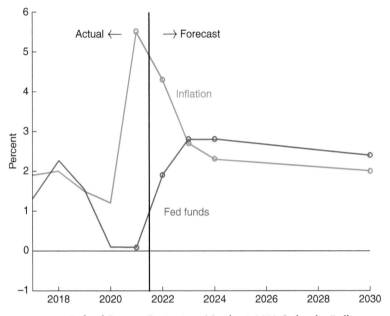

FIGURE 5.4. Federal Reserve Projections March 15, 2022. I plot the Fed's "Long-Run" Projection at 2030.

Source: Federal Reserve, March 16, 2022: FOMC Projections materials, accessible version at: https://www.federalreserve.gov/monetarypolicy/fomcprojtable20220316.htm.

inflation has not moved so the Fed can leave the nominal interest rate alone and the true real rate of interest, measured by expected future inflation, will not be that low. We cannot say that the Fed is following a Taylor rule that responds to expected future inflation rather than past inflation, $i_t = \phi E_t \pi_{t+1}$, and the Fed just happens not to forecast any future inflation. (As natural as such a rule may sound, it has some unpleasant dynamic properties. The conventional Taylor rule responds to current inflation for a reason.)

Before we make too much fun of the Fed's projections, note the market seems to believe much the same thing—this period of interest rates below inflation will not stoke further inflation. Figure 5.5 presents the 5-year Treasury and 5-year breakeven rates. If anything, the recent rise in Treasury and breakeven rates seems most

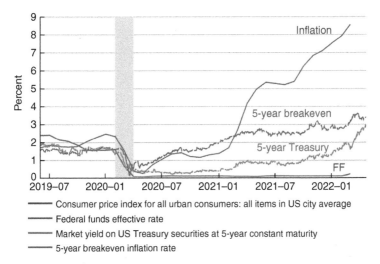

FIGURE 5.5. Market Forecasts
Source: BLS, Board of Governors via FRED.

likely to be a reaction to the Fed's announcements that it is going to start raising interest rates, and is not connected to inflation. Professional forecasters' job may be to forecast the Fed's forecasts in order to forecast interest rates, not actually to forecast inflation.

Where does the Fed's projection come from? What logic does the Fed use? Might it be right?

To address this question, I write a simple model, consisting of a static IS curve and a Phillips curve (Cochrane 2022b, section 17.1.):

$$x_t = -\sigma(i_t - r - \pi_t^e) \qquad (1)$$
$$\pi_t = \pi_t^e + \kappa x_t \qquad (2)$$

where x = output gap, π = inflation, i = interest rate, and r = steady state real rate. There are two variants: adaptive expectations $\pi_t^e = \pi_{t-1}$ and rational expectations $\pi_t^e = E_t \pi_{t+1}$. A model with a dynamic IS curve gives much the same result, but I can solve the simpler model with a line or two of algebra.

The model's equilibrium condition is

$$\pi_t = -\sigma\kappa(i_t - r) + (1 + \sigma\kappa)\pi_t^e. \tag{3}$$

With adaptive expectations the equilibrium condition is

$$\pi_t = (1 + \sigma\kappa)\pi_{t-1} - \sigma\kappa(i_t - r).$$

With rational expectations, the equilibrium condition is

$$E_t\pi_{t+1} = \frac{1}{1+\sigma\kappa}\pi_t + \frac{\sigma\kappa}{1+\sigma\kappa}(i_t - r).$$

I calculate unemployment via Okun's law as $u_t = 4 - 0.5x_t$.

Now, fire up each model, start with last year's 5.5% inflation, put in the Fed's projected interest rate path, and let's see what inflation comes out.

The top panel of figure 5.6 plots the result for the adaptive expectations model. I think this model captures the widespread intuition behind Fed criticism. Wherever it came from, the inflation shock creates a period of negative real interest rates as long as the Fed does not move. A negative real interest rate boosts inflation further, and around we go. If the Fed follows its current trajectory, inflation spirals out of control. Eventually, of course, the Fed will give in, raise rates in a hurry, and cause a large recession, something like a repetition of 1980 or worse.

The bottom panel of figure 5.6 makes the same calculation with rational expectations. The inflation that defines the real rate in the IS and Phillips curves is now the next period's expected inflation. Picking $\sigma = 1$, $\kappa = 0.5$, I match quite well the Fed's forecasts. The Fed, and markets, seem to believe the rational expectations, New Keynesian version of the model.

The central intuition comes down to the Phillips curve: Hold the unemployment rate and output gap fixed, and recognize we are in a bit of a boom, with positive output gap x and below-natural

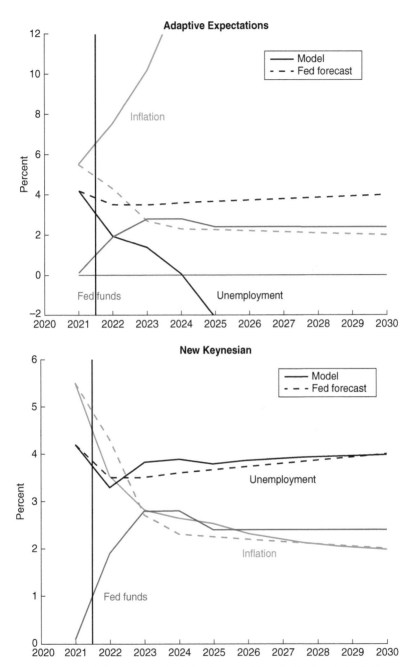

FIGURE 5.6. Fed Projections and Model Forecasts Given the Projected Funds Rate
Source: Author's calculations.

unemployment. In the adaptive expectations model, $\pi_t = \pi_{t-1} + \kappa x_t$, output is high when inflation is high *relative to past inflation.* Output is high when inflation is *increasing.* In the rational expectations model, $\pi_t = E_t \pi_{t+1} + \kappa x_t$, output is high when inflation is high *relative to expected future inflation.* Output is high when inflation is high but *decreasing.* That's the Fed's view of the current situation.

By starting this impulse-response function with observed 2021 inflation, I avoid all the initial condition and equilibrium selection issues of New Keynesian models, and the New Keynesian vs. Fiscal Theory question. If we ask any model for the response to any shock, there is a big issue of how does inflation react at the moment of the shock. But we observe that response, 5.5%. So now we can compute the rest of the projection (impulse-response function) taking this initial inflation response from the data, and neatly avoid all those controversies.

The rational expectations logic works from future to past. If people expected really high inflation in the future, then inflation would be even higher today. The fact that inflation was *only* 5.5% in 2021 despite low unemployment tells us that people expected less inflation in 2022 and beyond.

This is really the core issue. Forward-looking or rational expectations mean that we solve models backwards in time, that today's inflation reveals expectations of tomorrow's inflation, just as today's stock price reveals expectations of tomorrow's stock price. Unwillingness to follow that logic accounts for most of the divergence of opinion about Fed policy.

Figure 5.7 presents the point in another way: To attain the Fed's projected path for inflation, starting with 5.5% inflation in 2021, what *should* the interest rate projection be? To make this calculation, I solve the equilibrium condition (see equation 3 above) for the interest rate

$$i_t = r + \frac{1+\sigma\kappa}{\sigma\kappa}\pi_t^e - \frac{1}{\sigma\kappa}\pi_t.$$

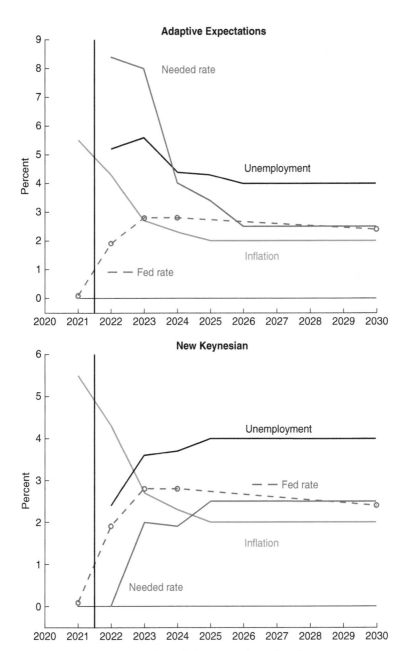

Adaptive Expectations

Needed rate

Unemployment

Inflation

Fed rate

New Keynesian

Unemployment

Fed rate

Inflation

Needed rate

FIGURE 5.7. Interest Rate Path Needed to Attain the Fed's Inflation Target
Source: Author's calculations.

Then I use the Fed's inflation forecast for π_t and π_t^e, the latter either one period ahead or one period behind.

The top panel of figure 5.7 shows that in the traditional adaptive expectations version of the model, we need sharply higher, Taylor-rule-style interest rates, 8.5%, not the Fed's projected 2%. Those higher nominal rates create higher real rates, which bring inflation down. They also cause a recession, with unemployment rising over the 4% natural rate. The recession is not so bad in my plot, because the simulation starts at last year's personal consumption expenditures (PCE) inflation, 5.5%, not, say, the March 2022 8.5% inflation, or the 10% or 12% inflation that figure 5.6 says will break out by 2023 if the Fed continues to move slowly. The recession is also mild because the model is incredibly simplified, and because I chose quite a low price-stickiness parameter (high κ) in order to fit the rather surprising speed of the Fed's projected return to normal in the rational expectations version of the model. Larger initial inflation, a larger price-stickiness parameter designed to fit the world with this model, and a more detailed model, can easily deliver a much worse recession.

By contrast, the New Keynesian model says that in order to hit the Fed's inflation forecast, interest rates can stay low, and indeed a bit lower than the Fed projects. And that path is perfectly consistent with unemployment slowly reverting to the natural rate, a soft landing.

All of these graphs are projections, forecasts, impulse-response functions. They assume that whatever "shock" started up inflation is over. They assume no additional "stimulus" will come from external events. Such events would be reflected in disturbances to the model's equations. The actual future course of inflation also depends on what future shocks hit us—continued fiscal stimulus, supply shocks due to war, government policy, and so forth.

Are the Fed's (Implicit) Beliefs Nutty?

No. There is a more serious debate to be had here than is often acknowledged. By writing a model that captures both traditional and Fed analysis, we can have a productive debate. We know the underlying assumption, and the key theoretical question we need to debate: *How forward looking are expectations?*

Do bond markets ($i_t = r_t + E_t \pi_{t+1}$) set rates based on forward-looking or backward-looking inflation expectations? Do price-setters and wage-setters ($\pi_t = E_t \pi_{t+1} + \kappa x_t$) do so? Does the Phillips curve shift based on past inflation or expected future inflation? Do people making consumption and investment decisions ($x_t = E_t x_{t+1} - \sigma r_t$) use forward-looking or backward-looking expectations to judge the rewards to saving and the cost of capital? If forward looking, what model of the world or forecast do they use?

Surely, permanent, exploitable, immutable, mechanically adaptive expectations in all these settings died in the mid-1970s. New Keynesian rational-expectations models have been around since the early 1990s. They are the standard workhorse of central banks and academic monetary policy analysis. Having a rational expectations view is, at least, not outlandish or incoherent.

On the other hand, it is hard to insist on perfectly forward-looking behavior, and especially rational expectations of the effects of novel shocks ($5 trillion of helicopter money, a pandemic, lockdowns, and so forth). Empirical Phillips curves contain at least some backward-looking terms, which may also reflect wage index-ation. Some new research tries to put less-than-rational expectations into New Keynesian models, in order to rescue something like traditional beliefs, though at the cost of substantial mathematical complexity. (García-Schmidt and Woodford 2019, Gabaix 2020; on the latter, see Cochrane 2016.)

As figure 5.6 emphasizes, the question, *How forward looking are expectations* is related to a deeper one: *Is the economy stable or unstable under an interest rate peg, or a target that moves less than one-for-one with inflation?* Is the Taylor principle necessary for *stability* (nonexplosive dynamics), or does it just reduce volatility (variance)? The answers are not obvious.

If the answers to these questions seem obvious, consider the experience of the zero-bound era, plotted in figure 5.8. The same logic that predicts an inflation spiral today, starting from a period of inflation, predicts a deflation spiral starting from a deflationary shock. More generally, the same logic predicts that if the interest rate does not move in response to inflation, then inflation must spiral in one direction or another. Many commenters predicted such a spiral during the zero-bound era, loudly and correctly, with this model in mind. It never happened. Interest rates did not move, for years on end, and could not move in the downward direction, yet the deflation spiral never broke out. This model failed a test as clear as we get in macroeconomics. (See Cochrane 2018 for much on this point.)

Perhaps central banks have internalized the zero-bound experience. If the widely forecast *deflation* spiral never broke out at the zero bound, why should they worry about the analogous *inflation* spiral now? The spiral prediction cried wolf.

In sum, the Fed's forecasts and its slow response are not necessarily nutty, rosy scenarios, failures to act, politically convenient denial, and so forth. Before criticizing based on the standard adaptive expectations model, let us at least acknowledge that there *is* a model that makes sense of the Fed's forecasts, that model's equations have dominated academic macroeconomics for 30 years, and they make sense of the zero-bound experience. Now, we can debate if that model is right, or will be right in this instance. We can now debate its predictions by examining its assumptions and its ability to fit other episodes.

My opinion—or at least a compromise view consistent with theory and evidence—is that the economy is stable in the long run,

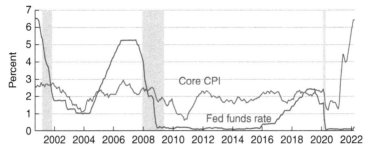

Shaded areas indicate US recessions.

——— Consumer price index for all urban consumers: all items in US city average
——— Federal funds effective rate

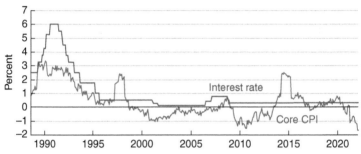

——— Consumer price index: all items excluding food and energy for Japan
——— Immediate rates: less than 24 hours: central bank rates for Japan

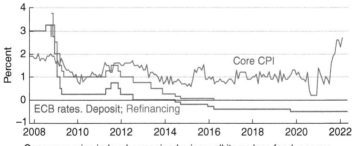

——— Consumer price index: harmonized prices: all items less food, energy,
    tobacco, alcohol: total for the Euro area
——— ECB deposit facility rate for Euro area
——— ECB main refinancing operations rate: fixed rate tenders for Euro area

FIGURE 5.8. Core CPI and Federal Funds Rate in the Zero-Bound Era: US,
Japan, and Europe

Source: BLS, Board of Governors, Organisation for Economic Co-operation and
Development (OECD), European Central Bank (ECB) via FRED.

and the long-run predictions of the rational expectations model are right. Rational expectations are also right on average, which was always the central point: the Fed can fool people a few times, but once it gets in the habit of exploiting adaptive or other nonrational expectations as a matter of systematic policy, people catch on. Rational expectations are more likely in times of high and variable inflation when people pay more attention. Rational expectations are more likely as a description of policies that last a long time. A decade of high interest rates to fight volatile inflation is more likely to feature forward-looking expectations, while a few initial months of a onetime shock may leave people puzzling about what to expect. Expectations may not have moved fully this time, but don't expect that to be a robust, permanent, exploitable, and reliable feature of the economy.

However, there is also a substantial and temporarily negative effect of interest rates on inflation. Such an effect is not captured by my little model, but is captured by more elaborate models, even with fully rational expectations. An example follows.

Central banks can temporarily push down inflation by high interest rates, and do so. That short-run negative effect is more visible in historical episodes such as 1980 than the subtle long-run positive effect that we only see in rare occasions such as the zero-bound era when interest rates do not move for years on end. So it is possible that both sides are right; that failing to act promptly will not lead to an unlimited inflation spiral, though inflation may well get worse before it gets better, and that the Fed could lower inflation in the near term with interest rate increases.

For the rest of this paper, I adopt the New Keynesian rational-expectations version of the model. I adopt it as a working hypothesis, not immutable truth. Let us figure out what it says about how inflation will evolve, what the effects are of Fed policies, and how inflation might be ended if it gets out of control. I also adopt as a working hypothesis the view that fiscal constraints matter now as they might not have mattered in the past, that the Fed cannot call on an unlimited amount of fiscal tightening to support its monetary policy efforts. The fact that this inflation was sparked by fiscal policy, and the fact of large debts and ongoing deficits means that we will have to pay more attention to fiscal-monetary policy coordination than in the past.

INFLATION PERSISTENCE
AND UNPLEASANT ARITHMETIC

How long will inflation last? Even granting the Fed's rational expectations view, the dynamic response to sticky prices gives a certain momentum to inflation. It is *not* true that once you remove the stimulus, inflation stops on a dime.

A related question is: How does inflation respond dynamically to a fiscal shock? The standard New Keynesian model posits passive fiscal policy, implying there is no such thing as a fiscal shock. Here I adapt that model to include a fiscal shock, and study the persistence of that shock.

What happens in the Fed's (implicit) rational expectations New Keynesian model if the Fed does wish to tame inflation by substantially raising interest rates? This is a standard question, but I add a wrinkle: Suppose that the Fed cannot count on a "passive" fiscal response that produces abundant fiscal surpluses in response to Fed policy. We shall see a form of unpleasant arithmetic emerge.

Response to a Fiscal Shock

I use the most standard New Keynesian model, this time with a full dynamic IS curve:

$$x_t = E_t x_{t+1} - \sigma(i_t - E_t \pi_{t+1}) \qquad (4)$$
$$\pi_t = \beta E_t \pi_{t+1} + \kappa x_t \qquad (5)$$

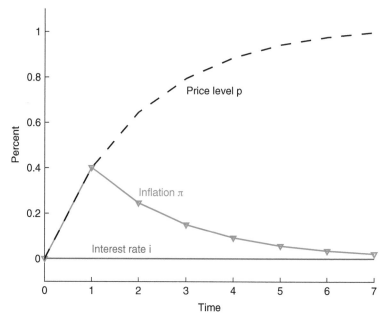

FIGURE 5.9. Response to a Deficit Shock Equal to 1% of Outstanding Debt: Sticky Prices with No Monetary Policy Response
Parameters $\sigma = 1$, $\kappa = 0.25$, $\beta = 0.99$, $\rho = 0.98$.
Source: Author's calculations.

Figure 5.9 presents the response of inflation to a shock that leads to an eventual 1% rise in the price level. That response is given analytically by

$$\pi_t = (1 - \rho\lambda_1^{-1})\lambda_1^{-(t-1)} \tag{6}$$

where

$$\lambda_1 = \left[(1 + \beta + \sigma\kappa) + \sqrt{(1 + \beta + \sigma\kappa)^2 - 4\beta} \, \right] / 2.$$

I interpret the shock below as a fiscal shock, as I believe we have experienced. But as before, this is the response to any shock, including a "supply shock" in the Phillips curve, that leads to 0.4% initial inflation and then goes away. It is the same calculation as above using the simpler model. It thus makes a few points immediately:

First, the essence of the simple model calculation does in fact hold with the standard dynamic IS curve (equation 4). Even if the Fed does nothing, inflation slowly goes away on its own. The standard New Keynesian model is *stable* under an interest rate peg.

Second, sticky prices lead to a drawn-out inflation, even though the shock ends in the first period. It is *not* true that once the "stimulus" ends, inflation goes away *quickly* on its own. Thus, we have a second quantitative question facing our evaluation of the Fed's benign inflation projections: *How sticky are prices? How steep is the Phillips curve?*

To fit the Fed's projections with the simple model in figure 5.6, I chose $\sigma = 1$, $\kappa = 0.5$. Using Okun's law, and holding constant expected future inflation, those parameter values mean that a 2% output gap corresponds to 1 percentage point unemployment and 1 percentage point more inflation, a 45° slope to the Phillips curve. That's pretty steep, or pretty price flexible. Figure 5.9 doubles price stickiness to $\kappa = 0.25$. That means 1 percentage point of unemployment means 0.5 percentage points of inflation, holding fixed future inflation, a flatter Phillips curve. Together with the full model dynamics, you see that figure 5.9 predicts much longer-lasting inflation than figure 5.6.

How steep is the Phillips curve? Well, in the 2010s, we observed very high unemployment, and then a slow, steady, and large decline in unemployment, with very little movement of inflation. Even unemployment equal to its current 3.6% in late 2019 did not spark any inflation. People wrote papers about how amazingly flat the Phillips curve was. Prices seemed very sticky. Now, we have just seen inflation rise from 2% to 8.5% with little movement in a very low rate of unemployment. It seems prices are very flexible, and the Phillips curve is steep. Which is it? Perhaps the Phillips curve is somehow state dependent. The Calvo fairy visits more often in Argentina. Perhaps the whole Phillips curve concept is garbage, a cloud of points not a curve of any slope. Perhaps inflation dynamics don't have that much to do with output and employment. Perhaps we should move to a search-theoretic model of labor market (Hall and Kudlyak 2021), with more detailed, real-business-cycle-style modeling of aggregate supply.

Third, the calculation of figure 5.9 allows a concrete description of what I mean by a "fiscal shock," and how it sets off inflation. Recognize the fiscal side of the model (equation 4)–(equation 5), the evolution of government debt,

$$\rho v_{t+1} = v_t + i_t - \pi_{t+1} - \tilde{s}_{t+1}. \tag{7}$$

Here, v is the real value of one-period nominal debt, $\tilde{s}$ is the real primary surplus divided by the steady state value of debt, and ρ is a constant of approximation slightly less than one, which may be taken as $\rho = e^{-r}$ where r is the steady state real rate. Real government debt rises when the real rate of return $i_t - \pi_{t+1}$ is high, and declines when surpluses relative to debt $\tilde{s}_{t+1}$ are high.

We can unite equation 7 with the rest of the model and solve by the usual matrix method. Or, we can solve it forward separately. Iterating equation 7 forward, taking the innovation $\Delta E_{t+1} \equiv E_{t+1} - E_t$, and imposing the transversality condition $\lim_{T\to\infty} E_t \rho^T v_{t+T} = 0$, we have

$$\Delta E_{t+1} \pi_{t+1} = -\Delta E_{t+1} \sum_{j=0}^{\infty} \rho^j \tilde{s}_{t+1+j} + \sum_{j=1}^{\infty} \rho^j (i_{t+j} - \pi_{t+1+j}). \tag{8}$$

The innovation to inflation equals the innovation to the discounted present value of surpluses.

To produce figure 5.9, I assume that the surplus takes a onetime unexpected move, $\tilde{s}_1 = -1$. This is a one percentage point change in the ratio of surplus to value of debt, which at a 100% debt-to-GDP ratio is also a one percentage point change in the ratio of surplus to GDP. We get the same result whether the change is to current or expected future surpluses; it is a one percentage point change in $\sum_{j=0}^{\infty} \rho^j \tilde{s}_{1+j}$.

The graph thus can model the response to the event we saw: a $5 trillion, 25% of GDP, 30% of initial debt, onetime shock to deficits. In this way of thinking, however, the big unknown is, how much do people expect the initial deficit $\tilde{s}_1$ to be repaid by higher subsequent surpluses $\tilde{s}_{1+j}$? If people expect all of the initial deficit to be repaid, there is no fiscal shock at all. If people expect none of it to be repaid, then the shock to the sum on the right-hand side of equation 8 is equal to the initial deficit. Reality lies in between.

However, again, we *observe* the initial inflation, 8.5%. That fact allows us to *infer* the size of the fiscal shock, and thus how much eventual inflation we will have.

If prices were not sticky at all, then the fiscal shock leads to a onetime price level jump equal to the fiscal shock. The 10% cumulative inflation from May 2021 to March 2022, of which about 8% is unexpected, means that people expect that, of the 30% increase in debt, roughly 22% would be repaid by subsequent surpluses, and 8% would not; inflation thus ate away 8% of the debt.

But prices are sticky. In figure 5.9, for a 1% shock to the sum of surpluses, the *total* rise in the price level is the same, 1.0%, but it is spread over time.

Now, again, we observe initial inflation, not the size of the fiscal shock. If this graph is right, we have a good deal of inflation left to go. The first year only produces about 40% of the total eventual price level rise. In this model, people do not expect the majority of the $5 trillion deficit, 30% of debt, to be repaid. The total price level rise will be about 20% (8% divided by 0.4 = 20%).

With price stickiness, the fundamental story of a fiscal shock changes. In a flexible price model, we digest the plot simply: unexpected inflation and an unexpected onetime price level increase lowers the real value of outstanding debt, just as would a partial default. But this model still maintains one-period debt, so a slow expected inflation cannot devalue debt. Instead, with sticky prices there is a long period of negative real interest rates—as we are observing in reality. This period of negative real interest rates slowly lowers the real value of government debt. With sticky prices, even short-term bond-holders cannot escape inflation, even a slow predictable inflation. In the accounting of equation 8, the second term is a discount rate term. Lower real interest rates are a lower discount factor for government surpluses and raise the value of debt, which is an anti-inflationary force. Equivalently, lower real interest rates give a lower interest cost of the debt, that acts just like lower deficits to reduce initial inflation.

That price stickiness draws out the inflationary response to a fiscal shock is perhaps not that surprising. Many stories feature such stickiness, and suggest substantial inflationary momentum. Price hikes take time to work through to wages, which then lead to additional price hikes. Housing prices take time to feed into rents. Input price rises take time to lead to output price rises. But such common stories reflect an idea of *backward-looking* price stickiness. The Phillips curve in equation 5 is entirely forward looking. Inflation is a jump variable. Indeed, in the standard New Keynesian solutions, inflation can rise instantly and permanently in response to a permanent monetary policy shock, with no dynamics at all. (Add $i_t = \phi \pi_t + u_t$, $u_t = 1.0 u_{t-1} + \varepsilon_{i,t}$ and inflation, and interest rates move equally, instantly, and permanently in response to the shock.) Nonetheless, sticky prices draw out dynamics.

One might well add such backward-looking terms, e.g.,

$$\pi_t = \alpha \pi_{t-1} + \beta E_t \pi_{t+1} + \kappa x_t$$

and such terms are often used (Cogley and Sbordone 2008). These terms can add a hump-shaped response and spread the inflation response to the fiscal shock out even further.

In sum, even with a completely forward-looking rational-expectations model, as the Fed seems to believe, and even if the fiscal or other underlying shock is over, inflation is likely to continue for some time. Even if we do not wish to disagree with the basic sign and stability of monetary policy and expectations, the parameters implicit in the Fed's view seem pretty optimistic, in this simplistic analysis. This vision of fiscal policy is quite different from that in Summers's analysis, discussed above. Here fiscal policy acts as a stock, not a flow. Inflation results when there is more debt relative to people's expectations of its eventual repayment. In Summers's analysis, we take the flow current deficits, multiply by 1.5, and compare them to the GDP gap to determine inflationary pressure. Later, I'll come back to the central question going forward: Which view of fiscal stimulus is right?

MONETARY POLICY TO FIGHT INFLATION

The Fed will respond, however, and has already begun to do so. What happens when the Fed starts raising interest rates? How much can raising interest rates lower inflation? I continue to use the New Keynesian model, giving the Fed the benefit of the doubt on that question, and in the spirit of offering advice consistent with its recipient's worldview.

Unpleasant Interest-Rate Arithmetic

To model how raising interest rates lowers inflation, we need a model in which the Fed *can* lower inflation somewhat by raising interest rates, without relying on a contemporaneous contractionary fiscal shock, all while keeping rational expectations and the consequent implication that inflation will eventually settle down. The latter ingredients make the Fed's projections sensible. To that end, I add long-term debt to the model. The model is

$$x_t = E_t x_{t+1} - \sigma(i_t - E_t \pi_{t+1}) \tag{9}$$

$$\pi_t = \beta E_t \pi_{t+1} + \kappa x_t \tag{10}$$

$$i_t = \theta_{i\pi} \pi_t + \theta_{ix} x_t + u_{i,t} \tag{11}$$

$$\rho v_{t+1} = v_t + r_{t+1}^n - \pi_{t+1} - \tilde{s}_{t+1} \tag{12}$$

$$E_t r_{t+1}^n = i_t \tag{13}$$

$$r_{t+1}^n = \omega q_{t+1} - q_t \tag{14}$$

$$u_{i,t} = \eta u_{i,t-1} + \varepsilon_{i,t}. \tag{15}$$

This is a simplified version of the model in *The Fiscal Theory of the Price Level* (Cochrane 2022b, section 5.5). The variable r_{t+1}^n is the nominal return on the portfolio of all government bonds. Equation 13 imposes the expectations hypothesis. Equation 14 relates the return of the government debt portfolio to the change in its price, where ω describes a geometric term structure of debt. The face value of maturity j debt declines at rate ω^j.

We can think of the Fed's response in two ways: It may follow a rule that responds to inflation, raising $\theta_{i,\pi}$, or it may raise the interest rate as a persistent discretionary response, a shock $\varepsilon_{i,t}$ that sets off a persistent disturbance $u_{i,t}$. Given the path of interest rates in equilibrium, we obtain the same output and inflation with either specification. It is conceptually easier to start with the latter.

So, to consider what the Fed can do about inflation, figure 5.10 plots the response of inflation to a persistent monetary policy shock $\varepsilon_{i,t}$, with no rule parameters ($\theta_{ix} = \theta_{i\pi} = 0$), and *holding fiscal surpluses or deficits constant*. Conventional New Keynesian responses to monetary policy shocks include strong "passive" fiscal policy responses. But that's not interesting here. We have had a fiscal policy shock, and as we look forward, fiscal constraints on monetary policy will loom. The first question for us and the Fed is: What can it do to address inflation *without* counting on a substantial fiscal policy response to its moves?

Alternatively, the model is linear, so we can break it into its parts by asking: What is the effect of the fiscal shock that lowered $\tilde{s}_1$ (figure 5.9) and what are the effects of potential fiscal coordination that raises $\tilde{s}_{t+j}$ (figure 5.9 upside down)? Then, separately, we ask: What are the effects of monetary policy and a raise in interest rates with no change in fiscal policy? To ask how inflation will evolve in

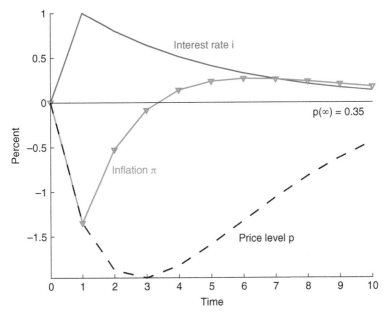

FIGURE 5.10. Unpleasant Arithmetic—A Response to a Monetary Policy Shock with No Change in Surplus or Deficit
Parameters $\sigma = 1, \kappa = 0.25, \beta = 0.99, \theta_\pi = 0, \theta_x = 0, \rho = 0.98, \omega = 0.8, \eta = 0.8$.
Source: Author's calculations.

the near term if the Fed tightens, we superimpose this response on the response of the economy to the fiscal shock with no change in monetary policy (figure 5.9), and likewise, ask how a joint fiscal-monetary tightening would look.

The higher interest rate in figure 5.10 lowers inflation. It also lowers output, as inflation is lower than future inflation. But inflation slowly creeps back up again, and inflation is higher in the long run. This long-run rise would be easy to miss in an estimated impulse-response function, and estimates have not tried to orthogonalize monetary and fiscal shocks.

This graph shows that, without modifying fiscal policy, the Fed can only move inflation around, buying lower inflation in the short run with higher inflation in the long run. Without changing fiscal policy, the Fed faces a form of "unpleasant arithmetic," to use a memorable phrase from Sargent and Wallace (1981). Sims (2011) called this pattern "stepping on a rake," and offered it as a diagnosis of the 1970s. Interest rate hikes initially quell inflation, but without a coordinated fiscal tightening, they later raise inflation.

Iterating forward equation 12, using equations 13 and 14, and taking innovations, the identity in equation 16 generalizes in the case of long-term debt to

$$\sum_{j=0}^{\infty} \omega^j \Delta E_{t+1} \pi_{t+1+j} = -\sum_{j=0}^{\infty} \rho^j \Delta E_{t+1} \tilde{s}_{t+1+j}$$

$$+ \sum_{j=1}^{\infty} (\rho^j - \omega^j) \Delta E_{t+1} r_{t+1+j} \qquad (16)$$

where $r_{t+1} \equiv r_{t+1}^n - \pi_{t+1}$ is the ex post real return on the portfolio of government bonds (Cochrane 2022b, section 3.5). Unexpected inflation, now summing current and expected future inflation, weighted by the maturity structure of government debt, devalues government bonds, and unexpected deflation raises their value. That inflation or deflation must correspond to a change in expected primary surpluses, or a change in the discount rate. Equivalently, higher interest costs on the debt in the last term act just as lower surpluses in the second term; higher interest costs on the debt must be paid by higher surpluses if they are not to cause inflation.

This identity clarifies the unpleasant interest rate arithmetic. Given that there has been a negative fiscal shock—deficits that people do not expect to be repaid by subsequent surpluses—the first term on the right-hand side is lower. Bondholders must lose via inflation or low returns (or default, though not in this equation, but easy to include).

Start by holding expected returns constant, which occurs with flexible prices. Then, bondholders must lose via inflation on the left-hand side. But with long-term debt $\omega > 0$, a change in expected future inflation can now devalue long-term bonds when they come due, in place of a one-period price level jump that devalues short-term debt. By setting the interest rate target, the Fed can choose more inflation now or more inflation later; shifting the burden from short-term bondholders to long-term bondholders. But the Fed cannot alter the fact that there must be some inflation, now or later. The first term on the left-hand side expresses the sort of budget constraint for inflation now vs. inflation later that Sargent and Wallace (1981) made famous. Moving inflation to the future might also give some breathing space for fiscal policy to reverse, for Congress and the administration to wake up and solve the long-run budget problem, or to hope for an opposite fiscal shock.

The future inflation rise is larger than the current inflation reduction. The "$p(\infty) = 0.35\%$" notation in figure 5.10 shows that despite no change in surplus at all, this intervention *raises* the eventual price level. Future inflation enters the left-hand side weighted by the maturity structure of government debt, so it takes more future inflation to buy away some current inflation. Unpleasant interest rate arithmetic carries a greater than or equal to sign, not an equality.

With changing real interest rates and expected returns, bondholders can lose via the second term on the right-hand side as well, as I analyzed above for one-period debt. With sticky prices, inflation gives a period of low real returns to bondholders. This mechanism adds to the unpleasantness of interest rate arithmetic. With sticky prices, higher nominal interest rates are like higher real interest rates, raise debt service costs, and thus *raise* inflation.

How is this analysis different from Sargent and Wallace (1981)? There are four main channels of fiscal-monetary interaction: seigniorage, interest costs on the debt, revaluation of nominal debt due to unexpected inflation and deflation, and non-neutralities in the economy—including the tax code, non-indexed contracts, sticky government salaries, etc. Sargent and Wallace consider only the first channel in a model that includes money and only real debt. The model in my analysis has no money and, therefore, no seigniorage, but it includes interest costs on the debt and a revaluation of nominal debt.

Unpleasant interest rate arithmetic is thus fundamentally different from unpleasant monetarist arithmetic. A quantitative analysis of fiscal-monetary interactions should include the fourth component as well.

The models and exercises of the last two sections still embody long-run stability of inflation under an interest rate target. The inflation line eventually converges to the interest rate line. Once a burst of inflation has inflated away bonds, corresponding to a fiscal shock; once long-term bonds have matured; once prices move; once whatever other short-term effects get in the way, and (very important) if there is no *further* bad fiscal news—if new deficits are repaid by subsequent surpluses—the Fed is fully in control of the price level. At a long enough horizon, the one-period debt and flexible price version of the identity,

$$i_t = E_t \pi_{t+1}$$

$$\Delta E_{t+1} \pi_{t+1} = - \sum_{j=0}^{\infty} \rho^j \Delta E_{t+1} \tilde{s}_{t+1+j}$$

apply. The Fed can arrange a change in $\Delta E_{t+1} \pi_{t+2}$ by raising $E_t i_{t+1}$, and can set that future inflation to whatever it likes, with no change in surpluses.

Long-run stability has important implications. If the interest rate path eventually trends negative, then the Fed can, without fiscal help, bring the price level fully back to where it was below the fiscal shock.

Moreover, if the Fed does nothing at all, inflation will eventually settle down. Inflation will be stable under a k percent interest rate peg, as it was stable under a 0.25% interest rate peg. Fiscal shocks and other shocks will cause inflation, but that inflation will eventually pass. An interest rate peg is not necessarily optimal. If the Fed understands short-run dynamics, it can offset and smooth inflation; raising rates in the short run, and then lowering them in the long run. This proposition is a natural interest-rate-based counterpart to Milton Friedman's k percent money growth proposal. Friedman also acknowledged that if the Fed understands short-run dynamics, it can artfully move money growth to stabilize inflation even more. But Friedman did not trust the Fed to understand those dynamics or to act on them wisely. An unreactive interest rate is a similar policy in these models.

A Policy Rule

We may ask the same question differently: What would happen if the Fed follows a Taylor-type rule, responding more quickly to observed inflation? Figure 5.11 gets at this question by calculating the response of the model (equations 9 through 15) to a 1% fiscal shock, but including a policy rule with $\theta_\pi = 0.9$, i.e., $i_t = 0.9\pi_t$. Compare the result to figure 5.9, which computes the response to the same fiscal shock but leaves interest rates alone.

The interest rate now rises to a point just below the inflation rate, since I specified θ_π slightly less than one. The effect of this monetary policy response is to reduce the initial inflation impact of the fiscal shock, from about 0.4% to 0.25%, but to further smooth inflation over time, raising inflation in the long run. Comparing figure 5.9 and figure 5.11, we see unpleasant arithmetic in action.

The Taylor rule in this model serves a very useful purpose. By spreading inflation forward over time, it reduces the volatility of immediate inflation in response to other (in this case, fiscal) shocks. In many models with sticky prices, like this one, small, smooth inflation is less disruptive than larger, sharper inflation. Reducing *volatility* is, in the larger picture, what the Taylor rule is all about, not remedying *instability* of old Keynesian models or *indeterminacy* of New Keynesian models with passive fiscal policy.

But the Taylor rule does not eliminate inflation. There has been a fiscal shock, a deficit that will not be repaid. At some point some debt must be inflated away. Unpleasant arithmetic still applies. Monetary policy alone can shift inflation around over time, and it can smooth inflation. But monetary policy cannot eliminate a fiscal inflation entirely.

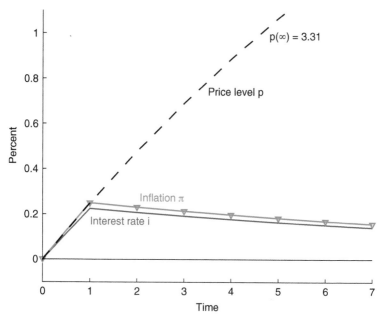

FIGURE 5.11. Response to a 1% Deficit Shock, with a Monetary Policy Rule
Parameters $\sigma = 1$, $\kappa = 0.25$, $\beta = 0.99$, $\theta_\pi = 0.9$, $\theta_x = 0$, $\rho = 0.98$, $\omega = 0.8$.
Source: Author's calculations.

Figure 5.11 builds on another main point of figure 5.9. With
sticky prices, and now with sensible policy rules, a onetime fiscal
shock leads to a very long and drawn out inflation, not to a onetime
price level jump.

How much inflation will we experience? We could interpret
this graph somewhat loosely as, what happens given that people
expect the Fed eventually to start following such a rule. (We really
want a rule with lagged response, $i_t = \phi i_{t-1} + \theta \pi_t$, as empirical Taylor
rules uniformly find, and which would account for much of the
Fed's slow response.) We *observe* the initial 8% inflation shock and
infer the size of the fiscal shock. If this is the world we live in, we are
only beginning to see the inflationary response to our onetime fiscal
shock! The 3.31% total price level increase in response to a one percent

fiscal shock, and the 0.25% impact, means that our fiscal shock will lead to a $8/0.25 \times 3.31 = 106\%$ cumulative inflation in response to the 30% fiscal shock.

How can the cumulative inflation be even larger than the initial deficit? It is possible that an initial deficit $\tilde{s}_1$ leads to expectations of larger unfunded deficits to follow, as with an AR(1) process. But that is not the case here, as I specify completely the size of the fiscal shock.

In fact, the cumulative inflation in this model is 3.38%, three times *larger* than the 1% fiscal shock, and the 1% cumulative inflation of the last two models. The Fed, in this simulation, spreads inflation forward to fall more heavily on long-term bondholders, whose claims are devalued when they come due, and thereby lightens the load on short-term bondholders, who do not experience much inflation. But the rule spreads inflation forward even further than that, as the maturity structure of the debt with coefficient $\omega = 0.8$ is shorter than this inflation response. We enter the territory where higher interest rates lead to higher inflation all on their own. A more sophisticated rule could achieve the same reduction in current inflation by eventually lowering interest rates. For now, if this is our world, not only will we see the nearly 30% total price level rise suggested by the previous model, we will see a total price level rise nearly three times greater.

HOW WILL INFLATION END?

Unpleasant arithmetic and monetary-fiscal coordination also pose some severe constraints on how inflation might end. They also remind us, however, of some hopeful analysis and episodes of how inflation can end swiftly without the pain of 1980.

Let us imagine a few more years have gone by, and inflation has continued, to 10% or similar levels, as it did by the late 1970s. And imagine that inflation is fully reflected in wage growth and in high nominal interest rates and bond yields. How can inflation be put back in the bottle?

Some of the basic points:

- Every successful disinflation has featured coordinated monetary, fiscal, and microeconomic policy.
- That coordination will be crucial in a future US disinflation.
- Without fiscal coordination, a purely monetary approach to lowering inflation, based on higher interest rates, will fail.

Fiscal constraints will matter for a monetary disinflation. This inflation was, more clearly than the 1970s, sparked by a fiscal blowout. Fiscal policy remains stuck in persistent structural primary deficits, with unsustainable entitlement spending looming. Monetary policy will operate in the shadow of 100% of GDP debts that are growing exponentially, 5% of GDP primary deficits, and growing entitlement gaps. Figure 5.12 plots the CBO's projections to emphasize these points. In 1980, the debt-to-GDP ratio was 25%. The fiscal constraints on monetary policy will be at least four times larger this time.

The CBO projections are conservative. They assume nothing goes wrong. The debt surge of the Great Recession and the COVID-19 pandemic were not forecast in the pre-2008 CBO projections. But since 2008, we have become cemented in a bailout/stimulus regime. Any significant shock is met by new rivers of borrowed or printed money. There will be shocks—war, disease, private or sovereign debt, financial collapse. I graph suggestively what debt-to-GDP might actually look like after the next two shocks.

Moreover, the US is now stuck in a period of sclerotic long-run GDP growth; cut roughly in half starting in the year 2000, and as a consequence, slower growth in tax revenues. The boom of the late 1980s and 1990s, which dramatically raised surpluses, does not seem to be at hand.

How will fiscal policy constrain a monetary disinflation? There are four main channels. First, of course, the government loses seigniorage revenue. But seigniorage is close to irrelevant today.

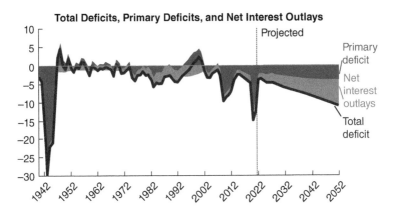

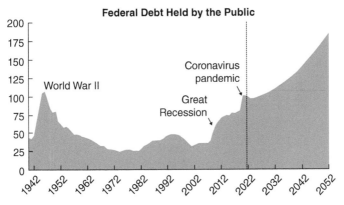

FIGURE 5.12. CBO Projection for Debt-to-GDP Ratio and Deficits. The debt forecast assumes nothing bad will happen and that's likely optimistic.
Source: Congressional Budget Office.

Second, higher interest rates raise interest costs on the debt. Suppose the Fed were to raise interest rates 5%. We have a 100% debt-to-GDP ratio, and rising. With interest rates at 5%, that means 5% of GDP interest cost, $1 trillion per year, of extra deficit. If it is to lower inflation, then, the monetary contraction must come with $1 trillion per year fiscal contraction as well. If it does not, then the fiscal forces behind inflation get worse. That our government has sadly chosen primarily to roll over short-term debt, and the

Fed has chosen to further shorten the maturity structure by buying trillions of long-term debt and turn it into overnight debt, means that interest costs flow much more quickly on the budget than they would otherwise, strengthening this channel.

Third, disinflation is a windfall to bondholders. That windfall must also be paid, an additional expense requiring fiscal contraction. At 100% debt-to-GDP, a 10% disinflation requires 10% of GDP to be transferred from taxpayers to bondholders. For the moment, long-term bond yields have not risen to match inflation, so a golden opportunity still remains to disinflate without this fiscal cost.

Fourth, disinflation is by itself trouble for government finances, as inflation helps the government. I do not model these effects.

The second and third effects are captured by the identity in equation 16, which I repeat here for convenience:

$$\sum_{j=0}^{\infty} \omega^j \Delta E_{t+1} \pi_{t+1+j} = -\sum_{j=0}^{\infty} \rho^j \Delta E_{t+1} \tilde{s}_{t+1+j}$$

$$+ \sum_{j=1}^{\infty} (\rho^j - \omega^j) \Delta E_{t+1} r_{t+1+j}$$

To durably disinflate, and not just move inflation around over time; to produce a negative term on the left-hand side, we must have increased fiscal surpluses, the first term on the right-hand side. If that disinflation comes with higher expected returns on government debt, the third term on the right-hand side, the rise in surpluses, must be that much larger.

The disinflation of 1980 was not just monetary. It was a joint monetary, fiscal, and microeconomic reform. The monetary contraction of the early 1980s was quickly followed with two tax reforms, in 1982 and 1986, that dramatically slashed marginal rates, while broadening the base. The 1991 tax change raised marginal rates, but not back to earlier levels. Deregulation was at least aimed at increasing economic growth. Whether for these reasons or just good luck, economic growth rose, tax revenues rose, and so did surpluses.

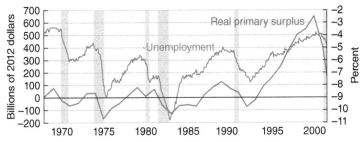

Shaded areas indicate US recessions.

—— Federal net lending or borrowing plus interest payments, 2012 dollars
(NIPA)
—— -Unemployment rate (right)

FIGURE 5.13. Real Primary Surplus and Negative Unemployment Rate 1980–2000
Source: US Bureau of Economic Analysis (BEA), BLS via FRED.
Note: Primary surplus is Federal net lending or borrowing plus federal interest payments, con-
verted to 2012 dollars via GDP deflator.

Figure 5.13 presents the real primary surplus through the 1980s
and 1990s. Despite the often-referenced "Reagan deficits," *primary*
deficits were not that large in the Reagan years. Most of the reported
deficit was sharply higher interest costs due to the higher interest
rates. I include the negative of the unemployment rate, to allow an
ocular business cycle adjustment. Adjusted for the recession, the
deficits of the early 1980s are at least no worse than those of 1975.
(I plot the surplus itself, not the surplus-to-GDP ratio. It is actual
surpluses that pay off debts.)

The main point: starting in 1982 and 1986, the US entered a period
of strong primary surpluses that lasted until 2000. At least with ex
post wisdom, the disinflation of 1982 corresponded to a strong fiscal
contraction, a rise in the present value of surpluses. (Cochrane [2019]
decomposes the value of government debt to make a calculation and
an ex ante calculation using Vector Autoregression [VAR] methods.)

Interest costs on the debt rose in the 1980s, posing a fiscal head-
wind. The rise in surpluses was strong enough to overcome that rise in
interest costs as well. In addition, investors who bought 10-year bonds

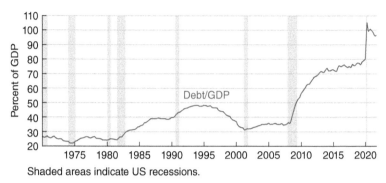

Shaded areas indicate US recessions.

——— Federal debt held by the public as percent of gross domestic product

FIGURE 5.14. US Debt-to-GDP Ratio

Source: Office of Management and Budget (OMB) via FRED.

at 15% yields in 1980, expecting inflation, got repaid in an environment of 3% inflation. That windfall came courtesy of the US taxpayer.

Figure 5.14 plots the debt-to-GDP ratio. That ratio rises with deficits and also with higher interest payments on the debt. We see the continued rise in debt-to-GDP in the 1980s due to interest costs, but that the strong surpluses of the 1990s paid those interest costs as well.

Did people know this would happen? What gave them confidence that the US would in fact pay off its debt at the much larger value implied by disinflation? Something did, and that expectation was right. Ex post, at least, 1980 involved a joint monetary, fiscal, and microeconomic reform.

Contrary episodes abound in Latin American history (Kehoe and Nicolini 2021). Inflation surges, caused by intractable deficits. The central bank attempts a monetary stabilization, which slows inflation for a while. The underlying fiscal problem is not solved, however, and inflation comes back more strongly. In particular, higher interest costs on the debt with no corresponding fiscal reform can lead to higher inflation quickly. The US had a monetary reform that was followed by fiscal and microeconomic reform—the latter growing the tax base. There were a few years of high interest rates in between. One might read the recession and period of high interest rates as a period of uncertainty whether the needed fiscal reforms and growth would indeed occur.

Onetime reversible "austerity" does not solve the fiscal problem. Equation 16 reminds us that a disinflationary reform needs to last decades; it must raise the *present value* of future *surpluses* (tax revenue less spending). And raising distortionary tax rates, which may take a decade or two to translate to lower growth, is at best climbing up a sand dune. Even on the left side of the Laffer curve, behavioral response yields less revenue and less growth for each rise in the tax rate.

Failed Stabilization

Without fiscal coordination, an interest rate rise will fail to control inflation. Equation 16 is an inescapable identity. To make this point concrete, figure 5.15 graphs the results of an interest rate rise in a perfectly standard New Keynesian model—no fiscal theory funny business here. (This figure, calculation, and discussion are adapted from Cochrane 2022b, chapter 17.)

The model is the standard New Keynesian model:

$$x_t = E_t x_{t+1} - \sigma(i_t - E_t \pi_{t+1})$$
$$\pi_t = \beta E_t \pi_{t+1} + \kappa x_t$$
$$i_t = \phi \pi_t + u_t$$

Fiscal policy is passive, providing whatever surpluses are needed to validate inflation chosen by monetary policy. I use the unexpected inflation identity (equation 16), to solve for the needed passive fiscal policy of surpluses, and using $r_{t+1} = i_t - \pi_{t+1}$. The only innovation from standard New Keynesian analysis is to look at the required fiscal contraction that accompanies a monetary tightening. (This amounts to adding up the fiscal shock of figure 5.9 and the interest rate shock of figure 5.10, but for rhetorical purposes I want to combine them and present them in an utterly standard New Keynesian framework.)

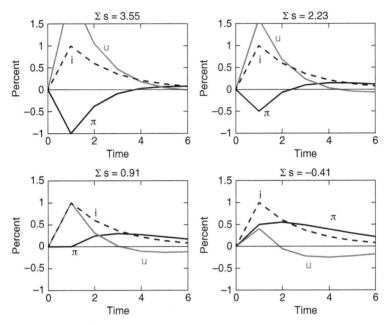

FIGURE 5.15.   Inflation Response to an Interest Rate Rise

Source: Author's calculations.

Notes: Each panel presents a different choice of the disturbance u_t, which produces the same interest rate path. The title $\Sigma s = \cdots$ gives the percent change in the sum of surpluses required by passive fiscal policy for each case. Parameters are $\eta = 0.6$, $\sigma = 1$, $\kappa = 0.25$, $\beta = 0.95$, $\varphi = 1.2$.

Suppose the Fed raises interest rates by a positive and serially correlated disturbance u_t. Figure 5.15 presents the result. The figure presents a surprise AR(1) rise in the interest rate, with serial correlation $\eta = 0.6$, a standard transitory monetary policy experiment.

However, there are multiple disturbance paths $\{u_t\}$ that produce the same interest rate path, but different inflation paths. In each case, I reverse engineer a $\{u_t\}$ disturbance to produce the same AR(1) interest rate path, and a chosen value of initial inflation π_1.

Start in the top left panel. I choose the disturbance $\{u_t\}$ to produce the AR(1) interest rate and a –1% initial inflation. This panel gives the standard New Keynesian result: A higher interest rate lowers inflation, here by exactly 1%. The disturbance u_t follows an AR(1)-like process. It moves more than the interest rate, since $\phi\pi$ and negative inflation drag the actual interest rate down below the disturbance u_t.

Fiscal policy is passive, but the fiscal response has to happen. In this case, as reported in the figure title, cumulative surpluses have to rise 3.55 percentage points of GDP. (I use $\rho = 1$ and 100% debt-to-GDP ratio.) Surpluses have to rise one percentage point of GDP to pay the 1% deflationary windfall to bondholders. They have to rise an additional 2.55 percentage points of GDP because of the long period of high real interest rates, which you can see from a higher i_t line than π_t line, which represent a higher discount rate or higher real interest costs of the debt.

Multiplying by 5, a 5 percentage point interest rate rise and 5 percentage point disinflation require an 18% of GDP austerity program, $4 trillion. Will the administration and Congress passively accede to this request? If they do not, the attempt must fail; the path is not an equilibrium.

What can the Fed do differently? It can follow a different disturbance $\{u_t\}$ that produces the same interest rate path, but requires less fiscal support. In the top right panel, I reverse engineer a disturbance u_t that produces the same interest rate path, but only −0.5% disinflation. The disturbance is smaller and has different dynamics. Since this disturbance produces less disinflation, it also requires less fiscal austerity, 2.23 percentage points of GDP rather than 3.55 percentage points. But for a 5% interest rate rise, this path still requires Congress and the administration to cut back by $5 \times 2.23 = 11.15\%$ of GDP, or $2.2 trillion.

In the lower left-hand panel, I reverse engineer a disturbance u_t that produces the same interest rate path, but produces no disinflation at all. Though interest rates follow the same AR(1), inflation starts at zero and then slightly *rises*. But this path still requires passive fiscal policy to turn to austerity, by 0.91 percentage points of

GDP. Higher real interest rates still provoke a discount rate effect, or higher real interest costs, which surpluses must overcome.

In the bottom right panel, I reverse engineer a disturbance process u_t that produces +0.5% inflation, along with the same interest rate path. This time, passive fiscal policy includes a slight fiscal loosening. Congress and administration cheer, but we clearly have done nothing to fight inflation.

The lesson of this example is that in the stock New Keynesian model, thought of and solved in completely New Keynesian fashion, the same interest rate path may or may not cure inflation. For a higher interest rate to disinflate, it must be accompanied by fiscal contraction. If that contraction does not or cannot happen, the Fed cannot lower inflation by raising interest rates.

Future Fiscal Shocks

There is an even scarier scenario. I have assumed no further fiscal shocks; that from now on fiscal deficits ($s < 0$) will now be matched by expectations of later surpluses, at least up to the moment that monetary policy demands additional surpluses to pay for interest costs on the debt or a bondholder windfall. But the fiscal shock we just experienced is, in my reading, a case of a deficit that people did not expect to be repaid, a $s_t < 0$ not matched by $s_{t+j} > 0$, leading to inflation. Government debt exceeded people's estimate of what the government will repay, so they inflated debt away until the real value of debt declined to match that expectation. Will they now believe that the government can repay larger future deficits? Or, having crossed the Rubicon once and been inflated back to the water's edge, are we in the territory that any future fiscal expansion will be inflationary?

Moreover, while normal deficits might be tolerated, what about the next shock? In the next economic shock—war, pandemic, private or sovereign financial trouble—can the government really borrow or print an additional 30% of GDP, and this time people expect that additional debt to be repaid? Or will we reach the fiscal limit even more quickly next time? We may have lost fiscal and monetary space to react to a shock. If the government wants to borrow or print another $5 trillion, and nobody wants to hold the debt, either inflation or a debt crisis erupt immediately.

In stating this view I raise another central theoretical question, one dividing my fiscal analysis from that of Summers: Is the fiscal limit a flow or a stock constraint?

As I have posed it, inflation breaks out when the quantity of *debt* exceeds people's expectations of repayment. In Summers's analysis, inflation breaks out when the flow *deficit*, times a multiplier, exceeds the GDP gap. So long as that flow is not exceeded, additional deficits really do not matter. Debt sustainability is an issue for long-run analysis not pressing on today's inflation.

Related to this is another crucial empirical question: Are we quickly going to return to an era of low real interest rates on government debt? Or are we going to repeat the 1980s, with a decade or more of high real interest rates? The inexorable trend of declining real interest rates started in 1980, suggestively coincident with a big monetary change. The trend may not be written in stone as most people think.

The deficits of 2008 did not turn to inflation, and by the identity of equation 16 a large reason was the unexpectedly low real interest rates of the 2010s, which lowered debt service costs. Can we count on a quick return to low real interest rates, causing low debt service costs to continue? There certainly seems to be little room for a further decline in real interest rates of the magnitude experienced between 2007 and 2009!

Happier Scenarios

We take for granted that if inflation does become embedded, a disinflation must involve a 1980s style recession. Let us remember the much happier possibilities, considered then, and verified since. That possibility is embedded in a Phillips curve driven by expectations of future inflation. At least in times of big reforms, the anchor point of the Phillips curve can move rapidly and favorably.

Inflation targets have been remarkably successful. Figures 5.16 and 5.17 show inflation around the introduction of inflation targets in New Zealand and Canada. On the announcement of the targets, inflation fell to the targets quickly, and stayed there, with no large recession, and no period of high interest rates or other monetary stringency, such as occurred during the painful US and UK stabilizations of the early 1980s. Sweden had a similar experience. Just how were these miracles achieved?

These episodes are the introductions of inflation targets. Now, inflation targets consist of more than just instructions to central banks to focus more on inflation. Central banks and politicians make announcements and promises all the time, which people take with skepticism well seasoned by experience.

Inflation targets are an agreement between central bank, treasury, and government. Yes, they instruct central banks to worry about inflation and thereby not to worry about other things. But inflation targets are also commitments by treasuries and governments, and specifically a commitment—implicit or explicit—to run fiscal policy so as to pay off nominal debt at the agreed-to inflation target, no more and no less, and to raise surpluses so as to pay any interest costs on the debt that may result from central bank monetary policy. Each of these inflation targets was implemented as a package of tax, spending, and microeconomic reforms. These *fiscal* and *microeconomic* commitments are as important to lowering inflation as is the central bank's *monetary* commitment.

The inflation target functions as a gold price or exchange rate target, which commit the legislature and treasury to pay off debt at a gold or foreign currency value, no more and no less. But the inflation target aims at the CPI directly, not the price of gold or exchange rate, eliminating that source of relative price variation.

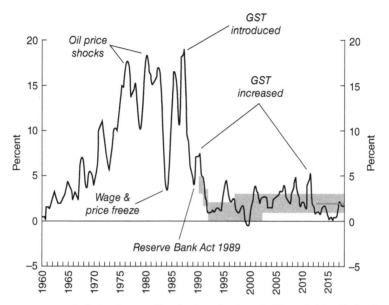

FIGURE 5.16. Inflation Surrounding the Introduction of a Target in New Zealand
Source: McDermott and Williams (2018).
Note: Shading indicates the inflation target range.

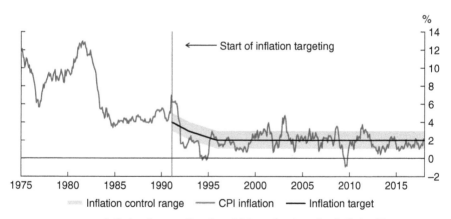

FIGURE 5.17. Inflation Surrounding Canada's Introduction of an Inflation Target
Source: Murray (2018).
Note: Consumer price index inflation, year-over-year, monthly data %.

Figure 5.16 provides evidence of this view, with the annotation "GST [goods and services tax] introduced" and "GST increased." The inflation targets emerged as a part of a package of reforms including fiscal reforms, spending reforms, financial market liberalizations, and pro-growth regulatory reforms (McDermott and Williams 2018).

That fact accounts for their near-miraculous success. One would have thought, and most people did think, that the point of an inflation-targeting agreement is to insulate the bank from political pressure during a long period of monetary stringency. To fight inflation, the central bank would have to produce high real interest rates and a severe recession such as accompanied the US disinflation during the early 1980s. And the central bank would have to repeat such unwelcome medicine regularly.

Nothing of the sort occurred. Inflation simply fell like a stone on the announcement of the target, and the central banks were never tested in their resolve to raise interest rates, cause recessions, or otherwise squeeze out inflation. Well, "expectations shifted" when the target was announced, and became "anchored" by the target, but why? Not by ever more colorful speeches about "anchoring," not by "forward guidance" speeches, and not by WIN buttons or the many other jawboning campaigns that public figures have used in attempts to manipulate expectations by hot air. Expectations shifted because the targets came with a new and durable *fiscal* and *microeconomic* regime, that cured the fiscal problems underlying inflation in the first place. They are a disinflationary fiscal shock, the mirror image of figure 5.9.

An inflation target failed instructively in Argentina in 2015–19. In the analysis of Cachanosky and Mazza (2021) and Sturzenegger (2019), the basic problem was that the necessary fiscal commitment was absent. Argentina's failure reinforces my point that a successful inflation target is as much a commitment by the treasury as a commitment by and commandment to the central bank.

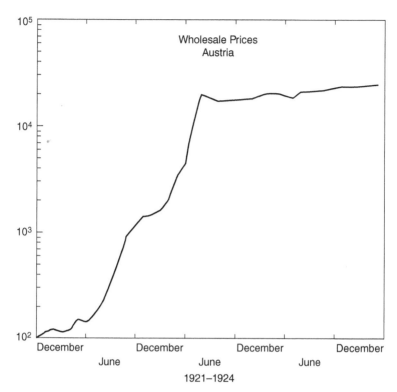

FIGURE 5.18. The End of Austria's Hyperinflation
Source: Sargent (1982).

This success of inflation targets is in this reading an application of the classic Sargent (1982) analysis of the ends of inflations. Figure 5.18 reproduces the end of the Austrian hyperinflation, as a visual reminder. When the long-run *fiscal* problem is credibly solved, inflation drops on its own, almost immediately. There is no period of monetary stringency, no high real interest rates moderating aggregate demand, no recession. Interest rates fall, money supply may rise, and deficits may rise temporarily as well, with the government newly able to pledge surpluses. As such, inflation targeting episodes are as revealing about lack of mechanical stickiness in expectations, specifically in the Phillips curve, as they are about the fiscal foundations of those inflation expectations.

But as Sargent reminds us, expectations do not shift on promises or speeches. People need to see that the regime has changed durably. The current discourse on inflation seems to have lost this history. Clearly, in much contemporary monetary policy, the conventional lessons of the 1970s and 1980s in the US have been somewhat forgotten. The Fed's average inflation targeting, with a focus on letting inflation rise to battle unemployment, seems to codify what most of us were taught to be the mistakes of the 1970s. But let us also not forget the wider lessons of history, and the durable lessons of the rational expectations revolution. *An economically painless disinflation is possible, if it combines fiscal, monetary, and microeconomic reforms that constitute a new and fiscally sound regime.* I qualify as economically painless because it certainly is not politically painless. The sort of tax reform, social program reform, and regulatory reform needed to straighten out US fiscal and monetary affairs are simple for us to design, but would be political suicide in today's environment. Perhaps, as in the late 1970s, or in the inflation targeting countries, enough inflation and stagnation will change that political consensus.

CONCLUSION

Where did inflation come from? The smoking gun suggests the $5 trillion fiscal helicopter drop of 2020–21, which was made particularly potent by its quick monetization and by sending people checks.

Is the Fed behind the curve? That depends crucially on the question, *Are expectations forward looking or backward looking?* The Fed's projections are in fact consistent with a forward-looking New Keynesian model.

How long will inflation last? That depends a good deal on how sticky prices are. Even under the Fed's view that inflation will melt away without a period of high interest rates, inflation can have substantially more momentum than the Fed's projections indicate.

How can the Fed ameliorate inflation? Without a change in fiscal policy, the Fed faces unpleasant interest rate arithmetic. It can lower inflation in the short run, but only by raising it in the long run. Creating a long drawn-out low inflation in response to a fiscal shock is, however, arguably better than allowing a large sudden price level jump. The Taylor rule also functions as a volatility-reducing rule.

When it is time to disinflate, it will require joint monetary, fiscal, and microeconomic (growth-enhancing) reforms. The fiscal constraints will be much tighter this time, with 100% or more debt-to-GDP and larger primary deficits than they were in the 1980s. Without fiscal coordination, to remove the fiscal source of inflation, to pay higher interest costs on the debt, and to pay bondholders in more valuable money, a purely monetary coordination can fail. With those reforms, a painless disinflation is possible.

Since fiscal expansion caused inflation once, will it do so again? In my stock and present value view, this is a clear danger, either in our regular fiscal policy, or the frightening possibility that a desired 30% of GDP or more deficit to fight the next shock will fail, and provoke essentially a sovereign debt crisis.

References

Cachanosky, Nicolás, and Federico Julián Ferrelli Mazza. 2021. "Why Did Inflation Targeting Fail in Argentina?" *Quarterly Review of Economics and Finance*, 80 (May 2019; revised December 2021): 102–16.

Cochrane, John H. 2016. "Comments on 'A Behavioral New-Keynesian Model' by Xavier Gabaix." Presented at the NBER EFG meeting, October 21.

———. 2018. "Michelson-Morley, Fisher, and Occam: The Radical Implications of Stable Quiet Inflation at the Zero Bound." *NBER Macroeconomics Annual* 32 (April): 113–226.

———. 2019. "The Value of Government Debt." NBER Working Paper, July 23 (revised October 16, 2021).

———. 2022a. "Fiscal Inflation." In *Populism and the Future of the Fed*, ed. James Dorn, 119–30. Washington, DC: Cato Institute Press.

———. 2022b. *The Fiscal Theory of the Price Level*. Manuscript (updated June 16), forthcoming. Princeton, NJ: Princeton University Press.

Cochrane, John H., and Kevin A. Hassett. 2021. "Inflation: The Ingredients Are in the Pot, and the Fire Is On." *National Review Online*, April 26.

Cogley, Timothy, and Argia M. Sbordone. 2008. "Trend Inflation, Indexation, and Inflation Persistence in the New Keynesian Phillips Curve." *American Economic Review* 98, no. 5 (December): 2101–26.

Gabaix, Xavier. 2020. "A Behavioral New Keynesian Model." *American Economic Review* 110 (August 1): 2271–327.

García-Schmidt, Mariana, and Michael Woodford. 2019. "Are Low Interest Rates Deflationary? A Paradox of Perfect-Foresight Analysis." *American Economic Review* 109 (January): 86–120.

Hall, Robert E., and Marianna Kudlyak. 2021. "Why Has the US Economy Recovered So Consistently from Every Recession in the Past 70 Years?" Manuscript, May 2020 (revised June 2021).

Kehoe, Timothy J., and Juan Pablo Nicolini, eds. 2021. *A Monetary and Fiscal History of Latin America, 1960–2017*. Minneapolis: University of Minnesota Press.

McDermott, John, and Rebecca Williams. 2018. "Inflation Targeting in New Zealand: An Experience in Evolution." Speech delivered to the Reserve Bank of Australia conference on central bank frameworks, in Sydney.

Murray, John. 2018. "Bank of Canada's Experience with Inflation Targeting: Partnering with the Government." Brookings Institution, January 8. https://www.brookings.edu/wp-content/uploads/2017/12/murray-slides.pdf.

Sargent, Thomas J. 1982. "The Ends of Four Big Inflations." In *Inflation: Causes and Effects*, ed. Robert E. Hall, 41–97. National Bureau of Economic Research Project Report. Chicago: University of Chicago Press.

Sargent, Thomas J., and Neil Wallace. 1981. "Some Unpleasant Monetarist Arithmetic." *Federal Reserve Bank of Minneapolis Quarterly Review* 5 (Fall): 1–17.

Sims, Christopher A. 2011. "Stepping on a Rake: The Role of Fiscal Policy in the Inflation of the 1970s." *European Economic Review* 55: 48–56.

Sturzenegger, Federico. 2019. "Macri's Macro: The Elusive Road to Stability and Growth." *Brookings Papers on Economic Activity*, ed. Janice Eberly and James H. Stock (Fall): 339–411. Washington, DC: Brookings Institution Press.

Summers, Lawrence H. 2021. "The Inflation Risk Is Real." *Washington Post*, May 24.

CHAPTER SIX

How Monetary Policy Got So Far Behind the Curve: The Role of Fiscal Policy

Tyler Goodspeed

To ascertain the proximate causes of the historically high inflation we have observed in the United States in 2021 and 2022, it is essential to look at the role of fiscal policy, which was and still is, an important source of policy variation across advanced economies over the past two years, particularly in 2021. The central thesis of this analysis is that the primary cause of the initial increase in inflation in the United States from early 2021 through early 2022 cannot be a cause that is global in nature—supply chain delays, pandemic-related labor market disruptions, corporate profit-seeking, or expansionary monetary policy—because until the invasion of Ukraine by the Russian Federation, the increase in inflation in the United States was so much greater than that observed in other advanced and major economies.

Indeed, of the forty-six advanced and other major economies tracked by the Organisation for Economic Co-operation and Development (OECD), the increase in inflation in the United States in 2021 over its pre-pandemic 2019 level was greater than in all but Brazil, Turkey, and the Kingdom of Saudi Arabia, which historically have not constituted paragons of fiscal virtue. Moreover, when considering the timing of the divergence of US inflation from other advanced economies, the timing is illuminating. The Harmonised Index of Consumer Prices (HICP) is a standardized

FIGURE 6.1. Harmonised Index of Consumer Prices (HICP),
December 2002–February 2022

Sources: Eurostat via Federal Reserve Bank of St. Louis; Bureau of Labor Statistics via Haver
Analytics; author's calculations.

Notes: Year-over-year percent change. HICP excluding food and energy for United States.
HICP excluding food, energy, alcohol, and tobacco for Euro area.

measure of consumer price inflation that allows for apples-to-apples comparisons of consumer price inflation in the United States and the Euro area. The Bureau of Labor Statistics has been computing this indicator since the early 2000s. Figure 6.1 plots year-over-year growth rates in core HICP in the United States and Euro area from December 2002 through February 2022. In the twelve months through February 2021, inflation in the United States was roughly the same or slightly lower than in the Euro area—1.0% in the United States versus 1.1% in the Euro area.

In March 2021, we then experienced the largest fiscal stimulus during an economic expansion in US history—$1.9 trillion. This was equal to approximately 10% of the US economy and followed a $900 billion stimulus that had only begun to be disbursed in January 2021. The March stimulus consisted mostly of transfer payments to households, at a moment when households were already holding $1.7 trillion in above-trend savings from prior pandemic relief packages, and the US economy was already more than ten months into an economic recovery and had exited the nonpharmaceutical interventions of 2020, having already entered the postvaccine recovery stage.

In the twelve months since February 2021, the increase in the rate of core consumer price inflation in the United States was four times that in the Euro area. It does not require a terribly sophisticated model to explain this divergence in March 2021. As has also been demonstrated by Furman (2022), applying standard fiscal multipliers—at roughly the midpoint of nonpartisan Congressional Budget Office (CBO) estimates—to a fiscal stimulus of the magnitude of that administered in early 2021, would imply aggregate demand rising to a level that was 5–6% above the CBO's (2020) pre-pandemic forecast of potential output.

The immediate impact of this impulse was that personal consumption expenditures on goods—which had already returned to pre-pandemic trend by summer 2020 and had risen slightly above trend by the end of 2020, surged by nearly 11% (240% at an annualized rate) in the month of March 2021 alone. Personal consumption expenditure on goods went from 7% above trend to 19% above trend in one month. By any metric, that is an historic increase in demand. Though US ports and supply chains received considerable attention and criticism in 2021, they in fact performed relatively well in the face of unprecedented demand, handling approximately 20% more import volume in 2021 than in 2019. Typically, when we observe both price and quantity increasing, it is indicative that demand has shifted out by more than supply has shifted in.

However, supply is also relevant insofar as pre-pandemic forecasts of potential output likely overestimate potential output during and in the immediate aftermath of the pandemic. In particular, the March 2021 demand shock was impinging upon a supply side of the US economy that had, by my estimation, lost 1.5 million workers to early retirement. On impact those early retirements constituted an adverse structural shock to the US economy, first, because it removed 1.5 million workers from the labor force who, conditional on being in the labor force, have a higher probability of being employed versus unemployed. Second, in the short term, younger workers are imperfect substitutes for experienced older workers, which can generate structural skill mismatches.

The supply side of the US economy was also still impaired in March 2021 by an ongoing recovery in labor force participation, with 3.7 million Americans still reporting that they had not looked for employment in the preceding four weeks because of the pandemic. In addition, a cumulative shortfall in private nonresidential fixed investment of approximately $500 billion since the start of the pandemic implied a smaller US private capital stock than would otherwise have prevailed had business investment continued at pre-pandemic trend levels.

Moreover, not only was the supply side of the US economy still exhibiting signs of continued pandemic-induced impairment in March, but also the fiscal legislation introduced by the American Rescue Plan actually exacerbated that supply shortfall. In particular, it did so by raising implicit marginal tax rates on the return to work through an extension of supplemental federal unemployment insurance benefits and the introduction of full refundability on an expanded Child Tax Credit. At the margin, the American Rescue Plan effectively lowered the after-tax return to employment relative to unemployment. Higher implicit marginal personal income tax rates therefore likely contributed to transition rates from unemployment to employment that were abnormally low in 2021 relative the volume of job vacancies.

This is reflected in the persistence through 2021 of an unprecedented outward shift of the Beveridge curve. An outward shift of this magnitude meant not only that the US labor market in 2021was exhibiting the highest level of disfunction in the task of matching unemployed workers to vacant jobs than at any time

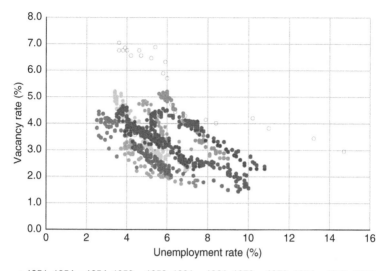

FIGURE 6.2. Beveridge Curve, 1951–2022

Sources: Bureau of Labor Statistics; National Bureau of Economic Research; Barnichon (2010); author's calculations.

Notes: Vacancy rates are from the composite Help-Wanted Index (HWI) constructed by Barnichon (2010) and updated through August 2021. Since August 2021, I use vacancy rates from the BLS Job Openings and Labor Turnover Survey, rebased to the August 2021 value of the composite HWI. Curves are plotted by business cycle, as dated by the National Bureau of Economic Research.

since the late 1970s—indeed, even worse than in the late 1970s—but also that any given unemployment rate was now associated with greater inflationary pressure, implying a higher natural rate of unemployment. As shown in figure 6.2, this was not the portrait of an efficient labor market, nor was it the portrait of a labor market with a natural rate unchanged from pre-pandemic estimates. Yet it was the labor market onto which the US federal government poured an additional $1.9 trillion in fiscal stimulus.

In 2021, the US economy, therefore, experienced an unprecedented stimulus to aggregate demand—particularly personal consumption expenditure on goods—at the same time that, at the margin, fiscal policy further exacerbated existing impairments to potential output. When such a large increase in aggregate nominal demand exceeds the real productive potential of the US economy, it results in a large positive residual. In 2021, that residual could be accounted for by the increase in price level, with legacy effects on inflation expectations.

Though it is generally inadvisable to conclude a paragraph, let alone a paper, with a quotation, I leave the reader with these words, written by the late Allan Meltzer on the origins of the "Great Inflation" of the latter half of the 1960s to the early 1980s. Policy makers in the late 1960s and early 1970s, he concluded in 2005,

> denied for several years that inflation had either begun or increased. They did not deny the numbers they saw. Like Gardner Ackley (Member of President Kennedy's Council of Economic Advisers, Chairman of the Council of Economic Advisers under President Johnson), they gave special explanations—a relative price theory of the general price level—in effect claiming that the rise in the price level resulted from one-time, transitory changes that they did not expect to repeat. Later, they added other explanations, especially that the cause of inflation had changed from the classic "demand pull" to the new "cost push." (Meltzer 2005, 160)

I ask the reader, does any of this sound familiar?

References

Barnichon, Regis. 2010. "Building a Composite Help-Wanted Index." *Economic Letters* 109: 175–78.

Congressional Budget Office. 2020. *The Budget and Economic Outlook: 2020 to 2030.* Washington, DC: Congressional Budget Office.

Furman, Jason. 2022. "Why Did (Almost) No One See the Inflation Coming?" *Intereconomics* 57: 79–86.

Meltzer, Allan H. 2005. "Origins of the Great Inflation." *Federal Reserve Bank of St. Louis Review* 87: 145–75.

CHAPTER SEVEN

CURRENT MARKET PERSPECTIVES

Beth Hammack

Well, thank you to John Cochrane and John Taylor for including me in this conference, and my apologies for not being able to be back at my alma mater in person. Unfortunately, after two long years, I have finally succumbed to COVID-19 this week. And so, I'm sorry not to be there with you. But obviously I'm sure you all appreciate why I can't be there.

My comments will be squarely, I think, in the "other" section of the commentary that we had put forward for "fiscal explanations and other." So, I'm going to give you a market perspective on inflation, where the Fed is, and where we might go from here.

I'll start with figure 7.1, which takes you through a similar path to what John Taylor showed you earlier, a look at the dot plots and the expectations the Fed has put forward about how both rates and inflation could evolve over time. What you can see from this is that inflation expectations have shifted quite materially since the fall of last year. As a result, the Fed's expectations for rate hikes also began accelerating as early as November 2021. That is when the Fed began to really change its tone on the inflationary environment, which the first panel at the conference today unanimously believed was way too late. When they started changing that tone on the inflationary environment and recognized that it might be more persistent than anticipated, there was a notable shift in the market. Then you add the Russia-Ukraine conflict to the picture, which we spent very little time talking about, but I really do think that was an exogenous shock

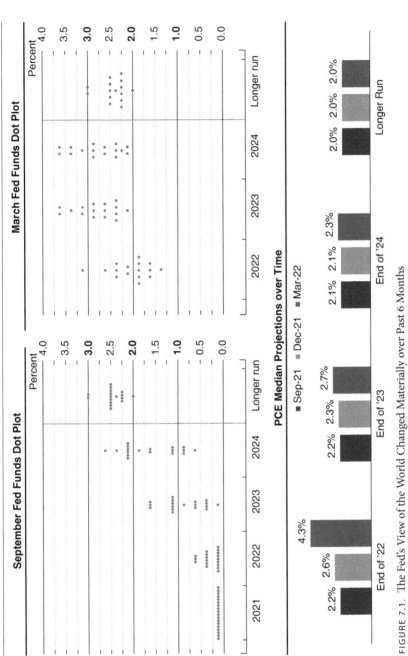

FIGURE 7.1. The Fed's View of the World Changed Materially over Past 6 Months

Source: Federal Reserve.

that exacerbated the food and energy price pressures. Both these things then meant that the Fed needed to pivot its stance even more quickly than it had anticipated, and to do it in a relatively short time frame. This monumental shift in tone, amplified by further hawkish commentary from a variety—a broad chorus really—of Fed governors and presidents, resulted in the heightened market volatility that I believe has slowed the efficient flow of capital in the markets.

It is helpful to consider credit spreads over the past thirty years. Current spreads are in line with historical 10-year averages. But the speed with which we've gotten here in the last six months has left investors off balance. As shown in figure 7.2, 10-year yields have nearly doubled since November 2021, and spreads across the credit spectrum have moved between 60% and 100% wider as well. And of note, we're currently seeing positive correlation between yields and spreads, which is atypical of market environments, and really is indicative of the increased investor demand for cash.

The velocity of this movement in the 10-year rate, and in the markets more broadly, has been quite remarkable. In prior periods of similar 10-year movements, in this case looking at six-month periods, where the 10-year note has moved both 125 basis points higher and experienced at least a 30% increase on a relative basis, the equity market was largely stable-to-rising during the same periods. This is indicative of a rebound in growth, and it's typically associated with declining volatility, tightening in credit spreads. However, in this most recent move, during the past six months, we've seen just the opposite. Yields are up, volatility is up, spreads are wider, and equities are down. The exit from the pandemic economy is quite unique, but this confluence of moves is tightening financial conditions and signaling a very challenging growth outlook at the same time.

Business expectations of sustained short-term inflation pressure are running well above current price models, driven by the recent commodity price shock. However, longer-term inflation expectations

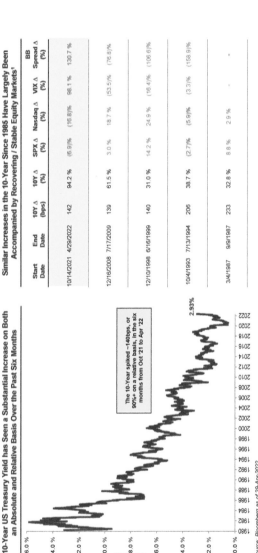

10Y Treasury Yields Have Increased at an Historic Pace in the Last Six Months

US equities typically rise and volatility declines during periods of rapidly expanding 10Y yields, but the last 6 months have been different

10-Year US Treasury Yield has Seen a Substantial Increase on Both an Absolute and Relative Basis Over the Past Six Months

The 10-Year spiked ~140bps, or 90%+ on a relative basis, in the six months from Oct '21 to Apr '22

2.93%

Similar Increases in the 10-Year Since 1985 Have Largely Been Accompanied by Recovering / Stable Equity Markets[1]

Start Date	End Date	10Y Δ (bps)	10Y Δ (%)	SPX Δ (%)	Nasdaq Δ (%)	VIX Δ (%)	BB Spread Δ (%)
10/14/2021	4/29/2022	142	94.2 %	(6.9)%	(16.8)%	98.1 %	130.7 %
12/16/2008	7/17/2009	139	61.5 %	3.0 %	18.7 %	(53.5)%	(76.6)%
12/10/1998	6/16/1999	140	31.0 %	14.2 %	24.9 %	(16.4)%	(106.6)%
10/4/1993	7/13/1994	206	38.7 %	(2.7)%	(5.9)%	(3.3)%	(158.9)%
3/4/1987	9/9/1987	233	32.8 %	8.8 %	2.9 %	-	-

Source: Bloomberg as of 29-Apr-2022
[1] Includes moves in the 10Y of at least 125bps on an absolute basis that were also greater than 30% increases on a relative basis. Dashes indicate comparable data not available for the period.

FIGURE 7.2. 10-Year Treasury Yields Have Increased at a Historic Pace in the Last Six Months are reasonably well anchored, though they are increasingly elevated as price pressures do persist.

Wage inflation, as we've talked about, is definitely a key cause for concern as shown in figure 7.3. The current jobs to workers gap is the largest since 1950. And it's driven a +5% acceleration in wages. A recent survey of US corporations found expectations for annual wage growth to moderate to 3.6% by year end. But that may be too optimistic given the magnitude of the current gap. There are early signs that some companies may have overhired in the recent period to get ahead of this trend. Most notably, this was a point of discussion during Amazon's recent earnings call, where executives indicated they are no longer chasing physical or staffing capacity. And while rhetoric like that may suggest there are sources of slack to come in the labor market, we still have a long way to go to close this current gap.

The magnitude of the Fed sentiment shift again has been quite notable. The shifting in tone, which began at the Fed's November meeting, might have been sufficient to stave off further inflationary pressure had it not been for the Russia-Ukraine conflict. The impact of that event and subsequent sanctions packages on the global supply chain, and on energy prices in particular, has resulted in expectations of accelerated tightening. Markets do best when they have time to adjust gradually. But volatility spikes when Fed-speak leans towards sharper, more aggressive moves. And you could see that clearly from the late-April movement, when you saw some rhetoric from the Fed that 75-basis-point hikes were on the table.

The current US financial conditions index is elevated but largely in line with pre-COVID levels. The market can digest a reasonable hiking plan to fight inflation. However, as I've noted, the abrupt change in stance is what's really causing investors to rethink their allocations, particularly to the equity markets. A significant portion of the tightening we've seen in the Goldman Sachs global financial conditions index (FCI) has come from the move in equities, mainly

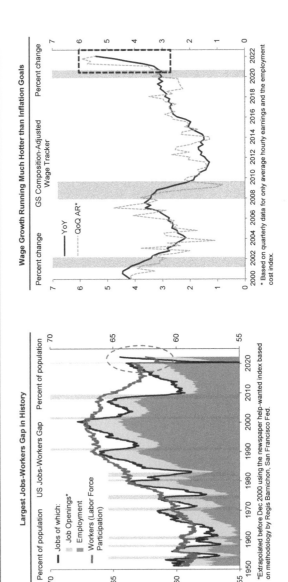

While companies expect wage growth to moderate to 3.6% by year end, that may be too optimistic given magnitude of current gap

FIGURE 7.3. Outsize Wage Growth Driven by Historic Jobs-Workers Gap

from technology and growth stocks. Long-term GDP growth and personal consumption expenditures (PCE) inflation expectations both point to modest future growth and a tempering of actual inflation. But the short-term volatility, driven by policy uncertainty, continues to slow the efficient flow of capital in our markets.

As a result, we're seeing investors pulling back. Flows out of equity and bond funds illustrate a lack of participation in the broader market by institutions, and US equity sentiment is currently (as of May 2022) at near-all-time lows. The reduction in institutional buyers from the equity market has slowed new equity issuance, particularly for growth companies and for those in the tech sector. Since 2020, we've had 150 tech IPOs, but so far this year, we've seen only one.

As a result, capital flows have left growth stocks and flooded toward value stocks and companies with demonstrated profitability. Investors are searching for safe-haven companies that are protected against inflation, and the benefit is accruing to the largest, most well-capitalized names, leading to a potential liquidity crunch among high-growth pre-profit companies who are most at risk of failing in a constrained market.

The composition of buyers in the market has also changed dramatically. Mutual funds are sitting on record amounts of cash, and hedge funds are running tight positions and pressing shorts. The most consistent market buyers have been retail, who now hold 39% of US equities, and corporations, whose 2022 buyback authorizations are projected to be a high-water mark for the previous five years. However, we've seen more than $20 billion of retail outflows in the last couple of weeks, and Robinhood Markets, Inc.'s recent earnings indicate retail trading activity is down 20% quarter over quarter, meaning that retail buying is starting to slow. The current market volatility, driven by a worrisome outlook on inflation and growth, is also impacting companies' investment priorities. Amidst heightened uncertainty, CEOs are spending capital buying back their own stock instead of leaning into capex. CEO confidence correlates well with capital expenditures and inversely correlates with volatility.

So where do we go from here? The good news, illustrated in figure 7.4, is that there is a clear path ahead, and hopefully the worst volatility could be behind us. Increased rates and broader FCI tightening should decrease growth sufficiently to rebalance the labor market and calm wage growth and inflation. However, the path to terminal rates may be just as important to the health of the market than where it ends up. As we've seen, the market has responded quickly to the Fed's tightening plans. However, continued unexpected changes to the velocity of those rate movements can spook investors. And while the Fed does have the power to put wage inflation in check, broader global supply chain disruptions continue to weigh on investors' minds. The key to market stability from here is a steadier pace of increases that are well anticipated by the market.

One final drop of optimism amid the volatility we continue to see is that private balance sheets remain reasonably strong despite the wind-down in government stimulus. Households and corporate balance sheets show signs of strength compared to periods preceding prior crises, and small businesses and partnerships, who needed the most help from COVID stimulus, are showing signs of resilience as well. Furthermore, balance sheets of the most highly levered firms are improving, and we're near recent highs in Q4. These healthy private sector balances widen the Fed's runway for a soft landing and bolster the view that a recession is not inevitable.

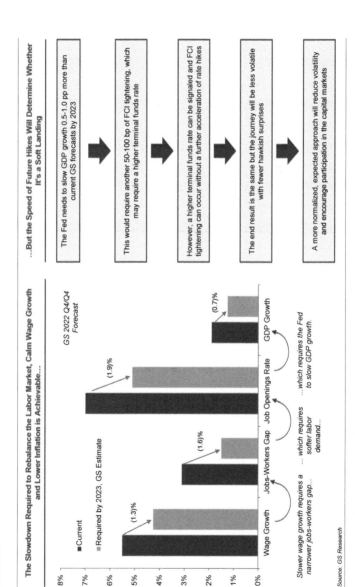

FIGURE 7.4. Where Do We Go from Here?

© **2023** Goldman Sachs. All rights reserved.

GENERAL DISCUSSION

CHARLES I. PLOSSER (INTRODUCTION): Welcome everybody. It's a pleasure to be back in person here at Hoover and for this conference, a conference I've been to many times. It is especially nice to see so many of you again. Our first panel was quite fascinating, a lot about monetary policy and a lot about inflation and whether the Fed is behind the curve. I have my own remarks about that, but I'll save those until a more appropriate time.

This panel is to broaden the discussion, to the extent that it hasn't already, into thinking about not just monetary policy actions but about fiscal policy. And we're delighted to have a panel to focus on some of those aspects of inflation and the role that fiscal policy might be playing. After all, Larry Summers raised this point and so did others. During the pandemic crisis, not only did the Fed reduce rates to near zero, but there was $6 trillion of new government debt issued between February 2020 and December 2021. What's interesting about that part is that over 50%, over $3 trillion, was actually purchased by the Federal Reserve. That rate of purchases of public debt is unprecedented even in war times. But it's certainly an extreme combination of fiscal policy stimulus and monetary policy, based on the volume of that new debt that the Fed actually purchased. So these things were clearly entwined in some important respects. And I think one of the challenges that we have as economists is disentangling some of those effects and what you might say is identifying the shocks, at least empirically.

First on our panel is John Cochrane, who obviously needs no introduction to this crowd, a senior fellow at Hoover, organizer of this conference for many, many years, and quite a vocal commentator. I love his title of his blog, *The Grumpy Economist*. My wife just says I'm grumpy, so I often identify with John's perspective. Another thing is that John has spent quite a bit of time talking about the fiscal theory of the price level. So I'll give a plug to his new book that is coming out, *The Fiscal Theory of the Price Level*. He's given that idea quite a lot of his attention. And so we're delighted to have him with us. John, along with John Taylor and Michael Bordo, have all been involved in the organization of this conference series and of this conference in particular. I'll note that all three of them are on the program today. Maybe that's just coincidence, I'm not sure. But maybe it also is a prerogative of the conference organizers. Anyway, I'm delighted to have John to present his own insights with us today.

Our next speaker is Tyler Goodspeed. He's a relatively new fellow at Hoover. Tyler's experience is in both economics, labor economics, as well as policy making. He came to Hoover shortly after stepping down as a member of the Council of Economic Advisers in the previous administration. So he has a particular perspective on policy making that I think will bring a lot of insights to our discussion.

And finally, we are joined by Beth Hammack. She is one of the lead members of the Global Financing Group at Goldman Sachs—a great deal of experience in financial markets. We're delighted to have her with us. And I suspect she's going to give us a bit of a perspective on the financial markets and the mechanisms going on there. So I think we've got the potential for a very good panel. And I'm looking forward to the discussion.

So I'm going to turn first to John.

*   *   *

KRISHNA GUHA: Thank you. So question for Tyler. The optimistic, perhaps absurdly optimistic, take on the Beveridge curve shifts that you spent a lot of time describing is that the sheer velocity, the sheer scale of the hiring that we've attempted to execute over the last year or so has put immense strain on the matching process. And as the economy cools toward less extreme growth rates, that matching process should improve significantly. And we might see a very pronounced shift of the Beveridge curve back toward pre-pandemic structures. How do you assess that? Is that wishful thinking, or is it a not unreasonable base case?

TYLER GOODSPEED: Thank you. Great question. I think it is a reasonable estimate. I think it is a reasonable expectation that the Beveridge curve will shift back in. There were very unusual circumstances in 2021 for several reasons. One, the enhanced unemployment insurance benefits. Two, the enormous accumulation of excess savings by households likely resulted in even those who were actively looking for work in the past four weeks in 2021 were probably able to be a little bit more selective in their job search than they would otherwise have been. Now that enhanced unemployment insurance benefits have expired, as households draw down some of those excess savings, I would expect that effect to dissipate. Also in 2021, there was—rather like the 1960s and 1970s—regional dispersion in employment growth, where you had relatively high unemployment and relatively low employment growth in California, New York, and relatively high employment growth and relatively low unemployment in Texas and Florida. Again, as we emerge from the pandemic, get back to a more normal macroeconomic state, I would expect that to ease. My point in illustrating the Beveridge curve was that that was the state of affairs in 2021 when this massive fiscal shock was applied.

MICKEY LEVY: I want to clarify a possible misperception about the trend in federal budget deficits and fiscal stimulus. The very nature of the pandemic and the sheer magnitudes of the fiscal responses suggest that the fiscal stimulus will have elongated lags, even as federal budget deficits recede. Charlie, you mentioned that there has been almost $6 trillion in deficit spending, but that is spending authorization and a nontrivial portion—approximately $500 billion at the federal level—that has not yet been spent. More has been saved by individuals and businesses that received income support.

While the rate of personal savings has receded, the stock of personal savings remains an estimated $2.5 trillion higher than pre-pandemic, about 12% GDP. Most of that onetime increase in savings eventually will be spent. Although good data on businesses is not available, business savings has also skyrocketed.

Here is another real irony in the not-spent story. State and local governments have saved virtually all of the half-trillion-dollar federal transfers they received through the CARES Act and the Biden administration's $1.9 trillion American Rescue Plan of March 2021. They have increased their holdings of US Treasuries, about $650 billion, and are now one of the biggest holders. Eventually those excess savings will be spent or taxes will be cut. They're spending some of those excesses now to subsidize gasoline price increases. Even as federal deficit spending comes down, the fiscal stimulus isn't over. Fed Chair Powell actually referred to the decline in budget deficits in his semiannual report to Congress, suggesting that fiscal policy is becoming restrictive. This delayed spending and stimulus is critically important to the future path of nominal spending and GDP, which are crucially important to the outlooks for inflation and the economy.

JOHN COCHRANE: Let me comment on that quickly. The five or six trillion we were referring to represents how many Treasuries have actually been issued, including half of them that have been issued and then turned into reserves. That's actually already out, I think. So what you're pointing out is, in addition to that, there is authorized spending that will lead to future issues of Treasuries beyond the five or six trillion that we already have in mind. So we have some baked-in stimulus hidden there. And you're exactly right.

Now, the other question—this really bears on this flow-versus-stock question about deficits and inflation that I closed with. It a really important issue. When the government issues Treasuries, people are supposed to think, "These are great investments, because the government is going to someday raise taxes or cut spending to pay me back." We hold them as investments; we don't try to sell and spend them. We might argue about crowding out of investment maybe, but Treasuries are supposed to be an investment vehicle that does not get directly spent. The fact that people on aggregate are seeing these Treasuries as kind of needless stuff that they need to get rid of fast before it goes away is unusual. And that's what lends me to this sort of fiscal limit, stock view of how much trouble we're in.

JAMES BULLARD: Jim Bullard, St. Louis Fed. I have a question for John Cochrane. I love the part of your presentation where you're talking about rational expectations versus adaptive expectations. Then you're talking about defining "behind the curve" as assuming adaptive expectations and then observing an inflationary spiral. There is a more rigorous literature on this that is kind of in between the two polar extremes that you presented, and has learning in it. That might also help explain why the interest rate peg at zero is supposed to be unstable but doesn't look unstable in Japan, as you showed in your picture, or even in the US in the last two years or so. What happened was that there was a certain monetary policy plus a really big shock. So, you get driven to somewhere else in the parameter space and it's not clear if that'd be stable or not, whether you come back or you get pushed off to the inflationary spiral. I think in more extensive analysis of this issue, you can probably make statements about "How big was the shock? Did it push you out of the basin of attraction?" And so on under the learning assumption. I think that's a very interesting way to define what we mean by "behind the curve," and then you could apply that to countries like Turkey or Venezuela, where they get so far out of line that they really do see the spiral.

COCHRANE: I dare to say you're absolutely right. But I'm not sure superadvanced nonlinear learning models are ready for policy!

Is inflation stable under an interest rate peg? It's surprising that we know so little about this basic question. I guessed, it's where I think you guessed: if you raise interest rates, that's going to lower inflation for a while, but then there are longer-run properties that we know less about. That short-run effect may have something to do with learning, forming expectations, in some sense becoming more rational. And it also has to do with financial frictions and the 15 other things that aren't in the simple model that I put down, that I wish we understood better. But it does mean the business of central banking is more squishy than we often say in public. We don't really know long-run stability, and we don't really know where the short-run negative effect of interest rates on inflation comes from and how reliable it is! I think Larry's comments were pretty good about that, let's not oversay what we actually know and can rigorously exploit.

I do think policy should be quite conservative. Academics like me can think three crazy things before breakfast. But policy makers should be a little more cautious.

RICHARD CLARIDA: Yeah. Excellent paper, John. Richard Clarida, a regular attendee at the Hoover conference. And thank you for holding them again.

John, as you know, I enjoyed your paper, but I'm gonna put both you and Tyler on the spot a little bit. So suppose we rewind the tape, and suppose in the US there's no FOMC. There's an inflation nutter central banker and you get to pick a Rogoff conservative central banker, and he or she has one objective, which is for year-end December 2021 core PCE to be at 2% conditional on the fiscal policy in place in 2021. So what's the level of the funds rate the nutter central banker would have set after the American Rescue Plan passed? Forget about inertia, just as in *Mission Impossible*, your mission, if you decide to accept, is to keep inflation in 2021 at 2%. So what's the funds rate that would have done that?

COCHRANE: Higher. I'll do a Larry Summers. Higher.

GOODSPEED: I was just going to say, I think there's a Larry Summers argument. The simple exercise that would have done a very good job at predicting inflation in 2021 would be to simply calculate what is the expected increase in nominal demand? What is the potential output of the US economy? What is the residual between those two? And I think the residual was about 5%. So you know, if you want to end the year with an inflation rate of 2%, and inflation expectations have risen by 5% . . . Or the price level is going to jump by 5% absent any intervention by the Fed, I mean, do the arithmetic there.

COCHRANE: I also want to emphasize, when you have a fiscal shock, there are limits to what the Fed can do. I think Milton Friedman won a little bit too much in thinking the Fed is always and everywhere completely in charge of inflation. When there's a fiscal shock, the Fed can move it around a little bit and delay it for a while, but when there's a fiscal shock, it's not all in the Fed's hands.

PLOSSER: I would like to exercise the chairman's prerogative here on following up on that point. So my question to you, John, is, you made a lot of the point that there's this joint fiscal monetary decision that has to be made. And in the case of the examples of New Zealand and Canada that you offer, there is a regime change. One of the important things about that is, how are they are made credible in the process? And how do you do that? I want to bring that back to today. In this experience, we had a big fiscal shock, $6 trillion of new debt issued. The Fed bought over half of that. Now my question is, in your view, would the outcome have been different had the Fed not bought all that government debt? Did that cause suspicion that in fact the bonds would not be paid back? And therefore, the mere fact that the Fed participated to the extent it did undermine the credibility of the payback, that inflation would be used instead of taxes to pay back the debt? And if so, getting the coordination to achieve both those things simultaneously is challenging? Am I misinterpreting what you're saying or not?

COCHRANE: In World War II, we issued an enormous amount of debt, and there was some inflation but not immense amounts of inflation. Why? Because people kind of understood, "We're fighting to save the world and eventually we'll pay back that debt." You can issue immense amounts of debt without inflation, if there's a plan for paying it back. So what was different about this one? One, so much of it went directly as checks to people. We need to add in our model that people are different, and sending checks to people is a lot more potent than selling bonds to investors. It carries different signals. I also think that in the 2008 recession, there was a lot of talk about stimulus today but deficit reduction tomorrow. You and I may have made fun of that. But there *was* talk about it. There was no talk about repayment this time. This time it was modern monetary theory, r is less than g, interest costs are low, we don't have to worry about fiscal expansion. Nobody was saying, deficit now repayment tomorrow. So I think there are 15 plausible things one can point to that help us to understand why this time resulted in inflation and other times did not.

Now, ex post, I'm spinning stories like everyone else is. I acknowledge the challenge. Why was this one so inflationary? How will we know when future debts are inflationary and when people have confidence that they will be repaid?

BETH HAMMACK: But I think you can't ignore the fact that you actually had borders shut, and you had things slowing down, you know, pretty tremendously. And post that, you've had even worse supply shocks given the Russia-Ukraine sanctions. And so I take your point that obviously the government did a lot and put money out there. And maybe the rhetoric wasn't quite as much around repayment, although there was a narrative that this was a different kind of war that needed to be met with significant support. But I think it's an interesting question, and I don't think it's totally . . . I think you can't ignore the external exogenous factors that drove us to be more significant than it may have been otherwise.

COCHRANE: Beth is absolutely right, 2008 was something like a demand shock. In the pandemic, people weren't failing to go out to restaurants because they didn't have enough money. They weren't going out to restaurants because the restaurants were closed. This was a supply shock. I think of it as a great snowstorm. In snowstorms GDP goes down not because there's lack of demand, but because there is lack of, for a better word, supply. So meeting a supply problem with demand certainly tells us a lot about why so much of the debt quickly went into inflation rather than more output.

MARKOS KOUNALAKIS: Hi, I'm at the Hoover Institution, Markos Kounalakis. Beth, this is addressed to you. And if you could address how you factor in the real estate asset class within the environment that you describe, that will be helpful.

HAMMACK: Sure. I didn't talk about real estate because it's not part of the broader financial conditions frame that we typically look at. But it certainly is an important sector in the economy. And it's one that, as I think we've all felt, has certainly been thriving, and given the significant price increases, I do think it's one that is the most interest-rate sensitive of any of the sectors, probably even more so than the technology sector. And so I think the increases that we've seen in rates, and frankly in term rates, which obviously moved much faster than overnight rates, will serve to bring it down and to cool it.

The other thing I would just caution as I think about the housing markets broadly, is that you don't have a lot of leverage coming into the market. So one of the things, again, that makes me feel more optimistic, and I might be the only optimist that you speak to today about the environment that we're in, is that we don't have a significant amount of leverage that's built up through the system this time, unlike prior episodes, where I think that would make more concern—other than government leverage.

THE FED'S DELAYED EXITS FROM MONETARY EASE

CHAPTER EIGHT

The Fed's Monetary Policy Exit Once Again Behind the Curve

Michael D. Bordo and Mickey D. Levy

Every business cycle has different characteristics that economic policy makers influence and respond to. The COVID-19 pandemic posed a negative shock to aggregate supply and aggregate demand. Pent-up demand and unprecedented fiscal stimulus and sustained aggressive monetary ease fueled a V-shaped recovery involving strong demand amid ongoing supply constraints. The result is that, as of mid-2022, the Federal Reserve finds itself in an uncomfortable situation that it failed to anticipate, but one that has occurred before in its modern history: it faces undesired high and rising inflation and is behind the curve, and it must tighten monetary policy just enough to reduce inflation but not so much as to generate a recession.

In this chapter, we assess the current situation through the lens of history, comparing the current inflation and the conduct of monetary policy to the recovery phase of prior business cycles. Focusing primarily on cycles since World War II, we highlight a persistent pattern of the Fed extending its monetary policy, easing too long, and delaying its tightening exits. Most frequently, this has led to rising inflation and then catch-up tightening that led to a recession more frequently than to a soft economic landing. While countercyclical monetary policy is a difficult task, the Fed does not seem to take away the appropriate lessons from history (Bordo and Levy 2022).

Prior to World War II, the Fed's focus on price stability under the gold standard and adherence to the real bills doctrine led it to prevent inflation but at the expense of depression and financial instability. The evolving policy anchors and the Fed's developing objectives resulted in major policy errors that contributed to the Great Inflation of 1965 to 1982. The current high inflation has some key differences that distinguish it from the 1970s, but the Fed's extended denial of any similarities between the two periods has allowed some of the more troubling characteristics of the Great Inflation to reemerge and threaten sustained economic growth. We provide empirical evidence that shows how the recent pervasiveness of inflation has begun to mirror the 1970s while intermediate-term inflationary expectations have risen but remain below the upward ratcheting of inflationary expectations during the Great Inflation found by Levin and Taylor (2013).

The Fed's current monetary policy mistakes did not just occur out of the blue. Rather, the Fed's new strategic framework and delayed exit from its emergency policy responses to the pandemic are a culmination of the evolution of its objectives and discretionary policy deliberations. The Fed's earlier anchor of price stability evolved into a low inflation target and more recently toward favoring higher inflation as a vehicle for avoiding the effective lower bound (ELB) while its long-standing tilt toward prioritizing low unemployment has become more pronounced. These asymmetries, which have been institutionalized in its new strategic framework (Levy and Plosser 2020), have contributed to its current dilemma.

The recent rise in inflation has been predictable, based on the expected excess demand that would be generated by the unprecedented expansive monetary and fiscal policy responses and the nature of the pandemic (Bordo and Levy 2020 and 2021; and Levy 2021). The Fed's failures to predict the higher inflation and acknowledge its sources in 2021 are puzzling.

Sections of this chapter, in turn: provide a historical perspective on business cycles, including a description and measures of the Fed's earlier delayed exits; analyze the similarities and differences between the current situation and the Great Inflation of 1965–82; consider factors that explain why the Fed has tended to be behind; and lastly, provide a recap of lessons from history and make recommendations that would help avoid future policy mistakes.

BEHIND THE CURVE
IN HISTORICAL PERSPECTIVE

The Federal Reserve has long had difficulty in timing its exits from countercyclical expansionary monetary policy. Bordo and Landon-Lane (2013) examined the historical and empirical record on the timing of the Fed's exits from recessions following the business cycles approach taken earlier by Milton Friedman, Karl Brunner, and Allan Meltzer.[1] In general, they found that since the Fed was founded in 1913 it has followed a pattern of waiting too long to tighten. The pattern has evolved over time. After World War I, the Fed under the leadership of Benjamin Strong focused on stabilizing the real economy and maintaining price stability, leading to the development in the US of countercyclical monetary policy. It did so within the frameworks of the gold standard and the real bills doctrine. Under this strategy once the economy began recovering, the Fed usually tightened when the price level increased, as adhering to the gold standard would require. It paid less attention to the real economy.

After World War II and the Employment Act of 1946, the Fed began pursuing its dual mandate, which attached importance to

---

1. Friedman (1953) first laid out the difficulty of using discretionary monetary policy to stabilize the business cycle, i.e., of fine-tuning. He showed that when the Fed used its policy tools to offset exogenous shocks in most cases it aggravated the business cycle. It mistimed policy actions because of long and variable lags between policy changes and its effects on output and prices. Friedman and Schwartz (1963) and others (Nelson 2019) supported this with their historical analysis. Brunner and Meltzer (1964) published a report for the US Congress documenting episodes in the post–World War II era when the Fed fell behind the curve. They criticized the Fed for following an incorrect policy doctrine, the Burgess Riefler Strong Doctrine—an extension of real bills (Bordo 2022). This monetarist evidence was used in their case against discretion and in favor of a monetary rule.

maintaining full employment and stabilizing the real economy along with the continued connection to the fixed dollar peg of the gold standard under Bretton Woods system. Price level stability remained important until the mid-1960s. The Fed's exits were similar with those of the mid-1920s.

After 1965, the Fed began jettisoning the gold peg under pressure to accommodate expansionary fiscal policy and fully abandoned it in the Nixon Shock of August 1971. The Fed's focus shifted towards full employment at the expense of rising inflation. During the Great Inflation, the Fed's exits from recessions became subsumed by higher inflation, tightening when inflation went up but never enough to stamp out inflationary expectations. The government's misguided wage and price controls failed to contain inflation and the Arab oil embargo imposed a negative supply shock. The upward ratcheting of inflation and inflationary expectations, enabled by accommodative monetary policy, undercut the Fed's credibility, leading to the US dollar currency crisis in 1978.

The Volcker disinflation shock in 1979–82 led to a new regime of low inflation and ushered in the Great Moderation during which the Fed's more balanced approach to inflation and employment resulted in more timely exits. The Fed's aggressive monetary tightening in 1994 lowered inflationary expectations and resulted in a stronger economic expansion—a picture-perfect soft landing. In the early 2000s, the foundations of the Great Moderation eroded as the Fed's fears of the risks of deflation led it to delay its exit from easy monetary policy. Its policies facilitated the debt-financed housing bubble and financial instability that resulted in the great financial crisis (GFC) of 2008–9. Following the GFC, inflation stayed low and the Fed sustained zero interest rates and used quantitative easing to keep bond yields low and reduce unemployment. Its concern about a downward spiral in inflationary expectations and the ELB led it to reassess its strategy, which resulted in a new strategic framework in 2020. That framework institutionalized its asymmetric prioritization of maximum inclusive employment over inflation and de-emphasized preemptive monetary tightening. The Fed's delayed exit from its emergency policy responses to the pandemic has allowed a surge in inflation and inflationary expectations that poses a serious challenge to sustained economic expansion.

The Historical Record

Bordo and Landon-Lane (2013) examined the Fed's exits from 1920 to 2007, comparing the timing of changes in policy—policy rate, monetary base, and money supply (in nominal and real terms)—with the timing of changes in macro variables—real GDP, prices, inflation, output gap, and unemployment. They measured the turning points in these variables compared to National Bureau of Economic Research (NBER) business cycle troughs.[2] Table 8.1 presents some salient variables pertaining to the Fed's exits.

For seven NBER cycles from 1920 to 1960, the table shows the turning points around the cyclical troughs in the price level (column 2) and the unemployment rate (column 3) compared with the turning points in monetary policy representing tightening measured by the nominal and real discount rate until 1953 and the federal funds rate thereafter (columns 4 and 5) and the nominal and real rate of growth of the monetary base (columns 6 and 7). When the Fed tightened, the policy rate would increase and the rate of growth of the monetary base would decline. The last column of the table ascertains the timing of the policy measures (whether on time, too soon, or too late) and the economic outcome.

---

2. Regression analysis was used to measure the timing of policy changes relative to the trough of a set of real variables and price variables. The results suggest that in the post–World War II era, especially after 1965, the Fed's tightening was more responsive to the level of unemployment than to inflation. In the pre–World War II period the Fed was more responsive to the price level than the real economy.

TABLE 8.1. Cyclical Turning Points in Monetary Policy, 1920 to 1960

(1) Cycle Peak to Trough (Trough)[a]	(2) Price Level: CPI[b] (Inflation)	(3) Unemployment[c]	(4) Discount Rate[d] (Fed Funds Rate)
1. 1920 Q1–1923 Q2 (1921 Q3)[f]	1922 Q1	1921 Q1	3, 7[g]
2. 1923 Q2–1926 Q3 (1924 Q3)	1924 Q1	1924 Q1	3, 3
3. 1926 Q3–1929 Q3 (1927 Q4)	1928 Q1	1928 Q1	−1, −1
4. 1929 Q3–1937 Q2 (1933 Q1)	1933 Q1	1932 Q1	−6, −5
5. 1948 Q4–1953 Q2 (1949 Q4)	1950 Q1	1949 Q4	1, 2
6. 1953 Q2–1957 Q3 (1954 Q2)	1954 Q4	1954 Q3	(0, 1)
7. 1957 Q3–1960 Q2 (1958 Q2)	(1958 Q2)	1958 Q2	(0, 0)

Source: Michael D. Bordo and John Landon-Lane, "Does Expansionary Monetary Policy Cause Asset Price Booms; Some Historical and Empirical Evidence," in *Macroeconomic and Financial Stability: Challenges for Monetary Policy*, ed. Sofía Bauducco, Lawrence Christiano, and Claudio Raddatz (Santiago: Central Bank of Chile, 2014), tables 1a, 1b, 2a, 2b.

[a] We omitted two cycles containing World War II years: 1937 Q2–1944 Q4 and 1945 Q1–1948 Q3.

[b] The turning point was determined by visual inspection for the first quarter after the start of the recession when the price level changes from having a negative slope to a positive slope.

[c] The turning point was determined as the first quarter after the start of the recession when the derivative of the unemployment series changes from positive to negative.

Pre–World War II: 1918 to 1941

In general, the timing and narrative evidence suggest the Fed waited until the price level (CPI or GDP deflator) rose before tightening, but in two cycles in the mid-1920s, the exit involved timely responses to both real and nominal variables. Friedman and Schwartz (1963) referred to these episodes as "The High Tide of the

(5) Real Discount Rate (Real Fed Funds Rate)	(6) Monetary Base Growth[e]	(7) Real Monetary Base Growth	(8) Comments and Result
—	3, 7	−1, 3	Too late, serious recession
4, 4	2, 2	4, 4	Too late, mild recession
−1, −1	0, 0	−1, −1	On time, mild recession
−6, −5	3, 4	3, 4	Too soon, real bills mistake, Great Contraction
4, 5	−3, −2	−3, −2	Too late, mild recession
(−1, 0)	−1, 0	−1, 0	On time, mild recession
(0, 0)	−1, −1	−1, −1	On time, mild recession

[d] The turning point was determined as the first quarter after the start of the recession when the interest rate started to increase from a period of falling or relatively level rates.

[e] The turning point was determined as the first quarter after the start of the recession when the monetary base growth rate started to fall from a time of increasing or relatively constant growth rates.

[f] NBER trough dates for each cycle.

[g] In each cell the first number represents the number of quarters after the price level trough, and the second number represents the number of quarters after the unemployment peak. Missing value represents a cycle in which no definitive turning point was identified.

Federal Reserve." In sharp contrast, Friedman and Schwartz viewed the Fed's responses in three other business cycles in this period as policy failures.

In the first cycle (1920–23 peak to peak), the Fed waited until inflation reached 15% per year before commencing tightening in late 1919. The mistiming is generally blamed on pressure from the Treasury on the Fed to keep interest rates low to support bond prices. When the Fed finally tightened, it led to the second deepest recession in US monetary history. The Fed's largest policy mistake was during the Great Contraction from 1929 to 1933. Its tightening cycle began in early 1928, not because prices were rising, but because of fears based on the real bills doctrine that the Wall Street boom in stock prices would lead to inflation. The ensuing recession that began in July 1929 turned into the Great Contraction when the Fed failed to appropriately address the four banking panics from 1930 to 1933 and allowed the money supply to collapse. The Fed's third mistake unfolded in 1936 when it doubled reserve requirements on commercial banks because it feared that banks would monetize their excess reserves and that would lead to high inflation. This "too soon" tightening led to the recession of 1937–38, the third deepest in US history.[3] These episodes provide valuable cautionary tales of the risks of misguided monetary policy.

1945 to 1965

World War II was financed by a combination of taxes, bond issuances, and the inflation tax of money issue. M1 and M2 surged during 1940–45. Compared to World War I, inflation during World War II was constrained by extensive price controls. Following the war, it was widely agreed that managing aggregate demand was an important role of the government, and the biggest concern was that aggregate demand would collapse and recession and deflation would follow, as in the post–World War I period.

Instead, pent-up demand surged, fueled by the lagged impact of monetary ease and sustained low interest rates, as the Fed was constrained from rising interest rates under the fiscal dominance

---

3. This cycle is not shown because the recovery phase from 1938 Q2 to 1945 Q1 was dominated by World War II and the Fed, under the control of the Treasury, did not conduct countercyclical monetary policy.

of the Treasury (Bordo and Levy 2020). Consumption, housing, and business investment spending boomed. The excess demand strained the transition from wartime to civilian production, and inflation surged after the wartime wage-price controls were lifted. The inflation of 1945–48 was temporary but intense, exceeding 10%, following the removal of wartime price controls.

The Fed belatedly tightened monetary policy in 1948 through higher bank capital and reserve requirements while the government's fiscal policy turned restrictive as defense spending fell faster than anticipated. This generated a mild recession and deflation in 1949.

The Fed regained its independence in March 1951 with the Treasury–Federal Reserve Accord and under Chairman William McChesney Martin followed a balanced approach to inflation and employment during the 1950s and early 1960s, with relatively successful exit policies (Meltzer 2010). The business cycles and recessions of 1953–54, 1957–58, and 1960–61 were relatively mild, similar to those in the mid-1920s. Like the 1920s, inflation was anchored by the gold standard constraint so that when the exits were delayed they did not lead to inflation but to a rise in the price level which then declined with recessions (see table 8.1).

Cyclical Episodes since the 1960s

Table 8.2 provides a description of the NBER business cycles since the 1960s and conduct of monetary policy around them. Reflecting the modern monetary policy regime, it includes for each expansion the trend in inflation and the unemployment rate (columns 2 and 3) and monetary policy reflected by the real fed funds rate and money supply (column 4). For an early and late stage of each cycle it measures in percentage points the deviation of the fed funds rate to an estimate of the Taylor rule (column 5). Column 6 describes the economic result of the Fed tightening.

TABLE 8.2. Cyclical Episodes of the Federal Reserve's Exits from Monetary Ease, 1961 to Present

	(2)	(3)	(4)		(5)	(6)
(1)	Inflation[a]	Unemployment Rate[b]	Fed Policy		Comments	
Cyclical Expansion	Start → End	Start → End	Real FFR[c]	Money	Fed Funds Rate minus Taylor Rate[d]	Result
1961 Q2–1969 Q4	1.2% → 5.5%	6.4% → 3.5%	0.9%–3.7%	↓ real MB & M2	1966–1969: −2.4pp	**1970 recession**
Note: 1965 Q4–1967 Q1	1.6% → 3.2%	4.5% → 3.8%	Credit tightening (Reg Q ceilings)		1971–1973: −1.6pp	Sharp slowdown, sustained expansion
1971 Q1–1973 Q4	5.6% → 6.2%	5.4% → 4.9%	1.5%–3.4%	↓ real MB & M2	1975–1979: −4.0pp	**Oil price shock & deep recession**
1975 Q2–1980 Q1	11.1% → 12.4%	7.3% → 6.0%	−2.1%–2.8%	↓ real MB & M2	1983–1987: +2.3pp	**Oil price spike & recession**
1980 Q4–1981 Q3	13.6% → 11.1%	7.2% → 7.4%	2.6%–7.2%	↓ real MB & M2 unchanged	1988–1989: +1.1pp	**Recession**
1983 Q1–1990 Q3	5.2% → 5.0%	10.1% → 5.4%	5.7%–4.2%	↓ real MB & M2	1991–1993: −0.3pp	**Mild recession**
Note: 1987 Q1–1987 Q4	1.7% → 3.7%	6.9% → 6.2%	Fed hikes until Oct '87 stock market crash then eases (↑ MB & M2)		1994–1999: +1.4pp	Extended expansion
1991 Q2–2001 Q1	4.3% → 2.5%	6.3% → 4.0%	2.7%–3.7%	↓ real MB, ↑ M2	2001–2006: −0.9pp	**Recession in 2001**
Note: 1994 Q1–1995 Q1	2.4% → 2.1%	6.8% → 5.8%	0.7%–2.7%	↓ real MB & M2	2007–2008: −0.7pp	Extended expansion

2002 Q1–2007 Q4	1.6% → 2.6%	5.1% → 4.6%	1.3%–2.5%	↑ real MB & M2		**GFC recession**
2009 Q3–2019 Q4	−0.3% → 1.5%	8.5% → 3.7%	0.5%–0.7%	decline in 2018–19	2009–2019: −1.7pp	**Pandemic recession**
Note: 2015 Q4–2018 Q4	0.2% → 2.1%	5.3% → 3.9%	−0.1% to −0.3%	↓ real MB, ↑ M2	2015–2018: −2.0pp	Extended expansion
2020 Q1–present	1.6% → 6.3%	3.7% → 3.6%[e]	0.3% to −6.3%[f]	surge in MB & M2	2022 Q1[g]: −8.1pp; Modified TR = −6.5pp	?

Sources: BLS, BEA, Federal Reserve Board, Haver Analytics; authors' calculations.

[a] CPI before 1991, PCE after 1991, 4-quarter average of year-over-year inflation.

[b] 4-quarter average unemployment rate.

[c] 4-quarter average of real fed funds rate.

[d] Fed funds rate minus Taylor rule estimate, average measured in percentage points.
Taylor rule: $r^* + \pi^* + 1.5(\pi_t - \pi^*) + 0.5^* \text{CBO GDP Gap}_t$, where $r^* = 2\%$, $\pi^* = 2\%$, and π is core PCE. See figure 8.1.

[e] March 2022 unemployment rate.

[f] As of February 2022.

[g] Based on Q1 core PCE inflation of 5.2% and Q1 effective fed funds rate of 0.12%. See figure 8.1 for modified Taylor rule equations and assumptions.

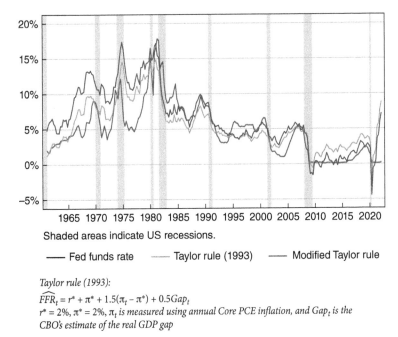

Shaded areas indicate US recessions.

—— Fed funds rate —— Taylor rule (1993) —— Modified Taylor rule

Taylor rule (1993):

$$\widehat{FFR}_t = r^* + \pi^* + 1.5(\pi_t - \pi^*) + 0.5Gap_t$$

$r^* = 2\%$, $\pi^* = 2\%$, π_t *is measured using annual Core PCE inflation, and* Gap_t *is the CBO's estimate of the real GDP gap*

Modified Taylor rule:

$$\widehat{FFR}_t = r^*_t + \pi^* + 1.5(\pi_t - \pi^*) + 0.5Gap_t$$

r^*_t *uses Laubach-Williams one-sided estimate of* r^* *(Laubach and Williams 2003 and Federal Reserve Bank of Atlanta 2022). Note:* r^* *from Q3 2020 onward is assumed to be equal to Q2 2020 level (0.36%);* $\pi^* = 2\%$, π_t *is measured using annual Core PCE inflation, and* Gap_t *is the CBO's estimate of the real GDP gap*

FIGURE 8.1. Taylor Rule Estimate and Actual Federal Funds Rate

Sources: Federal Reserve Bank of Atlanta; authors' calculations.

Figure 8.1 shows a comparison of the actual fed funds rate with estimates of several variations of the Taylor rule.[4] The gaps between the Taylor rule and fed funds rate are consistent with the descriptions of the business cycles provided below.

---

4. Both variations use the Congressional Budget Office's estimate of the GDP Gap and core PCE inflation rather than the GDP deflator used in the original Taylor rule (1993). Our second variation uses Laubach-Williams (2003) estimates of r^* in place of Taylor's $r^* = 2.0\%$ in his 1993 version. See figure 8.1.

The Beginning of the Great Inflation: 1965 to 1970

During the first half of the 1960s, the Fed under Chairman Martin was dedicated to both price stability based on its indirect link to the gold standard under the Bretton Woods system (Bordo and Eichengreen 2013) and full employment. But the policy-making environment was evolving. The historical objective of price stability was replaced by the view that moderate inflation was good for economic performance, and the anchor provided by the gold standard eroded. Keynesian policy prescriptions advocated activist macroeconomic policies that attempted to exploit what was perceived to be a reliable and stable Phillips curve trade-off between unemployment and inflation.

Beginning in 1965, under pressure from the Johnson administration, the Fed began accommodating the fiscal imperatives of the Vietnam War and President Lyndon B. Johnson's Great Society program. This generated excess demand and higher inflation (Levin and Taylor 2013). Inflation accelerated from 1.6% in 1965 to 5.9% in 1970. The Fed attempted to tighten credit during the summer of 1966 through higher bank capital requirements, and by not lifting Regulation Q on interest rates. This resulted in a "credit crunch" that slowed economic growth but did not cause a recession, forcing the Fed to step back.[5]

Meanwhile, accelerating spending on the Vietnam War and renewed monetary accommodation generated rising inflation. Inflationary expectations and bond yields rose. The Fed's delayed exit began only after President Johnson announced he would not seek reelection. The Fed's sharp tightening in 1969 involved a rise in real interest rates and a decline in the real monetary base and M2. Coupled with the extension of the Vietnam War surtax, a recession unfolded in 1970.

---

5. Some economic journalists referred to the Credit Crunch as a recession but the NBER never designated it as one.

The 1970s: Upward-Ratcheting Inflation

Arthur Burns became Chairman of the Federal Reserve in February 1970. He blamed inflation on nonmonetary (cost-push) factors including strong labor unions and greedy businesses, advocating wage and price controls to stem it. In response to the mild recession of 1969–70, and even though inflation was nearly 6%, the Burns-led Fed lowered interest rates aggressively, below inflation by early 1971. The result was a rapid growth in money. The Fed then raised the discount rate to slow credit and eased rates. In 1972, the Fed kept rates too low, allowing a sharp expansion in money aimed at supporting Richard Nixon's reelection bid (Meltzer 2010). At the same time there was significant fiscal stimulus. Although the Fed raised rates from 5% to 10% in the twelve months between the November 1972 election and the November 1973 Arab oil embargo, the lagged impacts of stimulus coupled with an acceleration in money velocity associated with the higher interest rates generated a surge in nominal GDP growth, to 9.8% in 1972 and 11.4% in 1973. This excess demand overwhelmed the wage and price controls, and CPI inflation rose from 3.3% in 1973 to 8% even before the Arab oil embargo generated soaring oil prices in November 1973. The Arab oil embargo contributed to a deep recession from late 1973 to early 1975 with real GDP declining by 4.7% while inflation rose to 11% in 1974 when the wage and wage price controls were lifted.

While inflation fell sharply following the recession, it troughed at 5.2% in late 1976, far above its mid-1973 low, while the unemployment rate was very slow to recede. The unemployment rate rose from 4.8% to a peak of 9% in the second quarter of 1975 and drifted only gradually lower to 7.8% at year-end 1976 even as the economy recovered.

The Fed lowered rates aggressively from an average of 10.5% in 1974 to 5.4% in late 1975 and kept them below inflation through September 1977. It belatedly raised rates faster, but only enough to keep pace with the sharply accelerating inflation rate, which rose to 6.6% in the fourth quarter of 1977, 9% in 1978, and 10.75% before the second oil price shock in mid-1979. Despite accelerating inflation, the high unemployment rate remained the top priority of Congress, and Burns did not attempt to stamp out inflation because he feared the implications of higher unemployment (Burns 1979). The Humphrey-Hawkins legislation, which was enacted as the Full Employment and Balanced Growth Act of 1978, established employment and inflation as the dual mandate for the Fed.

The ratcheting up of inflation during the Great Inflation took a heavy toll. From late 1965 to mid-1982, the CPI rose over 300%. Damage to the Fed's credibility culminated in a US dollar crisis in 1978. Higher inflationary expectations and bond yields generated sustained real declines in financial asset values, and the rising real costs of capital and depressed investment and potential growth. The higher inflation distorted the tax system, which was not indexed to inflation at the time.

Volcker's Aggressive Disinflationary Monetary Policies and the Great Moderation

In August 1979, President Carter appointed Paul Volcker, a well-known inflation hawk, as Fed chairman. Two months after taking office, Volcker announced a major shift in policy aimed at rapidly lowering inflation. He desired the policy change to be interpreted as a decisive break from the past policies. The Fed imposed a series of sizable hikes in the federal funds rate. The roughly seven percentage point rise in the nominal funds rate between October 1979 and April 1980 was the largest, most rapid increase in the Fed's history.

Although Volcker tightened monetary policy aggressively, because inflationary expectations were embedded and the Fed lacked credibility, the exit was costly, with back-to-back recessions in 1980 and 1981–82, and it took until 1983 to definitively lower inflationary expectations (Bordo, Erceg, Levin, and Michaels 2017 and Sargent and Silber 2022).

Volcker's successful disinflationary policies ushered in the Great Moderation. During this period the Fed took a more balanced response to inflation and employment, with more timely exits following monetary easing. The result was moderate inflation and virtually sustained economic expansion. The Fed began raising rates soon after the 1983 expansion began and well before inflation pressures ensued in mid-1983. It began raising rates before inflation turned up in late 1986 but eased in response to the stock market crash of October 1987. Soon after the crash, the Fed began raising rates in nominal and real terms when sustained economic growth lowered the unemployment rate and inflation picked up. It raised rates aggressively from 6.6% in March 1988 to 9.9% in March 1989, and the yield curve inverted.

Economic growth slowed sharply beginning in the second quarter of 1990, and a mild recession unfolded in late 1990 associated with the Gulf War spike in oil prices.

The Fed's most noted preemptive exit was in 1994. Following the so-called jobless recovery of 1991–93, the Fed raised rates sharply, from 3% to 6% from February 1994 to February 1995 in response to declining unemployment and signs of overheating labor markets when there were no signs of rising inflation. The Fed's tightening dampened inflationary expectations and successfully orchestrated an economic soft landing and ushered in strong performance in the second half of the decade. While Fed research touted this successful preemptive tightening, Fed Chair Greenspan expressed concerns about its negative impacts on the mortgage market and housing. The Fed delayed its monetary response to strong economic and financial performance and rising inflation in 1999 because of worries about liquidity needs around Y2K, opting to raise rates gradually. Following the collapse of the dot.com bubble, business investment fell and consumption growth slowed. In this environment, the Fed tightened too much in 2000, raising rates to 6.5%, far above the 2.6% inflation. The collapse in capital spending contributed to a recession that was accentuated by the shock of 9/11.

The 2000s: Worries about Deflation Contribute to a Delayed Exit

Following the bursting of the dot.com bubble and the 9/11 shock that extended the recession, inflation fell to 1%, and a new fear gripped the Fed: based on observations of Japan's bouts with mild deflation following the bursting of its equity bubble in 1990, the Fed began to fear the downside economic risks of deflation. Even though Japan's economic performance was far different from the United States', its experience resonated with the Fed, which feared that if deflation were to unfold, aggregate demand would spiral down and would be hard to reverse through monetary stimulus. The Fed thought that the risks of the costs of deflation far outweighed the risks of higher inflation, which it believed it could address through monetary tightening, so it strived to avoid any probability of deflation. This led the Fed to delay its exit from monetary easing, even as inflation moved back up. The Fed delayed raising rates and then raised them gradually, trying to avoid harming financial markets, in sharp contrast to the aggressive tightening of 1994. Keeping rates too low for too long facilitated the debt-financed housing boom that contributed to financial instability that later evolved into the GFC of 2008 (Taylor 2007 and Bordo and Landon-Lane 2014).

Post–Great Financial Crisis

In direct response to the extreme financial market dysfunction that centered on the mortgage market, the Fed engaged in large-scale purchases of mortgage-backed securities (MBS), quantitative easing or "QEI." Fed Chair Bernanke emphasized that QEI was credit policy, not broad-based quantitative easing, and said the Fed would unwind its holdings on a timely basis (Bernanke 2008). The Fed subsequently extended its zero-rate policy and ramped up its quantitative easing with purchases of MBS and Treasury securities well after the financial crisis had ended and the self-sustaining economic recovery had ensued. The low inflation allowed the Fed to focus on employment and extend its unprecedented monetary ease.

Inflation stayed low during the post-GFC expansion primarily because the expansive monetary and fiscal policies (the American Recovery and Reinvestment Act of 2009) did not stimulate sustained acceleration in aggregate demand. Nominal GDP growth remained below 4%, providing little support for higher prices or wages (Levy 2017). The Fed's QEs boosted bank reserves and the monetary base, but they did not translate into increased M2 or a credit expansion capable of generating stronger economic activity (table 8.2, column 4). Instead, changes in the Fed's operating procedures, including paying interest on excess reserves (IOER), and tighter capital and liquidity requirements, along with a shift to tighter controls and bank supervision imposed by stress tests, constrained credit (Ireland and Levy 2021). While the low interest rates boosted home prices and equity markets, the damages imposed by the financial crisis on the banking system, consumer finances, and the housing sector took years to repair. The Fed may have taken away the wrong lessons from this period, attributing the low inflation to the ex post observation that the Phillips curve had flattened. It subsequently presumed that inflation would stay low.[6]

The Fed raised rates very gradually beginning in late 2015 and began unwinding a portion of its bloated balance sheet beginning in 2017. By the third quarter of 2018, the Fed had raised rates to a range of 2.25–2.5%, modestly above PCE inflation of 2.4%. Following the

---

6. There were no cautionary voices within the Federal Reserve System to point out that historically, fiscal stimulus financed by monetary accommodation led to inflation.

Fed's delayed exit, the economy continued to grow at a moderate pace and inflation receded to 1.5%, close to its average of 1.4% since 2012. Although inflationary expectations remained fairly well anchored to 2% and the Fed continued to forecast that inflation would rise to 2%, the Fed harbored mounting worries that if inflation persisted below its 2% target, there was a risk of a downward spiral in inflationary expectations that would lower interest rates to the ELB and constrain the Fed's ability to respond to the next cyclical downturn. These concerns led the Fed to conduct a strategic review beginning in 2018. Underlying its strategic review, the Fed focused on the risks of lower inflation, and the more focus was directed at the goal of maximizing employment for all groups of people. The new strategic framework that was rolled out in August 2020 (Powell 2020) introduced a flexible average inflation targeting regime that incorporated an asymmetry that favored higher inflation, and dialed down the Fed's historic reliance on preemptive tightening to control inflation, while prioritizing and broadening the Fed's employment mandate to "maximum inclusive employment." It was a structurally flawed strategy (Levy and Plosser 2020).

The Pandemic and Subsequent Recovery

The negative shock to aggregate supply and aggregate demand and government shutdowns generated a short but massive decline of 9% in real GDP in the first half of 2020. The Fed's response was purposely more aggressive and expansive than its response to the GFC. It quickly lowered rates to zero, conducted massive purchases of Treasuries and MBS, and additionally established an array of direct business lending and grants programs coordinated with and capitalized by the Treasury and Congress (Bordo and Duca 2022). The Fed's asset purchases generated a surge in the monetary base. At the same time M2 surged, reflecting primarily government income support initiatives. Fiscal policy authorized over $5 trillion in deficit spending, more than 25% of GDP, largely in the form of checks distributed to individuals and small businesses, beginning with the CARES Act of March 2020. A sizable portion of the government's fiscal transfers in the ensuing twelve months were saved and deposited in banks. Associated with the decline in economic activity consequent upon the pandemic and government-imposed shutdowns, M2 money velocity declined.

The strong V-shaped economic recovery and sharp rise in inflation surprised the Fed. Nevertheless, the pandemic crisis had encouraged the Fed to be more interventionist, and its policies had helped lift the economy out of a deep contraction and were considered successful. The Fed maintained its emergency monetary policies of zero rates and ongoing purchases of Treasuries and MBS until March 2022. Its exit began long after inflation and inflationary expectations had risen sharply, and labor markets were characterized by accelerating wages and signs of extreme tightness. Measured against any inflation or employment benchmark, the Fed's exit has been more delayed than any in history. Most strikingly, as inflation rose sharply and the labor market recovery of all groups far exceeded expectations and exhibited clear signs of tightness and stress, the Fed ignored the data and insisted that tapering its asset purchases and raising rates would be delayed until "substantial progress" had been made toward its new employment mandate. By March 2022, the fed funds rate was 6.3% below PCE inflation (5.4% below core PCE inflation), the unemployment rate had fallen to 3.6%, and Chair Powell termed the extreme tightness of labor markets "unhealthy."

THE CURRENT SITUATION: SIMILARITIES AND DIFFERENCES FROM THE GREAT INFLATION

As the economy recovered from its second quarter 2020 trough, Fed officials presumed that there would be a repeat of low inflation the post-GFC conditions. When inflation began accelerating, the

Fed said it was transitory, attributing it to the base adjustments following the decline in the CPI and PCE indexes in March and April 2020 and to temporary supply shortages. Any comparisons to the 1970s were dismissed as inappropriate and uninstructive. The Fed's extended denial that inflation had anything to do with strong demand that was generated by monetary policy and unprecedented deficit spending contributed to the persistent acceleration of inflation and allowed some current conditions to become uncomfortably similar to the 1970s.

So far, the rise in inflation in 2021–22 has been similar in magnitude to the inflation of the late 1960s and early 1970s, but below levels during 1978–82. Through March 2022, CPI inflation had risen to 8.5% from 2.2% in 2019, while PCE inflation has risen to 6.6% from 1.5% over the same time frame (their core measures excluding food and energy have risen to 6.4% and 5.2%, respectively). These increases are similar to the rise in CPI inflation to 5.9% in 1970 from 1.5% in 1965.[7] Both inflation episodes were generated by a surge in government spending and accommodative monetary policy.

A detailed analysis of price increases of components of both the CPI and PCE price index show that current inflation has been pervasive across a wide array of goods and services, similar to the inflation of the late 1960s and early 1970s. Figures 8.2 and 8.3 show the acceleration of inflation in a growing number of components of the CPI and PCE. Through much of 2021, the rightward movement of the shares of the components indexes experiencing rising inflation was inconsistent with statements by Fed officials (Powell 2021) and the Biden administration that the inflation was attributable to sharply rising prices of select goods and services.

---

7. The CPI measures inflation for out-of-pocket consumer expenditures (it excludes expenditures that are paid for by employer-financed health insurance, Medicare, and Medicaid) and its components are not weighted by expenditure shares. The PCE components capture all personal consumption expenditures including those that are financed by third parties and are weighted by shares of spending.

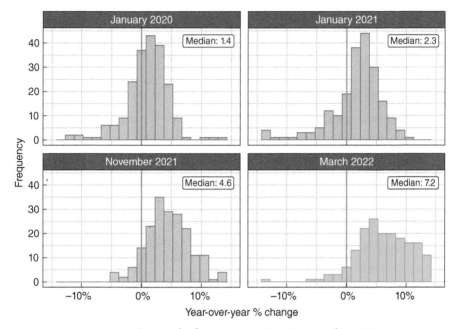

FIGURE 8.2. Distribution of Inflation across 200+ CPI Expenditure Categories

Sources: Bureau of Economic Analysis (BEA), Berenberg Capital Markets.

Note: Expenditure categories with year-over-year changes greater than 15% in magnitude dropped from the chart.

The growing pervasiveness of inflation and similarities to the 1970s are striking. Figure 8.4 shows the portion of CPI components experiencing inflation exceeding 3% and 5%, while figure 8.5 shows similar shares of components of PCE inflation. Through February 2022, the shares of CPI components experiencing inflation exceeding 3% and 5% rose to 82% and 65%, respectively, while the shares of PCE components with inflation exceeding 3% and 5% rose to 68% and 48%. These shares are as high as in the late 1960s and early 1970s, but remain below the late 1970s. Of note, while the shares of the PCE components experiencing high inflation are less than the CPI shares and below the shares experienced in the 1970s, the CPI measures out-of-pocket expenditures, which may influence inflationary expectations.

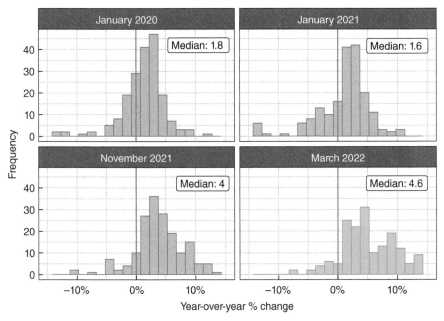

FIGURE 8.3. Distribution of Inflation across 191 PCE Expenditure Categories

Sources: Bureau of Labor Statistics (BLS), Berenberg Capital Markets.

Note: Expenditure categories with year-over-year changes greater than 15% in magnitude dropped from the chart.

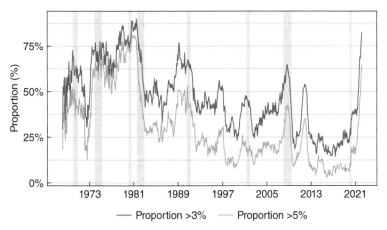

FIGURE 8.4. Portion of CPI Components Experiencing Inflation Exceeding 3% and 5%

Sources: BLS; authors' calculations.

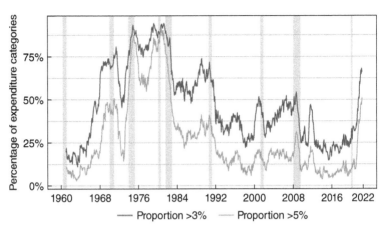

FIGURE 8.5. Portion of PCE Components Experiencing Inflation Exceeding 3% and 5%

Sources: BEA, Haver Analytics; authors' calculations.

The Fed's misreads of the economy and inflation have been disturbingly similar to the rhetoric of the 1970s. The Fed placed blame on special factors even when measures of aggregate demand including final sales to domestic purchasers had accelerated to their fastest pace in history. The Biden administration, similar to the Nixon administration, has blamed the inflation on greedy businesses (but not labor unions!). Fortunately, the Fed has acknowledged that wage and price controls failed. Instead of blanket controls, the Biden administration is attempting to lower prices of select goods by providing financial incentives to specific industries to increase supply and by imposing regulations on others aimed at controlling their prices. It is also releasing oil from the Strategic Petroleum Reserve.

Inflationary expectations have risen significantly in 2021 and 2022, but they remain well below those of the 1970s. Short- and intermediate-term expectations have risen markedly, while longer-run expectations have risen only modestly, suggesting that at least so far, the Fed's long-run inflation fighting credibility remains intact. Expectations of inflation in the next year have risen dramatically, to

TABLE 8.3. The Fed's Summary of Economic Projections of Inflation

Inflation forecast made in:	2021		2022		2023	
	PCE	Core PCE	PCE	Core PCE	PCE	Core PCE
December 2020	1.8	1.8	1.9	1.9	2.0	2.0
March 2021	2.4	2.2	2.0	2.0	2.1	2.1
June 2021	3.4	3.0	2.1	2.1	2.1	2.1
September 2021	4.2	3.7	2.2	2.3	2.2	2.2
December 2021	5.3	4.4	2.6	2.7	2.3	2.3
March 2022	—	—	4.3	4.1	2.7	2.6

Source: Summary of Economic Projections, Board of Governors of the Federal Reserve System.
Note: Measured Q4/Q4.

5.4% (University of Michigan) and 6.6% (Federal Reserve Bank of New York Consumer expectations), while three-year expectations have risen to 3.7% (Federal Reserve Bank of New York Consumer expectations). Market-based measures of inflationary expectations for five years have risen to 3.4% while inflation is expected to average 2.6% in years six through ten (based on the 5-year, 5-year forward curve).

The Fed's unwillingness to acknowledge the persistence of inflation is illustrated in the quarterly updates of its Summary of Economic Projections (SEPs) (table 8.3). In each succeeding quarterly SEP in 2021, the Fed raised its projection of inflation for 2021 to reflect inflation that had already occurred, but forecast inflation would fall sharply in 2022–23, despite assuming that it would be most appropriate that the Fed would not raise rates from zero until 2023. That forecast changed materially in March 2022.

Direct comparisons of inflationary expectations with the 1970s are limited by data availability. However, derived estimates of inflationary expectations during the Great Inflation by Levin and Taylor (2013) are materially higher than current levels. Current survey-based measures of inflationary expectations are higher than market-based measures, and may have a bigger influence on wage and price-setting behavior. Whereas market-based measures are determined by factors that influence yields on US Treasury securities and the TIPs markets—include changes in the Fed's holdings of these securities, commercial bank holdings, foreign central bank policies, the US dollar exchange rate, and foreign demand—consumer expectations may be more closely linked to household and business decisions that affect the inflation process (Reis 2021).

In sharp contrast to the upward ratcheting of bond yields between 1965 and 1982, bond yields remained far below inflation since the beginning of the pandemic. Yields on 10-year Treasury bonds were 1.5% in February 2020 and fell to 0.7% in October 2020. They have now risen to 3%. Ten-year Treasury yields rose from 4.2% in 1965 to 7.8% in early 1970. During the 1970s, they ratcheted up with higher lows and higher highs. Between June 1978 to June 1982, yields rose from a low of 8.6% and 15.3%.

The higher yields during the 1966–82 period pushed down stock valuations, and real total returns on stocks were negative over the entire period. In contrast, low bond yields since early 2020 have supported high stock valuations, although this now may be changing. Whereas the high rates during the Great Inflation raised the government's debt service costs and heightened concerns about persistent budget deficits, recent low interest rates have reduced government debt service costs and diluted concerns about rising government debt. Of note, nominal GDP growth was persistently high in the 1970s, rising to average 11.3% per year during 1978–81. This environment of persistent excess demand fueled the wage price spiral.[8]

---

8. While the oil price shocks and other negative shocks aggravated inflation, the rapid growth of nominal GDP could not have persisted without accommodative monetary policy. The high interest rates that reflected the upward ratcheting inflationary expectations raised the opportunity costs of holding money boosted money velocity that contributed to the excessive aggregate demand.

Inflation seems likely to persist at elevated levels, reflecting excess demand even after supply bottlenecks ease. Monetary and fiscal policy responses may have elongated lagged stimulative effects, reflecting the character of the pandemic, government shutdowns, and the magnitude of the policy excesses. The Fed's policy rate will likely remain well below inflation and an appropriate level estimated by a Taylor rule.

The current backlog of fiscal stimulus is sizable. A portion of the $5 trillion in deficit spending authorized has not been spent, and through year-end 2021 personal savings is an estimated $2.5 trillion (13.6% of disposable income) higher than pre-pandemic. An added wrinkle is that state and local governments saved virtually all of the $500 billion in Federal grants received through fiscal legislation in 2020–21. Their excess savings eventually will be spent or used to finance tax cuts, effectively providing lagged fiscal stimulus even as Federal budget deficits recede. Another $1 trillion of government spending has been authorized by the Infrastructure Investment and Jobs Act enacted in November 2021. Such investment is expected to have a higher fiscal multiplier than transfer payments. In addition, national defense spending is likely to rise. These sources point toward sustained excess demand even if supply chain disruptions dissipate.[9]

Through March 2022, the robust recovery of goods demand and the oil price spike have generated PCE inflation of 10.6% while PCE inflation of services have risen to 4.5%, as the recovery of spending on services has lagged. Services activities are now catching up, which points to continued inflation acceleration. Services sectors are labor intensive, pushing up operating costs. In addition, the largest component of services inflation is shelter costs, and inflation

---

9. Money velocity should recover from its abrupt pandemic collapse as the economy returns to normal and interest rates rise. Similarly, money velocity rebounded following World War II as the lagged impact of monetary stimulus during the war and pent-up demand generated a surge in spending as normal civilian life resumed.

of its two biggest components, owner-occupied rental equivalent (OER) and rental costs, is accelerating and may remain elevated, based on the historic lags following rising home prices (Levy 2022). Tight labor markets and higher expected inflation may combine to put upward pressure on nominal wages. The unemployment rate at 3.6% is below the Fed's estimates of its natural rate of 4%, and job openings of 11.5 million exceed job hires of 6.7 million, reflecting an unprecedented gap between labor demand and available supply. The job quits rate of 3.0% hovers near an all-time high. Real wages have been declining, as 8.5% CPI inflation has exceeded the 6.75% rise in average hourly earnings of private sector production and nonsupervisory workers. Higher inflation is influencing wages and a growing number of wage contracts at large corporations now include cost of living adjustments (COLAs). Nominal wages are expected to catch up to inflation, reflecting the tight labor market conditions, the pickup in labor productivity, and the feedback loop between wages and inflation.

In sum, the persistence and pervasiveness of inflation have begun to take on some of the negative characteristics of the 1970s.

WHY HAS THE FED BEEN CONSISTENTLY BEHIND?

The Federal Reserve's track record of delayed exits stems from a confluence of factors. Economic theories have evolved and become more conducive to activist macroeconomic policy making and the Fed's reliance on discretion has been prone to misjudgments. The Fed's interpretation of its dual mandate has evolved toward prioritizing maximum inclusive employment over inflation and has introduced asymmetries that require discretion in interpreting how to achieve its objectives. The Fed has expanded its set of monetary tools, including its heightened reliance on forward guidance to manage expectations and an expanded balance sheet, in ways that have confused its policy deliberations and introduced delays. It has complicated and muddled the Fed's communications. The Fed's assessments and forecasts of the economy and inflation occasionally have led to monetary policy mistakes. In addition, the Fed faces constant political pressures from elected officials to facilitate their short-term objectives. These political pressures have affected the Fed in significant ways during some critical periods.

Evolving Doctrines

Even following World War II when the government assumed the role of managing aggregate demand and the Employment Act of 1946 mandated the Fed to pursue maximum employment, monetary policy was grounded in price stability and a longer-run balanced budget anchored fiscal policy makers.

Replacing price stability as an anchor for monetary policy in the 1960s with the goal of moderate inflation and the Keynesian revolution, popularized by the Phillips curve that used inflation as a tool for reducing unemployment, fueled discretionary activist monetary policy. These new analytical frameworks promoted the role of the Federal Reserve Board staff that advocated the Phillips curve framework and activist countercyclical policy making. The prospects that the Fed could actively use monetary policy to achieve desired trade-offs between inflation and unemployment attracted like-minded policy makers. The realities of higher inflationary expectations in the 1970s and the Fed's loss of credibility unhinged the relationship between the unemployment rate and inflation and undercut any notion of a permanent stable Phillips curve. In response, the Phillips curve was modified and has remained as the Fed's benchmark, despite its analytical flaws and unreliability.[10]

10. While new ideas by the monetarists in the 1960s and 1970s and the rational expectations school in the 1980s and 1990s and research conducted at several Federal Reserve Banks, particularly St. Louis and Minneapolis, influenced thinking in the Federal Reserve System,

The trauma of the high inflation of the 1970s and Volcker's jarring disinflationary monetary policy ushered in the Great Moderation. During this period, the basic premise of the Volcker-Greenspan regimes was that low inflation was the foundation for achieving maximum employment, a clear departure from the doctrine of the 1970s. The Fed was quicker to reduce monetary accommodation at signs of inflation pressures. During this period, scholarly research focused on the benefits of rules that targeted low inflation and eventually settled on 2% (Taylor 1993). Others advocated the benefits of a framework for targeting low inflation without rules (Bernanke et al. 1999), also centering on 2%. Inflation targeting and guiding inflationary expectations toward the inflation target became the dominant anchor guiding monetary policy, operating as a constraint on the pursuit of full employment.

An ensuing pivot in the Federal Reserve System's thinking at the turn of the twenty-first century had a significant impact on monetary policy that remains central to monetary policy. The Greenspan-led Fed's concerns about deflation and its perception that the risks of deflation and the stagnation that would result were a far bigger concern than the risks of high inflation, became influential.[11] This new asymmetric view of risks around inflation resulted in the Fed's delayed exit from its 2001–2 countercyclical easing that proved costly for economic performance and financial stability. This asymmetric concern re-emerged as a dominant theme in the decade following the GFC.

Subdued inflation following the GFC allowed the Fed to aggressively pursue maximizing employment. In 2012, Fed Chair

---

the Phillips curve remained as the dominant framework for conducting monetary policy (Bordo and Prescott 2019).

11. Chairman Greenspan referred to "low probability but high-cost outcomes" (Greenspan 2003) and argued that while deflation would create a downward spiral in aggregate demand that would be hard to escape from, while higher inflation posed fewer risks because the Fed "would know how to address the problem." Then governor Bernanke articulated how the Fed could resort to quantitative easing at the zero lower bound (Bernanke 2002).

Bernanke stated that a key objective of QEIII was to lower the unemployment rate (Bernanke 2012), a noted departure for then unconventional monetary policy. Fed Chair Yellen was even more aggressive in pursuing low unemployment and posted a new labor market dashboard on the Fed's website. The persistently sub-2% inflation fueled Fed's worries about the risks of a downward spiral in inflationary expectations and asymmetries imposed by the ELB.

These ELB concerns along with the prospects that sustained monetary ease could promote maximum inclusive employment became a cornerstone of its new strategic plan. The new strategic framework institutionalized the Fed's asymmetries, including prioritization of its enhanced maximum employment mandate and flexible average inflation targeting that favored inflation above 2%.[12] Underlying its new strategy, the Fed acknowledged that the Phillips curve was flat, which allowed it to eschew the preemptive monetary tightening that had been critical to its high priority of managing inflationary expectations. The strategy's tenuous theoretical foundations, including heavy reliance on forward guidance and precise management of expectations, and the absence of any numeric targets was impractical for conducting sound monetary policy (Plosser 2021). It contributed to the Fed's excessive extension of its crisis management policies.

---

12. Fed Chair Powell's description of the Fed's new strategic plan in his August 2020 Jackson Hole speech emphasized its enhanced maximum inclusive employment. "The stories we heard [at the *Fed Listens*] events became a potent vehicle for us to connect with the people and communities that our policies are intended to benefit." "With regard to the employment side of our mandate, our revised statement emphasizes that maximum inclusive employment is a broad-based and inclusive goal. The change reflects our appreciation for the benefits of a strong labor market, particularly for many of the low- and moderate-income communities. In addition, our revised statements say that our policy decision will be informed by our 'assessments of shortfalls of employment from its maximum level' as in our previous statement. This change may appear subtle, but it reflects our view that a robust job market can be sustained without causing an outbreak of inflation." Vice Chair Clarida restated these points and concluded, "This is a robust evolution in the Federal Reserve's policy framework." (Clarida 2020).

Misreads and Unreliable Forecasts

Forecasting is very difficult and fraught with challenges. The Fed's models do not seem to have captured critical variables that have driven important shifts in the economy. They largely ignore money supply and the monetary transmission channels in its forecasting. The Fed, presumably for political reasons, has not forecast prior recessions. Nor has the senior Fed staff who manage the Fed's macroeconomic models, according to the minutes of FOMC meetings that are released with a five-year lag. Prior to the GFC, the Fed's macro models did not capture the economic implications of failing credit conditions and the spreading of financial instability and the precarious nature of the short-term funding market. As the housing and mortgage market unraveled, the Fed's forecasts were consistent with its assertion that the problems facing the housing sector would not spill into the economy.

The Fed's misread of how sharply inflation was rising in 2021–22 was not its first. In the 1970s, the Fed attributed the upward ratcheting of inflation to special factors rather than to monetary accommodation and did not account for the mounting negative impacts of rising inflationary expectations. Following the GFC, the Fed's senior staff model and SEPs significantly overestimated inflation. When inflation remained low, the Fed attributed it to a flatter Phillips curve, while it paid insufficient attention to factors and policies that may have bottled up the monetary policy transmission mechanism and inhibited the impact on nominal GDP.

As the economy recovered from the pandemic, the Fed presumed that inflation would stay low as it did post-GFC. When inflation rose, the Fed attributed it to supply shortages, and stuck to a forecast that it would decline back toward the Fed's target. In doing so, it understated any stimulative impacts of an increasingly negative real fed funds rate and the surge in M2, and the unprecedented increase in fiscal deficit spending. The Fed did not acknowledge the fastest growth of aggregate demand in modern history. It is uncertain whether the Fed's models estimated that the trillions of dollars of fiscal stimulus financed by the Fed's monetary ease would have no impact on the economy or inflation, or used judgment and overrode its models. The oversight of readily available data raises more questions. In light of the challenges facing forecasting and the sizable uncertainties posed by the pandemic, incorporating into policy deliberations more rigorous use of scenario and probability analyses of forecasts would be wise (Bordo, Levin, and Levy 2020).

Political Pressures and the Fed

Political pressure on the Fed has been a constant influencer. As William McChesney Martin has stated, the Fed is "independent within the government." Elected officials—the White House and members of Congress—try to impose their own personal interests on the Fed and clearly influence monetary policy. Congress chartered the Federal Reserve and is charged with supervising it. The Fed's history is replete with a series of powerful members of Congress's House and Senate banking committees with unfavorable views of the Fed and lack of knowledge about how monetary policy affects the economy who tried to steer the Fed in pursuit of their own political agendas. These politicians have affected the Fed in many ways. Populist Wright Patman, a decades-long member of the House Banking Committee, exerted constant pressure on the Fed to keep rates low on the belief that higher rates were inflationary and benefited commercial banks at the expense of workers. Others proceeded and followed with their own agendas.

In the 1960s, Fed Chair Martin was a fiscal conservative whose instincts were to tighten monetary policy in response to the expansive "guns and butter" government spending that began in 1965, but he was bullied by President Johnson to delay raising rates. This proved costly, as higher inflationary expectations became embedded and set the stage for the 1970s. Burns's direct involvement in President Nixon's policy agenda influenced the Fed in the 1970s. Burns was intimately involved with President Nixon's strategies for dealing with labor unions, and the lengthy General Motors strike in 1970 reinforced Burns's views and led him to team up with Treasury Secretary John Connally and Nixon to impose the wage and price controls. Following Burns's assistance to Nixon's reelection in 1972, in 1976–78 he was heavily influenced by the heated political debate on the Humphrey-Hawkins legislation and did not exit policy accommodation.

Political impacts on the Fed are pervasive. Choices of Fed governors nominated by the president are driven by politics, and congressional members have influenced the choice of Federal Reserve Bank presidents. Congressional initiatives have forced Fed governance changes. The Dodd-Frank legislation significantly affected the Fed's operations and constrained its lender of last resort facility. The Fed has been forced to adjust its communications and accountability to meet Congressional demands. The Fed is frequently expected and called on to do more to boost the economy and lower unemployment. In the past, when budget deficit concerns constrained Congress from pursuing fiscal stimulus, the Fed was expected to be more accommodative. Since the pandemic began, the Fed's stimulative stance has paralleled the desires of the Trump and Biden administrations and Congress. Now, in 2022, as the Fed begins to raise rates, it may come under intense pressure on several fronts. As the Fed removes monetary accommodation, it may get blamed for the slower growth and weaker labor markets. The higher rates and bond yields will drive up the government's debt service costs, for which the White House and Congress may blame the Fed instead of accepting blame for their fiscal profligacy. Higher consumer debt costs and mortgage rates will hit household pocketbooks. History suggests that pressures may mount to limit its rate increases and not allow unemployment to rise.

LESSONS FROM HISTORY AND
THE PATH FORWARD

Throughout its history, the Fed has learned from several monumental mistakes. The Great Depression taught how monetary policy based on the wrong doctrine and neglect, turned a modest recession into a deep contraction. Following World War II, the Fed learned its important role in aggregate demand management. The 1970s taught the costly mistakes of persistently accommodative monetary policy that allowed high inflation and a de-anchoring of inflationary expectations. But the Fed has not heeded many other important lessons. One recurring source of the Fed's lapses that has led to undesired outcomes—high inflation resulting from extended monetary ease followed by delayed exits and more frequently than not, recessions— is its discretionary approach to the conduct of monetary policy. The Fed has continued to eschew systematic rules as policy guidelines, instead favoring discretion and relying on its judgment.

In many spectator sports, professional analysts measure unforced errors and often refer to them as game-breakers. An unforced error is a mistake of one's own doing that is frequently based on bad judgment. "If (s)he would have only followed the rules and lessons learned from years of experience and practice. . . ." Our analysis of modern business cycles and the Fed's monetary policies describes a series of unforced errors, some large that led to recessions and a few that resulted in economic soft landings. The Fed's current challenge is difficult. While there have been episodes of delayed exits in which the Fed raised rates and lowered inflation without interrupting the expansion—the best examples are 1966, 1987, and 1994—the Fed has never been put into a position like the current one in which it must reverse monetary accommodation when inflation is so high, except for the late 1970s. This is highlighted in figure 8.1 by the current historically wide gap between the Taylor rule estimate and the actual fed funds rate. History has taught that the Fed must raise its policy rate above the underlying rate of inflation. But under current circumstances, the Fed must distinguish between the underlying inflation generated by excessive monetary and fiscal policy and the inflation that has resulted from supply shortages. The Fed must be evenhanded in its assessment (Bordo and Levy 2022).

Whether or not the Fed is successful in managing a soft landing, the number of the Fed's unforced errors—in which the Fed's discretion led to poor judgment and costly errors—strongly suggests the need for a policy reset. Were the Fed to adopt more systematic rules-based guidelines—or behave in a more rule-like manner as it did in the Great Moderation—it would avoid big mistakes and have a useful framework for conducting monetary policy under abnormal circumstances. Secondly, the Fed needs to correct the flaws of its strategic framework, eliminate its asymmetries and adopt a balanced approach to interpreting and achieving its dual mandate. Forecasting will always be a challenge, but the Fed should reassess its mistakes and analyze why it has been prone to occasional sizable mistakes. Finally, the Fed must pay attention to history and absorb the appropriate lessons.

References

Berger, Albert E. 1969. "A Historical Analysis of the Credit Crunch of 1966." *Federal Reserve Bank of St. Louis Review*, September.

Bernanke, Ben. 2002. "Deflation: Making Sure 'It' Doesn't Happen Here." Remarks at National Economists Club, Washington, DC, November 21.

———. 2008. "Federal Reserve Policies in the Financial Crisis." Speech to Greater Austin Chamber of Commerce, December 1.

———. 2012. "Monetary Policy Since the Onset of the Crisis." Speech at Federal Reserve Bank of Kansas City Jackson Hole Economic Symposium, August 31.

Bordo, Michael. 2022. "Karl Brunner and Allan Meltzer; From Monetary Policy to Monetary History to Monetary Rules." In *Karl Brunner and Monetarism*, edited by Thomas Moser. Cambridge, MA: MIT Press.

Bordo, Michael, and John Duca. 2022. "An Overview of the Fed's New Credit Policy Tools and Their Cushioning Effect on the COVID-19 Recession." *Journal of Government and Economics* 3 (2021): 100013.

Bordo, Michael D., and Barry Eichengreen. 2013. "Bretton Woods and the Great Inflation." In *The Great Inflation: The Rebirth of Modern Central Banking*, edited by Michael D. Bordo and Athanasios Orphanides. Chicago: University of Chicago for the NBER.

Bordo, Michael, Christopher Erceg, Andrew Levin, and Ryan Michaels. 2017. "Policy Credibility and Alternative Approaches to Disinflation." *Research in Economics 7*, no. 33: 422–60.

Bordo, Michael D., Owen Humpage, and Anna J. Schwartz. 2015. *Strained Relations: US Foreign Exchange Operations and Monetary Policy in the Twentieth Century*. Chicago: University of Chicago Press.

Bordo, Michael, and John Landon-Lane. 2013. "Exits from Recessions: The US Experience 1920–2007." In *No Way Out: Persistent Government Interventions in the Great Contraction*, edited by Vincent R. Reinhart. Washington, DC: American Enterprise Institute Press.

———. 2014. "Does Expansionary Monetary Policy Cause Asset Price Booms; Some Historical and Empirical Evidence." In *Macroeconomic and Financial Stability: Challenges for Monetary Policy*, edited by Sofía Bauducco, Lawrence Christiano, and Claudio Raddatz (Santiago: Central Bank of Chile).

Bordo, Michael D., Andrew T. Levin, and Mickey D. Levy. 2020. "Incorporating Scenario Analysis into the Federal Reserve's Policy Strategy and Communications." NBER Working Paper 27369, June.

Bordo, Michael D., and Mickey D. Levy. 2020. "Do Enlarged Deficits Cause Inflation: The Historical Record." NBER Working Paper 28195, December.

———. 2021. "The Short March Back to Inflation." *Wall Street Journal*, February 4.

Bordo, Michael D., and Athanasios Orphanides, eds. 2013. *The Great Inflation: The Rebirth of Modern Central Banking*. Chicago: University of Chicago Press for the NBER.

Brunner, Karl, and Allan Meltzer. 1964. "Some General Features of the Federal Reserve's Approach to Policy: A Staff Analysis." Subcommittee on Domestic Finance, Committee on Banking and Currency, US House of Representatives, 88th Congress.

Burns, Arthur. 1979. "The Anguish of Central Banking." Per Jacobsson Lecture, September 30.

Cagan, Phillip. 1974. *The Hydra-Headed Monster: The Problem of Inflation in the United States*. Washington, DC: American Enterprise Institute Press.

Clarida, Richard H. 2020. "Fed Vice Chair Richard H. Clarida on US Monetary Policy." Speech at the Peterson Institute for International Economics, August 31.

Federal Reserve. 2021. "Federal Reserve Press Release." December 15.

———. 2022. Minutes of the Federal Open Market Committee December 14–15, 2021," released January 5.

Federal Reserve Bank of Atlanta. 2022. "Taylor Rule Utility." Last modified May 27. https://www.atlantafed.org/cqer/research/taylor-rule.

Friedman, Milton. 1953. "The Effects of a Full Employment Policy on Economic Stability: A Formal Analysis." In *Essays in Positive Economics*. Chicago: University of Chicago Press.

Friedman, Milton, and Anna J. Schwartz. 1963. *A Monetary History of the United States 1867–1960*. Princeton, NJ: Princeton University Press.

Greenspan, Alan. 2003. "The Economic Outlook." Testimony before the Joint Economic Committee of the US Congress, May 21.

Ireland, Peter, and Mickey D. Levy. 2021. "'Substantial Progress,' Transitory vs. Persistent and the Appropriate Calibration of Monetary Policy." Shadow Open Market Committee, October 1.

Laubach, Thomas, and John C. Williams. 2003. "Measuring the Natural Rate of Interest." *Review of Economics and Statistics*, MIT Press, November.

Levin, Andrew, and John B. Taylor. 2013. "Falling Behind the Curve: A Positive Analysis of Stop-Start Monetary Policies and the Great Inflation." In *The Great Inflation: The Rebirth of Central Banking*, edited by Michael D. Bordo and Athanasios Orphanides. Chicago: University of Chicago Press for the NBER.

Levy, Mickey D. 2017. "Why Have the Fed's Policies Failed to Stimulate the Economy." *Cato Journal* 37, no. 1: 39–45.

———. 2021. "Fed Complacency Feeds Inflation." *Wall Street Journal*, November 1, and "High Inflation Needs a Policy Solution," December 19.

———. 2022. "Accelerating OER and Services Prices to Keep Inflation High." Shadow Open Market Committee, February 11.

Levy, Mickey D., and Michael D. Bordo. 2021. "The Fed in the Sand as Inflation Threatens." *Wall Street Journal*, April 26.

Levy, Mickey D., and Charles Plosser. 2020. "The Murky Future of Monetary Policy." Hoover Institution Working Paper 20119, October 1, 2020, republished in *Federal Reserve Bank of St. Louis Review*, May 24.

Nelson, Edward. 2019. *Milton Friedman and Economic Debate in the United States, 1932–1969*. Chicago: University of Chicago Press.

Ohanian, Lee. 1997. "The Macroeconomic Effect of War Finance in the United States." *American Economic Review* 87, no.1 (March): 33–40.

Plosser, Charles. 2021. "The Fed's Risky Experiment." Shadow Open Market Committee, June 18.

Powell, Jerome. 2020. "New Economic Challenges and the Fed's Monetary Policy Review." Speech (via webcast), Federal Reserve Bank of Kansas City Jackson Hole Economic Symposium, August 27.

———. 2021. *Semiannual Monetary Policy Report to the Congress*. House Financial Services Committee, US House of Representatives, July 14.

Reis, Ricardo. 2021. "Losing the Inflation Anchor." Brookings Papers on Economic Activity, September 9.

Stein, Herbert. 1984. *Presidential Economics: The Making of Economic Policy from Roosevelt to Reagan and Beyond*. New York: Simon and Schuster.

Taylor, John B. 1993. "Discretion versus Policy Rules in Practice." Carnegie-Rochester Conference Series on Public Policy 39: 195–214. Amsterdam: North-Holland.

———. 2007. "Housing and Monetary Policy." Federal Reserve Bank of Kansas City Jackson Hole Economic Symposium, August.

DISCUSSANT REMARKS

Jennifer Burns

This response is taken from the transcript of spoken remarks at the conference and retains the character of live speech.

Hello, everyone. Coming to an event like this and eavesdropping on the conversations feels as though I'm stepping into the pages of the book that I'm writing on Milton Friedman. And I'm particularly glad to comment on this excellent paper by Mickey Levy and Michael Bordo. In this paper, as you know, Bordo and Levy go over a huge sweep of history and compress it down to the essentials. Reading the paper, I reflected on how various monetary policy regimes correspond in interesting ways with regimes of thought. So, in my comment I want to outline a few of those, traversing them fairly quickly, but offering a little more detail at certain points, ahead of the policy conversation.

I'm going to start in the 1960s with the advent of the Phillips curve, which originally was derived from British data. As Bordo and Levy noted, the curve persists to this day. But even as it persists, the way it's formulated and expressed has changed in important ways. One of the first, and most influential, expressions of the Phillips curve is the famous paper by Paul Samuelson and Robert Solow. What Samuelson and Solow did was to take this British curve and construct one for the United States, since the data seemed to fit. And so they created a curve showing "the different levels of unemployment that would be needed for each degree of price level change." And they went on to conclude that the price index should be allowed to rise by as much as 4% or 5% a year. So, it may be the Phillips curve, but it's coming out with an inflation figure that's quite far from contemporary 2% inflation targeting. Samuelson and Solow went on to say, well, if this level of inflation creates any disharmony, "it could be addressed with price and wage controls." And then they speculated that maybe even inflation would be harmless under these circumstances, while further noting, "school teachers, pensioners, and others" would "devise institutions to protect their real incomes from erosion by higher prices." Now, it's not a coincidence that they picked schoolteachers, pensioners, and others. They were thinking of people on fixed incomes who suffer the most in an inflationary situation.[1]

What's noticeable is their glib confidence that should high rates of inflation occur—quick, we can whip up some institutions that will compensate. If people in those fixed-income situations can get their incomes to go up with inflation, it sort of won't matter. Wages will rise and prices will rise, but there won't be a real difference. In this paper, Samuelson and Solow also explicitly resist what came to be known as the accelerationist thesis, associated at the time with Friedman, that inflation has a tendency to go faster and faster. And so, as they claim, "It may be that creeping inflation leads only to creeping inflation."[2]

In later years, Samuelson and Solow asserted that the paper, which I've simplified here, is much more nuanced and was misread. But the paper is really easy to misread, especially because they include a chart, which they labeled, "A Menu of Choice between Different Degrees of Unemployment and Price Stability."[3] It's very easy, since they call it a "menu," for people to think of it as a menu. You expect to be able to order up the exact thing that you want from it.

It's also important to know this formulation was really important to policy. James Tobin of Yale, who authored the very influential 1962 CEA report that defined full employment as 4% for the first time, reflected later that the 4% full employment target was chosen

---

1. Paul A. Samuelson and Robert M. Solow, "Analytic Aspects of Anti-inflation Policy," *American Economic Review* 50, no. 2 (May 1960): 192, 194.

2. Samuelson and Solow, "Anti-inflation Policy," 185.

3. Samuelson and Solow, 192.

"with an eye on the Phillips curve." And in the data they had, 4% unemployment coincidently corresponded to 4% inflation. As Tobin noted, nobody got in trouble for having 4% inflation, so politically that was a safe target. In summary, it's easy to see a real connection between that paper, the CEA report, and goals of policy.[4]

Beyond the menu metaphor, I want to highlight the implied idea, in this early version of the curve, that you can program the economy: put in numbers, and a predictable outcome will arise. In many ways that is emblematic of the early 1960s, this moment of optimism and the "can-do" spirit—for example, we can and will make it to the moon. This was before the great crash in faith in government and institutions. So, there is an early-1960s flavor to this formulation. On the other hand, it's also a universal human hubristic assumption that we can see what's coming and control it. We may see some of that overconfidence still at work today, as some of our other panelists have discussed.

The Phillips curve also fits into a broader universe of understandings of inflation current at the time. In the 1960s, a popular idea was cost-push inflation, the idea that inflation is due to the rising cost of materials and the rising cost of wages. As a result, you get a wage-price spiral. There was also a demand-pull explanation. More similar to contemporary ideas, this explanation highlights aggregate demand getting ahead of the capacity of the economy. Now in the 1960s, the cost-push tends to be the more dominant approach. In part, this is because aggregate demand stimulation is really the name of the game for a lot of policy makers. If stimulating aggregate demand led to growth, which everyone wanted, there's not a lot of incentive to look at the downside. Also, the idea of cost-push inflation is more plausible in an environment where 20–25% of the workforce is unionized. The ability of unions to push through wage

---

4. James Tobin, *The New Economics One Decade Older* (Princeton, NJ: Princeton University Press, 1972), 17.

increases that would really ripple through the economy makes more sense than in today's context of a union membership closer to 10%. So those are some of the larger regimes of thought—from sixties optimism to cost-push to the Phillips curve—that form the background for earlier monetary policy regimes and our understanding of inflation.

I want to turn now to the mysterious case of the Fed chairman for most of the 1970s, Arthur Burns. Burns came into the Fed with a reputation as an inflation fighter. Instead, his term saw the "Great Inflation," a period of high inflation, sustained over many years. And this created some really interesting dynamics in his relationship with Milton Friedman, who was one of his oldest friends. Here's a brief clip from a letter that Friedman wrote him only a few months after he had taken over as the chairman. Friedman wrote, "Never in my wildest dreams did I believe that the central bank virus was so potent that it could corrupt even you in so short a time."[5]

What was going on with Arthur Burns? Mike Bordo and I differ a little bit on this. Mike tends to emphasize the political nature of Burns's term. I focus a bit more on the ideas that were guiding him. Burns was an institutionalist and a pragmatist—someone who had a theory not to have a theory, which, in the particular case he was in, left him a bit rudderless. Regardless, it is a great irony that Burns and Friedman were so close personally, and that Burns comes into a position of such potential power and influence right as Friedman's ideas on monetarism—which I'll simplify quickly as inflation is always and everywhere a monetary phenomenon—are getting greater credence. Yet, Friedman's ideas are almost completely ignored. Burns actually, and explicitly, rejects the idea that

---

5. Milton Friedman to Arthur Burns, May 18, 1970, Folder 8, Box 138, Milton Friedman Papers, Hoover Institution Library & Archives, Stanford University.

the Fed really has anything to do what's happening. As he writes to Nixon, "Monetary policy, I feel, has done its job fully."[6]

As this is unfolding, a series of famous Brookings Institution studies are published. They mainly look at the Phillips curve; specifically, they are testing Friedman's critique of the Phillips curve. As new data on inflation in the 1970s emerges, Friedman's argument about the curve—that it might work in the short run, but not the long run—becomes increasingly accepted. And that, in turn, will make monetarism in general more influential. So we have a fascinating case: the great inflation coincides with Friedman's ideas gaining greater acceptance, at least in academic and think tank circles, but not in the actual policy-making circles or in Burns's thinking.

There's another irony here, in that all this is happening even as what some people call the "fourth Chicago School" is rising. Concurrently, there is discussion of the so-called policy ineffectiveness proposition coming out as a major theoretical innovation. I find it a delicious irony that this conversation begins right before Paul Volcker arrives as Fed chair and puts monetary policy right back at the center of American conversation, politics, and history.

Volcker was not a monetarist. He was in tune with the basic debates, and he did say he was going to start targeting monetary aggregates, one of the most important aspects of monetarism. Now there's a whole debate, which I cover in my book, about how genuine or how cynical that particular policy was. Were aggregates a veil because he really wanted to go after interest rates? I tend to think his interest in monetarism started out more genuine than the standard account implies. The first takes on the Volcker Shock were written without the benefit of the documentary material we now have. Regardless, although Friedman and Volcker aren't personally close like Burns and Friedman were, there is definitely an influence.

---

6. Burns to Nixon, June 22, 1971, reprinted as Appendix B in George P. Shultz and John B. Taylor, *Choose Economic Freedom: Enduring Policy Lessons from the 1970s and 1980s* (Stanford, CA: Hoover Institution Press, 2020), 73.

There's yet another irony here. Just as monetarism is being applied, or some version of it is being applied, the data underneath it starts breaking down. So, if the early 1970s were the triumph of monetarist ideas, the early 1980s are the Waterloo. The monetary aggregates are no longer doing anything that relates to the broader macroeconomy. Even as Friedman wins the war on the importance of monetary policy, his more specific policies did not hold up well. Yet as I also discuss in my book, many of his ideas feed into what has become central banking consensus, from expectations management to Taylor rules.

I'll move quickly now over a few more policy and intellectual regimes. We see a shift to interest rates during the Greenspan years, and this corresponds to a shift in academic focus toward interest rates. Now, there is some leftover monetarism, such as letters from Alan Greenspan to Friedman saying nice things about M2. You can see it in some of the speeches and footnotes. And Friedman was certainly a fan of Greenspan. Yet like Volcker, Greenspan is more applied than theoretical. Moving on to Benjamin Bernanke, I just want to flag him as an academically trained economist. The focus on interest rates continued during his regime, both in policy and in academia. His was the era of the Taylor rule. I think Bordo and Levy do a good job of dissecting that era, and what follows with Janet Yellen, so I'm not going to add more.

Fast-forwarding to today, with Fed Chair Jerome Powell, we really have a return to what I think of as the banker-practitioner tradition: somebody who has not come out of a university faculty but rather from a more applied background. And if we look to the regime of intellectual thought, what is changing or what is emerging? I have to mention the emergence of modern monetary theory, which, as some of you must know, is really a reworking of Abba Lerner's functional finance. As I was preparing for this talk, I remembered that Milton Friedman had reviewed a book by Abba Lerner. Friedman was at the time pretty much unknown, and hadn't published much himself, but he did a big review essay, talking specifically about Lerner's functional finance. Here's what he called it: "A brilliant exercise in logic." This was *not* a compliment. Friedman's point was that Lerner's ideas were too abstract, too disconnected from empirical evidence and history. He goes on to conclude, "What looks like a prescription evaporates into an expression of good intentions," which I think is actually a pretty good summary of a creed that its supporters summarize as: anything we can imagine, we can afford.[7]

By way of conclusion, let me pull back here and reflect on a few things. The changes in thinking about monetary policy have been profound. And they have some relation to policy, but it's not really clear what it is. When you look back over the history, in some cases you see the Fed and policy makers using academic insights, and in some cases not. In some cases, it's a good idea that they used them. In some cases—such as in the account we get from Michael and Mickey—maybe it has been too much theory, and that is not as good as staying attuned to the moment.

In my book, I separate the academic economists interested in monetary theory, of whom Friedman is really emblematic, from the bankers and practitioners and those people who are putting the ideas into practice. I also think about the Federal Reserve System writ large—the researchers, the scholars, the network, and the intellectual climate—not just the actual members of the policy-making bodies.

And so, I have three questions for you. First, as you think generally about this relationship between what I'm calling the research wing and the practitioner wing, between the people who come up with ideas and frameworks about inflation, and then the men and women who try to put them into action, what are some features

---

7. Milton Friedman, "Lerner on the Economics of Control," *Journal of Political Economy* 55 (October 1947): 413.

of this relationship? What factors connect and separate these two fields? Is it different mentalities, different training, different incentives? Second, what would be the ideal relationship? Because as I described, looking at the history there's a mix: sometimes too much theory is bad, and sometimes not enough theory is bad. Is there a balance here to strike? The third question I'd like to leave you with: If you could make one or two changes, institutional or cultural changes between the academic research wing and this practitioner community, what would they be?

Thank you so much.

GENERAL DISCUSSION

KEVIN WARSH (INTRODUCTION): How did we get into this inflation mess, and how do we get out of it? It is difficult to gain perspective on events so immediate. Our panel, nonetheless, is tasked with wrestling with this central question. We have a duty to speak clearly about the ideas and institutions we hold dear: the United States economy and the Federal Reserve are at a tipping point.

An anxious conformity of voices—inside and outside of official policy-making circles—should avoid rationalizing reality or redirecting responsibility. I will endeavor to frame the current policy conjuncture. And then turn it over to my colleagues to provide important historical insights and offer lessons learned that may be applicable at this critical moment in economic history.

Allow me first to introduce my fellow panelists. Michael Bordo is a staple of Hoover monetary conferences past, a professor of economics at Rutgers, and the author of an important recent book on the historical performance of the Fed.

Mickey Levy is the chief economist at Berenberg. Mickey served as the chief economist at Bank of America during the prior financial crisis. In a past time of peril, he provided invaluable data on the real economy, and he is a longtime source of insight to policy makers, myself included.

We're also honored to be joined by Jennifer Burns. Jennifer is a professor of history here at Stanford and a trusted colleague of mine at Hoover. Jennifer's academic work is directed at the thinkers and ideas of the twentieth century and their influence on politics and policy.

Jennifer's intellectual biography of Milton Friedman is to be published soon. I can't help but wonder whether Milton would be surprised that some of the errors of the 1970s would again be so resonant. Given the imprudent conduct of monetary and fiscal policy in the past several years, I am curious what he would have proffered as the preferred policy path forward. Jennifer will help give voice to a mentor to so many of us assembled here. The twenty-first century is off to a rocky start. Four major shocks—the terrorist attacks of 9/11, the global financial crisis, the plague of COVID, and the land war in Europe—have left an indelible mark on the economy and policy-making institutions. The series of shocks over two decades catalyzed the most extraordinary, unprecedented expansion of monetary and fiscal policy in history. And the periods of relative peace and prosperity between shocks failed to correspond with concomitant reductions in policy accommodation. The asymmetry in the policy response is disconcerting.

Condi Rice spoke at the outset of the conference about the Russian invasion of Ukraine. An important takeaway from her discussion of national security: the price for stopping a dictator goes up over time. Well, the same is true of inflation. The surge in prices was fixable at considerably less cost a year ago, even six months ago.

Inflation—now running more than four times the rate of the Fed's promised inflation target—is a clear and present danger to the economy. The level, rate of change, and variance of prices are interfering with the decision making of households and businesses. And it is causing a dramatic cost-of-living squeeze for most Americans.

In some sense, the highly elevated levels of inflation owe to errors in tactics, timing, and risk management made by the Federal Reserve in the last year. But the broader sources of error— strategic, doctrinal, and institutional choices made by policy makers—have been long in the making.

In the last decade, monetary policy makers became increasingly precise in their definition of price stability, namely inflation of 2.0%. They also became more exacting about their preferred measure of inflation that would be tantamount to its target. Policy makers mistakenly believed that they possessed a reliable, robust model to forecast inflation dynamics. The central bank's understanding of the true underlying causes of inflation, however, are far fuzzier.

First, large structural forces (e.g., demographics, globalization) pushed inflation down since the early 1980s. The central banks were significant beneficiaries of many of these forces, largely outside of their control. The structural forces are now reversing. I know of no theory that assigns the central bank credit for the Great Moderation of inflation over this long period but absolves it of responsibility of the current inflation surge.

Second, many in the central bank community came to believe that inflation was running around 2% per year because central banks ordered it so. Inflation expectations have an important role to play in the inflation forecasting business, but expectations are not established by edict. Inflation-fighting credibility—and the expectations that flow from it—are earned over time. They can be lost more quickly.

Third, the dominant workhorse (dynamic stochastic general equilibrium) models used by the Fed (including FRB/US) are designed to be mean reverting. That helps explain why a year ago the Fed believed inflation would fall back to 2.0%—it had happened before. But the Lucas critique is directly applicable here. If policy makers change regimes, that is, change markedly how they they conduct policy, then the mean-reverting forecasts will invariably be in error.

Fourth, r-star, the neutral equilibrium real interest rate, is a useful theoretical monetary policy construct for considering the proper conduct of policy. But policy makers err when they make r-star their north star. Unlike a star in the sky, r-star is unobservable. And it changes its position in the horizon in response to changes by policy makers in the conduct of policy.

Finally, the Fed announced a major regime change in the conduct of monetary policy in August 2020. The regime change was an important catalyst for the subsequent inflation surge. The Fed promised to increase the inflation rate, which was running a mere three-tenths of a percent below its numerical objective. Most notably, the Fed relegated the tried, trusted, true idea that monetary policy affected the economy with "long and variable lags." Instead, the authorities said policy would be inert until the Fed fully achieved its new objectives.

Hence, we should not be surprised that the extraordinary conduct of monetary policy in recent years—for all seasons and all reasons—ushered in an era of surging prices, which first manifested in financial assets like equities before spreading to goods and, ultimately, services.

We should be surprised, however, that the Fed's reaction function to the inflation shock differed so materially from the shocks of 2008 and 2020. To date, we find the central bank's response plodding and begrudging in comparison.

Inflation is a choice, a choice for which the Fed is chiefly responsible.

In a sign of our times, most in Washington believe someone else is to blame for the inflation surge. So we hear a lot about Congress's fiscal profligacy, the ravages of COVID, and the war in Ukraine. These are relevant factors. But the central bank is no victim. The causes of inflation are varied, but the Fed chooses what it will permit to find its way into the generalized price level.

Former Supreme Court justice Antonin Scalia said once, "We aren't last to decide a case because we're right. We're right because we're last." The same is true of the Fed. The central bank has the benefit of observing fiscal decisions by the Congress and global linkages. Then it decides what actions to take to establish the nominal price.

Other contributing sources of central bank error are procedural but no less worthy of mention. I sense a far greater divergence of views around the FOMC than captured by their quarterly forecasts and public speeches. The term of art is "preference falsification." Some policy makers somehow may abide by a set of views contrary to their own best judgment. And whether that's owing to comity, contrivance, or convenience, policy making is impaired if there is not a candid and frank deliberation around the table and in the public square.

Is it plausible that early last year no one at FOMC thought the fed funds rate would rise until 2024? Or this past September that there'd only be one rate rise in 2022?

In times of critical decision making, I worry about an anxious conformity of views. We should be discomfited when a critical institution in aggregate is delivering considerably less than the sum of its immensely talented professionals.

Finally, permit me to say a word about the central bank's risk management. Being a member of the FOMC is not a prize for the perfect. All individuals—and institutions—make misjudgments. The best institutions, however, conduct their policy deliberations to minimize big errors so that they avoid significant deadweight losses in welfare.

With Milton Friedman's biographer by my side, we should recall his admonition that central bankers should conduct policy to minimize substantial deviations in output and inflation from its objectives. The operative word here is "substantial."

At the time the Fed adopted its new pro-inflation policy regime in 2020, the Fed noted that it was falling short of its inflation objective by just a fraction. And, yet, its leaders bet the ranch. It's not entirely fair to measure an institution by the outcome of its decision. But, it is fair to question the decision making itself. Too much emphasis is placed on modal forecasts and not enough on tails of the distribution. And ultimately, the central bank bears a special responsibility to mitigate large tail risks. That's the job.

At the outset of the conference, John Taylor asked the right forward-looking question: Where do we go from here?

Another regime change in policy will likely be needed to fix the inflation problem. Unless the inflation is resolved imminently and resolutely, today's inflation will rank among the most significant economic policy errors in the last half century. US households and businesses will bear the primary costs of the policy mistake, especially the least-well-off among us. Substantial harm is already done.

We need a regime change in the conduct of monetary policy, not least to show households and businesses that price stability will be achieved, come hell or high water. The Fed should rid itself of its existing forward guidance, where the authorities continually revise and reveal their then-preferences for policy in the coming meetings. Instead, as first proferred last year by my friend and fellow central banker from days of old Mervyn King: the only forward guidance the Fed should put on offer is that they will achieve price stability—no ifs, ands, or buts. Imagine the clarity when paired with credibility.

I also recommend that the central bank ditch the existing notion of data dependence. Policy must be forward looking, not periodically reliant on stale data that is indicative of how the economy once was. My old Fed colleague and dear friend Stan Fischer used to say, "We move policy early because we're late." And yet in the Fed newfangled regime, they choose to move late as a design feature.

As I mentioned earlier, we have a duty to speak clearly about the ideas and institutions we hold dear. We convene as policy makers (past and present), market participants, academics, and historians to move the conduct of monetary policy in a better direction. Ideas must be refined, institutions reformed, and credibility fortified.

So today isn't the time to pile on. Rather, it's high time, if not long past time, to put on the table what needs to be done.

With that perspective on the current policy conjuncture, allow me next to turn to our resident historians to offer a perspective on the current moment.

* * *

MICKEY LEVY: One observation based on our research of history that just jumps out is the Fed's series of mistakes that do not reflect the appropriate lessons of past cycles. The current episode calls for a policy reset. As Kevin mentioned at the outset, policy makers can't get every judgment right but should strive to avoid the major mistakes. Accordingly, a high priority should be the adoption of some kind of rules-based policies in place of total discretion. A rules-based policy framework would provide policy guidance based on the lessons from history. It would still provide flexibility for discretion. If the Fed deviates from the rules, it would provide a basis for explaining why. Rules could provide valuable guidelines during normal times as well as abnormal times, like the one we've just been through. This issue of rules versus discretion has been around for a long time, and the current situation stemming from the Fed's misguided judgments is a wake-up call that once again, heavily reliance on discretion has been the source of a major policy mistake.

MICHAEL BORDO: I greatly appreciate Jennifer's comments. I have read her book on Milton Friedman and I highly recommend it. In answer to her question, central banks evolved in the early modern period and later to provide finance to the new nation-states, to manage the gold standard, to serve as lenders of last resort, and later to stabilize the macroeconomy. Along with the evolution of central banks came the development of economic thinking on the role of money and on central banks in maintaining stability in the value of money and financial stability. Many of the early economists also were central bankers, so economics has always been tied to central banking. Some of the basic theories like the quantity theory of money and the price-specie flow mechanism had a great influence on central banks. This may be because central bankers were initially drawn from the financial sector, including some of the great pioneer monetary economists like David Ricardo and Henry Thornton, who well understood from their private practice the role of money in the economy. As economics has become more technical there have been occasional disconnects between theory and practice, but the coevolution between policy and theory has persisted. Whether the theories were correct and whether they were always understood by central bankers is another issue, which is at the heart of some of the major policy errors, like the present one.

RICARDO REIS: In his introductory remarks, Kevin worried that there has been a worrying consensus within the FOMC in the last 12 months. In your paper, you follow the usual convention of referring to periods in history by the name of the chair of the FOMC: Burns, Bernanke, etc. Realizing that this is an impossible question to answer in a few minutes, can I ask you to describe how much consensus or disagreement there was within the FOMC during the periods that you highlight? Was there a healthy debate within the institution? Were the regional Fed presidents playing a role of adding diversity of views, and pushing against when mistakes were made? Or does history confirm Kevin's hypothesis of consensus coming associated with mistakes?

BORDO: I have been working with Ned Prescott from the Federal Reserve Bank of Cleveland on the issues of the structure and governance of the Federal Reserve System. The regional Feds have become an important part of the policy-setting process since the 1950s. In the 1960s the Federal Reserve Bank of St. Louis was a key conduit for the monetarist views of Friedman, Schwartz,

Brunner, and Meltzer. The St. Louis Fed was treated as a maverick by the establishment of the Board of Governors, but as the Great Inflation exploded in the 1970s their views had a great impact, leading to the Volcker shock that ended it. A similar story can be told for the role of the Federal Reserve Bank of Minneapolis in the 1980s and '90s in transmitting rational expectations into Fed policy deliberations. The federal structure of the FRS has been instrumental in the introduction of new ideas into policy making.

WARSH: In my assessment of Fed history, the chairman of the institution has aggregated power and authority over time. It's not a perfect relationship over time, but it is the broad trajectory, especially since the Greenspan era. That's why it is fair nomenclature to describe the periods as the "Bernanke Fed," the "Yellen Fed," and the "Powell Fed." The central bank, as an institution, has dominated the front pages since 2008 to be sure. So it's hard to overstate the influence of the chairman. Nonetheless, my judgment is that there's a large dispersion of views inside the institution itself. There might be something like a thousand PhDs at the Federal Reserve today. While the large majority of economists arrive from much of the same intellectual timbre and the same academic institutions, there is a pretty healthy dispersion of views. But the organization's decision-making process—the deliberations—seem to remove the outliers and cast them aside. This is done ostensibly in the name of conformity, comity, convenience, or contrivance. It comes with the best of intentions but has some very problematic consequences.

In my own experience at the Bernanke Fed—especially during the crisis—we would end up speaking with one voice, which is good. But there was a fierce debate inside the room. And it wasn't always inside the FOMC: there was a meeting before the meeting, often in the chairman's office. You would get your "day in court." In my case, I'd make my argument and would lose as often as I'd prevail. But there was an opportunity for a fierce, truth-seeking debate.

The Fed today needs to ensure that the deliberation process leads not to parochialism or groupthink. And historians will someday judge if a lack of genuine deliberation led the Powell Fed to this troubling moment.

LEVY: My perception is within the FOMC meetings there's an extremely healthy debate. But the actual decisions on policies are skewed toward the chair and the Board of Governors. This brings up the whole issue of governance. I think the institution needs to have more modernized governance rules that, among other things, would take advantage of the 12-Federal-Reserve-Bank system. The bank presidents should be voting members at every FOMC meeting and be involved in other critical monetary policy decisions. This morning's panels referred to the Fed's quarterly Summary of Economic Projections (SEPs), which are important inputs to the Fed's deliberations and important communications vehicles to the public. They also reflect a tilt within the Fed's organizational structure. The SEPs are dominated by the FRB/US model, because the governors, when they submit their quarterly estimates, cannot deviate very much from the FRB/US model, which are developed by Board staffers. So deviations from the FOMC median forecasts heavily reflect the views of the Federal Reserve Bank presidents, who are underrepresented in FOMC voting on monetary policy.

WARSH: In the name of transparency, we end up with less transparency. Rich, care to weigh in?

RICHARD CLARIDA: Great panel. Jennifer, great survey. You, Mickey, and Mike, you talked about 1966 as a successful soft landing. I think of 1966 as a disaster. The Fed hiked aggressively in '66 out of concern the economy was overheating, and then they caved. The Livingston survey of inflation expectations in '65 is running around 1%, and by the end of '67, after it reverses course and cuts interest rates, inflation expectations were on the way to 5[%]. So it may or may have been a soft landing, but it was, you know, ex post, a spectacular policy mistake. So for the soft landing credit, perhaps we at least include an asterisk or a footnote. Thank you.

LEVY: Rich, I agree with you. The Fed's tightening was less about hiking rates but more about the credit squeeze as inflation pushed rates above Regulation Q interest rate ceilings on savings deposits Q. So it wasn't a great period for a lot of reasons.

WARSH: I don't think Rich wanted to follow up on our discussions about the transparency inside the Federal Reserve. [laughter]

JAMES BULLARD: Jim Bullard, St. Louis Fed. I have two parts to this. One is the '83–84 episode. I was wondering what you guys thought about that. If you look at the effective fed funds rate, it goes up 300 basis points. Ex post real interest rates are extremely high. I've often wondered about this period from the perspective of the kind of models we're writing up here. They would predict an astonishingly deep recession in 1984–85. Instead you got this huge boom, all through the 1980s. You got a very strong dollar obviously in '85 and so on.

This was a moment, to me, where inflation expectations were far more unmoored than they have been in recent times. So, that tightening was more game theory and less econometrics. It was more about establishing the idea that the central bank was going to get inflation under control, and you'd better pay attention if you're working in this economy. Indeed, inflation basically came down—was still kind of volatile through the '80s. So I think that that's an interesting episode. The current episode is very different, and inflation expectations are threatening to become unmoored, as opposed to in many of our models, where we just assume inflation credibility is very solid and we're talking about relatively small deviations around the steady state.

I can't let this go without talking about the influence of the regional banks. I'll give a recent example about what I think the role is. I'll give the Charlie Evans example. Evans—since Charlie is not here, I will be very complimentary to him, because he can't respond—gave a speech about thresholds. He said, "Okay, we're going to have this forward guidance. And we're going to have these thresholds. We're not going to raise the policy rate until one of these thresholds is met." This was going to be a way to get a "lower for longer" policy rate. When he first gave that speech, no one else in the Fed was talking about this. Then he gave his speech again, gave his speech again, talked about it more, and it eventually started to show up in the policy options. Then, lo and behold, six months after that, that actually became Fed policy. This was an example where you could float an idea through this channel. If Bernanke had floated that idea, markets would have gone crazy right away. But that isn't how it works, right? You've got the staff in Chicago thinking this up, and you've got Charlie promoting it, and then it became actual US monetary policy. I think a great advantage of our system is that you can have that kind of diversity of thinking across the board.

LEVY: Jim, great point on 1983. We had just come out of back-to-back recessions, inflation had come down. The back-to-back recessions were the cost of purging inflationary expectations from economic behavior. But Volcker was very frustrated that inflationary expectations and bond yields hadn't come down. The economic recovery was robust. Although the unemployment rate remained very high, the Fed hiked rates aggressively. Growth slowed, but there was an economic soft landing. Volcker slamming on the brakes emphasized the Fed's commitment to keeping inflation low and set the stage for what was to come in the Great Moderation, when the Fed shifted gears from the 1970s and emphasized the importance of stable low inflation. We've come a long way since then, and the Fed has seemingly lost those important lessons. It's really been wonderful working with Mike on this paper and revisiting the history and just thinking about how much things have changed. When I say "things," it's not just policies but theoretical foundations. Before the 1960s, as Mike said, the foundations were price stability and balanced budgets. The evolution of intellectual thinking and policy implementation from those anchors to where we are now has been monumental.

JENNIFER BURNS: In response to Richard Clarida's comment, I just have to remember the anecdote of William McChesney Martin going out to LBJ's ranch and getting a really bumpy ride around the ranch that was kind of symbolic of the other ride you might have. Right? So there was some pressure there.

BORDO: The Federal Reserve has benefited from its regional structure in bringing new ideas into its policy development and in having a wide array of people involved in the policy-making process. But policy mistakes, as is the case today, still happen. The question arises as to why the Fed, with its huge number of well-trained economists, has done so poorly in allowing inflation to take off. It is as if the experience of the 1970s was totally ignored. Is it because they have not been following rule-like policies, as John Taylor has argued? Is it because of political pressure? Is it because they adopted a strategy of flexible average inflation targeting, which was a solution to an outdated problem? Whatever the answers that history will later reveal, it still raises the question of why an organization with thousands of bright, well-educated people got it wrong.

INFLATION RISKS

CHAPTER NINE

The Burst of High Inflation in 2021–22: How and Why Did We Get Here?

Ricardo Reis

Inflation in most western advanced economies has been rising at a fast pace since the middle of 2021. It was tempting (and too common) at the time to dismiss this rise in one of two ways. During the first half of 2021, some noted that there was a normal catch-up of the price level after its sharp fall in 2020 during the pandemic. But this correction became a persistent acceleration by the second half of 2021, which gained further momentum in the first half of 2022, well beyond any reasonable catch-up. Another dismissal came from remembering how central bankers had worried that inflation might be stuck at too low of a level between 2014 and 2019, for instance hovering around 1% and 1.5% in the eurozone. Maybe a year or so of higher than 2% inflation was to be welcome. But, in April of 2022, the one-year inflation rate was 9.0%, 6.3%, and 7.5% in the United Kingdom, the United States, and the eurozone, respectively. Quantitatively, inflation is so far above target that concerns of the recent past that inflation was too low seem trivial.

This essay grew out of speeches and lectures given at Markus' Academy, the 2022 ECB and Its Watchers conference, the BIS annual meetings, the 2022 annual Bradesco/BBI conference, the Norges Bank, the Hoover Institution's 2022 Monetary Policy Conference, and the CICC Global Institute. I am grateful to participants at these conferences for many comments, and to Marina Feliciano, Brendan Kehoe, and Borui Niklas Zhu for research assistance.

Policy makers are worried, as they should be. More than a decade ago, Charles Evans, the president of the Federal Reserve Bank of Chicago and the current longest-sitting member of the Federal Open Market Committee, said in a speech: "Imagine that inflation was running at 5 percent against our inflation objective of 2 percent. Is there a doubt that any central banker worth their salt would be reacting strongly to fight this high inflation rate? No, there isn't any doubt. They would be acting as if their hair was on fire" (Evans 2011). Today, the reality of inflation is already well beyond Evans's imagination, and some central bankers are feeling the heat in their heads. How did we get to this dramatic situation?

The following discussion puts forward four factors behind the recent rise in inflation. The guiding framework is the principle that, ultimately, monetary policy can control inflation. That control is far from perfect, coming with unavoidable misses, and often it is desirable to let inflation deviate from 2% for some time to try to meet other objectives. But, common to all four factors, is a presumption that inflation rose because monetary policy became used to a state of affairs in the past decade and took too long to shift its stance. Rather than highlighting isolated mistakes in judgment, I point instead to underlying forces that created a tolerance for inflation that persisted even after the deviation from target became large. These factors suggest reforms for the future, as well as ways to put out the fire. Perhaps they are of use to the central bankers proving that they are worth their salt. I focus the discussion and the references on the ECB and the Federal Reserve, although the points apply more broadly to other central banks in advanced economies.

THE CONTEXT: TWENTY-FIVE YEARS OF PRICE STABILITY

Before looking at what happened in 2021–22, it is important to step back, and recall how exceptional the previous three decades

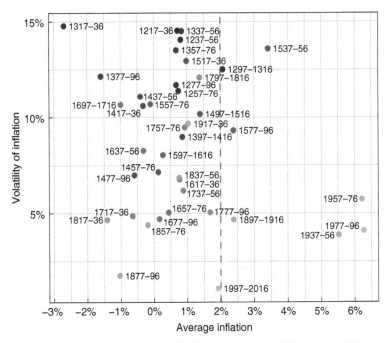

FIGURE 9.1. Eight Hundred Years of Inflation in the United Kingdom, 1217 to 2016

Notes: Data on the annual change in the consumer price index, from the Millennium Dataset of the Bank of England, grouped in twenty-year intervals. Horizontal axis has average inflation, and vertical axis has the standard deviation, both over twenty-year periods.

had been. Between 1995 and 2020, almost every major advanced economy enjoyed a remarkable period of price stability. I first produced a version of figure 9.1 in 2017 for a conference discussing the twenty years of independence of the Bank of England. It shows eight centuries of inflation in the United Kingdom, split into twenty-year periods for which I computed the average and the standard deviation of inflation. Eight hundred years is a long time, and it included many experiments with monetary policy: from the gold standard to floating exchange rates, with monetarism and Bretton Woods thrown in the mix. Some of them got close to the recent past in terms of achieving an average inflation rate near 2%, but they had much higher volatility. A few had low volatility, but those came with persistent deflation. None worked as well in delivering low and stable inflation as the regime of the last twenty years. Never had monetary policy been so successful at controlling inflation as it had been in the two decades before the pandemic (Miles et al. 2017).

What does this successful regime consist of? In my view, it is based on three pillars. The first is granting central banks independence from the ministry of finance, so that managing the public debt and helping to balance the public finances is no longer a job for monetary policy, and no longer overrides concerns about inflation. It is also important to have independence from governments seeking reelection so that monetary policy is not systematically used to stimulate the economy temporarily, a pursuit that often proves fruitless but results in high and volatile inflation.

The second pillar is the required balance to the first: for a public institution to have the power that we confer upon central bankers, then its mandate must be narrow, its actions transparent, and its performance measurable and routinely measured. The public has given central banks an inflation target that satisfies all these criteria.

The third pillar is the primacy of interest rates as the main tool of monetary policy, set in transparent and predictable ways. For most of this time, the interest rate was a short-term rate closely controlled by the central bank, but the period after the great financial crisis saw central banks "go long" by pursuing policies that would temporarily steer long-term interest rates in government bonds. Throughout, central bankers followed clear principles—like the Taylor rule or gradualism—that made their actions rule-like in allowing the private sector to understand where policy was heading and why.

There are endless debates on whether these three pillars are necessary or sufficient to deliver price stability. But it is unlikely it was a coincidence that inflation was so low and stable in a whole host of countries that followed these same three pillars, at different times and in different circumstances. I raise them because I fear that in the near future valid criticisms of central bankers' choices in the last year, or understandable outrages at how high and persistent inflation becomes, can lead to overreactions and entirely new regimes that come with volatility and may fail. The last twenty years showed that independent central banks setting interest rates to hit inflation targets can succeed. The water may need some cleaning or some change, but the baby should stay in it.

THE FIRST FACTOR: SHOCKS AND MISDIAGNOSES

The years 2021 and 2022 saw large and unusual shocks hitting the economy. The job of central banks was especially difficult, and choices were made amidst great uncertainty on what the state of the economy was in real time and what the nature and persistence of the shocks affecting inflation were.

The first and major shock was, of course, the pandemic of 2020. At first, it justified a remarkable degree of monetary stimulus since there were legitimate fears of a depression. The Federal Reserve announced a schedule of asset purchases that made its balance sheet expand to a record share of GDP. The ECB gave forward guidance that deposit rates would stay negative extending well beyond one year. Perhaps overinfluenced by the experience of the great financial crisis, many expected long-lasting scars from the COVID recession. Avoiding a slump demanded a strong response.

Instead, the economy rebounded quickly before 2020 was even over. Between the trough in 2020 Q2 and the end of 2021, real GDP rose by 14.9% in the United States and 17.5% in the euro area. The unemployment rate fell by more than 10% in less than twelve months in the United States. Instead of scars and hysteresis, the economy showed an ability to intertemporally substitute production and consumption. After the lockdown of the second quarter of 2020, the economy responded in the third quarter with intense reopening and economic activity. The private sectors became better at this intertemporal substitution with time, and when a larger health shock came at the end of 2020 with the Alpha wave (in number of infections, deaths, or any other health indicator) together with new lockdowns, the fall in production was smaller for the euro area, and inexistent for the United States. Figure 9.2 shows how quick, relative to its depth, the recovery was in comparison with the other recessions since the start of the century.

Macroeconomic policy deserves credit for this fast recovery. The social insurance programs of 2020 likely contributed to minimizing the scars and prevented consumers from becoming persistently pessimistic and unwilling to work or consume. Almost no bank failed during this time, and there was no significant crisis in any relevant financial market.

At the same time, the recovery came with inflation. The framework of the Phillips curve says that deviation from steady state inflation can come from three direct channels. The first is the expected inflation by households and firms. The second is a deviation of real activity from a potential level of output that is determined by technology and costs. The third is a markup shock that introduces a gap between the potential and efficient levels of output. While different models of price stickiness come with different concrete causes behind each of these three forces, this organizing framework has repeatedly been useful to interpret inflation dynamics arising from shocks.

The fast recovery is an example of the second force driving inflation up. Because tighter monetary policy can work through the same force in the opposite direction, it can stabilize the output gap and inflation with it. However, monetary policy was kept loose in 2021. Additionally, the direct transfers to households and firms in 2020 had led to an accumulation of savings and an explosion in broad monetary aggregates that provided the balances for a boom in spending once the economy reopened. The fiscal stimulus at the start of 2021 in the United States (the American Rescue

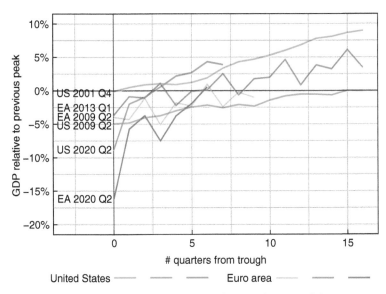

FIGURE 9.2. The Recovery from Recessions in the United States and the Euro Area
Note: Change in real GDP per capita from trough for four years afterwards unless a new peak is reached according to the recession dates of the Centre for Economic Policy Research–Euro Area Business Cycle Network and the National Bureau of Economic Research.

Plan of 2021) further raised aggregate demand, likely to a level above the potential output of the economy. The amount of fiscal and monetary stimulus in 2020 was perhaps excessive, although this judgment comes with the benefit of hindsight. A more pertinent criticism is that policy did not reverse course until at least the end of 2021, even as the signs that the fast recovery was leading to overheating became clearer. This slow reversal is perhaps best explained by the forward guidance given in 2020, serving as a constraint in 2021 on what central banks thought was admissible without defrauding expectations.

A second set of shocks compounded the inflation problem in 2021. They had their origin in the supply sector. At different times during the year, ports became clogged, the production of microchips hit capacity constraints, and global value chains broke down as new waves of the pandemic led to a closing of borders. These bottlenecks are shocks to the supply of goods in the economy that reflected themselves differently in different countries. Yet, the diagnosis of central banks was similar across the advanced economies. In terms of the Phillips curve, policy makers interpreted all these shocks as temporary markup shocks, the third channel. As such, they concluded that they should not reverse the stimulus stance of monetary policy and not jeopardize the recovery. The standard monetary policy prescription against a temporary markup shock is to let inflation rise above target so that, even if actual output rises above potential, it stays close (or slightly below) the efficient level of output.

This diagnosis was suspect, both at the time and in hindsight. Many of these shocks can just as well be interpreted as shocks to the potential level of output. For instance, the problem with global supply chains affects the actual technology used to produce goods, not just the market power of firms. Moreover, if the shape of globalization is going to change, as some have argued, this will most likely affect the productive capacity of the economy. So, if inflation was rising because of the second channel through lower potential output, as opposed to the third through higher deviations from the efficient level of output, the policy prescription would be instead to tighten monetary policy and to keep inflation on target. Simply put, persistent and recurrent negative supply shocks to potential output will make the economy poorer: inflation cannot change this, nor can monetary policy.

Energy prices were the third shock. They had been rising since 2021, and sharply increased in 2022 with the Russian invasion of Ukraine. The ECB responded again as if this was a temporary markup shock, as opposed to a shock to potential output. Policy tolerated a sharp increase in inflation, predicting it to be short lived. It was a defensible priority to strive to avoid mistakes of the past, when hikes in oil prices would raise inflation, trigger tighter monetary policy, and cause a recession.

Yet this "see through the shock" policy is a prescription of the literature only if inflation expectations are anchored. Otherwise, the sharp increase in the prices of energy will have an oversize impact on household expectations as the first channel of the Phillips curve becomes operative, further pushing inflation up. Not only did central banks again interpret a supply shock as being a shock to markups, as opposed to potential output, but they relied on expectations being anchored. Yet, large changes in household costs of energy are salient to households and can easily unsettle their expectations.

Three times in a row in a short period of time, a set of shocks pushed inflation up. Three times in a row, monetary policy interpreted them using the lenses of the Phillips curve in the direction that concluded that monetary policy should be kept loose. Three times in a row, this diagnosis was plausibly right but disputable, and the risk was that inflation would rise too much and too persistently. After the fact, in all three cases this risk became reality. A policy framework should be robust to shocks, and it should correct misdiagnoses. So many successive errors in the same direction indicate more systematic problems. The next three factors point to three such problems.

THE SECOND FACTOR: EXPECTATIONS

No central banker would deny the importance of inflation expectations for the control of inflation. Over the last decade, expected inflation was very sticky, so that its measurements reflected mostly noise with little signal. Household surveys of inflation expectations invariably returned an answer of 2%, which in every wave was polluted by measurement error. Only through careful econometric work were researchers able to uncover interesting patterns that allowed for scientific progress in understanding expectations and inflation. In turn, data from financial markets likewise reflected mostly changes in risk attitudes as well as financial shocks, which introduced noise beyond the expected inflation signal. Inflation expectations were solidly anchored because of the success of the past. Staffers at the forecasting team of central banks were justified in ignoring expectations data in their econometric models (Coibion, Gorodnichenko, and Kamdar 2018).

The experience of 2020 confirmed this view. Despite a few months of sharp deflation, followed by sharp month-to-month inflation, expectations of inflation stayed remarkably stable. The trust that central banks placed in the anchor is evident in the speech by Jerome Powell at the August 2021 Jackson Hole Economic Policy Symposium. The speech discusses data from inflation expectations and concludes that: "Households, businesses, and market participants also believe that current high inflation readings are likely to prove transitory and that, in any case, the Fed will keep inflation close to our 2 percent objective over time." (Powell 2021). There was nothing to see, and the anchor was firmly in the seabed.

In fact, before inflation started rising, central bankers were mostly worried about the possibility that expectations might be anchored at levels of inflation that were too low. In the presentation of the Federal Reserve's new framework in the 2020 Jackson Hole speech, Powell discussed the problem of an "adverse cycle of ever-lower inflation and inflation expectations." (Powell 2020). The ECB, in its revised monetary policy statement wrote: "In particular, when the economy is close to the lower bound, this requires especially forceful or persistent monetary policy measures to avoid negative deviations from the inflation target becoming entrenched." (European Central Bank 2021).

Relying on anchored inflation expectations and focusing on the downside risk has consequences for monetary policy. First, with expected inflation equal to a constant in the Phillips curve framework, one of the main drivers of inflation is absent. Second, a temporary rise in inflation expectations is welcome. If the fear is that of a deflation trap, then a rise in inflation expectations is a way to escape the adverse cycle in the Powell quote above. Third, a rise in actual inflation is likely to be transitory. If expectations stay anchored, they

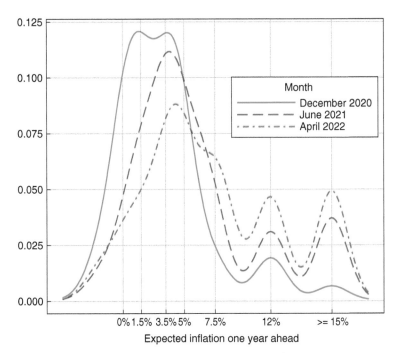

FIGURE 9.3. The Distribution of US Household Survey Inflation Expectations through 2021–22

Note: Data from the University of Michigan Surveys of Consumers, household expectations for one-year-ahead expected inflation.

pull inflation towards them, making most inflation shocks temporary. These three consequences are interlinked: If expectations are solidly anchored, then even sharp rises in inflation will only move them up a little, with no risk that the anchor would go adrift.

However, already halfway through the year 2021, the data showed that expectations were not so well anchored. In line with modern research, the key was to look beyond the measure of central tendency from household surveys and to focus on measures of disagreement. Figure 9.3 shows three snapshots of the distribution of one-year-ahead inflation expectations in the University of Michigan Surveys of Consumers household expectations. In the first half of 2021, the skewness started rising. That is, a rising share of households started expecting that inflation would be higher, even as the median changed little. Then, it was the standard deviation that rose decisively as more and more households joined the group of pessimists. By 2022, the shift of the distribution to the right was such that the median was rising quickly as well.

This three-stage movement in the distribution of expectations is not unique to 2021–22. Looking back to the end of the 1960s in the United States, again the distribution of survey inflation expectations shifted slowly to the right, and this was seen first through an increase in skewness, then a rise in standard deviation, and finally the rise in the median (Reis 2022a). This process took a few years back then, as opposed to less than one year in 2021–22, but qualitatively it was similar. In the other direction, between 1980 and 1985, as inflation sharply came down, again it was first skewness, then standard deviation, and finally median that moved as the distribution shifted to its new anchor. Another common feature of these three episodes is that the surveys of professionals lagged those of households, and after the fact turned out to be the more sluggish and less informative source of data. In normal times, the opposite happens, as household survey data lags professional surveys and is less accurate, but during these three past large changes in inflation, household data was more informative.

The data in 2021 revealed that a large change in expectations was under way. The expectations anchor had left the seabed after a couple of decades during which it had barely moved. Perhaps this was the result of the shocks that hit the economy, or perhaps it was a result of the loose monetary policy that accompanied them. Bad luck played a role, as some of the relative prices that moved the most in 2021 (like gas prices or cars) were among those most visible to consumers, who will tend to overreact to them when forming their expectations. Once central banks allowed inflation to rise, those realizations themselves fed into households anticipating higher expected future inflation. A temporary inflation shock becomes persistent if the expectations anchor moves with it.

THE THIRD FACTOR: CREDIBILITY

Sharp movements in expected inflation over the next year are alarming for the persistence of the shock. But if expectations of the distant future continue to be stable, the damage for inflation will be limited. The credibility of an inflation-targeting central bank is ultimately measured by whether expected long-run inflation is equal to its target. In the long run, money is neutral, the Phillips curve is (nearly) vertical, and expected inflation matches actual inflation. If the central bank manages to convince economic agents that inflation in the long run will be on target, then most of the work of keeping its actual value on target in the long run will have been done.

In 2021, it was justified to rely on having significant credibility. After all, such credibility had been earned after more than twenty years of inflation very close to 2%. Central banks can enjoy a "capital of inattention" in that people do not pay much attention to what the central bank is doing, trusting it will deliver inflation on target over the next few years. One important consequence of this credibility is that it will make the negative relation between inflation and real activity appear to be flatter. As people and firms are inattentive, and update their wages and prices less often, the extent of nominal rigidities in the economy rises, making monetary policy more powerful in affecting real activity. Relying on this credibility, the central bank can exploit short-run trade-offs between inflation and real activity to try to improve welfare. Policy makers will appear more "dovish" because mistakes in policies are more likely to cause recessions than to cause high inflation. In 2021, facing an unusual amount of uncertainty about the shocks hitting the economy and their ability to measure fast-moving indicators, central banks leaned heavily on their credibility by allowing inflation to rise above target to offset the impact of these shocks on real activity. As long as they had credibility, inflation would only rise moderately.

It is hard to survey households on what they expect inflation to be in the distant future. Instead, the dominant measure of credibility comes from financial markets. The most used measure is the 5-year, 5-year forward inflation expected rate. Using either inflation swaps or nominal and inflation-indexed bonds over 5- and 10-year horizons, it computes what the expected inflation will be starting in five years, on average over the succeeding five years. Looking at April 21, 2020, 2021, and 2022, this measure increased from 1.34% to 2.13% and then to 2.67%, respectively, in the United States. Since market measures include a premium for inflation risk, even the more recent number is maybe only slightly above a 2% inflation target.

However, again the average hides what is behind it in the distribution. Looking beyond the mean gives more cause for alarm. Recent research has developed methods to use option prices to inspect these distributions and, especially, to accurately capture the probabilities of the tails (Hilscher, Raviv, and Reis 2022). The top panel of figure 9.4 shows these distributions for the 10-year horizon in the United States throughout 2021. While the average rose little, there was a clear shift to the right. Especially during the second half of the year, this shift came with a quick accumulation of mass on the right tail. The distributions became increasingly asymmetric as upside risks to inflation became dominant.

The bottom panel of figure 9.4 focuses on that right tail by presenting probabilities that reflect how much market participants are willing to pay to insure themselves against an "inflation disaster," a scenario where inflation is persistently higher. To do so, these estimates adjust the tails from the top panel to take out the compensation for risk, and they set the horizon to 5-year, 5-year so as to focus on credibility, as opposed to pessimism about the immediate few years. The numbers therefore measure the current date market-perceived probability that average inflation will be more than 4%

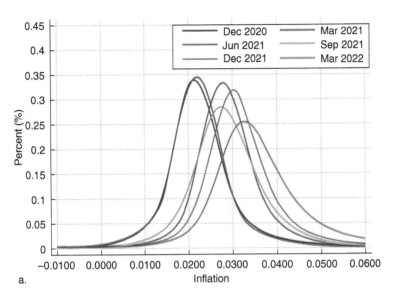

a.

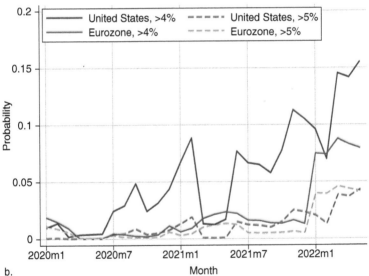

b.

FIGURE 9.4. Measurements of Credibility of the Federal Reserve from Options Markets

a. Probability densities for average risk-adjusted inflation over the next ten years

b. Tail probabilities of a 5-year, 5-year inflation disaster in US and EZ inflation

Notes: Estimates using the methods in Hilscher, Raviv, and Reis (2022). The top panel shows 10-year distributions including risk premia. The bottom panel shows actual forward probabilities over a 5-year, 5-year horizon.

starting in five years, over the following five years. If central bankers are risk managers, they should care more about these disasters than about the average outcome that was so often cited in 2021.

In the United States, this probability rose steadily from the middle of 2021 onwards. By the last date in this sample, April of 2022, it was 16%. Investors were paying a high price to insure against the chance that the Federal Reserve would, considerably and persistently, miss its inflation target between 2027 and 2032. This reveals a lack of credibility of the Federal Reserve. Credibility in the inflation target of the ECB stayed high until the end of 2021. But then, the perceived disaster probability jumped up very quickly to 8%. This is less than in the United States, but it still puts a considerable dent into the faith that credibility has remained intact.

Seeing these numbers, relying on credibility of the inflation target to offset policy shocks by letting inflation rise is a bold and risky move.

THE FOURTH FACTOR: R-STAR AND THE TOLERANCE OF INFLATION

In 2019, both the Federal Reserve and the ECB announced they would be revising the framework that guides their monetary policies. When presenting the result of this work at the 2020 Jackson Hole conference, Jerome Powell cited as one of its important motivations the "fall in the equilibrium real interest rate, or 'r-star.'" In turn, in the overview document that the ECB released presenting its own reviews, the first justification offered for why it was needed was that "structural developments have lowered the equilibrium real rate of interest."

This r-star refers to the real interest rate at which savings are equal to investment and output is at its potential. It is often interpreted and measured as the long-run steady state for real returns in the economy. Sometimes it is called the neutral rate of interest because, in New Keynesian models, having the nominal interest rate of the central bank above r-star plus the inflation target captures contractionary policy. Conversely, if the policy rate is below r-star plus 2%, then policy is understood to be expansionary, putting upwards pressure on inflation. R-star is difficult to estimate because it is observed in an equilibrium that is never reached but estimates that show it has fallen make it more likely that monetary policy is contractionary for any given level of the policy rate.

If r-star is indeed lower, it is more likely that when the central bank needs to lower policy rates aggressively to push up inflation, it will find itself unable to do so. It would require policy rates that are below their "effective lower bound" (ELB). Therefore, monetary policy will sometimes be insufficiently expansionary. In principle, this would lead to too little inflation. The central bank can "go long," trying to affect longer-term interest rates by using forward guidance and quantitative easing to provide further expansion, but this may not be enough.

Matters can get worse. If agents start expecting deflation, and the central bank cannot lower interest rates, then this breakdown of the Taylor principle because of the ELB makes deflation self-fulfilling. As Powell's 2020 speech noted, in that case, the economy may enter an "adverse cycle of ever-lower inflation and inflation expectations," leading the economy to become stuck in a deflation trap. A long academic literature suggests that, to escape this trap, central banks must find a way to commit to delivering high inflation, above the target, in the future. Future higher inflation would boost current inflation, and on average deliver inflation on target.

An emphasis on a low r-star also leads to a focus on providing stimulus to aggregate demand. In economies at the ELB, aggregate demand is too low. The economy is persistently operating below capacity, so that the looser monetary policy can be, the better. This logic extends to fiscal policy, and thus to embracing large deficits and to not worrying about the public debt (which, anyway, now

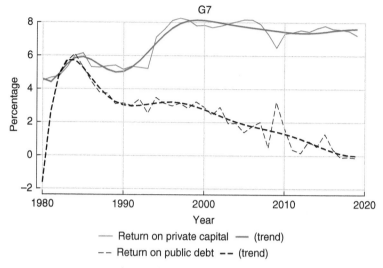

FIGURE 9.5. Estimates of R-star from Returns on Government Bonds and on Private Capital

Note: Estimates from Reis 2022b.

pays a lower interest rate). Policies based on supply, in contrast, are less important. At the ELB, the opportunity cost of liquidity is close to zero, so firms should have access to abundant liquidity and credit. Improvements in aggregate productivity may even backfire and lower output if they lower inflation expectations.

Putting it all together, if r-star has fallen, then central banks increasingly start to worry about deflation because of inevitably tight monetary policy even with interest rates near zero. They welcome inflation rising above target, and they focus on perpetually boosting real activity and providing more and more stimulus. Both the Federal Reserve and the ECB's mission reviews moved in this direction. But has r-star fallen?

Figure 9.5 shows that the ex post return on long-term government bonds has fallen in the G7 countries over the last twenty or thirty years. Short-term government bond yields were close to the ELB for many years including 2021. Monetary policy was certainly constrained in providing more stimulus. But the theoretical concept of r-star refers to an equilibrium between savings and investment in the overall economy. Why would this happen in the government bond market? In fact, in the standard neoclassical growth model that defines the output potential in many modern macroeconomic models, the interest rate on government bonds is irrelevant, as government bonds are not net wealth. It is the marginal product of capital (and time preferences) that determine where savings equal investment. The return on government bonds is only useful because with efficient and complete capital markets, it provides a risk-free measure of the relevant r-star, which conceptually is the return to capital in the economy.

Closer to the concept of r-star is to measure the return on investing in the private capital stock. Doing so using financial returns is a thankless task because, as the Modigliani-Miller theorem states, the return on capital can be split in many ways between different financial claims, and these have likely changed over time. Instead, figure 9.5 shows a measure of the return to capital using the income flows in the aggregate economy. Namely, it starts with value added in the economy, subtracts payments to labor and depreciation, and divides it by the private capital stock. It is therefore a measure of the average return from owning capital in the economy every year, whether those came from profits or costs of finance, or from the payout of loans, bonds, dividends, or others. This measure of r-star has been remarkably constant over the last twenty years. There is no downward trend in it.

There has been a trend increase in the difference between the return in the private economy and the return on government bonds. Perhaps this is a sign of misallocation of capital away from private investment in the capital stock and towards financial investments. It may also reflect an inability of capital markets to fund enough investment to bring the marginal product of capital down. Or, perhaps it reflects an increasing "specialness" of government bonds in providing safety, liquidity, convenience, or some other service that attracts an excess demand for them and justifies their paying an inferior return. Whichever it is, the data suggest that r-star may have been constant, or it may have fallen, but the difference between private and public returns has definitely risen.

This perspective—nondecreasing return to private capital and an increasing wedge between it and the return on public debt—changes the focus of monetary policy (Reis 2022b). First, promising to increase inflation in the future to raise inflation expectations becomes less appealing. Doing so still lowers the real interest rate on government bonds and boosts consumption at the ELB, so it is still an effective policy. However, now it only raises investments if it can reduce the real return on the private capital stock, which it may or may not be able to do. Therefore, all else being equal, it is likewise less stimulative. The costs of higher inflation may start offsetting its benefits.

Second, and related, the priority of escaping the ELB is no longer as overwhelming. Policies that raise the r-star measured with government bonds may relax the constraint on monetary policy. But if these policies do not close the gap to the return on private capital, or even raise the r-star measured with private capital, then they may backfire. They will crowd out investment and potentially lower real activity.

Third, to exit a situation of a persistent deflation trap and accompanying stagnation, lowering the gap between the return on private capital and the return on the public debt is an alternative strategy. This logic points to working on the supply side of the economy, focusing on what is disturbing the allocation of savings. It gives a different focus to the one underlying the recent mission reviews with their focus on aggregate demand. It instead leads to thinking harder about how financial regulation may be helping or hindering an effective allocation of capital, or to what extent asset purchases by central banks have aided or distorted the allocation of capital, to give two examples.

Finally, lower interest payments on the public debt allow for a higher level of public debt to be sustainable. But, if the source of these lower payments is a rising gap between the return on private capital and the return on government debt that is induced by the specialness of public debt, then monetary policy should ask how it contributed to that specialness. In particular, the remarkable achievement in stabilizing inflation over the last twenty years may be related to that rising gap. It has meant that one of the major risks in lending to the government, which is inflation, has disappeared. This suggests that if higher inflation comes with more volatile inflation, and hence higher inflation risk premia, then this may well close the gap between the two rates of return by raising the return that bondholders require on public debt. This would hurt debt sustainability. Delivering on the mandate of price stability becomes even more important (Reis 2022c).

CONCLUSION

The rise in inflation in 2021–22 is such a dramatic event that it will likely spur a large literature and a heated debate in trying to explain it over the next many years. Perhaps it may even trigger regime changes in how monetary policy is conducted. In the short run, it is surely leading to changes in policy to bring inflation back on target.

This article made some contributions to this analysis. It started by reminding that the institutional regime that is in place today, based on independent central banks with inflation targets that set interest rates predictably, has served the advanced economies very well over the previous thirty years. It seems unwise to throw it out after one year of high inflation.

Second, it put forward four structural causes for why inflation rose so much. Common to all of them is a presumption that if inflation rises, it is because the central bank allowed it to rise. Every year has its shocks hitting the economy and its challenges for central banks.

The past always seems rosier in comparison with the turmoil of the present. But theoretically, the institutional regime described above is predicated on the principle that ultimately the central bank can always use its tools to rein in inflation around its target on average over a few years. When the central bank allows inflation to deviate significantly from target in the short run, it is by choice, in trading off other objectives. Empirically, over the last two decades, dozens of countries all over the world adopted this institutional regime under all kinds of circumstances and facing all types of shocks. Almost all and almost always they were able to deliver low and stable average inflation.

The first of the causes for the failure this time was that the unusual and large shocks of 2020–22 were almost always diagnosed in a way that justified keeping monetary policy extremely loose. The fast recovery of 2021 was not enough to trigger a quick reversal on previous forward guidance since the focus was on real activity. The succession of supply shocks was all interpreted as temporary markup shocks as opposed to persistent changes in potential output. As a result, purposely allowing inflation to overshoot its target was seen as optimal and desirable. That is, until it became too large to justify.

The second cause was a steadfast belief that inflation expectations would stay anchored, as they had been for two decades. This belief led to relying on surveys of professionals and on the median expectation of inflation from household surveys to support this strong prior. The distribution of survey inflation expectations and the historical experience with regime shifts pointed elsewhere already in the second half of 2021, and this became clear in 2022. Missing the drift of its anchor, central banks underestimated the persistence that the deviations of inflation from target would have.

The third cause was an overreliance on the credibility of monetary policy. The capital of inattention that the central bank had earned in the past would have allowed it to focus on real activity or other parts of its mandate during an uncertain time. Yet, either by bad luck or by leaning too hard on this past credibility, some of it was lost, producing an upward spiral of inflation when output rose above potential.

The fourth cause was the influence of estimates of a falling and low r-star in the revision of the frameworks for monetary policy. These led to a determination to fight low inflation, and an increased tolerance for inflation above target, as well as a focus on stimulating the economy through aggregate demand. When inflation started rising, this contributed to not fighting it as vigorously as otherwise might have been the case. The r-star that comes from private returns has been constant, and the rising gap between those returns and those on public debt suggest that a different set of policies might have been warranted.

This paper proposed these causes as hypotheses. While there is a strong case that they played a role, future research will tell if they were quantitatively the most relevant. For now, facing the challenge of bringing down inflation, they suggest that policies in the near term may involve: (i) accepting lower levels of real activity in the future, (ii) acting vigorously and sharply in the near future with raising interest rates to reanchor expectations, (iii) restating as loudly and convincingly as possible the primacy of price stability as the goal that guides policy, and (iv) revising upwards the relative costs of high inflation while refocusing on aggregate supply policies.

References

Coibion, Olivier, Yuriy Gorodnichenko, and Rupal Kamdar. 2018. "The Formation of Expectations, Inflation, and the Phillips Curve." *Journal of Economic Literature* 56: 1447–91.

European Central Bank. 2021. "An Overview of the ECB's Monetary Policy Strategy," July 8. Available at: https://www.ecb.europa.eu/home/search/review/html/ecb.strategyreview_monpol_strategy_overview.en.html.

Evans, Charles. 2011. "The Fed's Dual Mandate Responsibilities and Challenges Facing US Monetary Policy." Speech at the European Economics and Financial Centre, London, September 7. Available at: https://www.chicagofed.org/publications/speeches/2011/09-07-dual-mandate.

Hilscher, Jens, Alon Raviv, and Ricardo Reis. 2022. "How Likely Is an Inflation Disaster?" CEPR discussion paper 17224.

Miles, David, Ugo Panizza, Ricardo Reis, and Ángel Ubide. 2017. *And Yet It Moves: Inflation and the Great Recession*. Geneva Reports on the World Economy 19, CEPR Press.

Powell, Jerome. 2020. "New Economic Challenges and the Fed's Monetary Policy Review." Speech at the 2020 economic policy symposium in Jackson Hole, Wyoming, August 27. Available at: https://www.federalreserve.gov/newsevents/speech/powell20200827a.htm.

———. 2021. "Monetary Policy in the Time of COVID." Speech at the 2021 economic policy symposium in Jackson Hole, Wyoming, August 27. Available at: https://www.federalreserve.gov/newsevents/speech/powell20210827a.htm.

Reis, Ricardo. 2022a. "Losing the Inflation Anchor." *Brookings Papers on Economic Activity*, forthcoming.

———. 2022b. "Has Monetary Policy Cared Too Much about a Poor Measure of R*?" Unpublished manuscript, presented at the Asian Monetary Policy Forum, May.

———. 2022c. "Steady Prices, Sustainable Debt." *Finance and Development* 59, no. 1 (March): 16–19.

DISCUSSANT REMARKS

Volker Wieland

In this chapter, Ricardo Reis comes to the conclusion that central banks—in particular the Fed and the European Central Bank (ECB)—could have acted earlier to slow down the rise in inflation but failed to do so. He identifies signals from the data on inflation, household expectations, financial market derivatives, and the returns on private capital that became visible in the first half of 2021 and strengthened throughout the year. In his view, four factors contributed to the delayed response of the central banks: (1) a misreading of relevant shocks; (2) insufficient attention to a rise in household expectations; (3) ignorance of signals of a loss of credibility in long-dated inflation swaps and inflation-indexed bonds, including implied tail probabilities; and (4) excessive focus on low equilibrium interest rate estimates derived from government bonds rather than private capital.

I share Reis's assessment that the Fed and the ECB could have, and should have, responded earlier by tightening monetary policy. Furthermore, I largely agree that the four factors he discusses played an important role in the policy debate and in central banks' decision making. In the following discussion, I provide additional perspectives on these and other factors that mostly support the case he makes, and I note a few caveats. In so doing, I discuss implications of the literature on monetary policy under uncertainty regarding some of the strategic and tactical choices made at the Fed and the ECB.

THE PATH OF INFLATION AND CENTRAL BANK ASSESSMENTS

In the United States, the consumer price index (CPI) inflation rose from 0.24% in May 2020 (percentage change from a year ago) to about

1.3–1.4% between September 2020 and January 2021. Then it quickly increased further to 2.7% in March 2021, 5.3% by June 2021, 6.2% by October 2021, and 7.1% by December 2021. As of May 2022, US CPI headline inflation reached 8.6%. The personal consumer expenditures (PCE) deflator series, which the Fed primarily focuses on, rose more or less in parallel from 0.4% in April 2021 to 6.4% in April 2022.

Reis correctly emphasizes that for a longtime policy makers stuck to the view that the rise of consumer price inflation was a temporary phenomenon that would subside fairly quickly. For example, according to CNBC, Chicago Federal Reserve President Charles Evans said on October 5, 2021, that the Fed soon will be facing the familiar charge of keeping inflation elevated to healthy levels, and likely will have to keep rates low. As late as November 18, 2021, Reuters reported that he said monetary policy is in a "good place," and that he still "believes currently high inflation will recede next year and end 2022 closer to 2% than many people think," allowing the Fed to stay patient on policy.[1] Other members of the Federal Open Market Committee (FOMC) voiced similar views throughout the summer and fall of 2021. As a consequence, most FOMC members saw little reason to raise the federal funds rate in 2022. As of September 2021, the central tendency regarding the anticipated value of the federal funds rate at the end of 2022 still stood at 0.1% to 0.4%.

In the euro area, inflation as measured by the harmonised index of consumer prices (HICP) was negative in the last few months of 2020. In January 2021, it moved to 0.9% from −0.3% in December 2020. From then on, it rose rather quickly: 1.3% in March 2021, 1.9% in June, 3.4% in September, 5.0% in December, and 5.4% in February 2022. Following the start of the Russia-Ukraine war, it rose further, reaching 7.4% by April 2022. Currently, it's estimated at 8.1% for May 2022.

---

1. Jeff Cox, "Fed's Evans Sees Inflation Falling below Central Bank's 2% Target after Current Rise Subsides," CNBC, October 5, 2021; and "Fed's Evans: Baseline View Is for 2023 Rate Hike, but 2022 Possible," *Reuters*, November 19, 2021.

As noted by Reis, policy makers at the ECB also stuck to the characterization of the 2021 rise in inflation as a short-lived phenomenon for a long time. To give an example, ECB board member, Isabel Schnabel, when asked on November 29, 2021, by the German TV channel ZDF how much longer the rise in inflation was going to last, responded: "Many people were not expecting prices to increase to this extent. But we believe that the inflation rate will peak in November and gradually subside next year, towards our inflation target of 2%. Indeed, most forecasts expect inflation to fall even below that 2% level. So, there is no indication that inflation is getting out of control."[2] With her assessment, Schnabel was by no means an outlier among the members of the Governing Council. Nor did it deviate from the ECB staff's projection. Only on December 16, 2021, did the euro system staff raise its inflation projection for 2022 to 3.2%, up from the ECB staff's projection of 1.7% in September 2021. This has been the ECB's largest inflation forecast revision to date.

OUTPUT GAPS, TEMPORARY COST-PUSH SHOCKS, AND INFLATION PERSISTENCE

Reis starts by arguing that central banks underestimated the inflationary impact of the rapid recovery following the pandemic and recession in 2020 with demand exceeding supply and driving up inflation. He also suggests that the impact of the inflationary shocks due to bottlenecks that arose in international sourcing and intermediate goods, as well as those due to energy prices, were misdiagnosed. Central banks characterized them as temporary cost-push shocks. They followed the presumably "conventional wisdom" that monetary policy should look through these shocks and the central bank should let inflation rise while keeping output close to the (unchanged) potential.

---

2. "Interview with Isabel Schnabel, Member of the Executive Board of the ECB, conducted by Mitri Sirin on 29 November 2021," European Central Bank, November 29, 2021.

Additionally, they thought inflation would be self-stabilizing and soon return to the credible inflation target of the central bank.

According to Reis, this was a misdiagnosis. Instead, these shocks can also be understood as negative productivity shocks that reduce potential output. As a result, aggregate demand exceeds potential output and pushes up inflation. In this case, the standard monetary policy prescription would have been to tighten monetary policy to bring demand back in line with potential output.

I agree that such a misreading of the impact of the shocks may well have been a reason for the inaction of the Fed and the ECB. However, I want to move beyond the point raised by Reis and question the wisdom of "looking through" cost-push shocks. In particular, it relies too much on a low degree of inflation persistence and a high degree of credibility for the central bank's inflation target.

To this end, it is helpful to consider simulations of a standard small New Keynesian model. I use the model developed by Clarida, Galí, and Gertler (1999), which embodies much of New Keynesian "conventional wisdom."[3] It consists of a forward-looking aggregate demand curve, a forward-looking Phillips curve, also mentioned by Reis, and an interest rate rule for monetary policy. An extended version of the model also includes lagged output in the aggregate demand curve and lagged inflation in the Phillips curve. This extended Phillips curve corresponds to:

(1) Extended Phillips curve:
Inflation = φ past inflation + (i – φ) expected future inflation
+ λ output gap + cost-push shocks

Compared to the Phillips curve discussed by Reis, the extended Phillips curve uses past inflation as an additional element. The

---

3. The model is one of 150 models available at our Macroeconomic Model Data Base, https://www.macromodelbase.com. The simulations shown can easily be reproduced with software we have made available online. For further information, see also Wieland et al. (2016).

parameter φ lies between 0 and 1 and regulates the importance of inflation persistence. With φ = 0, equation (1) corresponds to the simplest version of the New Keynesian Phillips curve.

To investigate the consequences of a monetary policy that "looks through" the inflationary impact of cost-push shocks, I compare the well-known Taylor (1993) rule with a version of the rule that assigns an eight times larger reaction coefficient on the output gap. With a reaction coefficient of 4 instead of 0.5, what is referred to below as the "accommodative rule," aims much more aggressively towards stabilizing aggregate at potential in the event of macroeconomic shocks, than the original Taylor rule. The parameter r* stands for the equilibrium real interest rate while π* refers to the inflation target.

(2) Taylor (1993) rule:
  fed funds rate = r* + inflation + 0.5 (inflation − π*)
  + 0.5 output gap

(3) Accommodative rule:
  fed funds rate = r* + inflation + 0.5 (inflation − π*)
  + 4 output gap

I start by simulating a positive cost-push shock in the purely forward-looking New Keynesian model (φ = 0) under these two policy rules. As shown in the first panel of the top row of figure 9.6, the shock pushes inflation up by close to 1 percentage point. The Taylor (1993) rule (blue line) keeps inflation a bit lower—by about 20 basis points—than the Taylor rule accommodated (red line). But in both cases, inflation collapses within four quarters. This is an example of the purely temporary impact that the Fed and ECB were anticipating. Of course, the Taylor (1993) rule raises the federal funds rate quite a bit while the accommodative rule moves it much less (middle panel, top row). As a result, the Taylor rule opens up a much bigger negative output gap (right panel, top row).

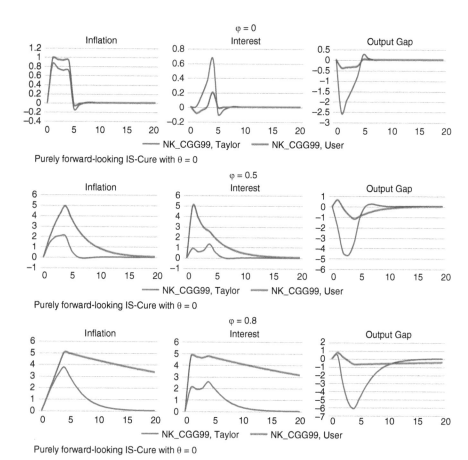

FIGURE 9.6. Simulation of a Positive Cost-Push Shock in a Forward-Looking New Keynesian Model

Source: Author's calculations using the Macroeconomic Model Data Base, https://www.macromodelbase.com.

The trade-off between the output gap and inflation stabilization is clearly unfavorable. This confirms the conventional wisdom of looking through a temporary cost-push shock.

However, once there is a significant degree of inflation persistence, the picture changes drastically. When lagged inflation receives the same weight as expected future inflation ($\varphi = 0.5$, middle row in figure 9.6), the cost-push shock leads to substantial increase in inflation of up to 5 percentage points under the accommodative rule relative to 2 percentage points under the Taylor (1993) rule. For this reason, the accommodative rule ultimately needs to raise the funds rate much more than the Taylor rule to rein in inflation. In a situation where inflation depends more on past inflation than inflation expectations ($\varphi = 0.8$, bottom row in figure 9.6), the cost-push shock drives inflation up for more than 5 years under the accommodative rule. These simulations assume that the inflation target of the central bank is 100% credible. This ensures that even in the simulation with high inflation persistence, real rates need not rise much to return inflation to its target eventually. In practice, however, a sustained rise in inflation raises doubts about the central bank's commitment. Thus, inflation expectations will become unhinged, and the central bank will lose control of inflation.

Bottom line: When faced with cost-push forces and uncertainty about inflation persistence, the central bank better react right away rather than wait and "look through" the rise in inflation.[4] And it may need to accept inducing a negative output gap to achieve price stability.

INFLATION EXPECTATIONS, ASYMMETRIC RISKS, AND CENTRAL BANK POLICY

Reis argues that central bankers remained mostly worried with the possibility that expectations might be anchored at too low of an inflation rate and failed to act while it became clear in 2021 that a substantial change in expectations was under way. Looking at the distribution of US household inflation expectations one-year ahead from the University of Michigan Surveys of Consumers, he shows a three-stage movement. In the first half of 2021, skewness was rising

---

4. Söderström (2002) shows that parameter uncertainty about the persistence of inflation calls for a more aggressive policy response, in contrast to the finding that multiplicative parameter uncertainty calls for gradualism (Brainard 1967; Wieland 2006).

already, resulting in a longer tail on the upside. As more and more households expected higher inflation, the standard deviation rose and eventually, so did the median.

Reis's findings for US household expectations are certainly thought-provoking. With regard to the euro area, I would like to draw attention to the Bundesbank's survey of household inflation expectations in Germany. It also provided a signal of what was ahead. Throughout 2021, this survey reported an increasing share of households expecting inflation to increase slightly or significantly over the next twelve months. By May 2021, the median also moved up from 2% to 3%. By October 2021, it had reached 4%.

An interesting recent paper by Dräger, Lamla, and Pfajfar (2022) reports on a randomized control trial (RCT) that was included in the September 2021 survey. They randomly exposed households to different information treatments such as (1) the current August 2021 inflation rate of 3.6%; (2) the inflation projection from the survey of professional forecasters; (3) a newspaper report from May 31, 2021, stating that ECB president Lagarde had "so far stressed that she thinks the increased inflation will be a temporary phenomenon"; and (4) a newspaper report from March 12, 2021, stating that Volker Wieland, member of the German Council of Economic Experts had said: "I think it's possible that we'll have similar inflation rates also in 2022 and the years after, that are between 2% and 3% annually." Interestingly, Dräger, Lamla, and Pfajfar find that communication using explicit numerical inflation projections limited spillovers from the current inflation rate to inflation expectations.

How should monetary policy account for asymmetric risks? According to the basic inflation forecast targeting framework, the central bank should only respond to the point forecast. Standard deviation and asymmetry of the inflation distribution are ignored. This policy prescription is derived in a framework with a linear economy, known parameters, normally distributed shocks, and a quadratic central bank objective function (see Svensson 1997). By contrast, distributions matter for policy once the framework is extended to allow for a nonlinear economy, non-quadratic objectives, non-normal distributions, and parameter uncertainty. In particular, non-normal errors and skew call for a more aggressive policy reaction according to Swanson (2000) and Christodoulakis and Peel (2009).

In this context, I would also like to point out an asymmetry introduced explicitly in the recent update of the FOMC's monetary policy strategy. It clarified that the Committee seeks, over time, to mitigate shortfalls of employment from the Committee's assessment of its maximum level. This strategy does not include a symmetric response when employment exceeds its natural or long-run level. This asymmetry in policy response to the unemployment gap is also made explicit in the balanced-approach (shortfalls) rule that was included in the July 2021 *Monetary Policy Report* to illustrate the FOMC's approach.

Interestingly, such an asymmetry in the monetary policy objective has been the focus of several contributions to the literature on optimal monetary policy (see Tambakis 1999, Cukierman 2002, Cukierman and Gerlach 2003, Cukierman and Muscatelli 2008). They model this asymmetry in terms of half-quadratic output gap preferences in the central bank loss function or a reaction to shortfalls only in the central bank reaction function. Cukierman and Gerlach (2003) write that "Even if policy makers are content with the normal level of employment there is an *inflation bias* if the central bank is uncertain about the future state of the economy and is more sensitive to policy misses leading to employment below the normal level than to policy misses leading to employment above it." Cukierman and Gerlach (2003) also found empirical evidence supporting half-quadratic preferences for output for OECD countries including the United States. In a way, the Fed's new strategy serves to corroborate the claim by Cukierman and Gerlach, while potentially contributing to an inflation bias and a policy that waits too long.

CREDIBILITY AND MARKET-BASED MEASURES
OF LONG-RUN INFLATION EXPECTATIONS

With regard to central bank credibility, Reis focuses mostly on measures derived from bonds and derivatives traded on financial markets, in particular, inflation swaps or nominal and inflation-indexed bonds over 5- and 10-year horizons. For the United States, this measure of expected inflation from five-to-ten years into the future had risen by about 1.3 percentage points from 2020 to 2022. With co-authors, Reis has developed methods for using option prices to estimate the distribution of such long-range market-based inflation forecasts (see Hilscher, Raviv, and Reis 2022). The results are striking. Just as in the case of household expectations, the distributions he derives shifted rightward throughout 2021. Tail probabilities for long-run inflation exceeding 4% or 5% in the long run moved up in the second half of 2021 for the United States, and at the start of 2021 for the euro area. Clearly the measures Reis calculates were signaling the need for convincing policy action. Nevertheless, central banks continued to rely on the credibility of their policy targets to keep inflation expectations anchored.

Turning to the euro area, the 5-year, 5-year forward expectation from inflation swaps increased from a low point of around 1% in the second quarter of 2020 throughout the year 2021 to about 2% by the end of that year. In 2022, it increased further towards 2.5%. It is surprising that this steady increase did not feature importantly in ECB communication.

By contrast, in 2014, a decline in these measures triggered aggressive policy easing. At the Jackson Hole conference in August 2014, ECB president Mario Draghi famously stated: "Over the month of August, financial markets have indicated that inflation expectations exhibited significant declines at all horizons. The 5-year, 5-year swap rate declined by 15 basis points to just below 2%—this is the metric that we usually use for defining medium-term inflation. But if we go to shorter- and medium-term horizons, the revisions have been even more significant. . . . The Governing Council will acknowledge these developments and within its mandate will use all the available instruments needed to ensure price stability over the medium term."

Throughout the year 2021, the 5-year, 5-year measure increased much more. While it approached the ECB's target from below, it was a clear signal that markets were anticipating a substantial increase in long-run trend inflation. This would have supported the case for an earlier start of gradual policy normalization. Instead, the ECB waited, thus responding asymmetrically to the increase in market-based long-run inflation relative to the earlier decrease in this measure.

One caveat is in order, however. The long-run market-based inflation forecasts are very sensitive to short-run developments. In particular, the 5-year, 5-year forward expectation for inflation has moved quite often in lockstep with energy prices, with the 5-year, 5-year measure coming down and then rising sharply with energy prices. This is quite apparent from figure 9.7. Energy prices, however, exhibit substantial short-run volatility. By contrast, survey expectations from professional forecasters have not moved very much in either direction.

Thus, the long-run market-based forecast of inflation probably does not offer that much more new information relative to short- to medium-term forecasts, and possibly the same applies to long-dated inflation options. Even so, the distributions Reis estimates provide very useful and important information for central banks to consider and may just be telling us more about a much closer horizon.

FOCUS ON THE EFFECTIVE LOWER BOUND AND A LOWER EQUILIBRIUM REAL INTEREST RATE

Since the financial crisis, central banks have been concerned with the effective lower bound on nominal interest rates, which forces

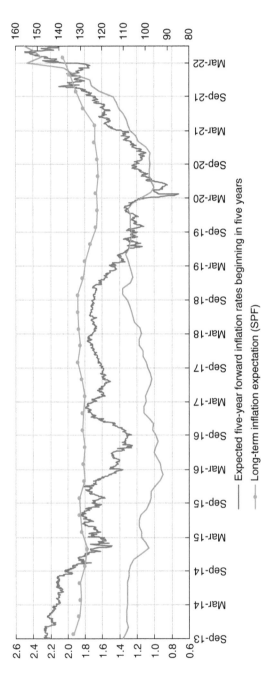

FIGURE 9.7. Long-Term Inflation Forecasts and Energy Prices in the Euro Area

Sources: European Central Bank, Thomson Reuters Datastream.

Notes: (1) Market-based long-term inflation expectations looking ahead five years. Derived from the fixed payments of inflation swaps that are exchanged for the annual inflation rates realized over the next five or ten years; (2) Survey of Professional Forecasters expectation for inflation looking ahead five years.

Legend:
— Expected five-year forward inflation rates beginning in five years
— Long-term inflation expectation (SPF)
— HICP energy (right-hand scale) (September 2015 = 100)

them to switch from the central bank rate to quantitative easing as primary policy instrument. Additionally, a perceived decline of the equilibrium real interest rate (r*) means that they worry about a greater likelihood of policy being constrained in this manner in the future. Approaches to dealing with this combined policy challenge constituted the main focus of the Fed's and the ECB'S recent strategy reviews, which were completed respectively, in 2020 and 2021.

Reis questions the empirical evidence for the decline of real equilibrium returns. He argues that it is derived primarily from the decline of government bond rates. Instead, he provides some empirical measures of the returns on private capital, which apparently have not declined. He speculates, for example, that this may be a sign of a misallocation of capital away from private investment in the capital stock and towards financial investments. Rather than increasing public debt to raise bond rates, he argues for lowering the gap between the returns on private capital and the returns on public debt by supply-side policies.

Reis's provocative challenge of entrenched central banker thinking is worth serious consideration. I would certainly support the call for renewed effort on supply-side policies. Yet, a caveat is in order. Much of central bank research on low equilibrium real rates does not rely on bond rates. It treats r* as an unobservable variable to be estimated from a simple aggregate demand and Phillips curve setup. The only rate used in estimation is the short rate. R* estimates from this framework declined from 2009 onwards partly because of lower potential growth estimates and partly because low interest rates did not stimulate inflation as expected (see Wieland 2018). These estimates are quite sensitive and may well rise again along with higher inflation and higher policy rates (see Beyer and Wieland 2019).

Yet in my view, the Fed and the ECB delayed too long even if one accounts for the proximity to the effective lower bound. Early research on monetary policy at low inflation showed that it is optimal to lower interest rates earlier and keep them near zero

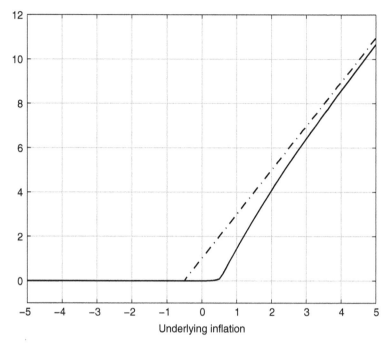

FIGURE 9.8. Optimal Interest Rate Setting with Zero Lower Bound and
Uncertainty about QE Effectiveness

Source: Orphanides and Wieland 2000.

Notes: The solid line shows the optimal policy for the federal funds rate with the zero bound
and uncertainty regarding QE effectiveness. The dash-dot line illustrates the optimal policy
in the absence of uncertainty.

longer than in a standard linear inflation targeting framework.
Orphanides and Wieland (2000) derived this policy implication
in an inflation-targeting framework with a zero lower bound on
nominal policy rates and multiplicative uncertainty about the effectiveness of quantitative easing.

As inflation declines, it is optimal to use the interest rate instrument more aggressively before switching to quantitative easing
where the impact is uncertain. Similarly, as inflation rises, the optimal interest rate policy stays at the zero bound for longer than the
benchmark linear policy. This is directly apparent from figure 9.8,

which replicates the optimal interest rate reaction function from Orphanides and Wieland (2000).

This analysis illustrates that "lower for longer" refers to the comparison with a linear benchmark that either ignores the uncertainty about the effectiveness of quantitative easing or ignores the effective lower bound altogether. Yet, the responsiveness of the optimal interest rate setting to inflation is the same whether inflation declines towards zero or whether it rises from zero to positive territory. In both cases, it is characterized by a movement along the solid line, though in opposite directions. ECB policy seems to have proceeded quite differently. From 2014 onwards, the decline in inflation was quickly followed by aggressive and substantial policy easing. Yet, when inflation rose in 2021, the central bank balance sheet continued to increase, and policy tightening was delayed.

References

Beyer, Robert C. M., and Volker Wieland. 2019. "Instability, Imprecision and Inconsistent Use of Equilibrium Real Interest Rate Estimates." *Journal of International Money and Finance* 94 (June): 1–14.

Brainard, William. 1967. "Uncertainty and the Effectiveness of Policy." *American Economic Review* 57 (May): 411–25.

Christodoulakis, George, and David Peel. 2009. "The Central Bank Inflation Bias in the Presence of Asymmetric Preferences and Non-Normal Shocks." *Economics Bulletin* 29, no. 3:1608–20.

Clarida, Richard, Jordi Galí, and Mark Gertler. 1999. "The Science of Monetary Policy: A New Keynesian Perspective." *Journal of Economic Literature* 37, no. 4 (December): 1661–1707.

Cukierman, Alex. 2002. "Are Contemporary Central Banks Transparent about Economic Models and Objectives and What Difference Does It Make?" Federal Reserve Bank of St. Louis, 15–35.

Cukierman, Alex, and Stefan Gerlach. 2003. "The Inflation Bias Revisited: Theory and Some International Evidence." *Manchester School* 71, no. 5: 541–65.

Cukierman, Alex, and Anton Muscatelli. 2008. "Nonlinear Taylor Rules and Asymmetric Preferences in Central Banking: Evidence from the United

Kingdom and the United States." *B. E. Journal of Macroeconomics* 8, no. 1 (February): 1–31.

Dräger, Lena, Michael J. Lamla, and Damjan Pfajfar. 2022. "How to Limit the Spillover from the 2021 Inflation Surge to Inflation Expectations?" Working Paper Series in Economics 407, University of Lüneburg, Institute of Economics.

Hilscher, Jens, Alon Raviv, and Ricardo Reis. 2022. "How Likely Is an Inflation Disaster?" *Review of Financial Studies* 35, no. 3: 1553–95.

Orphanides, Athanasios, and Volker Wieland. 2000. "Efficient Monetary Policy Design near Price Stability." *Journal of the Japanese and International Economies* 14, no. 4: 327–65.

Reis, Ricardo. 2020. "The People vs. the Markets: A Parsimonious Model of Inflation Expectations." CEPR Discussion Paper 15624.

———. 2021. "Losing the Inflation Anchor." Brookings Papers on Economic Activity, September 9.

Söderström, Ulf. 2002. "Monetary Policy with Uncertain Parameters." *Scandinavian Journal of Economics* 104, no. 1: 125–45.

Svensson, Lars E. O. 1997. "Inflation Forecast Targeting: Implementing and Monitoring Inflation Targets." *European Economic Review* 41: 1111–46.

Swanson, Eric T. 2000. "On Signal Extraction and Non-Certainty-Equivalence in Optimal Monetary Policy Rules." *Finance and Economics Discussion Series* 2000-32, Board of Governors of the Federal Reserve System.

Tambakis, Demosthenes. 1999. "Monetary Policy with a Nonlinear Phillips Curve and Asymmetric Loss." *Studies in Nonlinear Dynamics and Econometrics* 3, no. 4: 223–37.

Taylor, John B. 1993. "Discretion versus Policy Rules in Practice." Carnegie-Rochester Conference Series on Public Policy 39: 195–214. Amsterdam: North-Holland.

Wieland, Volker. 2006. "Monetary Policy and Uncertainty about the Natural Unemployment Rate: Brainard-Style Conservatism versus Experimental Activism." *B. E. Journal of Macroeconomics* 6: 1–34.

———. 2018. "The Natural Rate and Its Role in Monetary Policy." In *The Structural Foundations of Monetary Policy*, edited by Michael D. Bordo, John C. Cochrane, and Amit Seru. Stanford, CA: Hoover Institution Press.

Wieland, Volker, Elena Afanasyeva, Jinhyuk Yoo, and Meguy Kuete. 2016. "New Methods for Macro-Financial Model Comparison and Policy Analysis." In *Handbook of Macroeconomics*, edited by John B. Taylor and Harald Uhlig. Vol 2. Amsterdam: North-Holland.

GENERAL DISCUSSION

ARVIND KRISHNAMURTHY (INTRODUCTION): We are experiencing a period of a rapid increase in measured inflation as well as an increase in the mean expectation for inflation rates over the next few years. Beyond these mean shifts, there has also been an increase in uncertainty over inflation outcomes, as Ricardo Reis's paper in this volume makes clear. It is worth highlighting this increased uncertainty, which reflects (1) model uncertainty and (2) uncertainty over economic outcomes.

The 2010s were a period of monetary experimentation, with massive increases in monetary aggregates, and forward guidance policies aimed to keep long-term interest rates low. Yet, inflation rates generally undershot the Fed's 2% target, albeit by small margins, and inflation expectations as measured from asset markets remained remarkably stable around 2%. The US experience of low inflation and low inflation expectations during a period of substantial monetary stimulus is echoed in the experience of Europe in the 2010s, as well as that of Japan going back another decade. These episodes call into question models of the inflation-generating process running through money mechanisms.

There has also been a reexamination of models of the inflation mechanism running from labor market tightness to increases in wages and prices, i.e., the Phillips curve. The relative insensitivity of inflation to changes in unemployment in the last two decades has led many economists to estimate that the Phillips curve has flattened substantially. What is the current slope of the Phillips curve, and how important is this relationship to models of the inflation process?

The model uncertainty faced by researchers has a counterpart in the deliberations of policy makers. The Fed, prior to the COVID recession, embarked on a reassessment of its monetary policy framework. This culminated in Jay Powell's August 2020 speech laying out the new monetary framework of flexible average inflation targeting.

I make these points primarily to highlight that in 2020, before the COVID recession, policy makers, researchers, and investors faced considerable uncertainty regarding their models of the inflation-generating process as well as uncertainty over the parameters of a new Fed Taylor rule.

Model uncertainty has been coupled with a series of unusual shocks that has increased economic uncertainty. How would an economy undergoing the shutdown of COVID react? How much of the heightened unemployment of the COVID recession was a response to reduced demand in the recession and how much a response to workers' shift in individual labor supply, driven by pandemic concerns? As the supply bottlenecks of COVID eased, would inflation rates normalize? And as the pandemic-driven economic effects in the US have diminished, the world has been faced with another shock, the war in Ukraine. Navigating monetary policy through these uncertain times is challenging, as we have heard from policy makers in this conference. For agents in the economy that set prices, inflation rates, and asset values, forecasting economic outcomes and policy reactions is doubly challenging.

To return to the point where I started: the challenge of inflation in the current environment is one not only of high mean inflation but also of significant uncertainty and inflation risk.

* * *

RICARDO REIS: I want to take a minute to emphasize a point that Volcker made: measures of expectations are noisy. Take measures of disagreement, like skewness, a third moment sometimes estimated on samples with 500 respondents. Month to month, it is going to move quite a bit simply due to noise, which should best be ignored.

Next, say you were brought up at the inflation desk of the Fed between 2000 and 2019. Because you have been living in a regime in which inflation is very strongly anchored at 2%, all you're getting from expectations jumping up and down is the noise. You would convince yourself that expectations are garbage in terms of forecasting inflation rate. However, when you have a regime change, like potentially in 2021, the expectations data is now moving a lot. Now, the expectations data is quite revealing, including its second and third moments. That happened during the [Chairman Paul] Volcker period. And that's what has been happening in the last year or so.

Similarly, with options, I am looking at tails. If I'd shown for instance the probability of deflation, where they're a little higher, month to month they can jump quite a bit and I would make nothing of it because it just jigs back and down. But when you see a probability like that tail of high inflation that used to jump up and down between 1% and 5% in seemingly random ways, and all of a sudden it moves to 16% to 20% for many months, then I'm paying attention. So this is just to say that you don't want to rely on these data for month-to-month forecasting. But it's only when you see these big movements that I think it's worth paying attention.

ROBERT HALL: It seems to me there's lots of evidence that the Phillips curve just recently has become a lot steeper. And the steepness of the Phillips curve in a New Keynesian setting in a model such as Ricardo's famous job market paper, the higher the dispersion of the environment of the firm, the more frequently it will adjust its price. There hasn't been much discussion at this conference about this point. But I take it from Ricardo's nodding vigorously he agrees that the figuring out what's going on today is going to involve a considerable increase in the steepness of a New Keynesian Phillips curve, maybe almost vertical given the speed with which wage and price inflation have changed recently.

REIS: I agree with that, but you've been much too generous toward me, Bob. I think it was Lucas, who argued forcefully that in a world that's very volatile, the Phillips curve becomes steeper. Absolutely, models of endogenous attention and price stickiness will have this property, and that may be consistent with the facts right now.

JAMES BULLARD: Jim Bullard, St. Louis Fed. So, I have a question for Ricardo. First of all, I love the options of pricing stuff. That was really good. But on the picture that has the returns to capital and then the returns to short-term Treasuries in real terms since the 1980s, we stared at that picture in St. Louis, but maybe we came to different conclusions than you did. There's a lot of issues here about the equity premium. There's a New Keynesian model that has capital in it. Don't you have to modify that model and then tell me where the r-star is in the Taylor rule, instead of just putting the m-star in the Taylor rule? So I think that that would be an issue. And then, you know, I guess the main reading of that diagram was, and I think is, that there's a demand for highly safe securities in the last two decades, or three decades. And this is what's going on. There's a demand for global liquidity, and there's not enough issuance around the world. There's a shortage of safe debt.

ARVIND KRISHNAMURTHY: Can I add one thing to that? The Fed sets the rate on the safe and liquid asset as opposed to the rate on m-star. So wouldn't that be the relevant thing to measure in a model?

REIS: Some telegraphic answers. First, the equity premium. If I had been measuring returns on the stock market, then I would worry a lot about that. Instead, I use national income and product accounts, so we're not talking necessarily about premiums on financial assets. Second, there could have been a change in aggregate risk since there's certainly a gap between m, a risky rate, and r, a safe rate. Seeing an enormous increase in the m minus r gap, either you think that there's been a dramatic increase in risk aversion or an increase in demand for safety. That seems implausible. Instead, maybe there's something that made either

Treasuries more attractive or the capital stock less attractive. If so, the efficiency of allocation between the capital stock and the public debt may have changed. That then implies that the dangers of the ZLB, whether there is a deflation trap or not, depends on how the m minus r gap behaves, not solely on how r behaves. That is my point. We are then discussing the diagnosis of that change, and it's not enough to dismiss it as saying, "Oh, it was just risk or an equity premium that has changed." You have to go on what generated it. And thirdly, related on the model, yes, I did not show the equations, but that's what I've been doing. I start with a New Keynesian model with capital and nominal rigidities, and the m minus r changing because of misallocation, and I end up with the three conclusions I told you: (1) the ZLB is not as bad, because the m margin is adjusting; (2) raising future inflation expectations does not have quite as much as a kick on real activity, and (3) aggregate demand multipliers are not so large. And then on Arvind . . .

KRISHNAMURTHY: I was pointing out that the Fed should care about r-star more than m-star because the zero lower bound on their policy rate concerns r-star.

REIS: I completely agree. There is an important distinction. For what the central bank sets, r-star is the key constraint on policy thing since your actions are on the yield curve. But, the question I raised is what are the effects of that constraint and of policy on overall economic outcomes? That determined how actively should you fight that constraint on the r and on the r-star. Whether m fell in tandem with the r or not, or if there's a gap, changes that answer. So thanks, for the question.

PATRICK KEHOE: Patrick Kehoe of Stanford. Ricardo, when you were talking about there being an increase in the variance of beliefs that predated the shift in the mean of beliefs, do you interpret that initial increase in variance as an indication that people's expectations became unanchored? And that's all you're picking up in the first bit, and that means people are ready to move their beliefs, and then they actually started moving later. And Volker responded, Do we have nonlinear maps between heterogeneous beliefs and outcomes in one nonlinear quadratic model? Is that how we're using the idea that before things move, people are getting less sure of themselves, and that what was the spreading out of the variances namely, more weight in the tails? And that shows me that it's going to move? Volker instead was talking about nonlinearities, but I don't think you actually said much about nonlinear maps between distribution to beliefs and outcomes.

REIS: There are two separate points, and I made one, and Volker made a different one. And so let me distinguish them to be clear. In the data, when you have these large changes in regime, it is as if some people figure it out right away and they move to the new regime. That's where you see the spread and the variance. That's where you see the skewness, and then the other ones catch up. When I was documenting these facts 20 years ago, I did so because in these models of sticky information, some guys figured it out faster and the other ones catch up. This is about how during shifts in the regimes you observe these dynamics in the population.

A separate point, which Volker made, is to what extent people are inattentive? And that is like the inaction models of inattention in my doctoral thesis. There's a fixed cost to paying attention, and the central bank has a "capital of inattention" when agents are in the inaction range. Then something big happens, they shift to attention, and policies have to address it. That's a totally separate thing.

MARC KATZ: Marc Katz, Broadfield Capital Management. You have in your slides sort of a propagation of an expected inflation curve. And if you look at a curve like that, it could really give you sort of a false sense of security about what future inflation may be for the same reasons that Treasury yields are unexpectedly low, for reasons that Jim talked about. But have you considered propagating a curve of expected m, i.e., expected nominal return on capital, to gauge the market's true concern about inflation? That versus just looking at inflation expectations by only propagating a risk-free curve?

REIS: That's a good question. I have no idea how to do it for m. For r, I was showing you 10-year rates, and people will make a distinction between the 10-year, the short term, and others. For the m, this is a return to capital. I don't know how to map this to a 1-year or 5-year horizon, let alone build a curve on it.

KATZ: Intuitively, it seems like expected returns on capital have increased dramatically recently, perhaps partially due to increases in expected inflation and required higher real returns.

REIS: When you mention expected returns on capital, you are referring to expected returns on equity, right? But there's many claims on the capital stock of the economy. And to what extent those converge or not to the ultimate returns on capital is something that I'm not super comfortable making assumptions on. But if you're willing to make some assumptions, yes, you could do that, as you say, from the prices of equities and others. I mean, what I do know from the work of my distinguished chair is that if you really try to strip out from the private sector everything that makes it the private sector—aggregate risk, everything—to try to come up as close as possible to Treasury, you still have an m minus r gap. There's something special about Treasuries, say convenience or safety.

ELENA PASTORINO: Elena Pastorino, Hoover Institution. And this is a question for Ricardo. You talked about the issue of credibility and the anchoring of inflation expectations. But after all, we live in a different monetary policy world after the very public "soul searching" that took place in 2019, at least on this side of the ocean, with the strategy review of the Fed. So in this new world, how should we be thinking about establishing credibility, especially in light of asymmetric inflation rules? In your opinion, what concrete steps should monetary authorities be undertaking in this dimension? Thank you.

REIS: That's a great question. Insofar as I showed you some estimates of those tail probabilities, you see them increasing after 2021. There are three hypotheses that I cannot distinguish. One, they rose because of the 2019–20 mission review, but it took a while for you to be able to see this in the data. Two, it was the policy choices (and maybe mistakes) that happened in 2021, which have been discussed here this morning. Three, that it was neither of these two, but long-term trends common across central banks, in terms of the monetary environment and others, including shifts in r and m. I don't know. We can discuss whether we like the new framework of the Fed or not. But the fact that we had such a huge pandemic shock right after it was adopted means that it's hard to test it. Maybe it was the best framework ever, it just got really unlucky? Or maybe it was a terrible framework and would have done worse anyway? So I guess I'm not answering your question, but I'm hopefully making the question more interesting, and then maybe someone will be able to answer it by solving the identification problem.

One thing that is interesting is that at the other side of the Atlantic, the big concern was this probability of deflation, and it was quite high, around 20%. It's quite interesting that when the ECB changes its strategy, that deflation probability falls, and then it kind of comes back up. So I'll just leave it at that.

WORLD WARS: FISCAL-MONETARY CONSEQUENCES

CHAPTER TEN

Financing Big US Federal Expenditures Surges: COVID-19 and Earlier US Wars

George J. Hall and Thomas J. Sargent

> *Inflation is repudiation. Deflation is assumption.*
> —Calvin Coolidge (1922)

The first part of this chapter summarizes Hall and Sargent (2022), a pattern recognition exercise in which we described similarities and differences between how the US government financed its "war" on COVID-19 and how it financed World War I and World War II. We asked, who paid for each of these three wars? Was it taxpayers? Bondholders? Money holders? The second part of the chapter consists of additional historical evidence that helps to answer some of the probing questions we received from conference participants. To assemble our answers, we rely heavily on findings reported in Hall and Sargent (2014, 2019, 2021) and Sargent (2012). Throughout the chapter, we use a consolidated government budget constraint as our organizing principle. Data visualization and tabular summaries are our principal techniques. We organize data as though they conform to a "common stochastic trends" process of a type

We thank conference participants and our discussant Ellen McGrattan for suggestions and questions. We especially thank Michael Bordo, James Bullard, John Cochrane, and Patrick Kehoe for their probing questions.

presented by Hansen (2012) and applied to asset pricing by Hansen and Scheinkman (2009). Thus, our main tools for pre-processing the data are taking logs and their differences. As promised by Hansen (2012), these transformations uncover apparently stationary statistical behavior lurking within a suite of randomly growing time series. Thus, see our figures 10.2 and 10.9 below, which serve as virtual poster children for a Barro (1979) tax-smoothing model.

WORLD WARS I AND II AND THE WAR ON COVID-19

We start with some similar private sector patterns across World War I, World War II, and the war on COVID-19. First, the war on COVID-19, like World War I and World War II, was a worldwide adverse shock. Second, all three wars were large shocks to the civilian workforce. In World Wars I and II, the government paid, and in many cases, drafted men to leave the civilian workforce and join the military. During COVID-19, the government paid people to leave the civilian workforce and stay home to slow the spread of the virus. Third, domestic and international travel and trade were sharply curtailed during all three of these wars.

In figure 10.1, we ask what percentages of the working age population were removed from the civilian workforce during these wars? The blue line plots active duty military as a percentage of the total population, and the red line plots the share of the population receiving unemployment insurance. The figure illustrates that 3% of the population was in active duty military during World War I. This share rose to 8.5% during World War II. During COVID-19, 7% of the working-age population was receiving unemployment insurance.

Next, we discuss a few public sector patterns. Consider figure 10.2. The blue line is government expenditures, and the red line is tax revenues, both as a share of GDP. Government spending in the twentieth-century world wars had both temporary and permanent components.

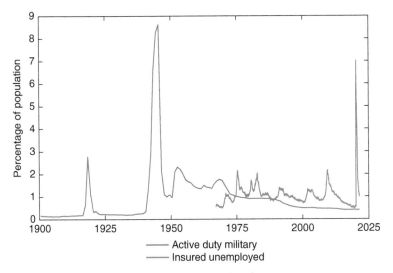

FIGURE 10.1. Active Duty Military and Unemployed Persons Receiving Insurance as Percentages of Total Population: 1900–2021

Sources: Department of Defense (active duty military); Federal Reserve Bank of St. Louis (insured unemployment), https://fred.stlouisfed.org/series/CCSA. Population is total population including armed forces overseas from the Census Bureau.

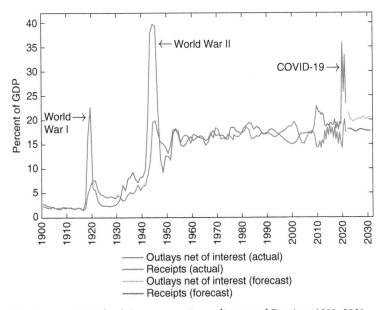

FIGURE 10.2. US Federal Government Expenditures and Receipts: 1900–2031

Sources: *Annual Report of the Secretary of the Treasury on the State of Finances*, 1940 report (1900–40); Office of Management and Budget (1940–2011); *Monthly Treasury Statement* (2011–22); *Interest Expense on the Debt Outstanding*. The forecasts of revenues and outlays for 2022–31 are computed using Congressional Budget Office forecasts, adjusted by the authors.

- Perhaps the most striking feature of this figure is the three spikes in expenditures for World War I, World War II, and COVID-19. While expenditures rose sharply during these wars, tax revenues rose by only a fraction of the total expenditures on the war. This pattern suggests that those wars were partly financed by interest-bearing debt and base money. For COVID-19, tax revenue barely budged, indicating that nearly all war costs were covered by the issuance of interest-bearing debt and base money.

- Immediately after World War I and World War II, both expenditures and tax revenue fell, but notably, after both wars, the government ran primary surpluses, implying that a portion of the wartime debt was repaid quickly. For the post–COVID-19 period, we anticipate a decade of primary deficits—not surpluses. The four major federal spending packages of 2020 and 2021 in response to COVID-19 authorized increases in spending for the next several years.[1] The gold and purple lines plot our forecasts of outlays and tax revenues for the next ten years based on Congressional Budget Office (CBO) projections. In sharp contrast to the post–World War I and World War II periods, in the post-COVID period, outlays are expected to exceed tax revenue for at least ten years.

- After World War I and World War II, expenditures fell, but they did not fall back to their prewar levels. Thus, the government grew as a share of GDP after each war. Based on CBO projections of spending and GDP growth, we anticipate the same after the war on COVID-19.

- Finally, note that the federal government's response to the Great Recession of 2008 looks similar in magnitude as a share of GDP to its response to the Great Depression in the 1930s.

As we noted in figure 10.2, each of these three world wars was financed in part by issuing interest-bearing debt. In figure 10.3, we

---

1. The CARES Act (signed into law on March 27, 2020); The Consolidated Appropriations Act, 2021 (signed December 27, 2020); The American Rescue Plan (signed March 11, 2021); and The Infrastructure Investment and Jobs Act (signed November 15, 2021).

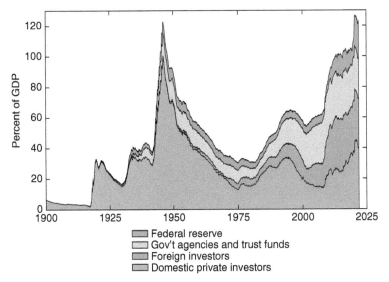

FIGURE 10.3. Par Value of US Treasury Debt by Ownership as a Percent of GDP: 1900 to 2021

Sources: US Treasury Monthly Statement of Public Debt; Federal Reserve Holdings of Treasury securities are from the Federal Reserve System Open Market Account (SOMA). Foreign holdings of US Treasury securities are from the Department of the Treasury's Treasury Bulletin (1939–99); and Treasury International Capital System (2000–21).

plot US Treasury debt as a percentage of GDP and decompose it by ownership. In all three of these wars, Treasury debt increased dramatically and quickly. But the ownership of the debt varied considerably across World War I, World War II, and COVID-19. During World War I, nearly all of the debt was held by domestic private investors (in blue). Fast-forward to 2021—as a very rough approximation—about a fifth of the debt is held by the Federal Reserve (in purple); about a fifth is held by government agencies and trust funds (in yellow); about a quarter is held by foreign investors (in brown); and about a third is held by domestic private investors. Today, a wider range of investors hold the debt than in previous wars.

Table 10.1 reports some of the numbers behind the data plotted in figure 10.3. As noted by other authors in this volume, in 2020 and

TABLE 10.1. Treasury Debt Ownership at Starts and Ends of Three Wars

	World War I		World War II		COVID-19	
	1914:5	1918:12	1939:9	1945:12	2019:12	2021:12
Federal Reserve	$0	$0.3115	$2.80	$19.41	$2,303.5	$5,580.0
	+0.312		+16.61		+3,276.5	
Gov't Agencies	0	0.1070	6.55	31.88	6,030.9	6,473.5
and Trust Funds	+0.107		+25.33		+442.6	
Foreign	—	—	—	2.40	6,844.2	7,739.4
Investors					+895.2	
Domestic	1.1893	20.6574	31.51	224.42	8,045.2	9,824.3
Private Investors	+19.468		+192.91		+1,779.1	
Total	$1.1893	$21.0759	$40.86	$278.11	$23,223.8	$29,617.2
	+19.887		+237.25		+6,393.4	

Sources: US Treasury Monthly Statement of Public Debt; Federal Reserve Holdings of Treasury securities are from the Federal Reserve System Open Market Account (SOMA). Foreign holdings of US Treasury securities are from the Department of the Treasury's Treasury Bulletin (1939–99); and Treasury International Capital System (2000–21).

Notes: The debt is measured at its par value in billions of nominal dollars. The number below and center is the change in the debt holding for each ownership class. Treasury records on holdings by foreign investors begin December 1939.

2021, the Treasury issued about $6.4 trillion in new debt. How did this debt get absorbed? The Federal Reserve increased its holding of US Treasury debt by about $3.3 trillion, or 51% of the increase in total debt outstanding. Domestic private investors increased their holdings by about $1.8 trillion, or about 28% of the total increase in US Treasury debt.

Next, we turn to the Federal Reserve System. During all three of these wars, the Federal Reserve supported the US Treasury market, and as a consequence of this support, expanded its balance sheet. In figure 10.4 we display the balance sheets of the Federal Reserve with assets on the left and liabilities on the right.

Panels 4a and 4b report the Fed balance sheet during the period around World War I. The first thing to note is that the balance sheet expanded dramatically during the war. The Federal Reserve did purchase Treasury securities outright, chiefly the Liberty Loans. In

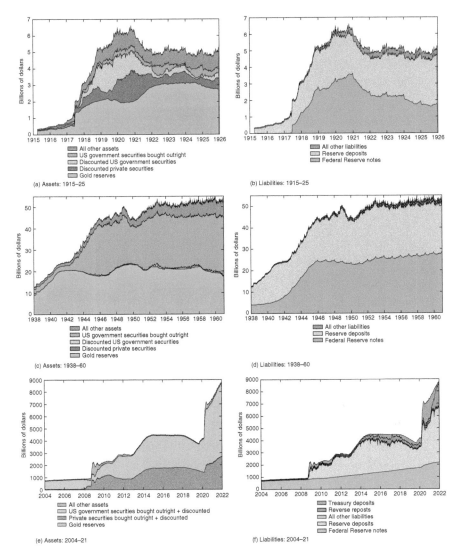

FIGURE 10.4. Federal Reserve Balance Sheets during Three Wars

Source: Tables of assets and liabilities of the twelve Federal Reserve Banks reported in each issue of the *Federal Reserve Bulletin* and the Federal Reserve's H.4.1 statistical release, "Factors Affecting Reserve Balances of Depository Institutions and Condition Statement of Federal Reserve Banks."

the asset graph, these purchases are denoted by the green area, but note this green area is quite small. The primary way that the Federal Reserve supported the US Treasury market was by making loans to banks at preferred interest rates. If those loans were used to purchase Liberty Loans, the Fed would hold those Liberty Loans as collateral on its balance sheet. The yellow area in the asset panel denotes these bonds held as collateral.

How did the Federal Reserve raise the funds to make these loans? On the liability side of its balance sheet, we see that currency outstanding (in green) rose, as did bank reserves at the Federal Reserve (in yellow). Of course, currency plus reserves is the monetary base. So the answer is: by expanding the monetary base.

During World War II, the Federal Reserve purchased US Treasury securities outright on a large scale. These purchases are depicted by the green area of the panel 4c. As a consequence of the Treasury's wartime policy of a fixed upward-sloping yield curve during World War II, private investors perceived little or no interest rate risk. Hence, private investors largely concentrated their purchases in longer-term notes and bonds. This left the Federal Reserve to concentrate most of its holdings in short-term treasury bills and certificates of indebtedness.

Again how did the Fed pay for its support of the Treasury market? As before in World War I, looking at the liability side of the balance sheet in panel 4d we see increases in both currency outstanding (in green) and bank reserves at the Federal Reserve (in yellow).

As others at this conference have noted and as we have discussed above, the Federal Reserve in 2020 and 2021 purchased $3.3 trillion in US Treasury securities (in green) and purchased over $1 trillion in private assets, primarily mortgage-backed securities (in brown), as shown in panel 4e. How did the Fed pay for these purchases? Once again, by increasing currency (in green) and by increasing bank reserves at the Federal Reserve (in yellow) as denoted in the panel 4f. But unlike the two world wars, the Fed also issued reverse repurchase agreements (in red) partly to increase liquidity in key markets, particularly the money market mutual fund market.

There are two other differences between the COVID-19 and World War II periods. First, during the current COVID-19 period, much of the Fed's holdings were weighted toward the longer-term notes and bonds. In contrast, during World War II, the Fed's holdings were concentrated mainly in shorter-term securities. Second, since 2008, the Federal Reserve has paid interest on bank reserves and the reverse repurchase agreements (reverse repos). So we ask whether we should include these bank reserves and reverse repos as part of the money supply or whether they belong as part of the interest-bearing debt of the federal government?

The analytical core of our paper is a decomposition of revenues for the three world wars. Before doing this decomposition, we make adjustments to the Treasury data to bring it in line with economic theory. The first adjustment is to net out debt held by the Federal Reserve and government agencies. That is, we want to record just the debt owned by private investors, both domestic and private. The second adjustment is to measure the debt at its market value instead of its par value. In figure 10.5 we plot the market value of the Treasury debt held by private investors as a share of GDP (in blue) and the corresponding par value (in red). These two series track each other quite closely, but they deviate at times of fiscal stress.

We note again that since 2008, the Fed has paid interest on bank reserves and reverse repos. If we add those two private sector claims on the Fed to our stock of interest-bearing debt, we get the green line. Interestingly, this summation brings the debt to GDP ratio to nearly 100%. Of course, the Fed used some of these bank reserves to purchase private assets; subtracting these asset purchases from the total debt yields the series plotted in light blue.

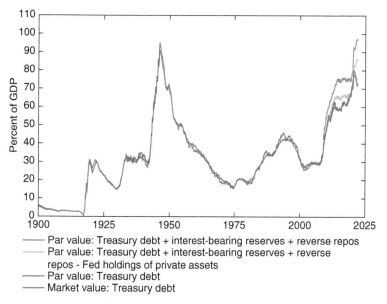

FIGURE 10.5. Par and Market Values of US Federal Debt Held by Domestic Private Investors and Foreign Investors as Percentages of GDP: 1900 to 2021

Sources: (1900–60) Hall et al. 2018; (1960–2021) CRSP US Treasury Database and the US Treasury Monthly Statement of Public Debt. We measure reserves balances and reserve repo agreements using the balances reported in the Federal Reserve's H.4.1 statistical release, "Factors Affecting Reserve Balances of Depository Institutions and Condition Statement of Federal Reserve Banks."

Notes: From October 2008 to December 2021, the green line plots the sum of the par value of privately held Treasury debt and interest-bearing reserves and reverse repos at the Federal Reserve. The light blue line subtracts the Federal Reserve's holdings of private assets from the sum reported in the green line.

Our third adjustment is to interest payments. Instead of using the accounting measure reported by the federal government, we measure interest payments by the ex post holding period returns earned by bondholders to take into account the capital gains and losses that John Cochrane discussed earlier this morning (in his conference presentation).

Our revenue decomposition is based on the period-by-period consolidated government budget constraint stated in equation 1.

On the left side of this equation are expenditures; on the right side are revenues.

$$G_t + r_{t-1,t}^B B_{t-1} + (A_t - A_{t-1}) = T_t + (B_t - B_{t-1}) + r_{t-1,t}^A A_{t-1} \\ + (M_t - M_{t-1}) + OM_t \qquad (1)$$

where

G_t = Government outlays (net of official interest payments)

B_{t-1} = Nominal market value of interest-bearing government debt held by private investors at the end of $t-1$

$r_{t-1,t}^B$ = Nominal value-weighted holding period return on government debt between $t-1$ and t

A_t = Private assets purchased by the Federal Reserve

$r_{t-1,t}^A$ = Nominal holding period return on Fed-held private assets between $t-1$ and t

T_t = Tax receipts

M_t = Federal Reserve credit

OM_t = Funding by other means

Funding by other means includes dollar deposits with and letters of credit to the IMF, changes in special drawing rights certificates issued to Federal Reserve Banks, and net activity of various loan financing activities.

We divide each term in equation 1 by nominal GDP and rearrange the term. Doing so yields equation 2:

$$\frac{G_t}{Y_t} + \left(r_{t-1,t}^B \frac{B_{t-1}}{Y_{t-1}} - r_{t-1,t}^A \frac{A_{t-1}}{Y_{t-1}} \right) + \left(\frac{A_t}{Y_t} - \frac{A_{t-1}}{Y_{t-1}} \right)$$

$$= \frac{T_t}{Y_t} + \left(\frac{B_t}{Y_t} - \frac{B_{t-1}}{Y_{t-1}} \right) + \frac{M_t - M_{t-1}}{Y_t} + \frac{OM_t}{Y_t} + g_{t-1,t} \frac{B_{t-1} - A_{t-1}}{Y_{t-1}}$$

$$+ \pi_{t-1,t} \frac{B_{t-1} - A_{t-1}}{Y_{t-1}} + (\pi_{t-1,t} + g_{t-1,t}) \left(r_{t-1,t}^B \frac{B_{t-1}}{Y_{t-1}} - r_{t-1,t}^A \frac{A_{t-1}}{Y_{t-1}} \right) \quad (2)$$

where $g_{t-1,t}$ denotes the net growth rate of real GDP and $\pi_{t-1,t}$ denotes the net inflation rate. As before, expenditures are to the left of the equal sign and revenues are to the right.

For each term in equation 2, we compute the average of the five years of observations before the war and use this value as a counterfactual; that is, it is our estimate of what the series would have been had the war not occurred. We call this the "peacetime baseline." We then sum up the differences between the observed series and the peacetime baseline. We do this term by term for every term in equation 2.

Table 10.2 reports the results of this decomposition. Consider World War I. The decomposition finds that for the two years that the United States was involved in World War I, it spent 36.93% of a single year's GDP on the war. It paid its bondholders 3/10 of 1% of a year's worth of GDP. The US also purchased private assets of 16/100 of one percent of a year's worth of GDP, bringing the total cost of the war to 37.39% of a year's worth of GDP. How did the US government pay for this? We decompose revenue raised into tax revenue, debt growth, money growth, GDP growth, inflation, and everything else. The terms in columns (5) through (10) add up to 37.39.

It may be more intuitive to look at the second row for each war, which reports the revenue sources as percentages of the total. How did the US finance its spending on World War I? The answer is 20.8% through raising taxes; 74.3% through issuing interest-bearing debt; and 6.9% through increases in the monetary base, with a residual of −2.0% explained by the remaining terms.

For the war on COVID-19, the US government spent 21.37% of a year's worth of GDP to fight the virus in 2020 and 2021.[2] The government paid its bondholders 2/10 of 1% of a year's worth of GDP, and the Federal Reserve purchased the assets of 5.85% of a

---

2. This represents actual spending—not just the authorizations.

TABLE 10.2. Decomposition of Wartime Revenues from Equation (2)

War			(1)	(2)	(3)	(4)	(5)	(6)	(7)	(8)	(9)	(10)
Start	End		Government spending	Payouts on net debt	Asset pur- chases	(1) + (2) + (3)	Tax revenue	Debt growth	Money growth	GDP growth	Inflation	Other
World War I												
1917:4	1918:11		36.93	0.30	0.16	37.39	7.76	27.79	2.59	0.03	0.68	-1.46
							20.8	74.3	6.9	0.1	1.8	-3.9
World War II												
1941:12	1945:8		116.48	2.00	—	118.48	35.80	54.53	11.96	8.99	6.05	1.14
							30.2	46.0	10.1	7.6	5.1	1.0
COVID-19												
2020:1	2021:12	reserves ⊂ M	21.37	0.22	5.85	27.45	0.95	-0.59	25.16	1.02	3.03	-2.12
							3.5	-2.2	91.7	3.7	11.0	-7.7
2020:1	2021:12	reserves ⊂ B	21.37	0.17	5.85	27.40	0.95	18.36	5.07	1.48	3.99	-2.45
							3.5	67.0	18.5	5.4	14.6	-8.9

Sources: See figures 10.2, 10.3, 10.4, and 10.5 for the World War I and World War II periods. Federal Reserve credit is the sum of bills discounted, bills bought, United States government securities bought outright and discounted, deposits in foreign banks, industrial and commercial loans, municipal warrants, and Federal Reserve bank float. For the COVID period, Federal Reserve credit is the sum of Bills Discounted and US Treasury Securities held by the Fed. For a more complete discussion of this measure, see Section 2 of the Data Appendix in Hall and Sargent (2022). The Federal Reserve policy rates are from https://www.federalreserve.gov/monetarypolicy/reserve-balances.htm.

Notes: For each war, the elements in the first row are in percent of GDP. Columns 5–10 sum to column 4. The numbers in the second row are percentages of the sum of war-related spending, net debt payments, and purchases of private assets (column 4) accounted for by each term on the right side of equation (2). Column 10 is the sum of other means, the cross product, and a residual. See the appendix for the definition of M.

year's worth of GDP. Summing these terms brings the total cost of the war to 27% of a year's worth of GDP.

How did the government pay for this spending? Increased tax revenue made up a mere 3.5% of the war payments. Debt growth is negative. Why is this? In the five years prior to COVID-19, the federal government ran large deficits, issuing debt that was primarily purchased by private investors rather than the Federal Reserve. The decomposition expects that this trend would have continued had COVID-19 not occurred. Thus, the decomposition implies that nearly all of the cost of COVID—91.7%—was financed by money growth.

As we noted earlier, some of the components of this newly created "money" paid interest, so we repeat the decomposition counting bank reserves at the Federal Reserve and the reverse repos as part of the stock of interest-bearing debt. If we do so, we shift about 70% of the revenues from the money growth category to interest-bearing debt. Thus, the cost of this most recent war was split: 3.5% by tax revenue, 67% by interest-bearing debt, and 18.5% by money growth.

Comparing the revenue decomposition across all three wars, we see that increases in tax revenues covered 20.8% of the cost of World War I, 30.2% of the cost of World War II, and only 3.5% of the war on COVID-19. Money growth covered 6.9% of the cost of World War I, 10.1% of the cost of World War II, and 18.5% of the cost of the war on COVID-19.

What impact did this money growth have on prices? In figure 10.6 we plot the log of the consumer price index (CPI) normalized to be 0 at the start of each war. Looking at the red line, we see that six years after the start of World War I, the CPI was 70% higher than it was in 1914. Then the US experienced two years of deflation. But by eight years after the war, the price level was still 55–60% higher than it was at the start of the war.

For World War II, we see a similar pattern. Prices rose early in the war, but price and wage controls dampened rates of increase in

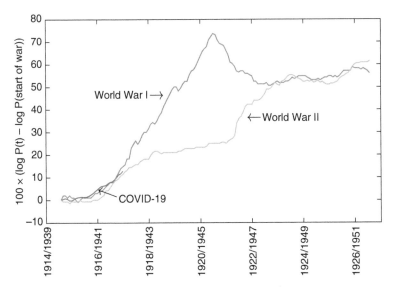

FIGURE 10.6. Natural Log of the Price Level during and After World War I, World War II, and the War on COVID-19

Source: BLS, Consumer Price Index for All Urban Consumers, Not Seasonally Adjusted, from FRED.

Notes: This figure displays $100 \times (logP_t - logP$ start of war), where P_t is the CPI for All Urban Consumers. Ticks on the x-axis correspond to January for the 1914 to 1926 period and March for the 1939 to 1951 period. For the COVID-19 war, the series begins January 2020 and ends May 2022.

the CPI. When the federal government lifted these controls in 1946, prices jumped. As was the case after World War I, eight years after the war, the price level was 55–60% higher than before the war. Today, we have only two years and five months of price data for the war on COVID-19 period. But prices during this period, plotted in blue, track the price increases from two previous wars.

How did bondholders do after each war? Not well. In figure 10.7 we plot the real (inflation-adjusted) value of $100 invested in a representative value-weighted portfolio of US Treasury securities in which the coupon and principal payments are continually reinvested. The red and gold lines represent the values of this representative portfolio during and after World War I and World War II, respectively.

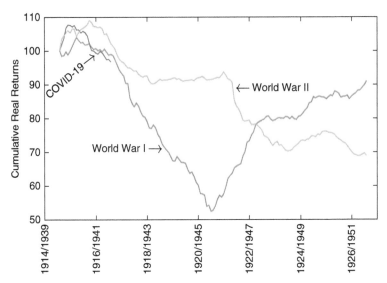

FIGURE 10.7.   Real Values of $100 Portfolio of Treasury Securities Invested at the Start of World War I, World War II, and the War on COVID-19

Sources: See figures 10.5 and 10.6.

Notes: This figure reports the cumulative real values coming from continually reinvesting in a value-weighted re-balanced portfolio of all outstanding US Treasury securities of an initial investment of $100 at the start of each war. Ticks on the x-axis correspond to January for the 1914 to 1926 period and March for the 1939 to 1951 period. For the COVID-19 period, the series begins January 2020 and ends December 2021.

Both lines are near mirror images of the normalized price levels plotted in figure 10.6. Six years after the start of World War I, the value of that portfolio was 50% of what it was at the beginning of the war.[3] During and after World War II, once again, bondholders did poorly. Price controls mitigated these losses, but bondholders received a large capital loss once price controls were released. As John Cochrane pointed out at the conference, these losses were transfers from the bondholders to the taxpayer. The blue line represents the value

---

3. One of those bondholders was Army Captain Harry Truman. He never forgot these losses. One of the reasons why the Korean War was tax financed was that President Harry Truman argued that wartime inflation was due to "our failure to tax enough." (Truman 1951).

of the representative portfolio during the war on COVID-19. In the two years since this war began, the portfolio's value tracked the values during the previous two world wars.

MORE HISTORY

In the remainder of this chapter, we describe historical precedents that shaped how twentieth-century policy makers framed decisions. Responses to the enormous disruptions associated with World War I did not start from a blank slate. Decision makers remembered how governments had coped during earlier wars, for example, in the United Kingdom during and after the wars from 1792 to 1815 against France, and in the United States during and after the Civil War. Those experiences had shaped a conventional wisdom about how to finance wars and how to manipulate returns on government debts through price level adjustments that could be engineered by temporarily suspending convertibility of government notes into gold but eventually resuming convertibility at prewar rates of exchange. Thus, an issue that confronted many countries after World War I was how to reconstruct a prewar gold standard. That same problem had also been faced in the nineteenth century. UK monetary-fiscal authorities after 1815 had awarded high real returns to government creditors by presiding over a fall in the price level sufficient to allow the Bank of England in 1821 to make its notes convertible into gold once again at the same rate that had been maintained before convertibility was suspended in 1797. US monetary-fiscal authorities did something similar after the US Civil War ended in 1865. Greenback dollars issued by the Union during the dark days of the Civil War at big discounts relative to gold dollars were ultimately made convertible into gold one-for-one starting in January 1879. Authors of these policies wanted wartime suspensions of convertibility to be temporary because they wanted markets to infer that future suspensions would also be temporary. Subsequent monetary and fiscal decision makers praised those episodes for fostering expectations among creditors that public debts would be honored, thus enhancing the marketability of public debts and providing future government officials opportunities to borrow at the low interest rates brought about by low default probabilities.

Digging deeper reveals that post–US Civil War debt repayment and currency policies emerged only after bitterly contested political struggles that had pitted the interests of government creditors against the interests of both taxpayers and the private borrowers who had issued bonds dominated in paper units of account. Those disputes probably taught post–World War I policy makers that the foundations of the conventional wisdom were fragile and subject to substantial political risks.

Various conference participants raised questions about how a monetary authority, or consolidated fiscal-monetary authority, acquires credibility. The idea that a government earns a reputation as a trustworthy creditor by honoring promises to award high returns to government creditors has been treated well by modern theories of how sovereign debts are valued and optimally managed. Theories of sovereign and domestic government debts are driven by assumptions about consequences of paying and defaulting, consequences that are affected by feedback on how government deficits are chosen. Outcomes hinge on assumptions regarding consequences of defaults and about incentives to repay.

DISTINGUISHING BETWEEN MONEY AND BONDS

Since the beginning of the Republic, US policy makers have thought hard about how to design evidences of federal debt. Attitudes about "bonds versus money" evolved during the first century under the Constitution of 1789, as conflicting interests and theories interacted with a string of experiences. These formed the background

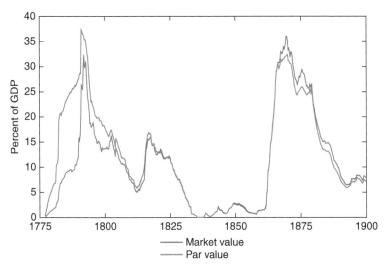

FIGURE 10.8. Par and Market Values of Treasury Debt Held by Private Investors
Source: Hall et al. 2018.
Note: Excludes bonds issued to Pacific Railway Companies.

for policy debates that were precursors to contemporary discussions of whether and how to pay interest on reserves. A fascinating drama unfolded entailing actions designed at first to poison, then to restore, and ultimately to sustain expectations that the US federal government's paper IOUs were as good as gold.[4]

As a preview of the outcomes, notice the large gaps between the market and par values of US government debt plotted in figure 10.8. Starting in 1775 with the issuance of the Continental Government's Loan Office Certificates until the end of James Madison's administration in 1817, US government debt traded at a deep discount relative to its par value. Further, note that beginning in the late 1860s, the market value of the debt *exceeded* the par value. Now contrast the large deviations between the market and

---

4. At the conference, Patrick Kehoe and Elena Pastorini wanted evidence about the social process that allows a monetary-fiscal authority to acquire and sustain a reputation.

par values observed in the eighteenth and nineteenth centuries with the relatively minor deviations observed in the twentieth century plotted in figure 10.5.

In 1790, the framers of the US federal government debated whether and how to discriminate the rates of return given to US creditors. James Madison wanted to allocate payoffs among current and former bondholders in ways that would withhold capital gains from more recent purchasers and compensate former holders who had experienced capital losses from selling their bonds. Alexander Hamilton (1790) opposed Madison's discrimination scheme because of its adverse effects on the expectations of prospective government creditors. Hamilton criticized Madison's proposal, first, because it would defeat Hamilton's goal of fostering a liquid market in US government bonds, and, second, because it would inappropriately reward former holders of government bonds who, by selling, had bet against the credit of the US; it would also unfairly punish current holders who, by buying, had expressed their confidence in US credit.

Hamilton won that argument, and Congress did not implement Madison's particular version of a discrimination scheme. But it did discriminate. In particular, in following Hamilton's recommendations about how to restructure US and state debts in 1790, Congress discriminated among creditor classes in ways that were designed to intentionally poison the US government's reputation for servicing some types of debt (the despised paper money known then as "bills of credit") while simultaneously enhancing its reputation for servicing other types of debt (interest-bearing medium- and long-term obligations, especially to foreign creditors).

US fiscal authorities' propensity to discriminate was destined gradually to diminish over time, a pattern revealed in how the United States financed its expenditures during the Revolutionary War, the War of 1812, and the Civil War. During all three wars, the federal government and the states issued debts that differed in their maturities, denominations, and units of account. A theoretical contribution of

Bryant and Wallace (1984) explains why federal and state governments might have wanted to award different rates of return to different classes of government creditors. Bryant and Wallace showed how such price discrimination can improve fiscal efficiency.

The units of account in which government debts can be expressed and enforced are central to a price-discrimination analysis of monetary and fiscal policy. Bryant and Wallace, in effect, assumed that a government can issue some securities that are expressed in a foreign government's unit of account or otherwise indexed against domestic inflation, and that it can issue other securities that are not.

Whether units of account should be arranged in this way is an issue that underlies a fascinating story, namely the evolution of US government officials' opinions about whether they should, or even legally could, issue small denomination zero-interest notes (paper money) and whether they should declare those notes legal tender for public and private debts. James Madison thought that making paper money a leading tender was reprehensible, while Ulysses S. Grant thought that it was useful. But making US paper money a legal tender meant something different to James Madison in 1787 or 1813 than it did to Ulysses S. Grant in 1869. In 1787 and 1790, issuing paper money portended depreciation and repudiation. In 1869 and 1870, when the Congress and the president took actions to make US-issued paper money as good as gold, paper money meant appreciation and resumption.

We can summarize the main features of this story as follows. The US Constitution prohibits states from issuing bills of credit; during the 1790s, federal issues of bills of credit, though not explicitly prohibited, were widely regarded as bad. There was also a broad sentiment against making anything other than specie a legal tender. Madison thought that denying legal tender status to government-issued paper money was a good way to limit its capacity to damage credit markets. Alexander Hamilton's restructuring of federal and state government's debt harshly discriminated against continental bills of credit. That saved federal tax revenues. And by impairing their reputation, it also had the salutary effect of discouraging future issues of federal bills of credit.

Despite that history, on February 25, 1862, the Union made greenbacks a legal tender for all private debts and some public obligations, an act hotly disputed at the time.[5] In 1869 the Supreme Court declared the act that made greenbacks a legal tender unconstitutional. Soon thereafter, President Grant appointed two new justices who concurred in the court's quick reversal of that earlier decision, thereby affirming that the federal government was empowered to make a paper fiduciary currency a legal tender. Instead of unleashing an era of high inflation fueled by government printing of paper money, President Grant and the Congress presided over an appreciation of the greenback that awarded people who held them higher returns than those who, when Union Armies had suffered setbacks, had speculated against the greenback. In 1790, people deplored federal paper money as "not worth a continental"; after 1879, people trusted greenbacks to be small-denomination warehouse certificates for gold. Reputational considerations were very much on the minds of public officials in both periods.

Tax Smoothing

We received questions about how our analysis relates to leading "tax smoothing" models. Our figure 10.2 prompted such questions because it reminded some conference participants of a computer simulation of a Barro (1979) tax smoothing model. Figure 10.9 confirms that nineteenth-century US observations look like that too. This pattern reflects that Secretary of the Treasury Albert Gallatin (1837) can be credited as an early co-author of the Barro model, and that subsequent administrations and Congresses adhered to Gallatin's advice.

---

5. See Lowenstein (2022).

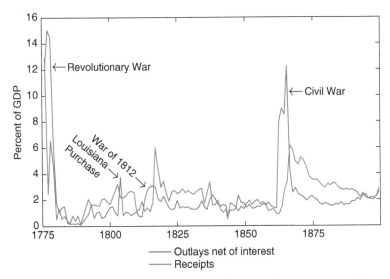

FIGURE 10.9. US Federal Government Expenditures and Receipts: 1775–1900
Source: *Annual Report of the Secretary of the Treasury on the State of the Finances*, 1940.
Notes: Outlays are net of official interest payments. During the Civil War, GDP includes the Confederacy.

Hamilton (1790) and the Congress rescheduled Continental and state obligations in ways that they hoped would give the federal government sustained access to domestic and international credit markets. That would expand the Federal government's subsequent options for financing temporary surges in government expenditures by borrowing, thereby allowing it to moderate the contemporary tax increases needed to finance those surges. This part of Federalist policy was embraced and extended by the Jefferson administration when it took office in 1801. In his 1807 report to Congress, Secretary of the Treasury Albert Gallatin (1837) used a line of reasoning that contains all of the components of a normative model of fiscal policy later formalized in models of Barro (1979) and Aiyagari et al. (2002). Gallatin's report recommended that tax rates should be set to "provide a revenue at least equal to the annual expenses on a peace establishment, the interest on the existing debt, and the interest on the loans which may be raised . . . losses and privations caused by war should not be aggravated by taxes beyond what is strictly necessary." (Gallatin 1837). Thus, Gallatin proposed that the best way to pay for a surge in government expenditures would be temporarily to borrow during the surge, to increase taxes permanently by enough to service the resulting debt, and after the expenditure surge had ended, to run a net of interest surplus sufficiently large to roll over the debt. Like Hamilton, Gallatin's presumption was that the debt would surely be serviced as promised, and that a good fiscal policy would adjust net of interest surpluses required to service the debt to smooth tax distortions over time.

US fiscal authorities embraced Gallatin's model throughout the nineteenth century. Gallatin and his successors presumed, and wanted markets to presume, that US government debts would always be paid in a timely manner; they promoted expectations that no circumstances would be offered as excuses for failures to pay. Essentially, they proposed to use risk-free government debt to smooth tax distortions across time, and they sought to sustain a reputation that their debt would be risk-free. They would smooth tax distortions across contingencies only to the extent that risk-free debt allowed them effectively to "self-insure" fluctuating government expenditures.

TO BUY INSURANCE AGAINST
EXPENDITURE RISK OR SELF-INSURE?

Some conference participants asked us about the applicability of the Lucas and Stokey (1983) model. In the representative agent Ramsey models of Lucas and Stokey (1983) and Chari, Christiano, and Kehoe (1994), a government optimally finances a stochastic stream of exogenous government expenditures by trading state-contingent claims with the private sector. The government thereby enters into a complete risk-sharing scheme with the private sector that allows it to smooth tax distortions across time and across random histories of government expenditures. Lucas and Stokey (1983) and Chari, Christiano, and Kehoe (1994) show that if the government does not have access to complete insurance markets, but can issue only risk-free nominal bonds, then it can achieve the same equilibrium outcomes by using history-contingent inflation and deflation to award real capital losses and gains to holders of government bonds. Here, denominating risk-free bonds in a nominal unit of account, then making nominal values respond appropriately to random shocks to government expenditures, are parts of an optimal fiscal and monetary policy. Sims (2001) used this logic to argue against "dollarization" schemes because they prevent sovereign governments from reaping the benefits that flow from using inflation to award history-contingent returns to government creditors.

Early American policy makers did not see it Sims's (2001) way. Influenced by the repudiation of the Continentals, they saw inflation as a deplorable way of abrogating contracts, not implementing a well-understood risk-sharing scheme between the government and the private sector. For more than eighty years after 1790, most American statesmen denied that there were benefits to be reaped by denominating government debt contracts, and forcing citizens to denominate theirs, in a nominal unit of account other than specie. This drove their hostility to making a federal paper money a legal tender.

THE CIVIL WAR

Union expenditures during the Civil War were unprecedented, generating four years of budget deficits over 8% of GDP. See figures 10.9 and 10.10 and compare the magnitudes of the Civil War deficits to the 2% of GDP deficits during the War of 1812. In response to the sudden increase in needed funds, Secretary of the Treasury Salmon P. Chase initially relied heavily on short-term borrowing.

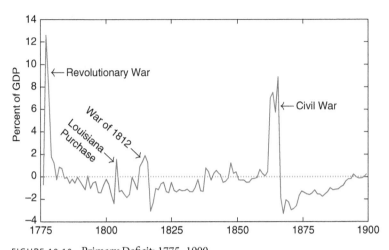

FIGURE 10.10. Primary Deficit: 1775–1900
Source: *Annual Report of the Secretary of the Treasury on the State of the Finances*, 1940.
Note: During the Civil War, GDP includes the Confederacy.

Much of this short-term debt was in the form of three-year "7-30s," Treasury notes paying an interest rate of 7.3%.[6]

In table 10.3 we repeat our revenue decomposition for the War of 1812 and the Civil War. During the Civil War, while the Treasury imposed a host of new internal taxes, including the first federal income tax, taxes only accounted for 6.8% of total expenditures. Increases in interest-bearing debt and money accounted for 59.6% and 19.6%, respectively. These proportions are remarkably similar

---

6. Remnants of hard money Jackson Democrats had long regarded the Whig Party as soft on paper money. Remnants of the Whig Party formed the backbone of the Republican party. Did this history bequeath a credibility problem to the new Lincoln administration in March 1861? Maybe. But, anticipating an idea of Rogoff (1985) that you can resist a temptation to inflate by strategically delegating monetary policy to an inflation hawk, Lincoln appointed as his secretary of the Treasury Salmon P. Chase, governor of Ohio, formerly a Jackson hard money Democrat and a future chief justice of the US Supreme Court. A decade later Chase would write the Supreme Court decision that declared unconstitutional Congress's 1862 action that awarded legal tender status to the paper money called greenbacks that he, as secretary of the Treasury, had issued to help pay for the war. The Congress had made them legal tender for all debts public and private, except payment of customs duties, the lion's share of federal revenues. The legal tender clause created many winners (debtors who owed dollars) and losers (creditors in dollars). See Lowenstein (2022) for much more about these events.

TABLE 10.3. Decomposition of Wartime Revenue: War of 1812 and the Civil War

War		(1)	(2)	(3)	(4)	(5)	(6)	(7)	(8)	(9)
		Government spending	Return on debt	Total spending	Tax revenue	Debt growth	Money growth	GDP growth	Inflation	Other
Start	End									
War of 1812										
1812:6	1815:2	7.34	-0.20	7.14	2.35	10.60	0.00	-0.16	0.06	-1.01
					-32.9	148.5	0.0	-2.2	0.8	-14.2
Civil War (Union)										
1861:4	1865:4	31.04	2.10	33.14	2.26	19.74	6.49	1.08	3.95	-0.37
					6.8	59.6	19.6	3.2	11.9	-1.1

Sources: See figures 10.8 and 10.9.

Notes: For each war, the elements in the first row are percentages of GDP. Columns 4–9 sum to column 3. The numbers in the second row are percentages of the sum of war-related government spending and returns to bondholders (column 3) accounted for by each term in 4–9. Peacetime baseline is the average value five years prior to the war.

to proportions for the financing of the war on COVID-19 reported in table 10.2.

To refinance these 7-30s into longer maturity securities, beginning in February 1862, the Congress authorized the Treasury to sell 5-20s, a bond redeemable in twenty years, but callable at par at the government's discretion in five years. (In effect, the Union government simultaneously borrowed and purchased a call option.) The 5-20s promised to pay interest in gold, but, in a masterpiece of ambiguity, were silent about whether the principle would be payable in greenbacks or in gold.[7] Uncertainty about the currency in which the principal of the 5-20s would be repaid was resolved only after a heated political debate after the war. It mattered whether they would be paid in gold or in greenbacks because prices denominated in greenbacks doubled during the Civil War. They receded enough from 1865 to 1879, that by 1879 the US could resume specie payments, de facto making the greenbacks warehouse certificates for a set quantity of gold. However, before the election of President Grant in November 1868, there was widespread doubt and debate about whether the principal owed to owners of 5-20s was due in paper or in gold. In June 1868, the 5-20s comprised 70.5% of the interest-bearing debt, and gold was trading at a 40% premium. The creation of the legal tender notes also created two types of debts: those promising to pay "lawful money" (i.e., greenbacks) and those promising to pay "coin" (i.e., gold). At its peak in September 1865, debt promising to pay in "lawful money" comprised over 54% of outstanding debt. During the War of Independence, the unit of account had been specie (Spanish dollars) and the paper money (the Continental currency) traded at a discount. However, from 1862 to 1879 prices for both goods and bonds (including those that promised to pay in coin) were quoted in "lawful money" (i.e., greenbacks) and gold dollars sold at a premium.

---

7. Lowenstein (2022) presents a fascinating account of the log-rolling process that designed the 5-20s. It sheds light on the political coalitions supporting many features of the 5-20s, but not the ambiguity about units of account for repayment of principal.

Rationalizing the 5-20s

We interpret the government's decision to issue 5-20s in the first place as indicating policy makers' wish to implement policies that would promote lower future interest rates on government debt. The 5-20s had a par value of 100, promised 6% coupons each year, matured after twenty years, and were callable at par at the government's discretion after five years. Wanting to raise large amounts, why would the Union sell a bond that involved simultaneously purchasing a call option? To understand the government's decision to issue 5-20s, it helps to posit heterogenous beliefs about future interest rates. If Union fiscal authorities imputed to most market participants different views about the likely future path of interest rates than theirs, then the call options associated with the 5-20s would have been a good buy for the Union government. Also, by buying a call option, the Union fiscal authorities could indicate to the market their intention to pursue continuation policies that would drive future interest rates lower than those forecast by the market, thereby rendering the call option more valuable than the market might otherwise have thought.

A persistent theme in US policy circles has been how to reduce interest paid on US government debt. Both sides of the late 1860s debate about whether to repay the principal on the 5-20s in paper or in gold could claim to advocate policies in the tradition of our first secretary of the Treasury. Hamilton (1790) had asserted that by restructuring the US debt as he had recommended, prospective interest rates on new issues of government debt would fall because default premiums would fall. But, by discriminating among government creditors, Hamilton had lowered interest rates in another sense, namely, by paying out substantially less to various classes of US creditors than had originally been promised. The magic that Hamilton's restructuring plan promised was that it would save money for US taxpayers by partially defaulting on some debts, while simultaneously promoting the prospect of lower default premiums on new and future issues of US government debt. That Hamilton managed that balancing act left room for advocates of very different debt management policies to claim that they were his true followers.

Thus, the Democrats and President Andrew Johnson meant one thing when they advocated reducing interest payments on the government debt, while the Republicans and Ulysses S. Grant meant something else. The Democrats wanted to reduce interest payments ex post by paying government creditors with a depreciated currency. By paying in gold, Republicans wanted to reduce risk premia on prospective issues of Federal debt, thereby reducing interest payments ex ante.

Deciding to repay the 5-20s in gold resulted in large real returns to bondholders. From 1869 to 1879 the real holding period returns to federal government creditors averaged 7.2% per year. Owners of the 5-20s received an average real annual return of 8.2% over this period. However, in contrast to Hamilton's refinancing in 1790, the high returns delivered to federal bondholders did not come at the expense of holders of paper money. Holders of non-interest-bearing "lawful money" legal tender notes and fractional currency saw the specie value of their assets appreciate through deflation. In June 1868, it took 140 greenbacks to buy 100 gold dollars. Five years later in 1873, the price had fallen to 116.5. In December 1878, greenbacks traded at par. In this way, the federal government "assumed" all of its promised obligations to holders of the greenbacks (see the above words of Calvin Coolidge). Contrast this "closing the gap" between market and par values to the persistent gap between the market and par values of the debt after Hamilton's 1790 rescheduling, summarized in figure 10.8 above.

Payne et al. (2022) argue that Hamilton's and Grant's strategy for reducing the cost of financing US Treasury debt succeeded. Over the nineteenth century, yields on US Treasury securities steadily declined, with the zero-coupon 10-year yield falling from 8% in 1800 to 2% in 1900. Further, prior to and during the Civil War, US

Treasury debt traded at a premium relative to UK debt, the "safe asset" of the era, but by the 1880s this risk premium had evaporated.

HISTORICAL FRAGMENT ABOUT PAYING INTEREST ON RESERVES

The Fed's policy since 2008 of paying interest on reserves, and now also on reverse repos, arose several times at the conference. Proposals to pay interest on reserves are interesting when viewed from perspectives supplied by nineteenth-century US proposals. As noted above, the framers of the US Constitution disapproved of any government's issuance of "bills of credit" that resembled money, either federal or state. So for them, proposals to pay interest on paper money were moot. An originalist and strict constructionists President Andrew Jackson and his successors Presidents Martin Van Buren and James K. Polk took steps to implement a 100% reserve regime: bank reserves were to be full-bodied gold and silver coins.[8] Paying nominal interest on those reserves was not on the table in that perfect commodity standard. But in the nineteenth century, whenever federal or state governments did issue paper money backed by fractional reserves, the issues about paying interest on money really lay close to the surface. This situation provoked the shifting opinions about exploiting gains from price discrimination among classes of government creditors that we have described above, and in more detail in Hall and Sargent (2014).

LEARNING FROM EXPERIENCE

Wartime surges in government expenditures have always provoked debates about how to pay for them. Those debates inspired classic theoretical contributions about the optimal mix of debt and taxes

---

8. See Rothbard (2002).

and whether the mix matters at all. The origin of theories of optimal tax-borrowing policies in those debates is an element of our defense against a charge of inappropriate presentism (interpreting the past from a perspective and with information not available to those who acted in history). Statesmen who made the tax and borrowing decisions studied here had purposes and theories in mind, intellectual forces that will be important parts of our story. Therefore, we are naturally ambivalent about whether the theories that guide our pattern recognitions are to be viewed as normative (how things should be) or positive (how things are). We use the theories both ways because key historical actors sometimes used them as rationalizations of their proposals. A poster child for this point of view is the coincidence of recommendations of the Barro (1979) model with Secretary of the Treasury Albert Gallatin's 1807 Report as well as subsequent actions of Gallatin and his successors.

For over two centuries, policy makers confronted their predicaments by combining their recollections of histories with their theories. They repeatedly struggled against the same forces. These include rollover risks associated with unanticipated changes in market conditions and interest rates that bedevil decisions about the maturity structure of debt being sold; issues about units of account in which to denominate coupon and principal payments; interactions between banking and fiscal policies; temptations to default; and issues forced on them by prospective government creditors, along with incentives to delay supplying credit in anticipation of better terms later.

We appreciate Gary Becker's (1962) view that constraints alone go a long way in explaining patterns in outcomes, regardless of decision makers' purposes or their rationality. When we spot differences across patterns of wartime financings, our theories naturally direct us to ask how much of these are to be explained by the decision makers' *purposes* or their *constraints* or their *theories*. Our research in Hall and Sargent (2021) described decision makers' evolving understandings. Thus, memories of how the Continental currency that had financed the War of Independence from Great Britain had eventually depreciated to one penny on the dollar convinced War of 1812 decision makers to take steps to avoid that outcome. Noncallable federal bonds issued to pay for the Mexican-American War appreciated in value after the war when interest rates fell, creating ex post regrets that the bonds had not been bundled with call options, something that the Union would do early in the Civil War. As we noted in figure 10.7, rising prices and thus rising nominal interest rates after World War I delivered nominal capital losses to owners of the Liberty Bonds that had been used to finance the war, teaching Captain Harry Truman a lesson that he would remember when, as president, he insisted the Treasury and Federal Reserve manage interest rates after World War II to prevent that from happening again. In Hall and Sargent (2021) we described many other instances of later statesmen learning from what came to be recognized as mistakes during past wars. Prevailing understandings evolved about how government securities should be designed and marketed; about types of taxes to be imposed; and about the roles of the legal restrictions such as price controls and portfolio restrictions recommended by Keynes (1940) and formalized by a theory of Bryant and Wallace (1984).[9]

In most wars, we see evidence of Gallatin-Barro tax smoothing (i.e., taxes responding much less than one-for-one with spending), but only during the Civil War and the war on COVID-19 do we actually see a close approximation to the split between taxes and debt that the model recommends for a purely temporary expenditure surge. We also see negative wartime bond returns followed by positive postwar returns in the War of 1812, the Civil War, and World War I as prescribed by the Lucas-Stokey model (see

---

9. Statisticians tell us that the only things we can learn about are parameters of a necessarily restricted model, so perhaps it is excusable that we see successive government authorities processing information about past government expenditure surges in order to modify and refine their theories.

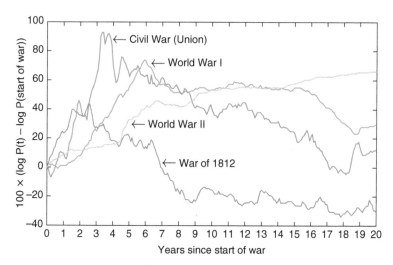

FIGURE 10.11. Natural Log of the Price Level during and after the War of 1812, the US Civil War, World War I, and World War II

Sources: Warren-Pearson Index, US Census Bureau (War of 1812 and Civil War); BLS, Consumer Price Index for All Urban Consumers, Not Seasonally Adjusted, from FRED (World Wars I and II).

figures 10.11 and 10.12). But as John Cochrane noted at the conference, this model directs that bondholders should receive an immediate capital loss at the outbreak of a war. To implement that Lucas-Stokey recommendation, there had to be a sufficiently large outstanding stock of debt at the time of the wartime surge in government spending. As shown in figures 10.5 and 10.8, the US had little debt at the start of the Civil War and World War I. Thus for these wars, the Lucas-Stokey action would not help the government's financial situation. In various episodes, Hall and Sargent (2021) discusses how Congress and Treasury secretaries experimented and innovated with various debt designs and management policies to induce potential investors to purchase bonds early in wars despite fears of wartime capital losses.

From observations before the war on COVID-19, we think that we detected some notable patterns. As table 10.4 reports, from the

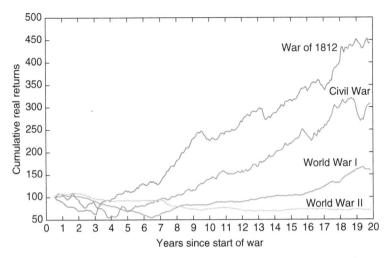

FIGURE 10.12. Real Values of $100 Portfolio of Treasury Securities Invested at the Start of the War of 1812, the US Civil War, World War I, and World War II
Sources: See figures 10.8 and 10.11.

TABLE 10.4. How US Paid for Five Wars as Percentages of Total Revenues

	Taxes	Bonds	Money
War of 1812	−32.9	148.5	0
Civil War	6.8	59.6	19.6
World War I	20.8	74.6	7.0
World War II	30.2	46.0	10.1
COVID-19	3.5	67.0	18.5

Source: Data repeated from tables 10.2 and 10.3.

War of 1812 to World War II, the US financed larger shares of wartime spending with taxes and smaller shares with debt. This trend did not continue for COVID-19. Seigniorage contributed a significant share of revenue in the Civil War, World War I, World War II, and the war on COVID-19. Over time, postwar real returns paid to bondholders have declined. After four major wars, the War of 1812, the Civil War, World War I, and World War II, average annual returns to bondholders were 12.0%, 8.5%, 5.5%, and −1.4%, respectively.

A BROADWAY MUSICAL?

THOMAS JEFFERSON (STANDING NEXT TO JAMES MADISON):
  But Hamilton forgets
His plan would have the government assume state's debts
Now, place your bets as to who that benefits
The very seat of government where Hamilton sits

. . .

ALEXANDER HAMILTON: If we assume the debts,
the Union gets new line of credit, a financial diuretic. How do
  you not get it?
If we're aggressive and competitive, the Union gets a boost.
You'd rather give it a sedative?

—Lyrics from "Cabinet Battle #1,"
Hamilton: An American Musical[10]

At the conference, Michael Bordo stressed that it mattered that the US was on a limping gold-exchange standard during World Wars I and II, while during COVID-19, links of the US dollar to gold had been completely severed. An important aspect of our account of pre-1900 US fiscal-monetary policies was a struggle about how firmly to link various types and denominations of federal government debts to gold. Perhaps parts of our story could inspire a Broadway musical "Madison" that rewrites a conventional wisdom encoded in the Broadway hit *Hamilton* in a way that presents a less confused Madison and a subtler Hamilton.

Thus, Hall and Sargent (2014) offers a provocative revisionist interpretation of the first 100 years of US government finance.

---

10. CABINET BATTLE #1 (from *Hamilton*). Words and Music by LIN-MANUEL MIRANDA, CLIFTON CHASE, EDWARD FLETCHER, MELVIN GLOVER and SYLVIA ROBINSON. © 2015 5000 BROADWAY MUSIC and SONGS OF UNIVERSAL INC. All Rights on behalf of 5000 BROADWAY MUSIC Administered by WC MUSIC CORP. All Rights Reserved. Used by Permission of ALFRED MUSIC.

A conventional wisdom sees Alexander Hamilton as a paragon of financial responsibility who in 1790 promoted US credit by executing an honorable and credit-enhancing rescheduling of debts incurred during the American Revolution. In doing that, Hamilton received little help from a less economically knowledgeable James Madison, who had advocated a misdirected discrimination scheme for tampering with payouts to US creditors, a scheme that would have permanently damaged US credit. But if we judge Hamilton and Madison by the actions over which they presided, a different picture emerges.

It was Hamilton who presided over widespread discriminations and repudiations, though perhaps he repudiated less than had been expected during the 1780s, undoubtedly earning him substantial gratitude from 1780s speculators in some US and state debts, but not in others (purchasers of those forlorn Continentals). It was James Madison who during the War of 1812 presided over an administration that declined to make short-term US debt a legal tender and, at the end of the war, awarded positive returns to holders of short-term US debt. Despite considerable difficulty in selling interest-bearing debt, in financing the War of 1812 the US government refrained from using that mainstay of government finance during the American Revolution, the inflation tax. That established precedents that influenced how Ulysses S. Grant and the Republican party chose to complete Union policy for financing the Civil War. Andrew Johnson and other late 1860s advocates of ex post *lowering* interest payments to Union creditors could have appealed to Alexander Hamilton's discriminatory haircuts as antecedents; but they wanted to repudiate the precedent set by the high returns paid out by the Madison administration and its immediate successors.

Of course, our revisionist history omits as much as it includes. The Madison administration faced different constraints and opportunities than did the Washington-Hamilton administration in 1790. The US was bigger and wealthier in 1812. And as a result of how markets interpreted what Washington and Hamilton had done, the US in 1812 faced reputations vis-à-vis its prospective creditors that differed from those that had confronted the Washington administration in 1790.

More generally, from the observations that we have surveyed here we can gather five enduring lessons:[11]

1. The ability of a government to borrow today depends on expectations about future tax revenues.
2. Free-rider problems exist for subordinate governments vis-à-vis a central government.
3. Good reputations can be costly to acquire.
4. Sometimes, it can help to sustain distinct reputations with different parties.
5. Confused monetary-fiscal coordination creates costly uncertainties.

References

Aiyagari, S. Rao, Albert Marcet, Thomas J. Sargent, and Juha Seppala. 2002. "Optimal Taxation without State-Contingent Debt." *Journal of Political Economy* 110, no. 6 (December): 1220–54.

Barro, Robert J. 1979. "On the Determination of the Public Debt." *Journal of Political Economy* 87, no. 5 (October): 940–71.

Becker, Gary S. 1962. "Irrational Behavior and Economic Theory." *Journal of Political Economy* 70, no. 1: 1–13.

Bryant, John, and Neil Wallace. 1984. "A Price Discrimination Analysis of Monetary Policy." *Review of Economic Studies* (Oxford University Press) 51, no. 2: 279–88.

Chari, V. V., Lawrence J. Christiano, and Patrick J. Kehoe. 1994. "Optimal Fiscal Policy in a Business Cycle Model." *Journal of Political Economy* 102, no. 4 (August): 617–52.

Coolidge, Calvin. 1922. Address on the anniversary of the birthday of Alexander Hamilton, before the Hamilton Club, at Chicago. January 11.

---

11. Versions of these lessons were also stated in Sargent (2012, 3–4).

Gallatin, Albert. 1837. "Report on the Finances 1807." *Reports of the Secretary of the Treasury of the United States* Vol. 1, 360. Washington, DC.

Hall, George J., Jonathan Payne, Thomas J. Sargent, and Bálint Szőke. 2018. "US Federal Debt 1776–1940: Prices and Quantities." https://github.com/jepayne /US-Federal-Debt-Public.

Hall, George J., and Thomas J. Sargent. 2014. "Fiscal Discriminations in Three Wars." *Journal of Monetary Economics* 61, no. C: 148–66.

———. 2019. "Complications for the United States from International Credits: 1913–1940." In *Debt and Entanglements between the Wars*, edited by Era Dabla-Norris. International Monetary Fund Chapter 1, 1–58.

———. 2021. "Debt and Taxes in Eight US Wars and Two Insurrections." In *The Handbook of Historical Economics*, edited by Alberto Bisin and Giovanni Federico Academic Press Chapter 27, 825–80.

———. 2022. "Three World Wars: Fiscal and Monetary Consequences." *Proceedings of the National Academy of Sciences* 119, no. 18: e2200349119.

Hamilton, Alexander. 1790. "Report on Public Credit." Presented to Congress on January 9.

Hansen, Lars Peter. 2012. "Dynamic Valuation Decomposition Within Stochastic Economies." *Econometrica* 80, no. 3 (May): 911–67.

Hansen, Lars Peter, and Jos A. Scheinkman. 2009. "Long-Term Risk: An Operator Approach." *Econometrica* 77, no. 1 (January): 177–234.

Keynes, John Maynard. 1940. *How to Pay for the War: A Radical Plan for the Chancellor of the Exchequer*. London: Macmillan and Co.

Lowenstein, Roger. 2022. *Ways and Means: Lincoln and His Cabinet and the Financing of the Civil War*. New York: Penguin Press.

Lucas, Robert Jr., and Nancy L. Stokey. 1983. "Optimal Fiscal and Monetary Policy in an Economy without Capital." *Journal of Monetary Economics* 12, no. 1: 55–93.

Payne, Jonathan, Bálint Szőke, George J. Hall, and Thomas J. Sargent. 2022. *Costs of Financing US Federal Debt: 1791–1933*. New York University.

Rogoff, Kenneth. 1985. "The Optimal Degree of Commitment to an Intermediate Monetary Target." *Quarterly Journal of Economics* 100, no. 4 (November): 1169–89.

Rothbard, Murray N. 2002. *A History of Money and Banking in the United States: The Colonial Era to World War II*. Auburn, AL: Ludwig von Mises Institute.

Sargent, Thomas J. 2012. "Nobel Lecture: United States Then, Europe Now." *Journal of Political Economy* 120, no. 1: 1–40.

Sims, Christopher A. 2001. "Fiscal Consequences for Mexico of Adopting the Dollar." *Journal of Money, Credit and Banking* 33, no. 2: 597–616.

Truman, Harry. 1951. "Text of Truman's Message to Congress Asking for $10 Billion in New Taxes." *New York Times*, February 3.

DISCUSSANT REMARKS

Ellen R. McGrattan

An important question in public finance is how best to finance unanticipated emergency government spending needs. The prime example is war financing, but recent experience has highlighted the fact that there are other kinds of emergencies that also necessitate large temporary increases in government spending. Hall and Sargent do not answer the question of how to do this optimally, but they do lay out a strong case that the COVID-19 experience shares many features with the two world wars of the twentieth century.

In my discussion, I revisit two questions that are central to their paper. First, is a pandemic akin to battling a world war? I argue that there are some important differences that Hall and Sargent do not discuss that lead me to conclude that it is not like a world war. Second, who will pay? Like Hall and Sargent, I cannot answer this, because only time will tell us. But I will dig a little deeper into the "who": namely, which taxpayers and bondholders have been bearing the burden of US public financing.

IS COVID-19 LIKE A WORLD WAR?

For many analyzing budgets of the US government, figure 10.13 provides smoking-gun evidence that the pandemic was a world war–like event. The figure shows the federal primary deficit— that is, the gap between federal spending and revenues, excluding interest payments—as a percentage of gross domestic product (GDP). In figure 10.13, two lines are plotted: one for the annual data, in dark blue, and one for quarterly data, in light blue. These lines are hard to distinguish until the end, when quarterly spending increased midyear 2020 and decreased midyear 2021 at the same time that GDP fell.

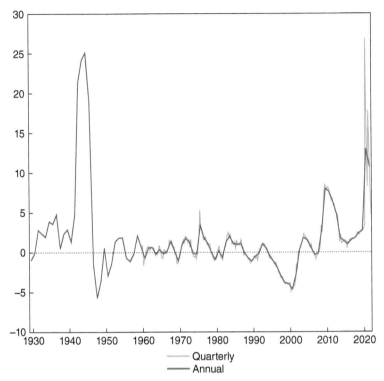

FIGURE 10.13. Primary Deficit as Percentage of GDP

Source: National Income and Product Accounts (NIPA), Bureau of Economic Analysis, US Department of Commerce. Included in NIPA are detailed government expenditures and receipts—both federal and state and local—compiled consistently back to 1929.

There is no argument that government spending greatly exceeded receipts during the pandemic. After all, figure 10.13 is simply a summary of NIPA data. However, in my view, this figure masks important differences between wars and pandemics. To address this, I will depart from Hall and Sargent in two ways. First, I will put greater focus on the spending needs during the periods of the world wars and the more recent pandemic period (2020–21). Second, I will avoid dividing government budget items by US GDP, given there are large expansions during world wars and large contractions during pandemics. I will instead analyze the

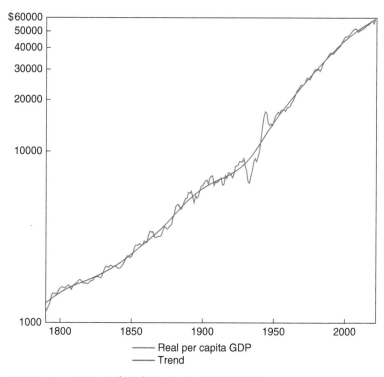

FIGURE 10.14. Historical Real Per Capita GDP (2012$)
Source: NIPA.

budget constraint after dividing by the trend in US GDP, displayed
in figure 10.14.

Figure 10.14 shows the historical real per capita GDP series over
the period 1790–2021 that Hall and Sargent use in their analysis. I
plot this on a log scale so that the fluctuations are visible. The second line in the graph is the time trend that I will use for detrending
all historical time series. This trend is constructed by applying a
very low-frequency filter.[1] Figure 10.15 shows the ratio of the two
lines and gives a graphical sense of output fluctuations over much
of the history of the United States. Not surprisingly, the prominent

---

1. I should note that the issues I raise below are not overturned by using alternative
low-frequency filters.

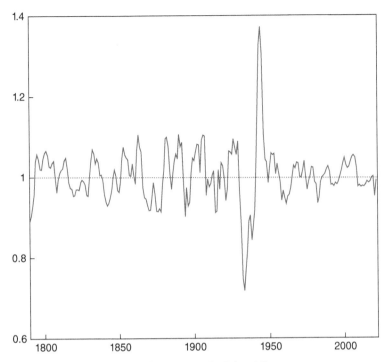

FIGURE 10.15. Detrended Real Per Capita GDP (2012$)
Source: NIPA.

episodes are the Great Depression of the 1930s and World War II
in the first half of the 1940s. Less prominent are World War I and
the pandemic, which are of shorter duration.

In figure 10.16, I plot the detrended real per capita GDP series
from figure 10.15, along with two measures of government spending
over the period 1929–2021.[2] To construct the detrended real, per capita spending measures, I first divide the relevant nominal spending
series by the GDP deflator to get a measure of real spending. I then
divide by the population (available in NIPA, table 2.1). Finally, I divide
the spending measures by the trend in figure 10.13. The nominal

2. Since the BEA data are revised regularly back to 1929, I compare only World War II with
the COVID-19 "war." Better measures of spending are needed to do the relevant comparison
with World War I.

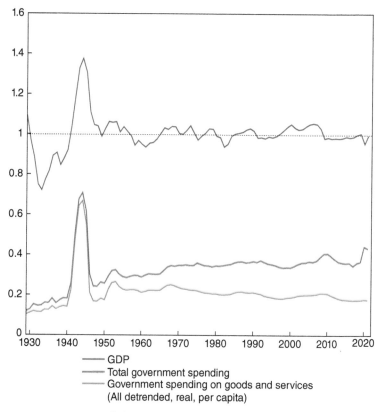

FIGURE 10.16. Detrended GDP and Spending (2012$)
Source: NIPA.

series underlying government spending on goods and services is the purchase of goods and services at the federal, state, and local levels. The nominal series underlying total government spending is the total purchase of goods and services at all levels of government plus interest payments, current and capital transfers, and subsidies.

In table 10.5, I reproduce the nominal BEA series from the NIPA tables that underlie the spending series during World War II and break out items relevant to the war. The spending is shown in billions of US dollars but can be easily converted to the deflated, per capita estimates used in figure 10.16 (and later). For example,

TABLE 10.5. Government Receipts and Expenditures, 1940–46 (Billions$)

	1940	1941	1942	1943	1944	1945	1946
TOTAL EXPENDITURES	20.5	32.4	70.5	103.6	115.9	107.6	62.4
Consumption expenditures	11.1	17.0	36.5	58.1	70.5	71.1	38.3
Of which:							
National defense	2.0	8.0	27.1	48.7	60.5	60.8	25.3
Current transfer payments	2.4	2.3	2.4	2.0	2.7	5.5	12.4
Of which:							
Veterans' benefits	0.5	0.5	0.5	0.5	0.9	2.8	5.3
Interest payments	1.7	1.8	2.1	2.9	3.6	4.5	5.6
Subsidies	0.7	0.5	0.5	0.6	1.0	1.1	1.4
Capital transfer payments	0.0	0.0	0.0	0.0	0.0	0.0	0.0
Gross government investment	4.4	10.8	29.0	39.9	38.2	25.3	4.7
Of which:							
Defense	0.8	7.4	26.4	38.1	36.8	24.0	2.7
Defense structures	0.6	3.6	10.3	5.8	2.5	1.7	0.3
Defense equipment	0.2	3.6	15.7	31.5	33.0	21.0	1.2
Defense IPP	0.0	0.2	0.4	0.7	1.3	1.3	1.2
TOTAL RECEIPTS	17.1	24.3	31.8	48.2	50.1	52.2	51.3
Current tax receipts	14.3	21.0	27.8	43.2	44.3	45.2	43.1
Contributions, social insurance	1.9	2.3	2.9	3.8	4.3	5.3	6.6
Income receipts on assets	0.1	0.1	0.1	0.1	0.1	0.1	0.1
Current enterprise surplus	—	—	—	—	—	—	—
Current transfer receipts	0.3	0.3	0.4	0.5	0.6	0.7	0.5
Capital transfer receipts	0.5	0.5	0.6	0.6	0.7	0.8	0.9

Source: NIPA.

Notes: Total expenditures include consumption of fixed assets and exclude net purchases of nonproduced assets. Veterans' benefits include pension, disability, and life insurance. Subsidies and current surplus of government enterprises not shown separately prior to 1960.

given the GDP deflator is equal to 9.5% at the peak of the war, we can convert the estimates into 2012 dollars by first dividing by the deflator and then dividing by the population of roughly 138 million to get an estimate for the per capita real spending. In other words, the $116 billion nominal total expenditures in 1944 is roughly equal to per capita spending of $8,800 in 2012 dollars, and the $50 billion nominal total receipts is equal to per capita revenues to the government of $3,800 in 2012 dollars. There are several note-worthy features of these spending measures. First, at the peak of the war, 86% of consumption expenditures and 96% of government investment expenditures were made on behalf of national defense. Current transfer payments are a minor category of spending that start to grow steadily only after the war. Half of the 1946 estimate is transfers to veterans. Also growing throughout the war are net interest payments.

Figure 10.17 shows the major categories of spending—all detrended, real, and per capita. This figure gives a good sense of the history of government spending since 1929. Wars—including World War II, the Korean War, and the Vietnam War—are times of elevated spending on goods and services. The pandemic is not. In table 10.6, I reproduce the nominal BEA series from the NIPA tables that underlie expenditure measures during the recent pandemic. As before, I report expenditures and receipts in billions of US dollars and break out categories relevant to the emergency spending. The last available data are from first quarter of 2022. In the case of the COVID-19 pandemic, there are twenty-two subcat-egories of spending listed that relate to different programs.

Programs that directly affect the accounting of government expenditures are included in four spending categories, namely, consumption expenditures, current transfer payments, subsidies, and capital transfer payments. One of the largest payouts of the Coronavirus Aid, Relief, and Economic Security (CARES) Act was

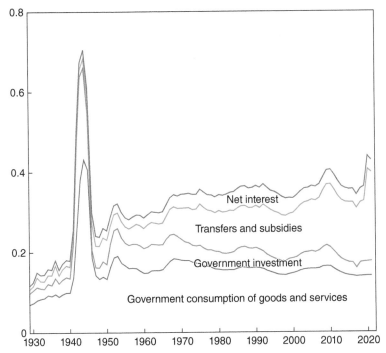

FIGURE 10.17. Detrended Spending and Components (2012$)
Source: NIPA.

the Paycheck Protection Program (PPP), which provided forgivable loans for small businesses and nonprofit institutions to help cover their payroll and other expenses during the pandemic. These payments show up as transfers to nonprofits and subsidies to businesses. PPP payments were also made to lenders to administer the loans and show up as government consumption of financial services. According to BEA estimates, the total funding for PPP was $726 billion over two years.

Another large spending initiative under the CARES Act was the Economic Impact Payments, which provided direct payments to eligible individuals. These transfers totaled $848 billion over two years.

TABLE 10.6. Government Receipts and Expenditures (Billions$)

	2019	2020	2021	2022 Q1
TOTAL EXPENDITURES	7,874	9,746	10,051	8,827
Consumption expenditures	2,974	3,078	3,250	3,375
Of which:				
Paycheck Protection lender fees	—	18	17	0
Current transfer payments	3,157	4,266	4,620	3,919
Of which:				
Paycheck Protection, NPISH	—	41	13	0
Economic Impact Payments	—	276	572	0
Provider Relief Fund	—	89	60	114
Coronavirus Relief Fund	—	150	246	1
Education Stabilization Fund	—	15	66	72
Lost Wages Supplement	—	36	1	0
Expansion of UI programs	—	395	293	3
Child Tax Credit	—	—	128	106
Increase in Medicare rates		10	14	15
Interest payments	890	829	807	845
Subsidies	73	761	493	150
Of which:				
Paycheck Protection, business loans	—	411	226	0
Provider Relief Fund for business	—	38	26	32
Coronavirus Food Assistance Program	—	20	6	1
Economic Injury Disaster Loans	—	20	7	2
Employees Retention Tax Credit	—	55	63	0
Tax credits to fund paid sick leave	—	105	8	0
Grants to air carriers	—	20	22	0
Restaurant Revitalization Fund	—	—	29	0
Support for public transit	—	15	14	20
Capital transfer payments	26	16	70	17
Of which:				
Emergency rental and homeowners	—	—	51	0
Gross government investment	740	782	802	825
Net purchases of nonproduced assets	14	14	9	−305
TOTAL RECEIPTS	5,919	5,926	6,691	7,424
Current tax receipts	4,055	4,021	4,623	5,217
Of which:				
Aviation Tax Holiday	—	−13	0	0
Contributions for social insurance	1,427	1,464	1,597	1,705
Income receipts on assets	207	216	236	269
Of which:				
Student Loan Forbearance	—	−30	−38	−38
Current surplus of government enterprises	−13	−17	−13	−14
Current transfer receipts	223	216	215	214
Capital transfer receipts	22	26	32	33

Source: NIPA.

Note: Total expenditures include consumption of fixed assets.

The Provider Relief Fund (PRF) has been supporting transfers and business subsidies—to date totaling $359 billion—to hospitals and health care workers treating uninsured individuals. The Education Stabilization and Coronavirus Relief Funds have provided $397 billion and $153 billion, respectively, in grants-in-aid to states and local governments for schools and other local needs during the pandemic.

A supplement of $37 billion drawn from the Disaster Relief Fund was paid by the Federal Emergency Management Agency (FEMA) for wages deemed "lost" in the pandemic. In addition to the new transfer programs, existing ones were expanded. There was an expansion of unemployment benefits and child tax credits, which increased current transfer payments. During 2021 and 2022:Q1, child tax credits were increased to $3,600 per child for children under age six and $3,000 per child between ages six and seventeen, which led to increases in current transfer payments. Reimbursement rates for Medicare service providers was also increased, which resulted in additional transfers of $39 billion over the period reported.

In addition to PPP and PRF subsidies, other subsidies to businesses were granted during the pandemic. The Coronavirus Food Assistance Program provided $27 billion in subsidies to farmers and ranchers impacted by supply chain disruptions. The Economic Injury Disaster Program provided $29 billion in loans to small businesses and nonprofit organizations experiencing a temporary loss of revenue. Tax credits totaling $231 billion were offered for employee retention and to fund sick leave.

There were also targeted subsidies in some sectors. Air carriers received grants totaling $42 billion. The Restaurant Revitalization Fund provided $29 billion in subsidies to owners of food and beverage–related industries including bars, restaurants, and their suppliers. The CARES Act provided $25 billion to state and local transit agencies.

Pandemic-related programs also affected capital transfers in which payments are made for liabilities incurred for services in earlier periods. In this category, the BEA includes the Emergency

Rental Assistance Program and the Homeowner Assistance Fund, both of which provided assistance for rental arrears and delinquent mortgage payments. To date, the government has spent $51 billion on this program.

Given the remarkable number of programs initiated during 2020–22, one can get lost in the weeds, and thus it helps to recap the clear message that the facts convey. The main spending of World War II was purchases of goods and services by the military. The spending was temporary—lasting four years. The main spending of the pandemic is in the form of new transfers and subsidies—to lots of different recipients—and expansions of some existing programs. Importantly, some of this spending will be hard to discontinue. Estimates in table 10.6 will be updated as new data are compiled by the BEA.

The more important data that has yet to be compiled is the eventual funding sources. I turn to this next.

WHO WILL PAY?

In figure 10.18, I plot total spending and total receipts. With total spending, I include net interest payments and gross government investment.[3] (See tables 10.5 and 10.6 for the underlying BEA data during World War II and the recent pandemic.) As is clear from the figure and tables, there is a significant and persistent funding gap. The only emergency provisions are noted in table 10.6, namely, the Aviation Tax Holiday, which lowered revenues by $13 billion in 2020, and the Student Loan Forbearance, which suspended interest payments on certain federally held student loans until August 2022. According to BEA estimates, the latter program costs roughly $38 billion annually in lost revenue.

---

3. If I were to include *net* government investment instead, then consumption of government fixed assets must be subtracted.

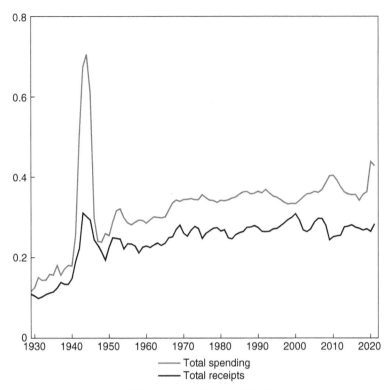

FIGURE 10.18. Detrended Spending and Receipts (2012$)
Source: NIPA.

Figure 10.19 shows the history of total receipts, by funding source. The figure shows that individual income and corporate taxes rose considerably during World War II, but as figure 10.18 makes clear, these tax receipts do not come close to funding the war. Sales and property taxes change little and, if anything, property taxes fall relative to trend during the 1940s and remain at that lower level after that. Over time, with corporations able to relocate production abroad and with a rise in pass-through business activity, the corporate income tax funding has diminished while individual income taxes have risen as a share of receipts. But, here again, the receipts are still far too low to cover the spending.

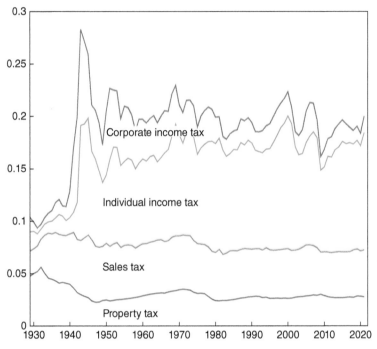

FIGURE 10.19. Detrended Receipts and Components (2012$)
Source: NIPA.

As a result, federal debt levels have soared. In figure 10.20, I plot total debt, debt held by private investors—both foreign and domestic—and debt held by foreigners. All series are in real, per capita terms and have been divided by the GDP trend level shown in figures 10.13 and 10.14. A value of 1 here means a real, per capita level of debt that is equal to real, per capita GDP. The figure makes clear that while foreign holdings of US debt have been rising over time, there is significant debt held domestically. Figure 10.21 provides a breakdown of these holdings. In this case, the data are reported in trillions of dollars (without any detrending) over the period 2011–21. The foreign holdings rise from a little under $5 trillion to $7.5 trillion. The net largest holder are mutual funds, which held little in 2011 but grew their positions

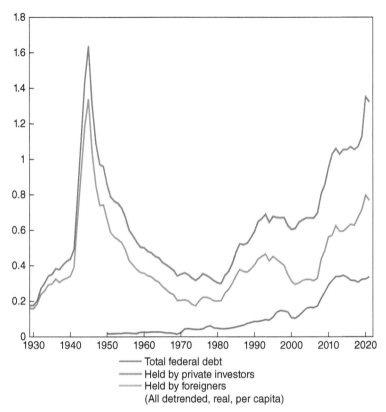

FIGURE 10.20. Detrended Federal Debt and Components (2012$)
Source: *US Treasury Bulletin.*

to $3.5 trillion. Adding banks, governments, pension funds, and insurance companies to this sum, we have another $4.5 trillion in 2021.

Financing the pandemic spending through an effective default on the federal debt—say, because inflation is now on the rise—will be difficult since so much debt is held domestically. Financing the pandemic with higher current taxes will be difficult given the "no new taxes" climate that has persisted for decades. That leaves the usual plan of action: ever-increasing debt levels and higher taxation on future generations.

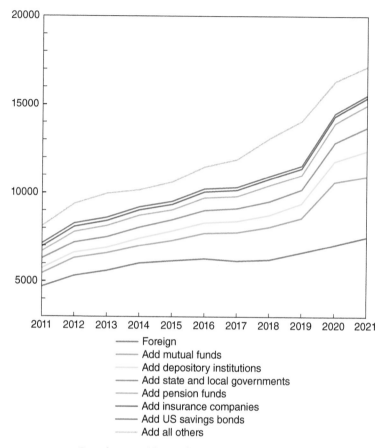

FIGURE 10.21. Cumulative Holdings of Federal Debt (Current$)
Source: *US Treasury Bulletin.*

NEXT STEPS

An interesting next step of the Hall Sargent research program is to work out optimal tax policy responses in the case of a war and in the case of a pandemic. Given the different spending requirements, I would be interested to know if the policy prescription is the same, regardless of the type of crisis.

GENERAL DISCUSSION

JOHN LIPSKY (INTRODUCTION): Something we do frequently is to think back to past occurrences and try to derive lessons that help illuminate our choices today. Of course, this is what historians do as a career. And, all of us, presumably, are guided in such endeavors by Mark Twain's notion that history doesn't repeat itself but that it often rhymes. And today, we are fortunate to be joined by two very distinguished poets of economics, who are going to examine aspects of the two world wars of the twentieth century to see if it is possible to derive some useful comparisons applicable to the COVID-19 pandemic. And that explains the title of the presentation we're about to hear: "World Wars: Fiscal-Monetary Consequences."

The presenters are—first—Professor George Hall from Brandeis. He is a professor of economics and also in the International Business School, and whose work focuses on fiscal policy and debt management, firm inventory investment and dynamic pricing, and business cycle dynamics. His coauthor is Professor Tom Sargent, the W. R. Berkley Professor of Economics and Business at NYU and a senior fellow here at Hoover. I presume that Professor Sargent is well known to this audience. After all, he was awarded a Nobel Prize in 2011. Moreover, his Wikipedia entry states that he is the twenty-ninth-most-cited economist in the world. George Hall is going to present the paper. Following the presentation will be comments by Professor Ellen McGrattan, who is a professor of economics at the University of Minnesota and also the director of the Heller-Hurwicz Economics Institute. Professor McGrattan's research is concerned with the aggregate effects of monetary and fiscal policy on GDP, investment, equity markets, and international capital flows.

*   *   *

JAMES BULLARD: I just have a question for the authors. The Barro literature would say that when you have a big expenditure that you have to make, maybe you should borrow and smooth the taxes. It looks like in these graphs that the US government did not impose a lot of taxes at the time. Is your gut instinct that this looks like optimal tax smoothing in which the inflation tax could be part of that optimal tax smoothing? Or is there some sense where there's faulty policy going on here?

KRISHNA GUHA: Thank you. I'm Krishna Guha with Evercore Partners. So I just wanted to ask the authors what relationship, if any, they established between the ways in which the wars were paid for and these big price level shifts that you observe at least in the historic episodes? Then relatedly, when we look at the current episode, and you're sort of looking at whether to classify the interest-bearing federal liabilities as part of consolidated government debt in effect, or as part of money, what are you left with? Are you assigning some special inflationary quality to what you're left with and calling money being the non-interest-bearing liabilities? Are you viewing it in a different way?

MICHAEL BORDO: World War I and less so World War II were fought in an environment where the gold standard prevailed. Under the gold standard the price level was anchored by the commitment mechanism of the fixed gold peg. Bordo and Kydland (1996) viewed the gold standard as a contingent rule which allowed temporary departures from gold parity to finance wars. Tax smoothing, as followed by the UK and the US, was complimentary to the gold standard. In the COVID-19 episode, the world was not on the gold standard, but the price level was supposedly anchored by credible central banks committed to low inflation. However with the current surge in inflation, the nominal anchor under the present regime may not be as credible or durable as under the gold standard. Would not this influence the debt dynamics?

WILLIAM NELSON: Thank you, Bill Nelson, Bank Policy Institute. George, just a factual question. So I've always thought of currency as being determined by demand and largely independent of anything that the Fed does or the rest of its balance sheet. And you see, in fact, the growth in currency undisturbed through the COVID event. But in both of the world wars, currency rises sharply. So, could you explain how that comes about?

ROBERT HALL: One of the jobs of the Fed is to keep currency and reserves on par with each other. So there's no independent control of their quantities. The Fed buys and sells currency in order to maintain exact parity. So, we shouldn't be talking about any buying or selling the Fed does separately. The Fed cannot determine either one of the components but only the sum. The price remains exactly the same. And changes in demand, therefore, show up as changes in quantities and not in price.

JOHN COCHRANE: Thanks, this was great. I want to bring us back a little bit to the topic of the conference and inflation. The big question is, of course, to what extent did this inflation look like the last one? There's a story that you finance wars with a Lucas-Stokey state-contingent default via inflation. That story is going around about COVID: "Don't worry about this inflation. It comes out of the pockets of the bondholders, and it's the right thing to do to finance a once-in-a-lifetime emergency with a once-in-a-lifetime state-contingent default via inflation." But there's a big puzzle here: That's supposed to happen at the *beginning* of the war, not at the *end* of the war, because if people see it coming, they don't take the bonds in the first place. So it's quite a puzzle that our pattern seems to be: sell bonds to unsuspecting people and then whack them three years afterwards with big inflation. Why don't people see it coming and refuse to buy the bonds?

Now on to Ellen's big question, which is the larger fiscal question facing us: Who's going to pay? You both pointed to the ongoing structural deficits due to entitlements. How does that work out? I'm not so sanguine as Ellen. First of all, how much high-income taxpayers could possibly bear it is an interesting question. The all-in marginal tax rate on the top end in California is over 70%. There is a Laffer curve out there somewhere; I don't know how much you can raise that. So middle-class taxpayers will bear the brunt, as they do in Europe, if that's the route it's going to go. Inflation is attractive, default on the debt through inflation. But as you're both pointing out, the problem is not so much the past debt, the problem is the ongoing and future surpluses. And default does nothing to solve that. Indeed it makes the problem worse. Default, or inflate. Now, where are we going to borrow that trillion bucks a year that we need to keep borrowing? There is also one option you didn't mention: spending. It has to be either taxes, default, inflation, or cutting spending. It's not so obvious to me that individual income taxes will just float up to solve the difference.

PATRICK KEHOE: I would like to follow up on what John Cochrane said. We heard a lot about the implications of the Barro tax-smoothing result. The Lucas-Stokey tax-smoothing paper also has implications for what John said. It would be useful to use that model as the baseline and see how much the historical events you study differ from the basic Lucas and Stokey prescriptions. That is, we could ask, Did the United States do a poor job on how we levied taxes in these periods? Or did we follow the Lucas-Stokey prescription of how a government should pay less to bondholders during the war and then pay more after the war? That is the interesting twist. It's not just did we tax-smooth as in the Barro prescription, it's did we find a way to pay less on debt during the war and more after the war ended? That'd be an interesting paper for you to follow up with: Take the simple Lucas-Stokey idea on how it is optimal to have contingent payments on the bonds—low during the war and high after the war—and see if actual policies essentially mimicked that pattern. We touched on it, but it'd be interesting if you could keep going with that idea.

Toward a Monetary Policy Strategy

CHAPTER ELEVEN

IS THE FED "BEHIND THE CURVE"? TWO INTERPRETATIONS

James Bullard

US inflation is exceptionally high, comparable to what was experienced in 1974 and 1983. Standard Taylor-type monetary policy rules, even if based on a minimum interpretation of the persistent component of inflation, still recommend substantial increases in the policy rate. This provides one possible definition of "behind the curve," and indicates the Fed is far behind.

However, all is not lost. Modern central banks are more credible than their 1970s counterparts and use forward guidance. Credible forward guidance means market interest rates have increased substantially in advance of tangible Fed action. This provides another definition of "behind the curve," and the Fed is not as far behind based on this definition.

CORE INFLATION IS COMPARABLE TO 1974 AND 1983

Core personal consumption expenditures (PCE) inflation from one year earlier was 5.2% in March 2022, which is the most recent reading as of this writing. There have been two other times since 1960 when this measure of inflation has been close to this level. One was 1974, and the other was 1983 (figure 11.1).

The 1974 Federal Open Market Committee (FOMC), which was looking at a core PCE inflation rate similar to today's, liked to talk

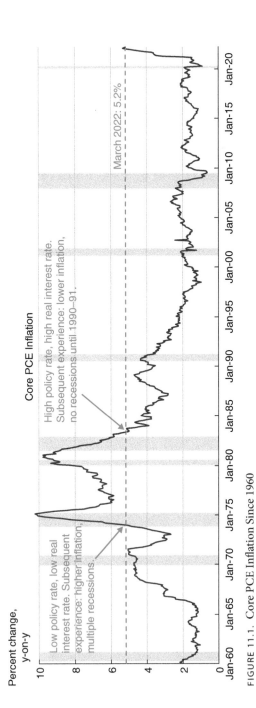

Percent change, y-on-y

Core PCE Inflation

Low policy rate, low real interest rate. Subsequent experience: higher inflation, multiple recessions.

High policy rate, high real interest rate. Subsequent experience: lower inflation, no recessions until 1990–91.

March 2022: 5.2%

FIGURE 11.1. Core PCE Inflation Since 1960

Source: Bureau of Economic Analysis (BEA).

Note: The gray shaded areas indicate US recessions. Last observation: March 2022.

about nonmonetary factors affecting inflation. The FOMC kept the policy rate relatively low in the face of rising inflation. The associated ex post real interest rate was relatively low. The subsequent experience was that core PCE inflation was above 5.2% for nearly ten years. The real economy was also volatile with multiple recessions.

The 1983 FOMC, which was also looking at a core PCE inflation rate similar to today's, had a different approach to monetary policy and spoke more about monetary factors affecting inflation. The FOMC kept the policy rate relatively high in the face of declining inflation. The associated ex post real interest rate was relatively high. The subsequent experience was that core PCE inflation was below 5.2% for the next ten years. The real economy also stabilized with no recession until 1990–91.

The contrast between the 1974 and 1983 experiences convinced many that it was important to avoid getting "behind the curve" on inflation.

FIRST INTERPRETATION OF "BEHIND THE CURVE"

The Fed has a statutory mandate to provide stable prices for the US economy. Associated with this mandate is an inflation target of 2%, stated in terms of the headline PCE inflation rate, which was 6.6% in March 2022, measured from one year earlier (figure 11.2). Because of particularly large movements in recent food and energy prices, some may argue that the Fed should consider the core PCE inflation rate instead, which, as we have seen, is currently 5.2%. Still others might argue that the truly persistent factors driving inflation are better captured by the Dallas Fed trimmed mean inflation rate, which was 3.7% in March 2022, measured from one year earlier.[1]

---

1. For more on inflation persistence, see Almuzara and Sbordone (2022).

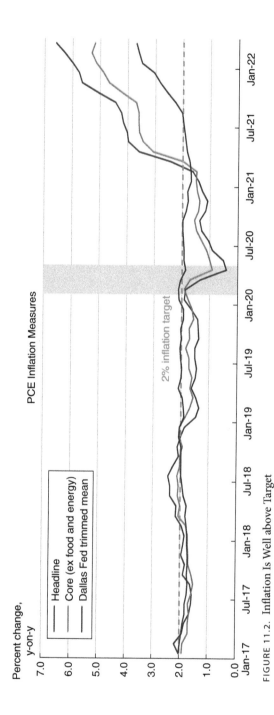

FIGURE 11.2. Inflation Is Well above Target

Sources: BEA and Federal Reserve Bank of Dallas.

Note: The gray shaded area indicates US recession. Last observation: March 2022.

In my definitions of "behind the curve," I will use the most generous (lowest) interpretation of the persistent component of current inflation, which is the 3.7% Dallas Fed trimmed mean value. This will help us define "behind the curve." The idea is to measure the degree to which the current level of the policy rate is less than some minimally reasonable level. We should keep in mind that this minimal definition excludes some inflation that is actually occurring, and that the Fed's inflation target is ultimately stated in terms of headline inflation.[2]

John Taylor (Stanford University) is famous for developing a "Taylor rule," which has been widely accepted in monetary policy discussions over the last thirty years (Taylor 1993, 1999). A Taylor-type policy rule with generous assumptions will give us a minimal recommended value for the policy rate given current macroeconomic conditions. We will then compare this minimal recommended rate to the actual policy rate to get a measure of the degree to which US monetary policy is "behind the curve."

In addition to an inflation measure, we need three ingredients in a non-inertial Taylor-type rule calculation:[3]

1. A value for the real interest rate (R^*); I will use an approximate pre-pandemic value of −50 basis points.[4]
2. A parameter value describing the reaction of the policy maker to deviations of inflation from target; I will use a relatively low value of 1.25.
3. A parameter value describing the reaction of the policy maker to deviations of output from potential; I will use zero when the output gap is positive, and one otherwise.[5]

---

2. See Bullard (2011) for a critical analysis of the use of core inflation in monetary policy discussions.

3. Adding inertia would not change the ultimate value of the policy rate but would suggest making a series of policy rate changes.

4. For more on this topic, see Bullard (2018).

5. This is a way to operationalize the "employment shortfalls" language in the FOMC's (2022) "Statement on Longer-Run Goals and Monetary Policy Strategy" in the context of a Taylor (1999) rule.

All the choices I have outlined can be interpreted as generous—
that is, as tilting toward a lower recommended policy rate. The
notion of "behind the curve," as I am defining it, is the position of
the policy rate relative to this minimalist benchmark.

The minimalist rule can be stated as:

$$R_t = R^* + \pi^* + 1.25(\pi_t - \pi^*) + \min(ygap_t, 0),$$

where R_t is the recommended policy rate; $R^* = -0.5$; $\pi^* = 2.0$; and
π_t is Dallas Fed trimmed mean inflation measured from one year
earlier. The output gap, $ygap_t$, is constructed by applying Okun's
law to deviations of the unemployment rate, u_t, from the median
Summary of Economic Projections (SEP) longer-run value, u_t^{LR}:

$$ygap_t = -2\left(u_t - u_t^{LR}\right).$$

This rule is consistent with the pre-pandemic policy rate. In particular, this generous Taylor rule would have recommended a policy rate of about 1.5% in late 2019, a value close to the actual policy
rate back then (1.55% in November and December 2019). More
conventional and less generous Taylor-rule specifications would
have recommended a much higher policy rate.

With these values in the minimalist policy rule, one concludes
that the recommended policy rate is the following:

$$-0.5 + 2.0 + 1.25(3.7 - 2.0) + \min(0.8, 0) = 3.63\%.$$

The current value of the policy rate is 87.5 basis points.[6] One concludes that the current policy rate is below the minimalist recommendation by 275 basis points. This provides one definition of the
idea that the Fed is "behind the curve." A higher value for R^* or a

---

6. This is the midpoint of the federal funds rate target range of 0.75% to 1% set by the
FOMC on May 4.

broader definition of inflation would suggest considerably higher recommended policy rate values, and the Fed would be further behind the curve.

SECOND INTERPRETATION
OF "BEHIND THE CURVE"

Modern central banks have considerably more credibility than they did in the 1970s, much of it stemming from an explicit commitment to inflation targeting. They also make more use of forward guidance. As a result, indications of future policy rate increases are incorporated into current financial market pricing, before policy actions are taken. This has been a key factor in current market pricing, as the 2-year Treasury yield and the 30-year mortgage rate have increased substantially and are above their pre-pandemic levels (figure 11.3).

Let's now return to the minimal Taylor-type rule calculation, which recommended a policy rate of 3.63%. In light of the forward guidance that has been given by the Fed since the fourth quarter of 2021, the 2-year Treasury yield may provide a better representation of where Fed policy is likely to be in the near future. The value of the 2-year Treasury yield as of May 5, 2022, was 2.71%, about 90 basis points shy of the rate recommended in the simple Taylor-type rule calculation. This suggests the Fed is not as far "behind the curve," although it would still have to raise the policy rate to ratify the forward guidance.

Recall that the recommended policy rate of 3.63% from the simple Taylor-type policy rule calculation involved some choices. In particular, a higher value for R^* or a broader definition of inflation would lead to the rule recommending a much higher value for the policy rate. For example, if one uses core PCE inflation instead of the Dallas Fed trimmed mean as the measure of the persistent component of inflation in the Taylor rule above, the recommended policy rate is represented by the blue line in figure 11.4. The shaded area between the two sets of recommended policy rates

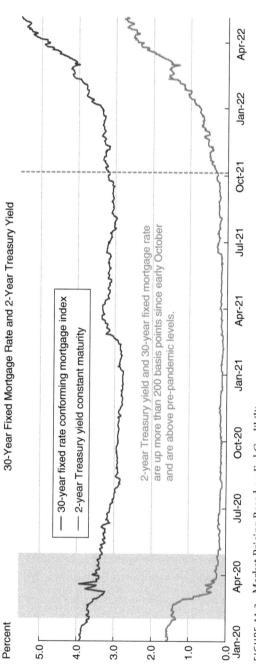

FIGURE 11.3. Market Pricing Based on Fed Credibility

Sources: Department of the Treasury and Optimal Blue, LLC, https://www2.optimalblue.com/obmmi.

Note: The gray shaded area indicates US recession. Last observation: May 5, 2022.

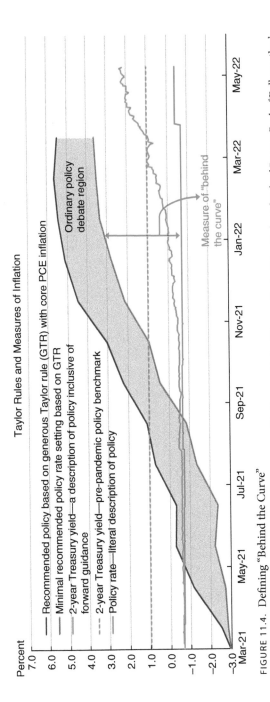

FIGURE 11.4. Defining "Behind the Curve"

Sources: BEA, Congressional Budget Office, Department of the Treasury, Federal Reserve Bank of New York, and Federal Reserve Bank of Dallas; author's calculations.

Note: Last observations: March 2022 and May 5, 2022.

is labeled the "ordinary policy debate region." The distance between the actual policy rate (red line) and a description of policy inclusive of forward guidance (2-year Treasury yield, solid green line in the figure) has been quite large recently. While the policy rate is lower than what it should be, both the actual policy rate and the measure incorporating forward guidance are moving in the right direction, toward the ordinary policy debate region. Therefore, the second interpretation probably still leaves the Fed behind the curve but by less than it appears based on the first interpretation.[7]

RISKS TO INFLATION EXPECTATIONS

One might argue that the current situation is more about waning Fed credibility with respect to its inflation target. According to the TIPS (Treasury Inflation-Protected Securities) markets, straight-read inflation expectations are rising (figure 11.5). The 5-year inflation compensation measure was 3.23% as of May 5, 2022.

In economic theory, expected inflation and actual inflation should be closely related. The current divergence between actual inflation readings and TIPS-based expected inflation will have to be resolved, possibly resulting in still higher inflation expectations.

CONCLUSION

Generously defined Taylor-type monetary policy rules, even if based on a minimum interpretation of the persistent component of inflation, still recommend substantial increases in the policy rate. By this first interpretation of "behind the curve," the Fed is far behind.

The first interpretation, however, does not take into account Fed credibility or its use of forward guidance. Credible forward

---

7. For additional analysis of Taylor-type rules and the role of Fed credibility in the current circumstance, see Papell and Prodan (2022). They conclude that the FOMC is currently about 100–125 basis points behind their rule recommendation.

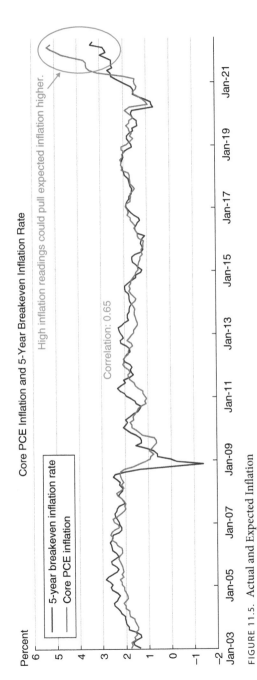

FIGURE 11.5. Actual and Expected Inflation

Sources: Federal Reserve Bank of St. Louis and BEA.

Note: Last observations: March 2022 and May 5, 2022.

guidance means market interest rates have increased substantially in advance of tangible Fed action. By this second definition of "behind the curve," the Fed is not as far behind, but it must now increase the policy rate to ratify the forward guidance previously given.

References

Almuzara, Martín, and Argia Sbordone. 2022. "Inflation Persistence: How Much Is There and Where Is It Coming From?" *Federal Reserve Bank of New York Liberty Street Economics* blog, April 20.

Bullard, James. 2011. "Measuring Inflation: The Core Is Rotten." *Federal Reserve Bank of St. Louis Review* 93, no. 4 (July/August): 223–33.

———. 2018. "R-Star Wars: The Phantom Menace." Remarks delivered at the 34th Annual National Association for Business Economics (NABE) Economic Policy Conference in Washington, DC, February 26.

Federal Open Market Committee. 2022. "Statement on Longer-Run Goals and Monetary Policy Strategy." Adopted effective Jan. 24, 2012; as reaffirmed effective Jan. 25, 2022.

Papell, David H., and Ruxandra Prodan. 2022. "Policy Rules and Forward Guidance Following the COVID-19 Recession." Unpublished manuscript, University of Houston, April 12.

Taylor, John B. 1993. "Discretion versus Policy Rules in Practice." Carnegie-Rochester Conference Series on Public Policy 39: 195–214. Amsterdam: North-Holland.

———. 1999. "A Historical Analysis of Monetary Policy Rules." In *Monetary Policy Rules*, edited by John B. Taylor, 319–41. Chicago: University of Chicago Press.

CHAPTER TWELVE

Strategy and Execution in US Monetary Policy 2021–22

Randal Quarles

The title of today's conference is "How Monetary Policy Got Behind the Curve—and How to Get Back," and the title of this panel is "Toward a Monetary Policy Strategy." This framing of the discussion clearly presupposes that the Fed is currently on the wrong track, but that it may not be too late to redeem the day by shifting course. I think that judgment is premature, in part because I think the Fed's strategy is misunderstood.[1] Those who were calling for the Fed to act in early 2021 were overly early. And while with the benefit of hindsight, I think it is clear the Fed did move too slowly in late 2021 and early 2022 to raise interest rates (a misstep that I supported at the time), this was an error of execution, not of strategy—a tactical misjudgment in the fog of war—and what is more, it is an error the Fed can correct, and is correcting, effectively and with dispatch.

The Fed's current strategy is laid out in its "framework" document, the declaration adopted by the Federal Open Market Committee (FOMC) in August of 2020, entitled "Statement on Longer-Run Goals and Monetary Policy Strategy."[2] This framework is just a page long and has two principal operative rules. The first is easily quoted: "Following periods when inflation has been running persistently below 2%, appropriate monetary policy will likely aim

---

1. In fairness, much of that misunderstanding stems from the Fed's own communication about its strategy after its implementation.
2. https://www.federalreserve.gov/monetarypolicy/files/FOMC_LongerRunGoals.pdf.

to achieve inflation moderately above 2% for some time." The second is an opaquely worded paragraph that is generally understood by the Committee (even if not by many native speakers of English) to mean that when the Fed sees unemployment below the non-accelerating inflation rate of unemployment (NAIRU), it will not act preemptively to constrain inflation (as it might have in the past), but will wait to see actual evidence of inflation before taking action that could dampen the labor market.

The first of these operative rules has generally been called "flexible average inflation targeting," but upon close examination, the word "flexible" in that informal title is clearly doing a *lot* of work; so much work, in fact, that it's not clear that the rest of the title— "average inflation targeting"—is that useful a descriptor of what the Fed is committed to by this statement. The statement says "the Committee seeks to achieve inflation that averages 2% over time," but it quite calculatedly does not refer to any *period* of time, and I certainly did not view us as trying to—much less as *committed* to— actually average inflation at 2% over any specific period of time. But an average that is not linked to any defined denominator over which it is being averaged is an odd sort of "average" indeed.

My resistance to an actual average over a defined period of time was not because I wanted the Fed to be unconstrained in its discretion, but rather because I viewed (a) the uncertainties in our measurement of inflation, (b) the mysteries around how inflation expectations are set, and (c) the bluntness of our tools to affect both inflation and inflation expectations as not supporting the degree of discretionary fine-tuning that actually aiming at 2% average inflation over any specific period of time would imply. I believed the Committee's framework statement would give us the ability to follow a longer-term, less reactive policy stance, *without* overly fiddling in light of minor departures from the target.

There were, obviously, some members of the Committee who were concerned that personal consumption expenditures (PCE) inflation had been running at an average of 1.8% over a number of years, which they believed could result in inflation expectations becoming anchored at that level. They wanted to run inflation at 2.2% for an equal number of years, apparently in the belief that this would be useful in anchoring inflation expectations closer to our 2% target. In my view, this was endearingly poindexterish, but complete voodoo.

My position, by contrast, was—and is—that for all practical purposes it is impossible to *tell* 1.8% from 2.2%. Both are close enough for government work, and we should be indifferent between them. I was fine saying policy would "likely aim" for inflation moderately above 2% "for some time" after a prolonged shortfall, but without any commitment to *achieve* 2% (we would only "likely aim"), and without even any commitment to aim for it long enough to mathematically average inflation at any specified level, only "for some time." And the reason I was fine with this phrasing of the statement was that I—and others—viewed "moderately above" as equivalent to "moderately below," and the reasonable, rule-like measures needed to achieve either outcome would not be wildly different. Moreover, my reluctance to agree to any specific period or to the actual outcome of a 2% average over *any* period came from a concern that if reasonable, rule-like measures didn't succeed in raising inflation to a level needed to mathematically average 2% over a specific, measurable period, the progressively more heroic efforts needed to achieve that increase would be progressively unlikely to land at a fine-tuned number. Instead, they would be more likely to end up unanchoring expectations entirely.

Now, obviously I believe that the language in the first operative principle of the Fed's framework statement accommodates the policy views I've described above—indeed, it was carefully crafted to allow for that view, among others—or I wouldn't have agreed to it. And the need to accommodate the gap between my view (and others like it on the Committee) with those folks in their lab coats with the Van de Graaff generators and smoking test tubes trying to average precisely 2% accounts for the Merovingian supineness of the language in the statement.

This may seem like a criticism of the framework. I don't mean it to be—quite the contrary. The framework emphasizes flexibility around 2% as a target at any point in time and does not actually tie the Fed to mathematically averaging 2% over any specific period, which actually leaves a greater ability to follow a more strategic, consistent policy than a commitment to actual averaging would. And it leaves significant latitude about the data to prioritize and the analytical tools with which to interrogate those data—including strict monetary policy rules, which the Fed can use as a benchmark or could even adopt—in operating within that framework. One can view this as a strength.

But the problem most people have seen with the Fed's current monetary policy framework is not with the first element we have been discussing—the "flexible average inflation targeting"—but with the second element: don't constrain employment until you actually see inflation, which I have called the "Israel Putnam principle": "Don't fire until you see the whites of their eyes."[3] Some are taking our current inflationary episode as an obvious refutation of at least that part of the Fed's framework.

I disagree, and I say that as one of the most consistent hawks on the FOMC during my time there. I used to take a perhaps unseemly pride that in any iteration of the FOMC's Summary of Economic Projections, or "dot plot," my dot was always right at the tippy top. But let's look closely at the data from one year ago, at the time when some say—indeed, said at the time—the Fed should begin to act. Inflation had begun to move materially above the 2% target—3.5% in March, 3.9% in April, hitting 5% in June. Yet, when one looked closely at the line item goods in the inflation basket, those numbers were being driven by one thing: used car prices. New car production

---

3. Israel Putnam was the General at Bunker Hill during the Revolutionary War generally credited with having given the "whites of their eyes" order.

had slowed to a crawl, principally because today's cars are basically rolling computers, and the COVID-19 constraint-induced shortage of computer chips was a strangling restraint on new car supply. As a consequence, if you wanted a car in the spring of 2021, you had to buy a used one. That sudden shift of relative demand between new and used cars resulted in a 25% increase in the price of used cars over two months, and that single factor drove the headline 5% annualized inflation rate at the beginning of June.[4] When one looked at all the other goods in the basket, there really wasn't any other element that was rising dramatically—there just wasn't any signal of widespread and non-supply-chain-driven inflation. Now, with the benefit of hindsight, we can say, "It was coming," but it was perfectly reasonable not to act at that point.

I do think, however, that we had enough data to realize this was broad-based, overstimulated-demand-driven inflation by mid-September 2021. Rich Clarida went through a number of those data points in his opening remarks this morning, others have cited some of them. I will focus here on the throughput figures for the main US ports in September. Over the summer, one common refrain was that bottlenecks at the ports—presumably resulting from the difficulty in clearing blockages created by COVID-related personnel shortages—were impeding the supply of goods into the United States, inevitably feeding inflation in the goods prices. A perfectly reasonably hypothesis. But by September, the figures we had for the amount of goods making it through the main US ports were actually running at, or above, pre-COVID levels. And the projected throughput by the end of the year was not just at pre-COVID levels, it was approaching record numbers for the amount of goods ever cleared through the ports in a single year. The bottlenecks were not resulting in a shortage of

---

4. It is a topic for a different panel to consider how often, and how much, the headline figures that drive the thinking of the public and even policy makers about inflation, are affected by anomalies in a single eccentric item in the inflation basket—cell phone pricing in the spring of 2017 and used car prices in the spring of 2021 being two prominent recent examples.

goods relative to pre-COVID supply—they were a result of demand at such levels that even record throughput could not satisfy it.

We on the FOMC did not, however, act in September. It is clear now that this was a mistake. But it was not a mistake dictated by the Fed's framework. Israel Putnam said, "Don't fire until you see the whites of their eyes," not "Don't fire until the redcoats march over you." Given the inflation rates over the summer of 2021, which had become comprehensive across the inflation basket by September, a 5-year backward-looking average of PCE inflation would have been running at well over 2%, and we obviously were seeing current inflation much higher than that. Thus, given the data we had in September, a proper understanding of the Fed's framework would not simply have *allowed* the Fed to move in September, it would have *required* it. And had the Fed pivoted last September and moved with the dispatch it is now showing, is there anyone who thinks the Fed would not be on top of inflation by next September?

This mistake is somewhat similar in character to the Archegos Capital Management kerfuffle from early 2021. Contrary to popular belief, the banks exposed to Archegos didn't actually have particularly weak risk management frameworks or poorly negotiated contracts with Archegos. For the most part, they had all the protections you would want, founded on a sophisticated understanding of that risk. And, for that reason, most of the US banks with Archegos exposure got out without loss. But those foreign banks that did lose, lost money because they didn't *follow* their frameworks. They improvised, and ad-libbed, and took limited initial steps, and ended up with their tails in a wringer.

In my view, the Fed's delay in the fall of 2021 resulted not from the Israel Putnam principle, but from a good faith misapplication of another, separate general principle of Fed practice, which is the sequencing of balance sheet and interest rate policy. The Fed, as a general matter, believes that balance sheet and interest rate policy should work in tandem: the Fed should not be providing accommodation through one tool while withdrawing it with another—in the oft-used analogy, that would be "stepping on the gas pedal and the brake at the same time." Given the accommodative consequences of the asset purchase program the Fed had begun in the spring of 2020—even though the purpose of the program had been to ensure market functioning rather than provide policy easing—the Fed believed it should taper those asset purchases to a stop before beginning to raise interest rates. And, given the potential for market disruptions if the tapering happened too abruptly, it would take several months before the purchases had slowed to zero.

Perfectly reasonable, but in hindsight I believe that was an important error in the Fed's policy in late 2021 and early 2022. This is somewhat similar to the general rule among pilots that you should coordinate the use of the plane's rudder and its ailerons. One of the first things you are taught as a young pilot is to avoid "cross-controlling" an airplane: pushing the rudder in one direction while applying the ailerons in the opposite direction. Most often, cross-controlling is inefficient, sometimes dangerous, and doing it is a mistake. There are, however, a few times when there is good reason to do exactly that—most typically when you find you are too high on final approach and need to steepen your descent into a short landing strip. It is called "slipping" the airplane; when done inadvertently, it is the sign of a rookie—when done intentionally and for the right reasons, it is a tool of a skillful pilot. I think with hindsight it is now clear that the Fed should have begun "slipping" monetary policy in the fall of 2021—raising interest rates in September or November even while the tapering of asset purchases was incomplete. The inefficiency of "cross-controlling" monetary policy for a relatively brief period would not have had materially bad effects, and the benefits of responding to a widespread demand-driven inflation with prompt interest rate increases would have been obvious.

In the end, though, I think this mistake will be remedied with dispatch. The interest rate increases that the Fed has begun, if continued as outlined, will be quite effective. In an environment where economic actors and market participants have been conditioned for almost fifteen years to expect extremely low interest rates, even modest nominal rate increases will result in quite high percentage increases in debt service, and the effect on the economy should be both swifter and more powerful than in many prior cases of the Fed's response to inflation. I think it will be clear by the fall that inflation is heading into the pen, and by the first part of next year it should be effectively corralled. There are lessons to be learned from this episode, certainly. But I think it is premature to conclude that one of those lessons is that either of the two operative principles of the monetary policy framework adopted by the Fed in August 2020 was a mistake or has become outmoded.

CHAPTER THIRTEEN

REFLECTIONS ON MONETARY POLICY IN 2021

Christopher J. Waller

I want to thank the organizers of the 2022 Monetary Policy Conference for inviting me to speak here today and add my response to the focus of discussion, "How did the Fed get so far behind the curve?" To do that, I am going to relate how my view of the economy changed over the course of 2021 and how that evolving view shaped my policy position.

When thinking about this question, there are three points that need to be considered. First, the Fed was not alone in underestimating the strength of inflation that revealed itself in late 2021. Second, to determine whether the Fed was behind the curve, one must take a position on the evolving health of the labor market during 2021. Finally, setting policy in real time can create what appear to be policy errors after the fact, due to data revisions.

Let me start by reminding everyone of two immutable facts about setting monetary policy in the United States. First, we have a dual mandate from the Congress: maximum employment and price stability. Whether you believe this is the appropriate mandate or not, it is the law of the land, and it is our job to pursue both objectives.

Second, policy is set by a large committee of up to twelve voting members, with a total of nineteen participants in our discussions. This structure brings a wide range of views to the table and a diverse set of opinions on how to interpret incoming economic data and how best to respond. We need to reconcile those views and reach a consensus that we believe will move the economy toward our mandate. This process can lead to more gradual changes in policy as members have to compromise to reach a consensus.

Back in September and December 2020, respectively, the Federal Open Market Committee (FOMC) provided guidance for lifting the federal funds rate off the zero lower bound (ZLB) and for tapering asset purchases. We said we would "aim to achieve inflation moderately above 2% for some time" to ensure that it averages 2% over time and that inflation expectations stay anchored. We also said that the Fed would keep buying $120 billion per month in securities until "substantial further progress" was made toward our dual-mandate objectives. It is important to stress that views varied among FOMC participants regarding what would constitute "some time" and "substantial further progress." The metrics for achieving these outcomes also varied across participants.

A few months later, in March 2021, I made my first submission for the Summary of Economic Projections (SEP) as an FOMC member. My projection had inflation above 2% for 2021 and 2022, with unemployment close to my long-run estimate by the second half of 2022. Given this projection, which I believed was consistent with the guidance from December, I penciled in lifting off the ZLB in 2022, with the second half of the year in mind. To lift off from the ZLB in the second half of 2022, I believed tapering of asset purchases would have to start in the second half of 2021 and conclude by the third quarter of 2022.

This projection was based on my judgment that the economy would heal much faster than many expected. This was not 2009, and expectations of a slow, grinding recovery were inaccurate, in my view. In April 2021, I said the economy was "ready to rip," and it did.[1] I chose to look at the unemployment rate and job creation as the labor market indicators I would use to assess whether we had

---

1. Jeff Cox, "Fed's Waller Says the Economy Is 'Ready to Rip' But Policy Should Stay Put," CNBC, April 16, 2021.

made "substantial further progress." My projection was also based on the belief that the jump in inflation that occurred in March 2021 would be more persistent than many expected.

There was a range of views on the Committee. Eleven of my colleagues did not have a rate hike penciled in until after 2023. With regard to future inflation, thirteen participants projected inflation in 2022 would be at or below our 2% target. In the March 2021 SEP, no Committee member expected inflation to be more than 3% for 2021. As I argued in a speech last December, this view was consistent with private-sector economic forecasts.[2]

When inflation broke loose in March 2021, even though I had expected it to run above 2% in 2021 and 2022, I never thought it would reach the very high levels we have seen in recent months. Indeed, I expected it would eventually fade, due to the nature of the shocks. All the suspected drivers of this surge in inflation appeared to be temporary: the onetime stimulus from fiscal policy, supply chain shocks that previous experience indicated would ease soon, and a surge in demand for goods. In addition, we had very accommodative monetary policy that I believed would end in 2022. The issue in my mind was whether these factors would start fading away in 2021 or in 2022.

Over the summer of 2021, the labor market and other data related to economic activity came in as I expected, and so I argued publicly that we were rapidly approaching "substantial further progress" on the employment leg of our mandate. In the June SEP, seven participants had liftoff in 2022 and only five participants projected liftoff after 2023. Also, unlike the March SEP, every Committee participant now expected inflation to be more than 3% in 2021 and just five believed inflation would be at 2% or below in 2022. In addition,

---

2. Christopher J. Waller, "A Hopeless and Imperative Endeavor: Lessons from the Pandemic for Economic Forecasters," speech delivered at the Forecasters Club of New York, New York, December 17, 2021, https://www.federalreserve.gov/newsevents/speech/waller20211217a.htm.

at that point the vast majority of participants saw risks associated with inflation weighted to the upside. The June 2021 minutes also describe the vigorous discussion about tapering asset purchases. Numerous participants agreed the new data indicated that tapering should begin sooner than anticipated.[3] Thus, in June, after observing high inflation for only three months, the Committee was moving in a hawkish direction and was considering tapering sooner and pulling liftoff forward.

At the July FOMC meeting, the minutes show that most participants believed "substantial further progress" had been made on inflation but not employment.[4] Tapering was not viewed as imminent by most participants. Again, individual participants had different metrics for evaluating the health of the labor market, and this approach influenced how each thought about policy. So, in my view, one cannot address the question of "how did the Fed get so far behind the curve?" without taking a stand on the health of the labor market as we moved through 2021.

Based on incoming data over the summer, my position was that we would soon achieve the substantial further progress needed to start tapering asset purchases—in particular, our purchases of agency mortgage-backed securities—and that we needed to "go early and go fast" on tapering our asset purchases to position ourselves for rate hikes in 2022 should we need to tighten policy.[5] I also argued that, if the July and August job reports came in around the forecasted values of 800 thousand to one million job gains per month, we should commence tapering our asset purchases at the September 2021 FOMC meeting. The July report was indeed more

---

3. Board of Governors of the Federal Reserve System, "Minutes of the Federal Open Market Committee, June 15–16, 2021," press release, https://www.federalreserve.gov/newsevents/pressreleases/monetary20210707a.htm.

4. Board of Governors of the Federal Reserve System, "Minutes of the Federal Open Market Committee, July 27–28, 2021," press release, https://www.federalreserve.gov/newsevents/pressreleases/monetary20210818a.htm.

5. Ann Saphir, "Fed's Waller: 'Go Early and Go Fast' on Taper," *Reuters*, August 2, 2021.

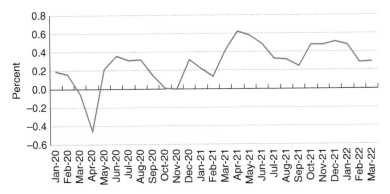

FIGURE 13.1. Monthly Change in PCE Prices ex. Food and Energy
Source: Bureau of Economic Analysis, US Department of Commerce.

than one million new jobs, but then the August report shocked us by reporting only 235 thousand new jobs when the consensus forecast was for 750 thousand. I considered this a punch in the gut and relevant to a decision on when to start tapering.[6] Nevertheless, the September FOMC statement noted the economy had made progress toward the Committee's goals and that, if progress continued, it would soon be time to taper.[7]

Up until October, monthly core personal consumption expenditures (PCE) inflation was actually slowing. As shown in figure 13.1, it went from 0.62% in April to 0.24% for the month of September. The September jobs report was another shock, with only 194 thousand jobs created. So, up until the first week of October 2021, the story of high inflation being temporary was holding up, and the labor market improvements had slowed but were continuing. Based on the

6. Of course, as we all know, the employment data was revised upward substantially, but that was not known to policy makers at the time, and it is important to explicitly make that point now—the data points were choppy and did not lend themselves to a clear picture of the outlook.

7. Board of Governors of the Federal Reserve System, "Federal Reserve Issues FOMC Statement," press release, September 22, 2021, https://www.federalreserve.gov/newsevents/pressreleases/monetary20210922a.htm.

incoming data, the FOMC announced the start of tapering at its early November meeting.[8]

It was the October and November consumer price index (CPI) reports that showed that the deceleration of inflation from April to September was short lived and year-over-year inflation had topped 6%. It became clear that the high inflation realizations were not as temporary as originally thought. The October jobs report showed a significant rebound with 531 thousand jobs created and big upward revisions to the previous two months.

It was at this point—with a clearer picture of inflation and revised labor market data in hand—that the FOMC pivoted. In its December meeting, the Committee accelerated tapering, and the SEP showed that each individual participant projected an earlier liftoff in 2022 with a median projection of three rate hikes in 2022. These forecasts and forward guidance had a significant effect on raising market interest rates, even though we did nothing with our primary policy tool, the federal funds rate, in December 2021. It is worth noting that markets had the same view of likely policy—federal funds rate futures in November and December called for three hikes in 2022, indicating an economic outlook that was similar to the Committee's.

So, given this description of how policy evolved over 2021, did the Fed fall far behind the curve? First, I want to emphasize that forecasting is hard for everyone, especially in a pandemic. In terms of missing on inflation, policy makers' projections looked very much like most of the public's. For example, as shown in table 13.1, the median SEP forecast for 2021 Q4/Q4 PCE inflation was very similar to the consensus from the Blue Chip Economic Indicators, which is a compilation of private sector forecasts published by Wolters Kluwer. In short, nearly everyone was behind the curve when it came to forecasting the magnitude and persistence of inflation.

---

8. Board of Governors of the Federal Reserve System, "Federal Reserve Issues FOMC Statement," press release, November 3, 2021, https://www.federalreserve.gov/newsevents/pressreleases/monetary20211103a.htm.

TABLE 13.1. Comparison of 2021 Q4/Q4 PCE Price Inflation Forecasts (%)

Month	SEP Median	Blue Chip Consensus
March	2.4	2.3
June	3.4	3.2
September	4.2	4.3
December	5.3	5.2

Source: Federal Reserve Board, Summary of Economic Projections and Blue Chip Economic Indicators (Wolters Kluwer).

Second, as I mentioned, you cannot answer this question without taking a stand on the employment leg of our mandate. There was a clear difference in views on this and on what indicators should be looked at to determine whether we had met the "substantial further progress" criteria we laid out in our December 2020 guidance. Some of us concluded the labor market was healing fast and we pushed for earlier and faster withdrawal of accommodation. For others, data suggested the labor market was not healing that fast and it was not optimal to withdraw policy accommodation soon. Many of our critics tend to focus only on the inflation aspect of our mandate and ignore the employment leg of our mandate. But we cannot. So, what may appear as a policy error to some was viewed as appropriate policy by others based on their views regarding the health of the labor market.

Third, one must account for setting policy in real time. The Committee was getting mixed signals from the labor market data in August and September. Two consecutive weak job reports did not square with a rapidly falling unemployment rate. Later that fall, and then with the Labor Department's 2021 revisions, we found payrolls were quite steady over the course of the year. As shown in table 13.2, revisions to changes in payroll employment since late last summer have been quite substantial. From the original reports to the current estimate, the change in payroll employment has been revised up nearly 1.5 million. As the revisions came in, a

TABLE 13.2. Change in Nonfarm Payroll Employment: Initial Report and Current Estimate (Thousands)

Month	Initial Report	Current Estimate	Revision
August	235	517	282
September	194	424	230
October	531	677	146
November	210	647	437
December	199	588	389
Total	1369	2853	1484

Source: Bureau of Labor Statistics, US Department of Labor.

consensus grew that the labor market was much stronger than we originally thought. If we knew then what we know now, I believe the Committee would have accelerated tapering and raised rates sooner. But no one knew, and that's the nature of making monetary policy in real time.

Finally, if one believes we were behind the curve in 2021, how far behind were we? In a world of forward guidance, one simply cannot look at the policy rate to judge the stance of policy. Even though we did not actually move the policy rate in 2021, we used forward guidance to start raising market rates beginning with the September 2021 statement, which indicated tapering was coming soon. The 2-year Treasury yield, which I view as a good market indicator of our policy stance, went from approximately 25 basis points in late September 2021 to 75 basis points by late December. That is the equivalent, in my mind, of two 25 basis point policy rate hikes for impacting the financial markets. When looked at this way, how far behind the curve could we have possibly been if, using forward guidance, one views rate hikes effectively beginning in September 2021?

GENERAL DISCUSSION

JOSHUA RAUH (INTRODUCTION): In this panel, three current or former Federal Reserve officials will talk about the future of monetary policy strategy. One common theme in their remarks will be the question as to whether the speed and scope of the Federal Reserve's actions to contain inflation have been adequate in the recent period.

We will first hear from Jim Bullard, president of the Federal Reserve Bank of St. Louis, who will pose the question, "Is the Fed behind the curve?" He will give us a mixed answer. Standard Taylor-type policy rules are clearly recommending substantial increases in the policy rate above where it is today, although it depends to some extent on the inflation measure used. Furthermore, central banks use forward guidance, and Mr. Bullard will in his remarks shed light on the role that credible forward guidance has already played in increasing market interest rates.

Randy Quarles, former member of the Federal Reserve Board of Governors, will take a step back and ask the question, "If we're moving toward a monetary policy strategy, what are we moving away from?" The Fed adopted a new statement on longer-run goals and monetary policy strategy in August of 2020. One of the principles therein is generally referred to as "flexible average inflation targeting." This approach targets average inflation over a period of time but does not bind the Fed mathematically to average 2% over any specific period. The second main principle in the Fed's August 2020 statement might be best described as "Don't constrain employment until we actually see inflation." Mr. Quarles will assess the contention that the August 2020 framework was in some way a mistake, concluding that in fact it is premature to draw that conclusion.

Christopher Waller, a current member of the Federal Reserve Board of Governors, will pick up on the discussion of whether the Fed has been behind the curve by focusing on the timing with which information, both about inflation and the health of the labor market, has come to light. When the first real departure of inflation from expectations occurred in March 2021, policy seems to have been guided by the expectation that it would eventually fade due to the nature of the shocks that were perceived as generating it. As of June 2021, the Committee was moving in a hawkish direction. The August 2021 jobs report then showed shockingly weak numbers. Yet progressive revisions in future months revealed that in fact the labor market had been quite a bit stronger, and that payroll growth had been quite steady over the course of the year.

All of this discussion is of course taking place in the context of a very substantial run-up in CPI inflation. I suspect the assembled group here will raise questions for our esteemed panel of central bankers as to how inflation could have deviated so substantially from the Fed's forecast, and whether there are further changes to the framework that might be implemented for the future. I convey our appreciation to the panel for engaging with us in this discussion.

*   *   *

DAVID PAPELL: David Papell, University of Houston. I want to relate the discussion this afternoon to the discussion in the first panel this morning by John Taylor and Rich Clarida, and particularly with Rich's graph that he showed from my paper with Ruxandra Prodan. We looked at prescriptions from six different policy rules: Taylor and balanced approach versions of original, shortfalls, and what we call consistent rules. The initial prescriptions are all bunched together. With the inertial rules, the liftoff would either be the second or third quarter of 2021 and, with the noninertial rules, the liftoff would be about one quarter earlier. Up to March 2021 everything is similar. Then, with the non-inertial rules, you see prescriptions like what John Taylor put on his graph. By March 2022, Taylor rule prescriptions are between 5 and 6%. Now that's a policy path that was out of the question. It would have required, depending on the rule, two federal funds rate increases of 100 or 200 basis points each over consecutive quarters or one rate increase of 300 basis points. It's not a path that the Fed could follow. The inertial rules were a path that the Fed could have followed by starting rate increases in the second or third quarter of 2021. By March 2022, the Fed was behind the curve by about 100 to 125 basis points based on the inertial rules. This had nothing to do with flexible average inflation targeting or by responding to shortfalls instead of deviations from maximum employment. It was not following the policy rules that led to being behind the curve. Last Wednesday, the Fed raised rates by 50 basis points. If the Fed increases the federal funds rate by 50 basis points in the next four to five meetings, they could get back to being on the curve. So it's not an impossibility. It's not that they have to get to 5 or 6%. It's definitely within the realm of what could be done.

JAMES BULLARD: I might just make one comment. The kind of calculations that I showed and that David just talked about are sensitive to this inertia issue. If you're going to put a lot of inertia in your rule, very low interest rates are going to look very good for a long time. So I regard the inertia parameter as kind of an ad hoc adjustment parameter. Inertial rules are popular because they fit the data pretty well pre-pandemic. And then we say, "Well, that was pretty good policy during that period." So we like that inertia parameter. But then you get this really big shock. And so what I was trying to calculate is, Where would we like to be? Then we can think about how fast we want to get there. And that's kind of a judgment call. And I would say the inertia parameter is encapsulating that judgment call about how fast to get there. But I still want to know: If I just had my druthers, if I could snap my fingers, where would I like to be right now given this data? The rest of the rule I think tells you that.

MICKEY LEVY: A quick comment and a quicker question. Jim, in your estimate of how far behind the Fed is, you suggested that only 90 basis points of further rate increases are needed. But that's 90 basis points above the 2-year note yield that reflects the fed funds futures curve that is pricing in numerous Fed rate hikes and now yields 2.75%. Accordingly, you must add to your estimate of a 90-basis-point shortfall all of the rate increases currently priced into the futures market. This raises your estimate of the fed funds rate to 3.75%.

My simple question is, with core PCE inflation of 5.2%, far above the Fed's 2% longer-run average target, do you think the Fed would accept a rise in the unemployment rate to 5 or 5.5% in order to get inflation down to 2%?

BULLARD: I think this is a question for Randy. But I'll answer your first question. It's totally true. If you're going to go to the 2-year Treasury yield as a metric, then you have to take into account that it's general equilibrium. Market participants are trying to game out what the Fed's going to do, and that's affecting the pricing. So when you say you're 90 basis points behind on the 2-year, you're not quite hawkish enough to get into that normal policy debate region. So you'd have to be a little bit more hawkish. Now some of that might be part of the market doesn't really believe us; they think we're going to stall out at some point or something. So I think as we push ahead here, we'll get more credibility, and we will be able to get into that region. But you're totally right that you can't just say, "Okay, well, two more hikes will get us there," because it isn't at all clear that that will do it.

RANDAL QUARLES: So, I will answer your question. I think that the answer is, yes. There are . . . I mean, there are many, many folks in this room who have been part of the institution of the Fed. I will . . . I will give a very, very short anecdote. I will constrain myself because this anecdote can become quite long, but I will give a very short anecdote that demonstrates why I think that they will stay the course because they're very committed to fighting inflation. I commuted from Salt Lake to the Fed. Well, I was going there because my family had not wanted to move back to Washington. And so, as a consequence, I didn't have any family in Washington, and I worked 'til late in the night. The building was not used to having a governor there at 10 at night. And I was unaware that there was a panic button underneath my desk that I kept hitting with my knee.

So the first night that happened, I hit the panic button with my knee, and a SWAT team comes running down the hallway and bursting into my office. And I have no idea what's going on. And they explained to me the panic button. Now you would think that once would have been enough. But no. So I did that regularly, and eventually they stopped responding.

But one night there was a new guard, a young man, who was not aware that I would hit the panic button with my knee, and so he came running down alone at 10 o'clock at night to see what terrorist was attacking the corner office. And so he got there, and I explained I do this all the time. I'm so sorry. But he was also something of an art critic, so he was interested in the art on the walls. And the Fed gives you some art. It's nothing from the Smithsonian, they get art from their collection. Nothing cost more than about $2,000. One of the things I had on my wall was a memento mori painting by Arthur Burns. Some of you may not know that Arthur Burns painted. George W. Bush is a much better painter than Arthur Burns. But I kept it to remind me. And so as he's asking about the various art, I explained, now this was by Arthur Burns. And I begin to explain to the young security guard who Arthur Burns was and why that painting is on my wall. And he says, "Oh my God, that's the guy who let inflation get out of control."

So the point is that this is an institution that from top to bottom knows that the one great sin that will be remembered by everyone 50 years later is if you let inflation get out of control. My young security guard did not remember what the unemployment rate was in 1971. He knew that Arthur Burns let inflation get out of control. And that will drive the commitment of the Committee to ensure that they get on top of this.

TYLER GOODSPEED: Two quick questions. First, what was the specific thinking behind the continuation of the purchase of mortgage-backed securities in 2021? And second, insofar as 2021 might have been a type-one error, in retrospect, do any of you think that 2018 was a type-two error?

BULLARD: On mortgage-backed securities [MBSs], I did argue publicly that we might consider just ending that part of the purchase program in the fall of 2021, on the grounds that the housing market was booming and that the purchases had been taken on at the height of the pandemic, thinking that the pandemic was going to cause problems in the housing market. But actually, the housing market went the other way and did very well. So it was mystifying, to me anyway, that by the time we got to Labor Day 2021 we were still doing this. Now, the counterargument was that MBSs and Treasuries are close substitutes and we weren't ready to announce the tapering decision: If you taper, why were you tapering one and not the other? And this kind of thing. But still, in retrospect, I would support my original idea. It didn't carry the day, but I think it would have been wise. We've really got a hot housing market here, and housing prices are up substantially. You've got an increased demand for housing, and you can't build enough houses. You're really pricing a lot of people out of the market. So I do think, in retrospect, it would have been better to get out sooner.

JOHN GUNN: I have really enjoyed the day, but one item has not come up. And it's—you're an appropriate panel to ask—and that is there's a huge change: In 2000, 80% of the global economy was in the developed world. By today, somewhere between 61 and 65% is in the developed world. The developing world is growing very rapidly. To some people—there's one academic paper anyway, I have no idea whether it's correct or not—that makes the point that the Chinese export boom to the United States that filled the shelves of Target and Walmart took 1 to 2% off the inflation rate. Now, we're in a situation where, due to technological innovation, meeting the 7 billion people in the developing world, they're moving rapidly at a growth rate that will be probably at least double that of the developed world. What do you, when you're thinking about—we're only 25% of the global economy, the United States—when you're thinking about what you're doing in Washington, do you factor in some subjective—I admit there's probably not too many numbers—but do you factor in some subjective items of what's happening in the rest of the world?

CHRISTOPHER WALLER: Well, I'd say that the typical way that we tend to look at the impact on the rest of the world on the US economy is through imports and exports and how trade flows affect GDP and our mandate. That's it. We don't set monetary policy for different countries; we don't try to fix their problems with interest rates. Whatever they do, however, it impacts us through GDP and inflation, that's how we responded.

JOHN COCHRANE: This is great. And thank you all. I want to ask a hard question: Let's get away from how fast the Fed raised interest rates or not and why. Inflation is 8%. That is a significant institutional failure. Now maybe it was nobody's fault. But when you target 2 and it comes out 8, that is a significant failure. If this were an army, you have an after-action report, a court martial, an inquest, and we'd figure out what went wrong.

So I'm curious. I see three conceptual questions that I want to know your view on. First, inflation forecasts: How could you get the forecast so wrong? Yes, most of the surveyed professional forecasters got it wrong too. But Larry Summers sat down with the back of his envelope, thought, 5 bucks of stimulus, multiply by 1.5, look at any plausible GDP gap, wow, here comes inflation.

If your inflation forecasts can be off by 8 percentage points, we need to figure out, Are the inflation forecasts really that impossible? If so, what are we doing making projections and asking and acting on projections? Maybe you need to change your procedures to forget about the projections if they're going to be that inaccurate. Either forming them or how you use them, it seems to me that a soul-searching and indeed a formal what-went-wrong effort ought to happen.

Second, anchoring. We hear lovely speeches about anchoring, but we just saw expectations are taking off. I've been wondering for ten years, is this an anchor or is this a sail, and it happens to be a calm day? I think we found out the answer to that question. And I've been wondering, Anchored by what? Anchored by more speeches about how there's anchoring? Sometimes the Fed will say, "Well, we have the tools," and never really tell us what the tools are.

Now, the only anchoring that makes sense to me is the reputation gained in 1980. People believe the Fed will do what it takes. If this means 20% interest rates, horrendous unemployment, and two back-to-back recessions, the Fed will do it. I never hear that out of the Fed. Deterrence only works if people know what the "tools" are and that you're ready to use them! I would think that some soul-searching on what anchoring is, how to better anchor, and how to make clear the steadfastness of that commitment would be something useful.

Third, r-star, which Ricardo brought up. There is a sense that the Fed was fighting the last war, as generals always do, but forgot about the war before that one, the war against inflation. But maybe not. To what extent do you believe that we are heading back toward a world of perpetual low real interest rates, the zero bound, that the Maginot line against deflation needs to be ready to go again two years from now? Ricardo's point is, I think, "Wait a minute, the marginal product of capital isn't that low." There was something special about government bonds in a noninflationary environment that may disappear. Low real rates, low r-star is not necessarily coming back. So as you think about the future, I would think that this conceptual mindset that we're going to be fighting deflation forever, which is what I really see was really quite well put together in the current monetary strategy, needs questioning.

In summary, forecasts, expectations, anchoring, and are we going back to zero?

BULLARD: On inflation forecasts, I have a very simple idea. We used econometric models estimated off the last two decades or so of data to forecast inflation. During that period, inflation was close to 2% pretty much the whole time. You got coefficients that were close to zero on most of the variables, except for the constant. In fact, probably the constant did the best, most of the work, in projecting inflation. Then you tried to use that model when you got a gigantic pandemic shock; it wasn't the right model to use. I think that's the simple explanation.

That kind of view is going to push all of the inflation movements into the noise term in the model. You're going to come back and say, "Well, my model doesn't fit this new data. So it must be all in the noise term. So it must be going to go away, it must be temporary." That's exactly what we got as advice. And I think it's turning out to not be correct now.

I think there's schizophrenia at this conference about the forward-looking versus backward-looking issue. That kind of comment sounds like: "We should just rely on hard tangible data that we actually have on inflation and react to that, because it's not going to be that easy to forecast." Indeed, the forecast may lead you badly astray if it turns out to be wrong and it's not that good. But on other occasions, people say, "You shouldn't wait till you see the whites of inflation's eyes. You should always be anticipating. You should always be acting a little bit ahead of time." This seemed to be the lesson that came out of the Volcker and Greenspan era. I think there's schizophrenia here. I'm not sure where everybody really comes down. Surely it's got to be some kind of combination or judgment about what's actually happening on the ground. You have to put heavy weight on what I actually have in hand. What's actually the data that I have? But then you also have to be thinking, What's a reasonable model of what's happening? Some judgment about what's happening and might happen in the future. And then make good calls. I think because we have a big Committee, we get a lot of input from a lot of different angles. And most of the time we do make good calls. Not this time, though.

On r-star, I think r-star's low for the foreseeable future unless you get a productivity boom coming out of this, which I wouldn't rule out. I think the pandemic did force us to use a lot of technology that we weren't used to using and probably spawned new ideas that may improve productivity going forward, and you might get higher growth rates. The demographics don't look that good going forward. Then you've got the issue of safe assets' scarcity. I don't think that's going to change. So the only thing I could think that can change on r-star is that productivity could move to the higher-productivity growth regime. That would be interesting and it would push up r-star a little bit, but the jury's out as to whether that's really great.

QUARLES: On your comment about expectations, anchoring, I would only say that I agree with you. The view that expectations have been so well anchored for so long, I've always been a little skeptical of that. Because if you walked out on the street before 2021 and asked anyone, "What is the level of inflation?" they would have had no idea what to say. If you had told them, you know, "How do you feel about inflation being 1.5%? How do you feel about inflation being 5%?" They wouldn't have given you an answer, because they had no clue as to what it was supposed to be. People in general—the folks in this room obviously think about that a lot—but for the people who actually drive the economy, the whole success of monetary policy was that they did not think about it. So in what sense were their expectations anchored anywhere? And indeed, the risk was, and perhaps we are beginning to see it, that as soon as you made them think about it, that the expectations would move off in an unpredictable direction. So that has long been a concern of mine. And I do worry that we're beginning to see that inflation expectations that we have always believed were so well anchored for so long were really, just, no one was thinking about them.

NICK TIMIRAOS: Nick Timiraos of the *Wall Street Journal.* I have two questions. One for Jim and Chris. One of the conclusions that came out of the framework review, and it seemed as if the Committee had already kind of absorbed this before you actually concluded the review, was because of the policy asymmetry of the lower bound, you should go big, go fast when you get there. And you certainly did that on QE and on forward guidance. And I wonder now if there's any buyer's remorse that might make you gun-shy, in the next downturn, about either the sequencing you had around that you have to take or before you raise rates, and also the magnitudes, the promises that you make with forward guidance. And then for Randy, I wonder to what extent did uncertainty over who was going to chair the Committee in the third quarter last year factor at all into the delay that you saw in getting to the pivot?

WALLER: So, I would say, looking at the strategy, one of the things that—and recall that I wasn't on the FOMC when the decision was made—that question is whether we should have stopped asset purchases in 2020 after it was clear the worst part of the pandemic appeared to be over, or did we feel that we needed that tool to help the economy recover in 2021? That's a question of whether we should have just stopped asset purchases in late 2020 and used forward guidance. Or should we have started tapering earlier as we saw the data coming in? That was my own personal preference, that we should have started much earlier in tapering to set us up for rate hikes later, and I argued that we needed to have the policy space. Maybe the economy wouldn't have recovered quite as well, but we needed the policy space as a risk management tool going forward. So I think tapering is the thing that really kind of got us in this bind. We couldn't lift off until we got it over with. It was a large amount of purchases. And we didn't start fast enough, and we didn't go fast enough at first. So that would be the way I think about lessons learned.

ANDREW LEVIN: I'm Andrew Levin from Dartmouth College. This has been a really great day. Thanks to John Taylor and John Cochrane and Mike Bordo for organizing it, and thanks to the panelists for participating. Rather than trying to second-guess what happened in 2021, I'd like to ask you about risk management going forward. According to the New York Fed's latest household survey, consumers now expect inflation over the next 12 months to be around 8 or 9%. That's their point forecast. And there's at least a possibility that they could be right. So it seems like the Fed would just be following a "hope for the best" approach by raising the funds rate to a level that's consistent with inflation declining all the way to around 3%. I'm much more concerned about the institutional risk that could materialize if we get to the end of the year and inflation is still running at high single digits. If the funds rate is only at 3.5%, and the real interest rate (adjusted for inflation) is −5%, then that would be a really big problem. Are you comfortable with facing that sort of institutional risk?

WALLER: That ain't gonna happen. I'll tell you that right now. What else you want me to say?

BULLARD: What I've said is, I want to get to a 3.5% policy rate expeditiously. Then at that point, we could see where we are and we could analyze issues like the ones you're talking about, e.g., whether inflation expectations are still going the wrong way. At that point, we'd be 100 basis points above what the Committee is saying the neutral benchmark is. Another idea I have is the front-loading idea—i.e., to get the policy rate to neutral and, for me, above neutral now—because that's what the optimal impulse response would be. You'd go up quite aways pretty rapidly, then you'd come back down from the higher level. We saw some of the impulse responses that Volker Wieland put up, for instance. That would be the pattern that you'd be looking for: some kind of increase now that would be enough to control the shock, then you come down from that point to the neutral rate. As opposed to what the Committee has been saying for a long time, that you're going to edge up to the neutral rate and stay there, I think my impulse response is a better idea of what we need to do here. But this is evolving day to day. The data has to come in, and we'll see how inflation and inflation expectations evolve going forward.

WILLIAM NELSON: Bill Nelson, from the Bank Policy Institute, and let me also add my thanks for a fantastic event today. So I have a kind of a practical question similar to Nick's question. So the Charlie Evans threshold-based forward guidance that was discussed earlier was two triggers, either of which would free up the Fed to tighten. So the language was: We're gonna remain at zero at least until unemployment falls below 6.5 or projected inflation rises above 2.5%. I might not have those numbers exactly right. But it was language that both extended the market's and the public's expectation for how long rates would be at zero but also was very robust to off the baseline path events, because it freed up the Committee if things went awry in either dimension, whereas the forward guidance that was used for the target range and for the balance sheet in 2020, both required double triggers. We will stay at zero until both the inflation rate is up to 2 and we're at maximum full employment. There were a few wiggle-room words, but not as many as in the threshold guidance, not as many escape hatches as Charlie's language. And the balance sheet guidance was the same, we will keep buying until we've made substantial progress on both legs. And that's language that is not robust to developments that are off the equilibrium path but stronger in many ways, although a bit less precise. Anyway, having had experience now with both types of qualitative . . . I mean, forward guidance that uses actual data, do you have any reflections on which you recommend the Committee use in the future?

BULLARD: Yeah, first of all, I'd agree with Chris's earlier comment that lifting this playbook on tapering—talk about tapering, taper, wait, then raise interest rates—from the Yellen era and trying to apply that to the post-pandemic economy was an error because it just did not fit. When Chair Yellen did it, it worked, and it made perfect sense because inflation was below target pretty much the entire time. But here we had a very different situation evolving, and we eventually had to chuck the whole playbook and eventually raised rates in March of this year. It was way sooner than what was previously thought of. I think that's a key thing.

The other thing to understand about the genesis of the flexible average inflation targeting and the idea that you weren't going to react until you actually saw some inflation is that we were tightening in the Yellen era with inflation below target. Why was that? Because we believed in the Phillips curve (I'm not that big of a believer in the Phillips curve) and we thought there was inflation ahead and, therefore, we were going to tighten preemptively. It wasn't that successful I think. It had stops and starts—we had

2015 and 2016. So we had problems with that approach. The attitude of the Committee was: We're not going to do that again.

But I also feel like the framework—I know there's a lot of talk about the framework here, so maybe I'll just leave you with this thought—is all about the effective lower bound. How to meet the challenges around the effective lower bound, how to make sure you're going to average 2 percent inflation considering the effective lower bound. So what I want to do is get you to draw a little diagram. When inflation is low, flexible average inflation targeting. When inflation is high, see Paul Volcker.

CHAPTER FOURTEEN

INFLATION BLUES: THE FORTIETH-ANNIVERSARY REVIVAL?

Monika Piazzesi

In 1983, legendary blues musician B. B. King recorded "Inflation Blues," a song that mirrored Americans' struggle to pay the bills and their frustration with the government's inability to address the rising cost of living. This was just after inflation soared to more than 14% at the dawn of the decade, while unemployment peaked at about 11% during 1982. Now, forty years after its vinyl debut, King's "Inflation Blues" is threatening an encore.

At the Federal Open Market Committee (FOMC) meeting on March 16, 2022, the Federal Reserve Bank announced its decision to raise its target for the federal funds rate from essentially zero to 0.25%. As of this writing, the current inflation rate for personal consumption expenditures (PCE) is much higher than the federal funds rate, with the latest numbers (from February 2022) being 6.4% for PCE inflation and 5.4% for core inflation (excluding food and energy). By keeping the fed funds rate so low relative to inflation, the Fed drove the *real* short rate—the difference between the fed funds rate and core inflation—into negative territory. When the real rate, which measures the return on savings adjusted for inflation, is negative, the incentive to save is extremely low while borrowing and—in turn—investment are encouraged.

How low the Fed believes the real rate to be during coming years can be inferred from table 14.1, which contains data from the Summary of Economic Projections (SEP), also released by the Fed on March 16, 2022. The SEP contains what FOMC meeting participants believe are the most likely outcomes for real gross domestic product (GDP) growth, the unemployment rate, and inflation for each year from 2022 to 2024 and over the longer run.

These projections imply that the Fed currently expects the real rate at the end of 2022 to be −2.2%, the projected difference between the fed funds rate, 1.9%, and core inflation, 4.1%. For the years 2023 and 2024, the Fed expects the real rate to be 0.2% and 0.5%, respectively. Over the longer run, the Fed estimates a 0.4% real rate.

The long-run real rate is of central importance for many questions we have about the economy. For example, whether or not households are saving enough for retirement depends on the real rate of return on their savings. Until a decade ago, the long-run real rate was around 2.50%. At that rate, household savings of $1,000 would more than double to nearly $2,100 in real terms over a period of three decades. If, however, the long-run real rate is only 0.4%, as the Fed now estimates (see table 14.1), $1,000 of savings will stay roughly unchanged in real terms after three decades. That is a big difference for households that are saving for retirement.

A January 13, 2021, speech by Richard H. Clarida, who stepped down as the Fed's vice chair in early 2022, explained that a long-term real rate of 0.5% is indeed what we now should expect in a normal environment with inflation at the 2% target and the economy growing at trend.[1]

There are many reasons for this big decline in the neutral real rate, or r-star, over the last decade in many industrialized countries.[2]

---

1. Richard H. Clarida, "The Federal Reserve's New Framework: Context and Consequences," speech delivered (via webcast) at "The Road Ahead for Central Banks," a seminar sponsored by the Hoover Economic Policy Working Group, Hoover Institution, Stanford University, January 13, 2021, https://www.federalreserve.gov/newsevents/speech /clarida20210113a.htm.

2. John C. Williams, "Three Questions on R-star," FRBSF Economic Letter, 2017-05, February 21, 2017, https://www.frbsf.org/economic-research/wp-content/uploads/sites/4 /el2017-05.pdf.

TABLE 14.1. SEP Median Forecasts

Variable	2022	2023	2024	Longer Run
Real GDP growth	2.8	2.2	2.0	1.8
Unemployment rate	3.5	3.5	3.6	4.0
PCE inflation	4.3	2.7	2.3	2.0
Core PCE inflation	4.1	2.6	2.3	2.0
Federal funds rate	1.9	2.8	2.8	2.4

These advanced economies have experienced a dramatic slowdown in the trend of real GDP growth. Lower growth rates are associated with a reduced need for savings to fund investment and thus a lower r-star. The slowdown in growth can be attributed to an aging workforce and lower productivity growth.

THE FED IS SLOW TO FIGHT INFLATION PRESSURES

Fed officials spent weeks giving speeches preparing the public for a liftoff in interest rates after keeping rates at zero for such a long time. Financial markets expected the subsequent 0.25% increase in the fed funds rate and now expect further gradual increases into 2023.

But the Fed's announcement is puzzling. Negative real rates stimulate the economy because borrowing is cheap, which encourages investment. In the environment in which they began raising rates, the economy does not need any further stimulus. Quite to the contrary, the economy has been running hot with levels of inflation that were last seen during the Great Inflation of the 1970s.

The current May 2022 inflation rate is sky high (from a US perspective, other countries are more used to these kinds of inflation rates) due to a combination of supply chain disruptions, pent-up household demand, wide-ranging government aid programs to support the economy during the COVID-19 pandemic as well as further large-scale asset purchases by the Fed. While economists disagree about the relative importance of each of these factors, inflation is currently also high in many other industrialized countries that did not adopt the same policies as the United States. Russia's ongoing war against Ukraine has further increased energy prices and thereby added to inflation pressures worldwide.

In his 2021 speech, Clarida explained the type of policy rule he would propose for thinking about the liftoff in interest rates, given the new policy framework adopted by the Fed. A policy rule describes what the Fed should be doing and what kind of fed funds rate it should set given where the economy is.

That policy rule is a Taylor-type rule (named after my Stanford colleague John Taylor). The rule sets the fed funds rate to a neutral rate of 2.5% (the 2% inflation target plus a 0.5% real rate) but raises the fed funds rate if inflation is higher than 2%. Clarida recommended a 1.5 response coefficient to inflation deviations from the 2% target. The policy rule looks like this:

Recommended fed funds rate = 2.5% + 1.5 × (inflation rate – 2%).

Since core inflation is, at this writing, currently 5.4%, the rule recommends a fed funds rate of 7.6%! It is obvious that we are far away from this goal even after the last FOMC meeting.

What should the Fed do? Clarida advocated that the Fed should not close the wide gap between its goal and the current fed funds rate in one giant step. Instead, he recommended that the Fed take a much more gradual approach. How gradual? The answer is an inertial Taylor rule, which says that the Fed should place a large 80% weight on where the economy is right now (before the Fed decision, that was a zero fed funds rate) and a modest weight of 20% on where the Fed should be (the 7.6% recommended fed funds rate, given the sky-high inflation rate).

The inertial Taylor rule says that in May 2022, the fed funds rate should already have been at 1.72% since the last FOMC meeting.

Given the inflation pressures, we should have thus seen a massive rate hike on March 16, 2022—seven times as high as the actual 0.25% decision.

The rule also helps to think about the Fed's plans going forward. The Fed's own estimate of 4.1% core inflation for the end of 2022 from table 14.1 implies a 5.65% interest rate target. Its 1.9% projection for the fed funds rate is much lower than that. These numbers reveal that the Fed thinks the economy will only be a third of the way toward its interest rate target by the end of the year. Moreover, the Fed expects inflation to drop by half over this year while projecting strong real growth: projected real GDP growth over the next years is higher than the 1.8% long-run projection in table 14.1.

These projections are highly optimistic. The Fed knows the economy is like a car driving downhill at a speed far above the speed limit. It also anticipates forces down the road that will further push the car to higher speeds. Moreover, the Fed is aware that its own actions will also further accelerate the car, while policy rules for the conduct of monetary policy would have called on the Fed to step on the brakes. But Fed officials are convinced that the car's high speed is only temporary—somehow the forces of nature will slow down the car and the car will roll to a stop right at the bottom of the hill.

To respond to strong real growth down the road, John Taylor's original policy rule puts a positive coefficient on deviations of output from trend, a variable called the output gap:

Taylor's recommended fed funds rate
= Clarida's recommended fed funds rate + 0.5 × output gap.

The Fed's projections of real GDP growth in excess of 1.8% long-run growth in table 14.1 can serve as a proxy for the output gap. Since projected growth is high, the Taylor rule prescribes a higher fed funds rate than Clarida. To summarize, all these policy rules suggest that the Fed is not stepping on the brakes enough.

THE GREAT INFLATION OF THE 1970S

The last time the Fed fell behind the curve was in the 1970s. Back then, Fed leaders Arthur F. Burns and then G. William Miller after him, reacted slowly to the rise in inflation. Both chairmen thought it was important to promote economic growth even if it resulted in inflation. Moreover, they believed that inflation was caused by forces outside the Fed's control, such as high energy prices. Therefore, they did not tighten enough—driving real rates to negative territory, just like today.

In joint research with Stanford PhD students Matteo Leombroni and Ciaran Rogers and my Stanford colleague Martin Schneider, we studied the "Great Inflation" of the 1970s more closely.[3] Figure 14.1 plots key household sector positions over the postwar period. The yellow shaded areas are three episodes for which we have more detailed household-level data on portfolios: the late 1960s, the late 1970s, and the mid-1990s.

Figure 14.1 shows that during the 1970s, the yellow shaded area in the middle, household net worth as a fraction of GDP fell by 25%, before recovering again to its late 1960s value. Our research attributes the drop in net worth to two key developments. First, baby boomers entered into asset markets. The average asset market participant thus became younger. Second, inflation eroded the value of bond portfolios, which are nominal assets, and made households poorer. Being young and poor lowers the propensity to save and thus diminishes net worth. The other lines in the figure are the three main components of net worth: housing, equity, and net nominal assets (the difference between any holdings of bonds and household debt).

---

3. Matteo Leombroni, Monika Piazzesi, Ciaran Rogers, and Martin Schneider, "Inflation and the Price of Real Assets," Department of Economics, Stanford University, January 2020, https://web.stanford.edu/~piazzesi/inflationAP.pdf.

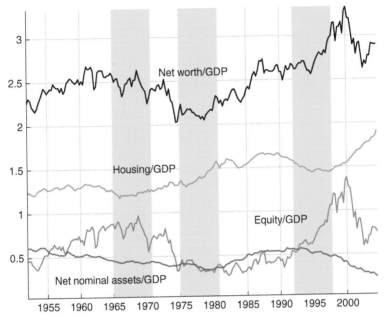

FIGURE 14.1. Household Net Worth in the United States as a Fraction of GDP
Source: Financial Accounts, Board of Governors of the Federal Reserve System.

Figure 14.2 shows portfolio weights in panel (a), in particular a 20 percentage point shift away from equity and into real estate during the late 1970s. This portfolio adjustment was associated with large moves by asset prices in opposite directions. Panel (b) shows that—relative to their fundamentals—house prices rose while equity prices fell. For housing, the line in panel (b) is the ratio of house prices to rents. For equity, the line is the ratio of equity values to dividends.

Our research points to several reasons that high inflation made housing such an attractive asset during the 1970s. First, the US tax code favors housing during high inflation: Mortgage interest deductibility is a bigger subsidy when mortgage rates are high. Moreover, capital gains on housing are largely tax sheltered. Finally, dividends on owner-occupied housing—the implicit rental value of

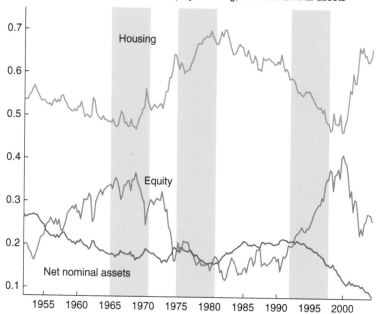

(a) Household portfolio shares on equity, housing, and net nominal assets

Housing

Equity

Net nominal assets

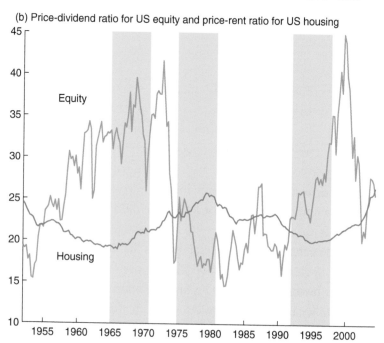

(b) Price-dividend ratio for US equity and price-rent ratio for US housing

Equity

Housing

FIGURE 14.2. Household Portfolios and Ratios of Asset Prices to Fundamental Values

Source: Financial Accounts, Board of Governors of the Federal Reserve System.

an owner-occupied house—are not taxed. All these features of the tax code matter more in times of high inflation because mortgage rates, capital gains on housing, and rents are higher.

A second reason behind the portfolio shift toward housing was strong disagreement about inflation among households. Based on data from the Michigan Surveys of Consumers, we document that younger households had much higher inflation expectations than older households. While the median 5-year inflation forecast was 6.3%, households aged below thirty-five years were forecasting 10% inflation, while households aged sixty-five years and above were forecasting 5% inflation. Since most house purchases are made by younger households, the average home purchase in the 1970s involved a buyer who believed that real borrowing costs are low. Therefore, those buyers were willing to pay more for housing.

Additionally, an important contributing factor to the massive shift out of equity was high uncertainty during the 1970s. With high energy prices and the Fed not keeping inflation under control, there was much uncertainty about whether businesses would be viable. This uncertainty, together with a tax code that favors housing when inflation is high, can quantitatively account for the shift of household portfolios away from equity toward housing.

BACK TO THE 1970S?

Are we in a time machine on our way back to the 1970s? A quick glance at rising ratios of house prices to rents seems to suggest that the answer to this question may be yes. However, uncertainty in the United States is relatively low at the moment. The public still trusts the Fed to rein in inflation. As a consequence, the ratio of equity values to dividends managed to stay high despite the currently high inflation. That is different from the 1970s.

The big question in the coming weeks will be whether the Fed will lose its reputation as an inflation fighter, especially if there are signs that inflation pressures may be more persistent. Right now, short-run inflation expectations are elevated, but the public believes the Fed will take us back to 2% inflation over the longer run.

We can see this trust, for example, in break-even inflation, defined as the spread between the interest rate on Treasury bonds and the interest rate on TIPS (which are government bonds that are protected against inflation). Break-even inflation over the next five years is 3.41% and 2.83% over the next ten years, quite low compared with the high inflation rate we are currently witnessing. If inflation expectations over the longer run increase, Treasury bond investors would demand to get paid a higher nominal interest rate by the US government relative to the interest rate on TIPS as a compensation for the lower expected real value of the associated bond payments.

Fighting inflation is not a pleasant task. When former Fed chair Paul Volcker raised interest rates to lower inflation, car dealers sent him coffins containing the keys of unsold cars and farmers protested in front of Federal Reserve Bank buildings.

Many Southern European countries before the introduction of the Euro did not have a top central banker with a reputation like Paul Volcker. As a consequence, inflation in these countries always fluctuated between very high and sky high—an important argument for the creation of the Euro and for the location of the European Central Bank in Frankfurt, Germany. The more time passes and inflation stays as high as it is currently, the more Fed Chair Jerome Powell risks to lose his own reputation to be tough on inflation.

Once that reputation is gone, our time machine will complete its journey and arrive in the 1970s. And that will have us all singing the blues. Let's hope for the best.

GENERAL DISCUSSION

JAMES BULLARD: Thanks, Monika. This is great. I have two questions. Would the Taylor rule that you want to use fit Fed policy in 2017, 2018, 2019? I think it would have prescribed super-high interest rates back then. We seem to get pretty good outcomes there, so I'm not sure we want to take that particular version of the Taylor rule. In fact, I showed a different Taylor rule earlier.

The other question is on the shares. It seems like you have a closed-economy model. They switch between equities, housing, and other assets. Is that really the way to think of it? US equities are the value of the US corporate sector globally, and I'm not sure you'd get a repeat of the seventies—given the much more open economy today, with free capital flows across borders and so on. So it's not so clear to me that I would come to quite the same conclusion that you did here. Also, on the housing side, if people really think that housing is a great hedge against inflation, you've got real estate investment trusts and other things that can enable even foreign investors to invest in the US housing sector.

MONIKA PIAZZESI: Yes, thank you. The question about the Taylor rule is well taken. If you take other Taylor rules, other types of policy rules, you'll get results that may look closer to what nominal rates are now. The way I'm thinking about this is that the Fed was sort of going through a period in which it basically was working off a reputation that was built up over many decades. And I would think that interest rates have been low for a while now, maybe too low. And now that we're having this inflation, if the Fed doesn't respond strongly now, the Fed is revealing its type of being a central bank that does not strongly fight inflation. And the question about, are we going to see this shift out of equity into housing again? An interesting fact is if you look at international plots—I didn't talk about this, but the shift out of equity into housing is not just in the US but internationally. In the seventies, this was a global phenomenon. If you look at all industrialized countries, they all had a housing boom. If you compute—I have a different paper that looks at this for all industrialized countries, and all these stock prices collapsed while housing increased massively. There was a housing boom in all European countries, for example. Everybody who experienced an oil price shock in the seventies and then had a lot of inflation was experiencing this phenomenon. Back then, all economies were pretty much closed. A good question is, how would this play out now? But I would think at least that the mechanism that housing hedges inflation because rents will always increase with inflation—the rental value of these houses will always increase with inflation. That is a protection that just housing gives you and not equity.

KRISHNA GUHA: Thanks. Krishna Guha. So two questions if I may. So first of all, I very strongly agree with your proposal here that we need a stabilizing Taylor principle, if you like, in the face of these inflation shocks. The question is whether that Taylor principle should be applied only to the point—today's federal funds rate—or to the path. So since the beginning of this year, the 10-year breakeven that you described has moved up 50 basis points. The 10-year yield has moved up 100 basis points. So arguably, the Fed's communications around the path of policy, combined with the market's expectations formation, is actually performing the function of a stabilizing Taylor-type principle. And so my question is, would you concur with that, and if not, why not?

Second thing has to do with the equities in a period of high inflation. So there's a Modigliani paper, I'm trying to remember which one it is. Modigliani-Cohn maybe?

PIAZZESI: Cohn, yes.

GUHA: Yeah, which essentially argues that the weakness in equities during the period of high inflation was a nominal illusion, and that the recovery of equity value in the later eighties and in the nineties, was essentially catch-up to what always had been the fair-value pricing of the equities. So do you agree with that or not?

PIAZZESI: Great question. Should we be looking at the path? I tend to think that we should look at many different policy rules. As Jim was saying, we need to consider a variety of rules, and then study what these policy rules would prescribe for policy and whether incorporating the path will matter. That is very interesting. The fact that in a period with high growth, real interest rates are negative and nominal interest rates are still close to zero while inflation is so high, that tells me that right now, we're not using the right policy rule. Of the many, I feel this is not the right one.

It's a great question to ask, what's the reason why equity is declining in times of high inflation. Modigliani-Cohn say that investors confuse nominal and real rates in times of high inflation. Therefore, they discount future dividends with high nominal rates, while they should be discounting future dividends with real rates, which are much lower in times of high inflation. I don't think that confusion is really needed to explain low equity valuations in the 1970s. Having said that, I believe that right now consumers are likely to be confused about nominal and real rates, because we have been in such a low-inflation environment for a long time. US households have lost their ability to process inflation. Because if you look at households in Argentina, they're very smart about how they're going about computing nominal and real rates, that's second nature to them. While in the US, households are not used to that anymore. Sometimes I'm having a hard time explaining the real rate to undergraduate students. They ask me, Why is it so important to look at real rates? So while people learn the difference between nominal and real when there is inflation, right now, after a long time of low inflation, they may no longer know the difference. Arvind?

ARVIND KRISHNAMURTHY: Monika, your housing point is both provocative and timely. And I'm going to ask you to comment on a couple of things.

We learned from the last crisis that the structure of the mortgage market, liquidity constraints, payment-to-income matter for housing market equilibrium. So, if I apply that lesson to the world currently, with market mortgage rates rising from 2.5 to 5.5 or 6%, that implies a substantial increase in mortgage payments, with income not catching up until inflation happens over time. So how does that fit with your observation regarding housing prices in the seventies? And, you mentioned international evidence. We have different mortgage markets and contracts in different countries. Does that help to understand what happened to housing markets in the '70s across different countries?

PIAZZESI: That's a great question. The US housing market is special in the sense that there are so many different ways in which the US government is subsidizing housing. There is the mortgage-interest tax deductibility, that's a bigger subsidy when the nominal interest rate is higher, even in real terms. If you're a US household, and you're thinking about buying a house, the high nominal interest rate is actually not that bad, because you get to deduct it from your taxes. The other feature that plays into this sort of thing is that housing is a nice asset during times of high inflation because capital gains on housing are basically tax sheltered. There's a high limit on when you actually start paying capital gains taxes when you sell your house, and that is also present in many other countries. While the tax subsidy for mortgages is not there for all countries, the tax advantage of capital gains on housing is there in many countries. And the fact that your rental equivalent as an owner is not taxed, that you're consuming the dividend on housing—you live in your house—and that is not taxed. That is another reason why in high inflation times housing is attractive as an asset. In other words, the tax code in many different countries makes housing more attractive in a period of high inflation.

AXEL MERK: Hi, I'm Axel. You mentioned confidence in the Fed, and I'd like to float a question at you how you measure that. And as food for thought, we talk about the 10-year breakeven rate, and I'm all but certain that nobody in this room knows what the inflation rate is going to be over the next ten years. And to me the breakeven rate is just that, it's a measure of how confident the market is to be able to contain inflation. But how does one disentangle that from the rate path that's already been announced versus the confidence? Because at the core, if we have a problem in the market, and we trust the Fed to take care of it, well, all will be fine. But if, as you point out, the market loses confidence, it's not. So how do you draw that distinction?

PIAZZESI: That's a great question. So here, basically, if you look at this graph, this is the breakeven inflation rate up until the start of TIPS trading. TIPS haven't been around and liquid for so long, which is why this is a relatively short data sample, it starts in 2004. This is from the St. Louis Fed database. If you look at it and 2%, it's not very often that breakeven inflation goes very high. What makes me worry is that breakeven inflation has recently been increasing and right now is at almost 3% for a longer horizon. That's where I see a loss in confidence. If everything was totally under control, if the Fed was completely in charge and households would trust the Fed, I think we should be seeing a 3% breakeven inflation plus or minus some small fluctuations, but basically 2%. Here, we're seeing a lot more.

DAVID PAPELL: David Papell, University of Houston. I'm not convinced that you should be apologetic for using Rich Clarida's rule for just before COVID. I'm looking on my phone at the *Monetary Policy Report* for 2021, and Rich's rule, which is basically the balanced approach shortfalls rule, inertial and non-inertial makes no difference here, is about equal to the federal funds rate by the beginning of 2019 and stays that way through 2019. And even in 2017 and 2018, it's closer to the federal funds rate than the Taylor rule or the balanced approach rule. So I don't think you should be apologizing for it.

PIAZZESI: I don't want to look like I'm apologizing. I'm using Richard's rule because I think it's terrific, and I'm also applauding him as a policy maker who helps us actually think about this phenomenon. The fact that policy makers explain to the public what kind of rule we should be looking at, I think it tells you everything about the US.

About the Contributors

MICHAEL D. BORDO is a Board of Governors Professor of Economics and director of the Center for Monetary and Financial History at Rutgers University, New Brunswick, New Jersey. He has held previous academic positions at the University of South Carolina and Carleton University in Ottawa, Canada. Bordo has been a visiting professor at the University of California–Los Angeles, Carnegie Mellon University, Princeton University, Harvard University, and Cambridge University, where he was Pitt Professor of American History and Institutions. He is currently the Ilene and Morton Harris Distinguished Visiting Fellow at the Hoover Institution. He has been a visiting scholar at the International Monetary Fund, the Federal Reserve banks of St. Louis, Cleveland, and Dallas, the Federal Reserve Board of Governors, the Bank of Canada, the Bank of England, and the Bank for International Settlements. He is a research associate of the National Bureau of Economic Research and a member of the Shadow Open Market Committee. He has a BA degree from McGill University, an MSc in economics from the London School of Economics, and a PhD from the University of Chicago. He has published many articles in leading journals and eighteen books on monetary economics and monetary history. His latest book is *The Historical Performance of the Federal Reserve: The Importance of Rules* (Hoover Institution Press, 2019). He is editor of a series of books for Cambridge University Press: *Studies in Macroeconomic History*.

JAMES ("JIM") BULLARD is the president and CEO of the Federal Reserve Bank of St. Louis. In that role, he is a participant on the Federal Reserve's Federal Open Market Committee, which meets regularly to set the direction of US monetary policy. He also oversees the Federal

Reserve's Eighth District, including activities at the St. Louis headquarters and its branches in Little Rock, Arkansas; Louisville, Kentucky; and Memphis, Tennessee. A noted economist and policy maker, Bullard makes Fed transparency and dialogue a priority on the international and national stage as well as on Main Street. He serves on the board of directors of Concordance Academy of Leadership, and he is a past board chair of the United Way USA. Bullard is coeditor of the *Journal of Economic Dynamics and Control*, a member of the editorial advisory board of the *National Institute Economic Review*, and a member of the Central Bank Research Association's senior council. He is an honorary professor of economics at Washington University in St. Louis, where he also sits on the advisory council of the economics department and the advisory board of the Center for Dynamic Economics. A native of Forest Lake, Minnesota, Bullard received his doctorate in economics from Indiana University–Bloomington.

JENNIFER BURNS is an associate professor of history at Stanford University and a research fellow at the Hoover Institution. The leading independent expert on Ayn Rand, she is author of the acclaimed biography *Goddess of the Market: Ayn Rand and the American Right* (Oxford University Press, 2009). Currently, she is completing an intellectual biography of Milton Friedman. At the Hoover Institution she directs the annual Summer Workshop on Political Economy. Burns is a graduate of Harvard College and the University of California–Berkeley. Podcasts of her American history courses are available through iTunes and on her website, jenniferburns.org.

RICHARD H. CLARIDA is the C. Lowell Harriss Professor of Economics and International Affairs at Columbia University, where he has taught since 1988. On September 17, 2018, he was sworn in as vice chairman of the Board of Governors of the Federal Reserve and served in that capacity until January 14, 2022. From February 2002 until May 2003, Clarida served as the assistant secretary of the US Treasury for economic policy, a position that required confirmation by the US Senate. In that position, he served as chief economic adviser to the secretary of the Treasury, advising him on a wide range of economic policy issues, including US and global economic prospects, international capital flows, corporate governance, and the maturity structure of US debt. In May 2003, then Treasury secretary

John Snow presented him with the Treasury Medal in recognition of his record of outstanding service. From 1997 until 2001, Clarida served as chair of the Department of Economics at Columbia University. Earlier in his career, he taught at Yale University and served in the administration of President Ronald Reagan as senior staff economist with the President's Council of Economic Advisers. He has published numerous and frequently cited articles in leading academic journals on monetary policy, exchange rates, interest rates, and international capital flows. Over his career, he has been invited to present his views and research to the world's leading central banks and has also served as a consultant to several prominent financial firms. He received his BS from the University of Illinois with Bronze Tablet honors in 1979 and his MA and PhD from Harvard University in 1983.

JOHN H. COCHRANE is the Rose-Marie and Jack Anderson Senior Fellow at the Hoover Institution. He is also a research associate of the National Bureau of Economic Research and an adjunct scholar of the Cato Institute. Before joining Hoover, Cochrane was a professor of finance at the University of Chicago's Booth School of Business and previously taught in its Economics department. He served as president of the American Finance Association and is a fellow of the Econometric Society. He writes on asset pricing, financial regulation, business cycles, and monetary policy. He has also written articles on macroeconomics, health insurance, time-series econometrics, financial regulation, and other topics. His books include the forthcoming *The Fiscal Theory of the Price Level* and *Asset Pricing*. Cochrane frequently contributes essays to the *Wall Street Journal*, *National Review*, *Project Syndicate*, and other publications. He maintains a blog, *The Grumpy Economist*. Cochrane earned a bachelor's degree in physics at MIT and a PhD in economics at the University of California–Berkeley.

TYLER GOODSPEED is a Kleinheinz Fellow at the Hoover Institution and US director at Greenmantle LLC. From 2020 to 2021, he served as chairman of the Council of Economic Advisers, having been appointed by the president as a member of the council in 2019. In that role, he advised the administration's economic response to the coronavirus pandemic as well as subsequent economic recovery packages. He previously served as chief economist for macroeconomic policy and senior economist for tax, public finance, and macroeconomics, playing an instrumental role in the design of the 2017 Tax Cuts and Jobs Act. Before joining the Council of Economic Advisers, Goodspeed was on the faculty of economics at the University of Oxford and was a lecturer in economics at King's College London. He has published extensively on economic and financial history, banking, and monetary economics, with particular attention to the role of access to credit in mitigating the effects of adverse environmental shocks in historical contexts. He received his BA, MA, and PhD from Harvard University and his MPhil from the University of Cambridge, where he was a Gates Scholar.

GEORGE J. HALL is the Fred C. Hecht Professor of Economics at Brandeis University, where he teaches macroeconomics. His research focuses on the history of US fiscal policy and firm-level inventory and pricing behavior. Before joining Brandeis in 2006, he served on the faculty at Yale University and the research staff of the Federal Reserve Bank of Chicago. He earned his BA at Oberlin College and his PhD in economics at the University of Chicago.

BETH HAMMACK is co-head of the global financing group within the Investment Banking Division (IBD) and a member of the Management Committee at Goldman Sachs. She is a member of the IBD Executive Committee, Firmwide Capital Committee, Firmwide Asset Liability Committee, and Global Inclusion and Diversity Committee, and she serves as a global executive sponsor of the Women's Network. In addition, she is a firmwide champion for Launch With GS, Goldman Sachs's $1 billion investment strategy grounded in the firm's data-driven thesis that diverse teams drive strong returns. Previously, Hammack was global treasurer of Goldman Sachs and chief executive officer of Goldman Sachs Bank USA, where she was responsible for the firm's funding, liquidity, and capital management strategy. Before that, she held a variety of leadership positions in interest rate products (IRP) trading, including global head of short-term macro trading, global head of repo trading, and co-head of US IRP cash trading. Earlier, she was a market maker on the IRP desk, where she traded a variety of instruments, focused primarily on options and later agencies. She joined Goldman Sachs in 1993 as an analyst in debt capital markets and was named managing director in 2003 and partner in 2010. She chairs the Treasury Borrowing Advisory Committee and serves on the boards of Northwell Health and Math for America. She is a former member of the Treasury Market Practices Group. She earned an AB in quantitative economics and history from Stanford University.

ARVIND KRISHNAMURTHY is the John S. Osterweis Professor of Finance at Stanford Graduate School of Business and a research associate at the National Bureau of Economic Research. He formerly taught at the Kellogg School of Management (1998–2014). Krishnamurthy studies finance, macroeconomics, and monetary policy. He has studied the causes and consequences of liquidity crises in emerging markets and developed economies and the role of government policy in stabilizing crises. Recently he has been examining the importance of US Treasury bonds and the dollar in the international monetary system. He has published numerous journal articles and received awards for his research, including the Smith Breeden Prize for best paper published in the *Journal of Finance*. He did his undergraduate studies at the University of Pennsylvania and his doctoral work at the Massachusetts Institute of Technology.

MICKEY D. LEVY is the chief economist for Berenberg Capital Markets LLC. He is a long-standing member of the Shadow Open Market Committee. He is on the Financial Research Advisory Committee of the Office of Financial Research. He is also a member of the Council on Foreign Relations and the Economic Club of New York. From 1998 to 2013, he was chief economist at Bank of America Corporation, where he was on the Executive Asset Liability and Finance committees. He conducts research on monetary and fiscal policies, their impacts, and how they influence economic and financial market performance in the United States and globally. He has authored numerous papers on the effectiveness of monetary and fiscal policies, their interaction, and longer-run risks. He testifies frequently before the US Congress on various aspects of monetary policy and banking regulation, credit conditions and debt, fiscal and budget policies, and global capital flows.

JOHN LIPSKY is a senior fellow of the Foreign Policy Institute at Johns Hopkins University's School of Advanced International Studies. Most recently, he was first deputy managing director of the International Monetary Fund. Previously, he was vice chairman of JPMorgan Investment Bank, chief economist at JPMorgan Chase, chief economist and director of research at Chase Manhattan Bank, and chief economist at Salomon

Brothers. Early in his career, he spent ten years at the International Monetary Fund. Currently, he is the chair of the National Bureau of Economic Research and the cochair of the Aspen Institute's Program on the World Economy. He is the vice chair of the Center for Global Development and of the Bretton Woods Committee. He also serves on the advisory board of the Stanford Institute for Economic Policy Research, is a director of the American Council on Germany, and is a life member of the Council on Foreign Relations. He received his PhD in economics from Stanford University.

ELLEN R. MCGRATTAN is a visiting fellow at the Hoover Institution, a professor of economics at the University of Minnesota, and the director of the Heller-Hurwicz Economics Institute. Her research is concerned with the impact of monetary and fiscal policy—in particular, the effects on GDP, investment, hours, productivity, the stock market, and international capital flows. Her recent work reexamines issues in macroeconomics and international finance in light of the fact that some investments are mismeasured. McGrattan is a consultant at the Federal Reserve Bank of Minneapolis, a research associate at the National Bureau of Economic Research, a fellow of the Econometric Society, a fellow of the Society for the Advancement of Economic Theory, president of the Society for Economic Dynamics, a member of the US Bureau of Economic Analysis Advisory Committee, and an associate editor of the *American Economic Review*. She received her undergraduate degree in mathematics and economics from Boston College and her PhD in economics from Stanford University.

MONIKA PIAZZESI is the Joan Kenney Professor of Economics at Stanford University and a professor (by courtesy) at Stanford Graduate School of Business. She is a research associate at the National Bureau of Economic Research's Asset Pricing Program, where she was the director of the program. She is also a fellow of the Stanford Institute for Economic Policy Research (SIEPR), the American Academy of Arts and Sciences, and the Econometric Society, and was a Guggenheim fellow during 2015–16. From 2006 to 2014, she was coeditor of the *Journal of Political Economy*. Before joining Stanford, she taught at the University of Chicago and the University of California–Los Angeles. She received the Elaine Bennett Research Prize and the Bernácer Prize for Research in Macroeconomics and Finance. She holds a diploma in economics from the University of

Bonn and a PhD from Stanford. Her research focuses on the interaction between the macroeconomy and financial markets. She works on monetary policy, credit, banking, housing markets, and expectation formation.

CHARLES I. PLOSSER is a visiting fellow at the Hoover Institution. He served as a public governor of the Financial Industry Regulatory Authority from 2015 to 2021 and as president and CEO of the Federal Reserve Bank of Philadelphia from 2006 to his retirement in 2015. He has been a longtime advocate of the Federal Reserve's adopting an explicit inflation target, which the Federal Open Market Committee did in January 2012. Before joining the Philadelphia Fed in 2006, Plosser was the John M. Olin Distinguished Professor of Economics and Public Policy and served as dean from 1993 to 2003 at the University of Rochester's Simon School of Business. He has served as a research associate of the National Bureau of Economic Research. Plosser served as coeditor of the *Journal of Monetary Economics* for two decades and cochaired the Shadow Open Market Committee with Anna Schwartz. His research and teaching interests include monetary and fiscal policy, long-term economic growth, and banking and financial markets. Plosser earned PhD and MBA degrees from the University of Chicago.

RANDAL QUARLES is chairman and founder of the Cynosure Group, an investment firm bringing together several of the United States' largest family offices to make long-term private investments. From October 2017 through October 2021, he was vice chairman for supervision of the Federal Reserve Board, charged with ensuring stability of the financial sector. From December 2018 until December 2021, he also served as the chairman of the Financial Stability Board (FSB), a global body established after the great financial crisis to coordinate international efforts to enhance financial stability. As FSB chairman, he was a regular delegate to the finance ministers' meetings of the G7 and the G20 and to the summit meetings of the G20. Earlier in his career, Quarles was a longtime partner at the Carlyle Group, a leading global private equity firm, and before that a partner at the international law firm of Davis Polk & Wardwell, where he was cohead of its financial services practice. He has been a close adviser to every Republican Treasury secretary for the last 35 years, including as under secretary of the Treasury in the George W. Bush administration. He has also served as assistant secretary of the Treasury for international affairs, deputy assistant secretary of the Treasury for financial institutions, and US executive director of the International Monetary Fund.

JOSHUA RAUH is the Ormond Family Professor of Finance at Stanford Graduate School of Business and a senior fellow at the Hoover Institution. He formerly served at the White House, where he was principal chief economist on the President's Council of Economic Advisers (2019–20) and taught at the University of Chicago's Booth School of Business (2004–9) and the Kellogg School of Management (2009–12). At the Hoover Institution, he has served as director of research (2018–19). Rauh studies government pension liabilities, corporate investment, business taxation, and investment management. His research on pension systems and public finance has received national media coverage in outlets such as the *Wall Street Journal*, the *New York Times*, the *Financial Times*, and *The Economist*, and he has testified before Congress on these topics. His PragerU video, "Public Pensions: An Economic Time Bomb," has been viewed over four million times on the PragerU website and over three million times on YouTube. He has published numerous journal articles and has received various awards recognizing his scholarship, including the Brattle Prize and the Smith Breeden Prize of the American Finance Association. His scholarly papers have appeared in journals such as the *Journal of Political Economy*, the *Quarterly Journal of Economics*, the *Journal of Finance*, the *Journal of Financial Economics*, the *Review of Financial Studies*, and the *Journal of Public Economics*. Before his academic career, he was an associate economist at Goldman Sachs in London. Rauh received a BA from Yale University and a PhD from the Massachusetts Institute of Technology, both in economics.

RICARDO REIS is the A. W. Phillips Professor of Economics at the London School of Economics. Recent honors include the 2021 European Economic Association for best academic economist in Europe under age forty-five, the 2017 Banque de France / Toulouse School of Economics junior prize, and the 2016 Bernácer Prize. Reis is an academic consultant at the Bank of England, the Riksbank, and the Federal Reserve Bank of Richmond. He directs the Centre for Macroeconomics in the United Kingdom and serves on the council or as an adviser of multiple organizations. He has published widely on macroeconomics. His main areas of research are inflation, inflation expectations, unconventional monetary policies and the central bank's balance sheet, disagreement and inattention, business cycle models with inequality, automatic stabilizers, public debt sustainability, monetary-fiscal interactions, sovereign bond-backed securities, and the role of capital misallocation in the European slump and crisis. He received his PhD from Harvard University and was previously on the faculty at Columbia University and Princeton University. He was a Hoover national fellow in 2006–07.

CONDOLEEZZA RICE is the Tad and Dianne Taube Director of the Hoover Institution and the Thomas and Barbara Stephenson Senior Fellow on Public Policy. In addition, she is a founding partner of Rice, Hadley, Gates & Manuel LLC, an international strategic consulting firm. From January 2005 to January 2009, Rice served as the sixty-sixth US secretary of state, the second woman and first Black woman to hold the post. Rice also served as President George W. Bush's assistant to the president for national security affairs (national security advisor) from January 2001 to January 2005, the first woman to hold the position. Rice served as Stanford University's provost from 1993 to 1999, during which time she was the institution's chief budget and academic officer. As professor of political science, Rice has been on the Stanford faculty since 1981 and has won two of the university's highest teaching honors: the 1984 Walter J. Gores Award for Excellence in Teaching and the 1993 School of Humanities and Sciences Dean's Award for Distinguished Teaching. She has authored and coauthored numerous books, most recently *To Build a Better World: Choices to End the Cold War and Create a Global Commonwealth* (2019), coauthored with Philip Zelikow. Among her other volumes are three bestsellers, *Democracy: Stories from the Long Road to Freedom* (2017); *No Higher Honor: A Memoir of My Years in Washington* (2011); and *Extraordinary, Ordinary People: A Memoir of Family* (2010). She also wrote *Germany Unified and Europe Transformed: A Study in Statecraft* (1995) with Philip Zelikow; edited *The Gorbachev Era* (1986) with Alexander Dallin; and penned *The Soviet Union and the Czechoslovak Army, 1948–1983: Uncertain Allegiance* (1984). Rice has a bachelor's degree from the University of Denver, a master's degree from the University of Notre Dame, and a PhD from the University of Denver, all in political science.

THOMAS J. SARGENT, a macroeconomist, joined New York University as the first W. R. Berkley Professor in September 2002, a joint appointment by the Economics Department at NYU's Faculty of Arts and Science and the Stern School of Business. He was awarded the 2011 Nobel Prize in Economic Sciences, shared with Princeton University's Christopher Sims, for his empirical research on cause and effect in the macroeconomy. Sargent was a professor of economics at the University of Minnesota from 1975 to 1987, the David Rockefeller Professor at the University of Chicago from 1992 to 1998, and the Donald L. Lucas Professor in Economics at Stanford University from 1998 to 2002. He has been a senior fellow at the Hoover Institution since 1987. He earned his PhD from Harvard University in 1968 and was a first lieutenant and captain in the US Army. He was a university medalist as Most Distinguished Scholar in the Class of 1964 and won the Nemmers Prize in Economics in 1997. He was elected a fellow of the National Academy of Sciences and a fellow of the American Academy of Arts and Sciences, both in 1983. He is past president of the Econometric Society, the American Economic Association, and the Society for Economic Dynamics. Among his books are *Rational Expectations and Econometric Practice*, with Robert E. Lucas Jr. (University of Minnesota Press, 1981); *The Big Problem of Small Change*, with François R. Velde (Princeton University Press, 2002); *Recursive Macroeconomic Theory*, with Lars Ljungqvist (MIT Press, 2004); and *Robustness*, with Lars Peter Hansen (Princeton University Press, 2008).

TOM STEPHENSON spent over thirty-five years as a venture capitalist with two high-profile firms, Fidelity Investments in Boston and Sequoia Capital in Silicon Valley, serving as managing partner at each venture firm for several years. Since the mid-2000s, he has devoted the bulk of his time to the world of policy, including a stint with the State Department as ambassador to Portugal. He is a longtime board member of the Hoover Institution and recently served as chair of its Board of Overseers. Mr. Stephenson is also an active director of Business Executives for National Security (BENS) and travels extensively to various hot spots around the world with BENS. At Hoover, he and the late George Shultz formed and cochaired an energy task force focused on market-based ways to address climate change and global warming. His energy and climate work at Hoover was augmented and complemented by his twenty-year service on Conservation International's board of directors. More recently at Hoover, he has helped set up a National Security Task Force to help address our many challenges from adversaries around the world.

LAWRENCE H. SUMMERS is the Charles W. Eliot University Professor and president emeritus of Harvard University. During the past two decades, he has served in a series of senior policy positions in Washington, DC, including as secretary of the Treasury for President Clinton, director of the National Economic Council for President Obama, and vice president of development economics and chief economist of the World Bank. He received a bachelor of science degree from the Massachusetts Institute of Technology in 1975 and was awarded a PhD from Harvard in 1982. In 1983, he became one of the youngest individuals in recent history to be named as a tenured member of the Harvard University faculty. In 1987, Summers became the first social scientist ever to receive the annual Alan T. Waterman Award of the National Science Foundation, and in 1993, he was awarded the John Bates Clark Medal, given every two years to the outstanding American economist under the age of forty. He is currently the Weil Director of the Mossavar-Rahmani Center for Business & Government at Harvard's Kennedy School.

JOHN B. TAYLOR is the George P. Shultz Senior Fellow in Economics at the Hoover Institution and the Mary and Robert Raymond Professor of Economics at Stanford University. He is also the director of Stanford's Introductory Economics Center. An award-winning teacher and researcher, he served as senior economist on the President's Council of Economic Advisers from 1976 to '77, as a member of the council from 1989 to 1991, and as under secretary of the Treasury for international affairs from 2001 to 2005. More recently, he was president of the Mont Pelerin Society and served on the Eminent Persons Group on Global Financial Governance created by the G20. His book *Global Financial Warriors* chronicles his policy innovations at the US Treasury. His book *First Principles* won the Hayek Prize in 2012. His most recent books are *Choose Economic Freedom: Enduring Policy Lessons from the 1970s and 1980s* (with George P. Shultz) and *Reform of the International Monetary System.*

CHRISTOPHER J. WALLER took office as a member of the Board of Governors of the Federal Reserve System on December 18, 2020, to fill an unexpired term ending January 31, 2030. Prior to his appointment at the board, he served as executive vice president and director of research at the Federal Reserve Bank of St. Louis since 2009. In addition to his experience in the Federal Reserve System, Waller served as a professor and the Gilbert F. Schaefer Chair of Economics at the University of Notre Dame. He was also a research fellow with Notre Dame's Kellogg Institute for International Studies. From 1998 to 2003, he was a professor and the Carol Martin Gatton Chair of Macroeconomics and Monetary Economics at the University of Kentucky. During that time, he was also a research fellow at the Center for European Integration Studies at the University of Bonn. From 1992 to 1994, he served as the director of graduate studies at Indiana University's Department of Economics, where he also served as associate professor and assistant professor. He received a BS in economics from Bemidji State University and an MA and PhD from Washington State University.

KEVIN WARSH serves as the Shepard Family Distinguished Visiting Fellow in Economics at the Hoover Institution and lecturer at Stanford Graduate School of Business. He is an adviser to Duquesne Family Office and serves on the board of directors of UPS and Coupang, the leading Korean e-commerce company. Warsh is a member of the Group of Thirty (G30) and the Panel of Economic Advisers of the Congressional Budget Office. He conducts extensive research in the field of economics and finance. He issued an independent report to the Bank of England proposing reforms in the conduct of monetary policy in the United Kingdom. Parliament adopted the report's recommendations. He served as a member of the Board of Governors of the Federal Reserve System from 2006 to 2011. Warsh served as the Federal Reserve's representative to the Group of Twenty (G20) and as the board's emissary to emerging and advanced economies in Asia. In addition, he was administrative governor, managing and overseeing the board's operations, personnel, and financial performance. Before his appointment to the board, from 2002 to 2006 he served as special assistant to the president for economic policy and executive secretary of the White House National Economic Council. Previously, he was a member of the mergers and acquisitions department at Morgan Stanley & Co. in New York, serving as vice president and executive director. He received his AB from Stanford University and JD from Harvard Law School.

VOLKER WIELAND holds the Endowed Chair of Monetary Economics at the Institute for Monetary and Financial Stability at Goethe University of Frankfurt, where he also serves as managing director. He was a member of the German Council of Economic Experts from March 2013 to

April 2020. In 1995, Wieland received a PhD in economics from Stanford University. Before joining the Frankfurt faculty in 2000, he was a senior economist at the Board of Governors of the Federal Reserve System. His research interests include monetary and fiscal policy, business cycles, macroeconomic models, and economic dynamics. He has published in leading economic journals such as the *American Economic Review*, the *Journal of Monetary Economics*, and the *Review of Economics and Statistics*. He has served as managing editor of the *Journal of Economic Dynamics and Control* and has received several awards and grants. Furthermore, he has been a consultant to central banks and international institutions. Recently, he has been coordinating the creation of the Macroeconomic Model Data Base, a public archive of macroeconomic models for comparative purposes.

About the Hoover Institution's Economic Policy Working Group

The Economic Policy Working Group brings together experts on economic and financial policy at the Hoover Institution and elsewhere to study key developments in the US and global economies, examine their interactions, and develop specific policy proposals.

For twenty-five years starting in the early 1980s, the US economy experienced an unprecedented economic boom. Economic expansions were stronger and longer than in the past. Recessions were shorter, shallower, and less frequent. GDP doubled and household net worth increased by 250 percent in real terms. Forty-seven million jobs were created.

This quarter-century boom strengthened as its length increased. Productivity growth surged by one full percentage point per year in the United States, creating an additional $9 trillion of goods and services that would never have existed. And the long boom went global with emerging market countries from Asia to Latin America to Africa experiencing the enormous improvements in both economic growth and economic stability.

Economic policies that place greater reliance on the principles of free markets, price stability, and flexibility have been the key to these successes. Recently, however, several powerful new economic forces have begun to change the economic landscape, and these principles are being challenged with far-reaching implications for US economic policy, both domestic and international. A financial crisis flared up in 2007 and turned into a severe panic in 2008, leading to the Great Recession. The economic expansion that followed that Great Recession lasted for more than a decade but ended severely as the forces of the coronavirus pandemic hit the US and world economy in 2020, leading to another recession. This episode and the nascent recovery raises fundamental questions about the role of economic policy. How we interpret and react to these forces—and in particular whether proven policy principles prevail going forward— will determine whether strong economic growth and stability returns and again continues to spread and improve more people's lives or whether the economy stalls and stagnates.

Our Working Group organizes seminars and conferences, prepares policy papers and other publications, and serves as a resource for policy makers and interested members of the public.

Index